THE MILK OF PARADISE

James Lees-Milne at eighty-five, August 1993, by Charles Yorke

The Milk of Paradise

DIARIES, 1993–1997

James Lees-Milne

Edited by Michael Bloch

JOHN MURRAY

© Michael Bloch 2005

First published in Great Britain in 2005 by John Murray (Publishers)
A division of Hodder Headline

2

A CIP catalogue record for this title is available from the British Library

ISBN 0 7195 6580 4

Typeset in 11.5/13pt Bembo by Servis Filmsetting Ltd, Manchester

Printed and bound by Clays Ltd, St Ives plc

Hodder Headline policy is to use papers that are natural, renewable and
recyclable products and made from wood grown in sustainable forests. The
logging and manufacturing processes are expected to conform to the
environmental regulations of the country of origin.

John Murray (Publishers)
338 Euston Road
London NW1 3BH

To Tony Scotland
'extrovert, open, bubbling'
and Julian Berkeley
who 'never says a stupid thing'

Contents

Preface

This twelfth and final volume of James Lees-Milne's diary covers the last five years of his life, from January 1993, when he was eighty-four, until a few weeks before his death on 28 December 1997, aged eighty-nine. Throughout this time he faced a constant struggle against the infirmities and discomforts of old age, including the ever-threatening spectre of cancer. Until her death in March 1994, he was also largely sacrificed to looking after his wife Alvilde, who had been rendered virtually helpless by a severe illness in March 1992. Nevertheless, his diary shows that, almost to the last, he maintained the keenest interest in art, literature, gossip, anecdote, human idiosyncrasy and current affairs, while continuing to enjoy new experiences, keep up with friends, and express his observations in sharp and entertaining prose.

Alvilde's death (which took place suddenly, in rather shocking circumstances) affected him in various ways. Although their marriage had had its ups and downs (and more than once had come close to breaking down altogether), they had drawn close to each other in old age; and Jim felt bereft at her loss. He was also assailed by guilt, feeling that he had been an insufficiently devoted husband. One curious result of this was that, although his nature had hitherto been predominantly homosexual (as had hers), he decided that he was now '100 per cent hetero-platonic', delighting only in the company of women; and although his head could still be turned by a pretty male face, he 'recoiled with a shudder' from his own gay past. On the other hand, her demise was a liberating experience, now that he no longer had to dedicate himself to her welfare or fear her disapproval. He therefore enjoyed something of a new lease of life, until his health began to deteriorate sharply in 1996.

Despite his troubles and preoccupations, Jim continued to be active as a writer, working either in his sitting room at Essex House,

Badminton or (until he gave it up a year before his death) in his beloved library in Lansdown Crescent, Bath. He no longer had the energy to produce a long narrative work such as a novel or a biography. But he was kept busy by journalism in the form of articles, obituaries and reviews. The only original book he wrote during these years, *Fourteen Friends* (1996), a collection of sketches of departed soulmates, is an uneven work, though containing much of value. He also tried his hand as a writer of ghost stories, until persuaded by the reception of his first effort (November 1994) that it was not his *métier*. His main literary activity, however, was the editing of his diaries for the 1970s. His much-acclaimed 1940s diaries had appeared in four volumes between 1975 and 1985; and he felt the time was ripe to start releasing the later series of journals which he had begun in 1971 and continued for the rest of his life. *A Mingled Measure* (covering 1971 and 1972) was published by John Murray in 1994; *Ancient as the Hills* (a curious title, as it covered 1973 and 1974 when he still had more than twenty years to live) followed in 1997; *Through Wood and Dale* (covering 1975 to 1978) appeared posthumously in 1998. As with the earlier volumes, he brought them out with mixed feelings, aware that they would annoy some people, yet hoping that they would cause him to be recognised as a significant chronicler of his times.

As Jim's literary executor, it has fallen to me to prepare his remaining diaries (1979 to 1997) for publication. It has been an unusual task, as I feature in the material to a degree which surprised me, and I discovered a man rather different from the one I had known. At the outset, it seemed far from certain that public interest would be sufficient to permit the completion of the series; but Jim's reputation as a diarist has grown steadily in the seven years since his death. I like to think that I have done the job much as he would have done it himself. In the case of the present volume, it has involved cutting out much on various grounds; but what remains may be regarded as some of the best of his diary writing, all the more poignant for being the product of old age.

I wish to thank the following people who have helped me during the five years that I have worked on Jim's diaries, some of whom have sadly not survived to read this volume: Freda Berkeley, Desmond Briggs, David Burnett, Ronald Creighton-Jobe, Juliana Deliyannis, Debo Devonshire, Patric Dickinson, Ian Dixon, Alexandra Erskine, Sue Fox, Robert Harding, John Harris, Selina Hastings, Bruce Hunter, John Kenworthy-Browne, Jonathan Kooperstein, Henry

McDowell, R. B. McDowell, Grant McIntyre, Philip Mansel, Hugh Massingberd, Tony Mitchell, Diana Mosley, Nigel Nicolson, Roland Philipps, Gail Pirkis, Stuart Preston, John Martin Robinson, Liz Robinson, Nick Robinson, Francis Russell, John Saumarez Smith, Tony Scotland, Dale Sutton, Giles Waterfield, William Waterfield, Moray Watson, Caroline Westmore and Rory Young. I am also grateful to the management of the Oriental Hotel in Bangkok and the Four Seasons Hotel in Sydney, while enjoying whose fantastic hospitality I got down to work on this volume.

Michael Bloch
mab@jamesleesmilne.com
February 2005

For information about James Lees-Milne's life and work, visit the Official James Lees-Milne Website at www.jamesleesmilne.com

... Beware! Beware!
His flashing eyes, his floating hair!
Weave a circle round him thrice,
    And close your eyes with holy dread,
    For he on honey-dew hath fed,
And drunk the milk of Paradise.

Samuel Taylor Coleridge, *Kubla Khan*

1993

At 11.59, turning out the light, I said in a loud voice which would have woken Alvilde, were she not so deaf, 'Hares!' – and then forgot to say 'Rabbits!', so no luck for 1993. 1992 was a filthy year, overshadowed by A's severe illness which began in March and is not over yet.

We lunched at Newark [Park], driving there through thick fog. Bob [Parsons]* and Michael [Clayton] gave one of their buffet luncheons, deliciously cooked by Michael who has grown a paunch and sickle-shaped sideboards, as if to accentuate the loss of his youth. The Harrises† there, whom I so like. Eileen clever, modest and wise. Is bewildered by the apotheosis of Bruce Chatwin,‡ whom she knew well and saw through. Marvels at how he managed to promote his own legend. John endeared himself to me by saying that my early architectural books§ were, like Sachie's¶ and Laurence Whistler's,** pioneering works, exciting the interest of the youth of the time, and preparing the way for the precise scholars of today. Decent of him to say so, but I think only partly true of my jejune efforts.

Now that I tend to fall asleep over novels, a curious thing happens. I doze off and briefly continue the story I have been reading in a sort

---

* American architect (1920–2000); tenant and repairer of Newark Park, N.T. property in Ozleworth Valley, Gloucestershire, where he lived with Michael Clayton (b. 1952).

† John Harris (b. 1931); expert and writer on architectural subjects; curator of RIBA Library and Drawings Collection, 1960–86; a neighbour of J.L.-M. in South Kensington during the 1950s (when both kept rooms in Geoffrey Houghton-Brown's house in Thurloe Square) and in Gloucestershire during the 1960s (when both had houses in Ozleworth Valley); m. 1960 Eileen Spiegel (b. 1932).

‡ Travel writer and novelist (1940–89); another Ozleworth Valley resident; died of Aids.

§ Between 1945 and 1970 J.L.-M. wrote some dozen books, covering English architecture from the sixteenth to the eighteenth centuries, the Baroque in Italy, Spain and Portugal, the monuments of Rome, and the buildings of his native Worcestershire.

¶ Sir Sacheverell Sitwell, 6th Bt (1897–1988); poet and writer on varied subjects, including architecture; m. 1925 Georgia Doble (d. 1980).

** Glass engraver, poet and writer on architecture (1912–2000); brother and biographer of Rex Whistler (1905–44), artist and designer.

of dream, before waking with a jolt. I then read on and find, not surprisingly, that the next passage does not coincide at all with the dreamed continuation I have just experienced.

Sunday, 3rd January

Watch John Gielgud* on television, in a half-hour talk with young actors and actresses. Radiant, worshipping eyes focused on this youthful old man of eighty-eight, with his smooth skin and absurd white moustache. So unlike the Gielgud I knew. Not in the least the old fogey, or patronising, or self-centred; but natural, amusing, educative. What a wonderful old man he has become.

Wednesday, 6th January

I had a feverish cold and stayed in bed yesterday, not meeting A. for fear of infecting her. Listened to *Four Last Songs* of Richard Strauss,[†] one of my favourite composers, and became intoxicated with the nostalgia evoked. Was transported back to Roquebrune;[‡] imagined myself sitting in a café with A., I in whites, she with greying hair and severe magisterial expression, being served breakfast by a white-aproned waiter. Around us the smells of brioches, coffee, pine trees, the clean early morning freshness of the sky; no birds singing, but in the distance the susurration of the sea and the hesitant piping of a shepherd's flute. The senses heightened, expectant of lovely future days without end. And then I heard the languid drip of water falling from our basin in the little enclosed garden onto the water hyacinth – all mixed up in the daydream conjured by the music in my feverish condition.

To my surprise I received a very nice letter this morning from Dame Elizabeth Murdoch,[§] saying she regrets 'very sincerely and

---

* Sir John Gielgud, actor (1904–2000), with whom J.L.-M., then an Oxford undergraduate, had a six-week affair in 1931 (as revealed in *Deep Romantic Chasm*).
† Poignant last work of the German composer (1864–1949), written in 1948 and posthumously premiered in London in 1950 by Wilhelm Furtwängler.
‡ Picturesque French mountain village overlooking Mediterranean between Mentone and Monte Carlo, where the L.-Ms lived from 1950 to 1961.
§ Elizabeth Greene (b. 1909; DBE, 1963); m. 1928 Sir Keith Murdoch (d. 1952), Australian newspaper owner; mother of controversial London-based media tycoon Rupert Murdoch (b. 1931), whose British newspapers included *The Times* and the *Sun*.

vehemently' the bad publicity the *Sun* has been giving to 'our Queen'. That she constantly points this out to her son Rupert, to whom she is forwarding my letter. So that's something achieved, I feel.

Saturday, 9th January

I remembered a vivid dream this morning. Was walking down a motorway, trying to get to Venice. Got there and stayed in a tiny room opposite the Arsenal, where there is in fact no building, only water. Was worried about luggage as I had to return urgently to England. Sympathetic people about, I think craftsmen. Suddenly I found myself in a gondola mooring in front of a bookshop; the window was down to the water and the rare morocco-bound volumes within were also surrounded by pools and jets of water, which, the proprietor explained to me, was the best way of keeping the books cool.

A. made a superb effort and gave a luncheon party for Diana Mosley,* Woman† and Hardy Amies.‡ Hardy has a pro to play tennis with him every Saturday if the weather is fine. As he is bent double, I asked him how he managed. He replied that it was possible to perform every action with the body bent except service, which he has to do pat ball. He seems a happy man, delighted with an article in today's *Telegraph* in which he gives his idea of the perfect weekend. Diana asked him how his firm was standing up to the recession. He said that never in his sixty years as a couturier had he experienced a better year financially, for the rich understand that the best clothes endure. All very fine for the rich who can afford the best, but will they continue to do so if the recession endures? Diana said that Heywood Hill's bookshop have also had their best year, and that *People and Places*§ was their best seller. Today's *Telegraph* also contains

---

* Hon. Diana Mitford (1910–2003), with whom J.L.-M., a schoolfriend of her brother, had been in love aged eighteen; m. 1st 1929 Hon. Bryan Guinness (1905–92; later 2nd Baron Moyne), 2nd 1936 Sir Oswald Mosley, 6th Bt (1896–1980); resident in Orsay near Paris.

† Hon. Pamela Mitford, 2nd of the Mitford sisters (1907–94); m. 1936 (as 2nd of his 6 wives) Professor Derek Jackson (d. 1982).

‡ Dressmaker By Appointment to HM The Queen (1909–2003; KCVO 1989).

§ A book of memoirs by J.L.-M. on his work in acquiring country houses for the National Trust, which had been published (to rave reviews) by John Murray the previous October.

a review by Nicky Mosley[*] of a book on wartime internment under
18B,[†] in which he defends Sir Oswald, emphasising his deep patri-
otism. This pleases Diana, who nevertheless refuses to forgive her
stepson for writing that book about his father.[‡] But oh how I love
her.

Monday, 11th January

We lunch with the Salmonds[§] at Didmarton, first calling on the
Westmorlands[¶] for an hour. David sitting in his chair by the fire.
Seemed amused, and to take in what was said to a limited extent. Like
George III, he keeping saying 'What, what, what?' with an interrog-
atory note. Jane appears to address all her remarks to him, without
expecting an answer.

Julian [Salmond] at lunch today – unusual. Always agreeable, intelligent, interested. Talk got on to the Yorks.[**] Brigid said he was difficult to live with, lacking in good humour. Believes that, if they
divorce, she will remain a duchess but drop the HRH. He talked of
the Desboroughs[††] whom he remembers well, spending much of his
childhood at Panshanger. All now gone.

Saturday, 16th January

A. is not very well, having recently given up the drugs she is supposed
to be taking in favour of homeopathic treatment. However, today she
managed with help from Peggy[‡‡] and me to prepare lunch for the

---

[*] Hon. Nicholas Mosley (b. 1923); writer; er s. of Sir Oswald Mosley and his 1st wife
Lady Cynthia Curzon (d. 1933); s. aunt 1966 as 3rd Baron Ravensdale.
[†] The Defence Regulation which, during the Second World War, authorised internment
without trial of anyone suspected of enemy sympathies.
[‡] The two-volume biography *Rules of the Game* (1982) and *Beyond the Pale* (1983).
[§] Julian Salmond (b. 1926), o. s. of Marshal of the RAF Sir John Maitland Salmond and
Hon. Monica Grenfell; m. 1950 Brigid Wright (b. 1928).
[¶] David Fane, 15th Earl of Westmorland (1924–93); Master of the Horse, 1978–93; m.
1950 Jane Findlay. He had suffered a stroke the previous August.
[**] HRH Prince Andrew (b. 1960; cr. Duke of York 1986); m. 1986 (diss. 1996) Sarah
Ferguson (b. 1959), niece of Brigid Salmond.
[††] Julian Salmond's maternal grandparents William Grenfell (1855–1945; cr. Baron Des-
borough, 1905) and Ethel ('Ettie') *née* Fane (1867–1952), of Panshanger Park, Hertfordshire;
leading members of 'the Souls', two of whose sons were killed in the First World War.
[‡‡] Peggy Bird, the L.-Ms' daily help.

Norwiches* and Droghedas.† This passed well, though she was very
bent and breathless. When the guests left, I took her for a drive round
by Sopworth and Didmarton; as soon as we got back, she went to bed.
I tried to read downstairs by the fire, but felt tormented with forebod-
ings as I looked at her empty chair. All I can do is minister to her every
whim and pour love into her.

Sunday, 17th January

Despite A's continuing frailty, we lunch with the Briggses‡ at Midford,
having ascertained beforehand from Isobel that the only other guest
would be Bill McNaught,§ a harmless individual. I watch her struggling to respond to McN's and Michael's conversation, she normally
so bright and responsive. On way home she says she cannot go out to
another meal until she is better. Conversation at Midford mostly about
the so-called Camillagate affair and the infamous publication of the
Prince of Wales's taped conversations.¶ All I have talked to on this
subject are unanimous in condemning the press's behaviour. Michael
Briggs however is critical of the Prince, who he says is so devoid of
humour as to be devoid of human understanding. Told us of some
function at which HRH, Bishop Stockwood,** the Lord-Lieutenant
and Michael were all present. Stockwood was saying how he adored
watered silk, fondling his episcopal garment; the LL riposted that he
had a fetish for feathers, drawing attention to his plumed hat.

---

* John Julius Cooper, 2nd Viscount Norwich (b. 1929); writer, broadcaster and
Chairman of Venice in Peril Fund; m. 1st 1952–85 Anne Clifford, 2nd 1989 Hon. Mary
('Mollie') Philipps (*née* Makins, dau. of 1st Baron Sherfield and formerly wife of Hon.
Hugo Philipps, later 3rd Baron Milford).
† Dermot ('Derry') Moore, 12th Earl of Drogheda (b. 1937); photographer (as Derry
Moore); m. 1st 1968–72 Eliza Lloyd, 2nd 1978 Alexandra, dau. of Sir Nicholas
Henderson, diplomatist. His parents, old friends of the L.-Ms, had died within a few days
of each other in 1989.
‡ Michael Briggs, businessman and aesthete, sometime Chairman of Bath Preservation
Trust, of Midford Castle near Bath; m. 1953 Isobel Colegate (b. 1931), novelist.
§ William P. McNaught; Curator of American Museum at Claverton near Bath.
¶ An intimate telephone call from the Prince of Wales to his mistress Camilla Parker
Bowles on 18 December 1992, just a week after he had separated from Princess Diana,
had been monitored and recorded by a 'scanner' and subsequently published in the tabloid
press.
** Anglican clergyman (1913–95), who as Bishop of Southwark from 1959 to 1980 was
renowned for his humanitarian ideals and love of Society and good living.

Overhearing this, the P. puckered his brow, became indignant, and asked them if they were serious. Totally at sea.

Monday, 18th January

Today I made three trips to Bath and back. First to dentist to have my plate adjusted. That was put right and I returned to find A. still in bed, her cheek and neck swollen and red. I fixed urgent appointment with her specialist Dr Thomas and drove her to Bath Clinic. He said at once she must go into hospital. A. surprised by this, I not in the least. While they put her through tests, I returned home and with Peggy packed her little bag and drove again to Bath. Thomas thinks her swelling may come from infected collar bone. He was worried I could see. I am miserable but determined to adopt a resigned and non-emotional attitude, reconciled to whatever fate has in store.

Victor Bruntisfield[*] has died. He was made in a heroic mould, in his golden youth beloved by all. Was a godson of Queen Victoria – unique survival I should have thought, though Kenneth Rose[†] tells me there are others still living. He inherited an ancient baronetcy in his teens; enlisted in the army at eighteen, winning the MC; was a whip in Baldwin's government; made a hereditary peer half a century ago. Extremely handsome and charming. I had dealings with him when he was one of Mrs Greville's[‡] executors, and remember his benign, radiant countenance across the table in the solicitor's office as we disposed of her immense fortune and countless possessions.

Tuesday, 19th January

At A's insistence, I go to London for Alfred Beit's[§] ninetieth birthday party at Brooks's. Over tea there I am joined by Francis

---

[*] Victor Warrender (1899–1993); Conservative MP and office-holder, 1923–43; cr. Baron Bruntisfield, 1942; m. 1st Dorothy Rawson, 2nd 1948 Tania Colin.
[†] Historian and journalist (b. 1924); 'Albany' of *Sunday Telegraph*.
[‡] The hostess Hon. Mrs Ronnie Greville bequeathed both her town house in Charles Street, Mayfair and her country house, Polesden Lacey near Dorking, Surrey, to the N.T. After her death in September 1942, J.L.-M., as related in his diaries, was occupied for several years in disposing of the London house and its contents, and preparing Polesden Lacey for eventual opening to the public.
[§] Sir Alfred Beit, 2nd Bt (1903–94); art collector and sometime Conservative MP; m. 1939 Clementine Mitford (cousin of the Mitford sisters).

Sitwell* who is delighted with Sarah Bradford's† life of Sachie, as is Bruce Hunter.‡ His only reservation is about some revelations of S.B. concerning Sachie's love life, particularly relating to Bridget Parsons.§ Apparently Georgia came upon them *in flagrante delicto*.

Alfred's party huge, sixty-eight guests. Nearly all from the old *gratin*,¶ with sprinkling of young *gratin* like Tatton Sykes.** Alfred arrived from hospital in an ambulance, carried upstairs in wheel-chair, and pushed into dining room where guests assembled. I seated happily between Mary Roxburghe†† and Kitty Giles.‡‡ I have never known the Duchess well, but we have many links. She is Bamber [Gascoigne]'s§§ great-aunt and finds him almost too good to be true. Spoke with admiration of Jamesey's¶¶ life of her grandfather Monckton Milnes. Appreciated that J. had a problem writing about her parents, her father a stereotyped character, her mother inclined to be rude to her inferiors through shyness.*** (Shyness hardly seems the right word for Lady Crewe's predicament.) Told of the brutality of her

---

* Yr s. (1935–2004; m. 1966 Susanna Cross) of Sir Sacheverell Sitwell, 6th Bt, whose house at Weston, Northamptonshire he inherited.

† Sarah Hayes (b. 1938); m. 1st 1959 Anthony Bradford, 2nd 1976 Hon. William Ward (b. 1948; succeeded 1993 as 8th Viscount Bangor); writer, whose *Splendours and Miseries: A Life of Sacheverell Sitwell* had just been published by Sinclair-Stevenson.

‡ Canadian-born literary agent (b. 1941); joined London firm of David Higham in 1962 and became J.L.-M's agent on death of D.H. in 1979.

§ Lady Bridget Parsons (1907–72), o. dau. of 5th Earl of Rosse; a great heart-throb also for J.L.-M., who had been in love at Eton with her brother Hon. Desmond (1910–37).

¶ 'The upper crust'.

** Sir Tatton Sykes, 8th Bt, of Sledmere, Yorkshire (b. 1943).

†† Lady Mary Crewe-Milnes (b. 1913); dau. of 1st and last Marquess of Crewe; m. 1935 (diss. 1953) 9th Duke of Roxburghe (d. 1974).

‡‡ Lady Katherine Sackville (b. 1926), o. dau. of 9th Earl De La Warr; m. 1946 Frank Giles, journalist.

§§ Arthur Bamber Gascoigne (b. 1935); author, broadcaster and publisher; m. 1963 Christina Ditchburn; er s. of J.L.-M's recently deceased friend Hon. Mary ('Midi') Gascoigne (1905–91).

¶¶ James Pope-Hennessy (1916–74); writer; intimate friend of J.L.-M. during 1940s; killed by 'rough trade' which he had invited into his flat in Ladbroke Grove.

*** Mary Roxburghe's grandfather Richard Monckton Milnes (1809–85), writer, poet, statesman and philanthropist, cr. Baron Houghton, 1863; his son Robert (1858–1945), 2nd Baron, Liberal Party statesman and HM Ambassador to Paris, 1922–8, cr. Marquess of Crewe, 1911, m. (2nd) 1899 Lady Margaret Primrose, yr dau. of 5th Earl of Rosebery (Liberal Prime Minister 1894–5), at whose instigation J.P.-H. wrote biographies of her husband and father-in-law.

Aunt Sibyl Grant* to her son, whom she persuaded her husband the General to disinherit. Kitty Giles talked of her prison visiting at Brixton. Knows the prisoners intimately, visits them in their cells. She concerns herself with their rights to be treated as civilised beings, though their reform is generally out of the question: 75 per cent of those discharged return.

Afterwards chatted with a host of forgottens. John Nutting,[†] so handsome, who has reviewed my book for *The Field*; John Bellingham,[‡] who always greets me as a cousin; the Brudenells.[§] Derek Hill[¶] told me that he told the Prince of Wales last week, 'Sir, I don't know how you go on.' HRH replied that that was not something he ought to be told – though there was worse to come. Derek says that bitch Kitty Kelley's** book on Prince Philip is going to be an absolute brute, revealing the names of the women involved in his life. All I can say is that he is a man of discretion, concerning whose private life I have never heard a word of criticism.

Thursday, 21st January

The Beits' guests are a gathering of the clan. They are tribal just like the African negroes. What makes them so conspicuous? Not so much their breeding or their appearance, rather their money and security. Their physical comfort and lack of financial worry leads to self-confidence, sophistication, good taste, in many cases a knowledge of the arts. It also explains their good manners, tolerance, iconoclastic

---

* Lady Crewe's sister (1879–1955); m. 1903 Charles (later General Sir Charles) Grant (1877–1950); described herself in *Who's Who* as 'poet, writer, designer and artist'; interested in 'the beyond'; lived at Pitchford Hall, Shropshire, where J.L.-M., visiting her during the war, found her eccentric almost to the point of insanity, but 'with a mind as sharp as a razor's edge'.

† Barrister (b. 1942; QC 1995); er s. of Sir Anthony Nutting, 3rd Bt (politician who famously resigned from Eden Government over Suez, 1956), whom he s. as 4th Bt, 1999; m. 1974 Diane, widow of 2nd Earl Beatty, châtelaine of Chicheley Hall, Newport Pagnell, Bucks (see entry for 3 July 1994).

‡ Old Etonian genealogist living in Ireland (b. 1929); m. 1989 Fiona Nugent; his mother, *née* Arthur, came from an Ayrshire family connected to J.L.-M's.

§ Edmund Brudenell (b. 1924) of Deene Park, Northamptonshire; m. 1955 Hon. Marian Manningham-Buller, dau. of 1st Viscount Dilhorne; the L.-Ms had stayed with them on several occasions during the 1980s and been amazed at their old-fashioned way of life.

¶ Landscape and portrait artist (1916–2000).

** American writer of scandalous biographies (b. 1942).

brand of humour, self-deprecation, and willingness to accept those outsiders wishing to be received whose manners make them acceptable. They are for the most part kindly and compassionate – yet withal proud. They won't admit to being superior, yet consider themselves so. Their society is undoubtedly agreeable, and it is possible for intellectuals to bask in it without becoming corrupted by their *train de vie*.

Debo rang.[*] Long talk. Full of solicitude for A., about whom she had heard through Woman. Said the Prince of Wales was to stay with them tomorrow, and wondered what they would talk about. I said, 'You will have to talk about the crisis for it will be on the tips of all your tongues. Be frank.' She said she had just lunched with Andrew Parker Bowles,[†] and was surprised to see no journalists outside the house. After ten minutes of mutual deploring, I said, 'I suppose we are being bugged.'

Sunday, 24th January

Clarissa[‡] came last night, and was very sweet. We went to fetch A. from the Clinic. Her recovery is striking, though swelling of leg and neck not yet entirely gone.

Friday, 29th January

A rare day of gentle sunshine with a whiff of the damned spring, so slight as not to be disturbing.

A. accompanied me to Tetbury [Gloucestershire] where I delivered my old car of four years and took possession of the new one. Mr Friend the head salesman asked me if I did not have another house in Bath. Just a library, I said, for I was a writer. He said, 'I shall look out for books under your name. I have never met an author before.' I drove home in the new car, a rather fancy turquoise colour chosen by A.,

---

[*] Hon. Deborah ('Debo') Mitford (b. 1920); m. 1941 Lord Andrew Cavendish (1920–2004), who s. 1950 as 11th Duke of Devonshire.

[†] Husband (m. 1973) of the Prince of Wales's mistress (and eventual second wife) Camilla *née* Shand, by whom he was divorced in 1994, the year he retired from the army with rank of brigadier.

[‡] Hon. Clarissa Chaplin (b. 1934); only child of A.L.-M., by her 1st marriage to 3rd Viscount Chaplin; m. 1957 Michael Luke (1925–2005).

feeling rather disloyal to the old friend who had served me well, and to whom I did not give a parting glance or even a pat.

Sunday, 31st January

'I see', says A., 'that they have invented a peel-less orange. I shall never eat one.' 'No,' I say, 'handled by all those Aids-ridden Africans.' 'At least', she says, 'oranges are germ-free when you take the peel off.'

Freya Stark* is a hundred, and a very disobliging biography of her has been published by a woman. I hardly know her and have always, I confess, been a trifle irritated by the worship of her, though she does write well, even if she does not explore the depths like Wilfred Thesiger.† We rented her house at Asolo one summer, and I wrote *Earls of Creation* [1962] at her writing-room desk, a beautiful thing like a round rent table which swivelled round, enabling one to switch from typing to consulting books of reference.

Thursday, 4th February

On Monday, John Harris telephoned that Geoffrey Houghton-Brown‡ had been sent to a nursing home in Wimbledon, next to the house where he was brought up. John has been kind in visiting and caring, for G. was his first protector in London, who gave him a room at 20 Thurloe Square and a job in his shop. I telephoned G. and could barely hear his tiny voice, but he seemed pleased to be remembered. This morning, I heard from John that G. died last night on the eve of his ninetieth birthday, having quietly fallen asleep, his friend and minder Fisher by his side.

Geoffrey was gentle and unassuming, too much so, yet a man of deep sensibility and conviction. An extremely pious Catholic until Vatican Council II when his faith, if not shattered, was so dented that his religion meant little to him thereafter, and he felt betrayed. He was very kind to me, letting me take a floor in his house in Alexander Place when I came out of the army during the war. I dare say I rather traded on his good nature and generosity, but we were

---

* Dame Freya Stark (1893–1993); writer and traveller; she died in Asolo in May that year.
† Explorer and travel writer (1910–2003; KBE 1995); Eton contemporary of J.L.-M.
‡ Dilettante and painter (1903–93), at whose house in Thurloe Square, South Kensington, J.L.-M. kept a flat from 1946 to 1961.

always good friends. He was as good as gold and quite a respectable artist, being a friend and disciple of the Australian painter Roy Le Maistre* who claimed to be the rightful King of England through the Stuarts. G. was an authority on eighteenth-century French furniture, but never wrote down his views on the subject. He lived all his adult life with the rather absurd Ronald Fleming, decorator, until the latter's death [1968].

While sad about Geoffrey, I found my hateful thoughts veering to speculation as to whether he had left me Henrietta Maria's heart in a small reliquary, knowing as he did of my interest in the Stuarts. I quickly brushed aside this selfish, acquisitive, beastly thought, as though at my age I needed or even wanted a token. One cannot prevent such sinful thoughts arising, only try to batten them down.

Saturday, 6th February

Susanna [Johnston]† lunched, full of gossip about Camillagate. She is furious with her brother‡ for having mocked the Prince in his *Times* column, which she considers almost as bad as the persecution of Camilla's children at school. When Sir William Hayter§ told S. that he was so disgusted with what the Prince had said that he could no longer have any respect for him, S. retorted angrily that the conversation was not one he was ever meant to hear. Quite right too – sex chat between participants is no more the business of others than how one behaves on the lavatory seat. No one should be judged by it.

Tuesday, 9th February

Father Michael Crowdy,¶ nice old boy but slightly cracked, called on me in Bath yesterday, hoping to reconvert me to Catholicism. He is a 'freelance', having quite rightly quarrelled with the bishops over the

---

* Australian Post-Impressionist artist (1894–1968); resident from 1930 in London, where his other 'disciples' included Francis Bacon.
† Susanna Chancellor; m. 1956 Nicholas Johnston, architect (b. 1929).
‡ Alexander Chancellor (b. 1940); journalist; editor, *Spectator*, 1975–84; columnist on *New Yorker* and *The Times*.
§ Diplomatist and scholar (1906–95); HM Ambassador to USSR, 1953–6; Warden of New College, Oxford, 1958–76.
¶ Priest ordained in 1954 (b. 1914); since 1982 assisting the (Lefebvrist) Society of St Pius X and based at their Bristol priory.

Latin Mass *et al.* I had to tell him that I had returned to the C. of E., and couldn't stomach the Catholic Church's opposition to birth control. He argued that few Catholics observe this ban, and that practising birth control is rather like telling lies – something we ought not to do, yet nevertheless do all the time. He then fell in my esteem by claiming that the population of this country is decreasing. I said that only that morning I had received a letter from the CPRE* warning about government plans to build two million more houses as soon as the economy permitted. We parted in a friendly spirit, but I hope he will leave me alone.

After he left I drafted my obituary of Geoffrey for the *Independent*. As I dictated it down telephone to bedint-sounding† transcriber, I felt rather disloyal to have described G. as a collector of reliquaries and French furniture who never played a game and was rather a cissy. I always knew he had a secret passion for rugby players and the like.

Thursday, 11th February

Poor A., who has become fearfully deaf, is having another hearing-aid fitted at a cost of almost a thousand pounds, having lost the previous one in the garden. Peggy and I have searched and searched. It was tiny like a minute piece of gravel. Meanwhile I have to repeat everything, and shout. I was saying that I had few if any friends left. What? And again, What? I find myself shouting, 'The whole damned lot are dead.'

Yesterday I went to London for Geoffrey's Requiem Mass at the Oratory, where he always used to worship. Quite a hundred mourners of all sorts. The coffin seemed curiously long for a man who was shorter than I am. Others went to Putney Vale cemetery, where he was to lie beside old Ronald. I walked sadly away to John Murray's, where Grant [McIntyre]‡ told me that my last book was the best they had published for several years. I thanked him aloud, while silently thinking that it is no wonder they are said to be going down the drain.

---

* Council for the Protection of Rural England; now Council to Protect Rural England.
† 'Bedint': adjective from the private language of Harold Nicolson and Vita Sackville-West, meaning 'common'.
‡ Director of John Murray, 1987–2003, and J.L.-M's editor there (b. 1944).

I called on M[ichael Bloch]* for tea, but he was not at home, so I shoved a note through his letter-box and walked on to Paddington. Had just entered a first-class coach of the 4.15 when I heard my name shouted and there was M. running along the platform, breathless and full of apologies. So sweet of him.

Saturday, 13th February

To London again yesterday to lunch at the Garrick with Clive Aslet.† A charming young man, Cambridge contemporary of Nick [Robinson],‡ and extremely handsome. I could not stop admiring his splendid even teeth. He wants me to contribute something to *Country Life* along the lines of *People and Places*. Was there a tour I would like to do for them, revisiting old haunts? I mentioned the Welsh borders – Radnor, Salop and Herefordshire – preferring the dim squires' manor houses, particularly those still inhabited, to the grand seats. I felt shy as always with the young, but O I liked him.

On foot to see Bruce Hunter in Golden Square. Good to see how many Georgian and Victorian houses remain, all worth a squint. The blue plaques always elicit interest, even of the dreariest past inhabitants. In Golden Square I went to look at the statue of George II. Face like Malcolm Muggeridge,§ sadly worn and streaked with bird messes. On the head was perched a black crow, which I tried in vain to shoo away. An old woman earnestly scavenging in a litter bin – the sort of thing which I suppose will never be eliminated even in the best-regulated society.

Monday, 15th February

That filthy paper the *Sun* has apologised to the Queen for leaking her Christmas Day talk and offered to pay £200,000 to her chosen charity.

---

* Writer (b. 1953); friend of J.L.-M. since 1979, at which time he had been a Cambridge postgraduate student; had spent much of the 1980s in Paris, writing books on the Duke and Duchess of Windsor at the behest of their formidable French executrix, Maître Suzanne Blum (1898–1994).
† Journalist (b. 1955); editor, *Country Life*, from 1993 (deputy editor, 1989–92); m. 1980 Naomi, dau. of Prof. Sir Martin Roth.
‡ J.L.-M's great-nephew (b. 1955), middle son of his niece Hon. Prudence *née* Arthur (d. 1976); publisher.
§ Writer, broadcaster and religious commentator (1903–90).

I like to think this may have been brought about by my letter to Dame Elizabeth Murdoch, which she told me she was forwarding to her beastly son.

Tuesday, 16th February

Nice young man from BBC, unpronounceable Polish name, came to talk about his proposals for celebrating the National Trust's centenary in 1995. He said that so many of the BBC staff were being made redundant that everyone was becoming ruthless, doing down their colleagues in the hope of clinging on to their own jobs.

Thursday, 18th February

Mary Keen* brought Woman and Myles Hildyard† to luncheon. Though not a beauty like her grandmother Lady Howe, Mary has an expression of the utmost benignity. Myles talked of our late friend Everard Radcliffe,‡ telling me that he hid the best furniture at Rudding [Park near Harrogate] when his father was dying so it would not be seen by the probate men and attract death duties. Three years before his own death, E. married the girl who had been engaged to his son Charlie. I knew Charlie's death had been a knock-out blow to E., and the cause of his own attempted suicide over the balustrade of the stairs into the central marble hall. Having miraculously survived this, he and his new wife then sold up and went to live in Switzerland where presumably the widow still lives. A good story for a novel. Myles recently had burglars at Flintham, who took a favourite clock and a small table before being disturbed by David. A friendly antique dealer warned M. that another antique dealer in York was advertising the clock for sale. Myles got it back, but the rascally York dealer was not prosecuted, despite having admitted the offence. Police couldn't be bothered, and Myles only too glad to get the clock back without having to pay a middle man.

---

* Lady Mary Curzon (b. 1940); dau. of 6th Earl Howe; garden writer; m. 1962 Charles Keen, director of Barclay's Bank.

† Squire of Flintham Hall, Nottinghamshire (1914–2005); war hero, local historian and sometime Honorary Representative of National Trust.

‡ Captain Sir Joseph Benedict Everard Henry Radcliffe, 6th Bt (1910–72); s. of Sir Everard Joseph Radcliffe, 5th Bt (1884–1969); m. 1st 1937 (diss. 1968) Elizabeth Butler, 2nd 1968 Marcia Maxwell. (He was to be the subject of an essay in J.L.-M's *Fourteen Friends* [1996]).

Friday, 19th February

Pat Trevor-Roper* lunched with me in Bath, having given a lecture
on eyes last night to the consultants at the Royal United Hospital. Was
emphatic that the Bath waters were no more effective than any old
waters the world over; that all spas were rubbish, in spite of 2,000 years
or more of Bath's reputation for therapeutic ingredients. Possibly
Droitwich had some virtues in that the waters are salt. I took him to
the station, stopping at his hotel for him to pick up what he called his
luggage. It was no larger than a sponge-bag. As he was wearing filthy
old trousers, a dirty red pullover and open shirt, these were presumably the vestments in which he addressed several hundred distinguished doctors and sisters. What can they have thought of this scruffy,
red-faced, rather niffy authority with his great reputation?

Friday, 26th February

Gervase [Jackson-Stops]† stayed last night, bringing his new friend, a
rather camp young man who is a learned horticulturist, currently
designing an ambitious garden at rear of Gervase's Menagerie with
temples and fanciful wilderness walks and rides. We all went to a party
at the Art Gallery in Bristol given by the N.T. for members in the
region who are gardeners or married to gardeners. Owing to A's disability, kind Mary Keen fetched us and drove us to Bristol. We had to
get there early, as the Prince of Wales was to be present. The poor
man carried a plate of snacks and glass of wine attached to a clip and
walked round meeting and talking to the guests one by one. He came
up to A., who was in a circle with me and John Harris, and said, 'We
have been so concerned about your illness. I hope you are better.' And
in passing, 'You simply must come to Highgrove [near Tetbury] and
see my garden. Come even if I am not there.' As A. said afterwards,
she wouldn't be let in if he wasn't there, and he hadn't exactly invited
her. The P. seemed far more relaxed than when I met him at
Chatsworth.‡ I observed him closely. Good complexion and youthful
skin. Was well-dressed, wearing the most covetable dark tan shoes

---

* Ophthalmic surgeon (1916–2004); co-tenant with Desmond Shawe-Taylor of Long
Crichel, Dorset.
† Architectural historian and adviser to N.T. (1947–95).
‡ See *Ceaseless Turmoil*, 18 January 1992.

with tassels. There is no doubt he *has* charm, notwithstanding Paul Johnson's* recent article in the *Spectator* that he lacks it, like most Hanoverians.

Sunday, 28th February

To luncheon with us came Alex Moulton,† Miranda‡ and her nephew Harry Morley, an extremely handsome and charming young man with perfect manners and a mind of his own, standing up to Alex's usual blimpish views about foreigners and Europe in an amused way. We took to him.

At the Bristol party, Emma Tennant§ told me that Woman found a belated fulfilment during Nancy's¶ terminal illness. In rallying to Nancy, who had always rather despised and bullied her, she proved to be the best nurse of all the sisters; and Nancy at the end wanted only her. *La Sainte Femme*, Emma calls her.

Friday, 5th March

Myles writes that while he was lunching here and telling of his burglary, a garden urn at Flintham was torn off a Coade stone pedestal and stolen.

To London for day. Met J[ohn] K[enworthy]-B[rowne]** at London Library, he reviewing *P&P* for *Apollo*. While I was standing at the desk, someone poked me gently in the behind and called my name. Minute and smiling, it was Frankie [Donaldson].†† I said we

---

* Writer and journalist (b. 1928).
† Dr Alexander Moulton of The Hall, Bradford-on-Avon, Wiltshire; engineer and inventor of the Moulton bicycle and motor-car suspension; friend of J.L.-M. since 1943.
‡ Miranda Morley; mistress (later 2nd wife) of David Somerset, 11th Duke of Beaufort, who (as related in *Ceaseless Turmoil*) had installed her in a house there.
§ Lady Emma Cavendish (b. 1943), er dau. of 11th Duke of Devonshire; m. 1963 Hon. Tobias Tennant (b. 1941), Oxford rowing blue and farmer, yr s. of 2nd Baron Glenconner.
¶ Hon. Nancy Mitford (1904–73); eldest of the Mitford sisters, who lived in France after 1945; writer.
** Expert on neo-classical sculpture, formerly on staff of N.T. and Christie's (b. 1931); close friend of J.L.-M. since 1958.
†† Frances Lonsdale, writer (1907–94); m. 1935 J.L.-M's Eton contemporary 'Jack' Donaldson (1907–98), Minister for the Arts, 1976–9, cr. Baron Donaldson of Kingsbridge, 1967 (see entry for 14 July 1994).

hoped perhaps she and Jack might stay a night with us during the summer. She looked amused and said, 'Do you and Alvilde like staying away now?' 'Not much,' I admitted. We lamented that we did not live nearer each other. Of our recent books, she wished the publishers could have sold them for £10 instead of £20, in which case we might have made some money.

I lunched with the Wagners* – main object of today's expedition – in their nice little house in a row behind the Physic Garden. All bolted and barred, entrance gates opened by residents flashing an instrument at them. Anthony sitting alone in nice large room. Totally blind, he looks distinguished with his white hair, which softens the slight austerity of heretofore. His eyes just slits under slanting brows. He was guided to luncheon table by nice South African girl who ate with us. He listens to talking books and radio, and I imagine continues to live because of Gillian. Told me that before proposing he warned her, twenty years his junior, that she might have to slave for a disabled old man. This has come to pass. She briskly walked in later having come from the Princess Royal's committee for children. Said the Princess was extremely quick and capable, and clever like Prince Philip. He said that during his long tenure of the office of Garter he got to know dozens of new men seeking arms and supporters. Most of the Labour peers wanted arms. He reminded me that it was through our parents' friends the Pearse-Duncombes† that we met as new boys in New & Lingwood's shop at Eton in 1921, when we were ordering our top hats, both aged twelve and a half.

Saturday, 6th March

Nicholas Ridley's‡ death a surprise to me, though photographs of him in newspapers show him gaunt and skeletal from lung cancer.

---

* Sir Anthony Wagner (1908–95); genealogist and writer on heraldry; Garter King of Arms, 1961–78, Clarenceux King of Arms, 1978–95; Eton contemporary of J.L.-M.; m. 1953 Gillian Graham (b. 1927; DBE 1994), writer and charity worker.
† Worcestershire hunting family.
‡ Conservative politician (1929–93), yr s. of 3rd Viscount Ridley; he had been obliged to resign from Mrs Thatcher's cabinet in July 1990 after Dominic Lawson, editor of the *Spectator*, published some anti-German remarks which he had uttered off the record; cr. life peer, 1992; m. 1st 1950 (diss. 1974) Hon. Clayre Campbell, dau. of 4th Baron Strathenden and Campbell, 2nd 1979 Judy Kendall.

Rosamond [Lehmann]* whose godson he was loved him dearly, and always thought him brilliant. I remember when he first joined the N.T. Executive Committee, a gasp went round the table at his good looks. They soon left him owing to his smoking. I thought him arrogant and charmless, but it seems he was loved by his staff. We used to exchange lunches with him and his first wife Clayre (whom he treated badly) when they lived near Bourton-on-the-Water, but never became intimate. I became irked by his off-hand, uncaring attitude to ancient buildings when he was Minister of the Environment, and had a skirmish with him when he announced that it did not matter how often country houses changed hands.† When we last met at a Foyle's luncheon, he was polite and friendly. He was a great man for the girls. Inherited some attributes of his grandfather Lutyens,‡ but as a painter was no great shakes.

Monday, 8th March

Reading St Thomas à Kempis§ I realise that a saint must be so disciplined that he is able to control his thoughts from evil. It is not enough to smile blandly on one's neighbour while thinking him an egregious bore. The saint may not even think any such thing.

Thursday, 11th March

To London to lunch with Ambrose Congreve,¶ who wrote out of the blue from Ireland inviting me on the strength of our having been contemporaries at Eton and his wife being a fan of my books. At Warwick House in precincts of St James's Palace, huge house where formerly we went to Ann Rothermere's** parties. Ambrose lives here one week every three months, *en prince*. Algerian manservant in uniform at door.

---

* Novelist (1901–90), with whom J.L.-M., on her death, considered he had been 'more intimate than with any other woman friend' (*Ceaseless Turmoil*).
† See *Ceaseless Turmoil*, 27 November 1988.
‡ Sir Edwin Lutyens (1869–1944); architect.
§ German divine (1380–1471); author of *Imitation of Christ*.
¶ Industrialist and philanthropist (b. 1907); of Mount Congreve, Co. Waterford, where he created a famous garden; m. 1935 Marjorie Glasgow (succeeding his father-in-law as chairman of the engineering firm of Humphreys & Glasgow, 1939–83).
** Ann Charteris (1913–81); m. 1st 1932–44 3rd Baron O'Neill, 2nd 1945–52 2nd Viscount Rothermere, 3rd 1952 Ian Fleming, novelist (1908–64).

Up vast and steep staircase to drawing room overlooking palace courtyard and Green Park. Smart butler and parlourmaid waiting. Highly
decorated rooms in style of 1740s, I guess not genuine. Pale yellow walls
and much gold, yet goodish taste. Ambrose verging on eighty-six, tall,
upright, robust, handsome with good complexion, the formerly red
hair now white. I recognised him instantly. Not deaf; in fullest possession. His wife, American heiress, is crippled and can't leave Ireland.

   We went downstairs to dining room. Odd arrangement, Ambrose
sitting at one end of table with myself on his right and another octo,
Michael Verey,* ex-merchant banker cousin of David V.,† on his left,
and his charming companion acting as hostess (niece? concubine?) at
other end, flanked by two young women. The lady next to me said
she was an old friend of Ambrose. How long, I asked? Twenty-six
years, she replied. I said I had known him for seventy. Of course, I
hardly knew Ambrose at all. But he said all his Eton friends were dead,
apart from Dunsany‡ who is dotty, and he liked to be in touch with
some survivors if they condescended to come to luncheon. Had Jack
and Frankie Donaldson recently. I take this as a kindly gesture from a
very rich man. Indeed, the *luxe* of Warwick House is for these days
astounding. My lady neighbour said that at Mount Congreve he
employs a hundred people, and has a huge garden. The house
(Regency) is huge too, and has been improved by him since accession.
To Verey, I heard Ambrose say, 'Do you suppose I did right in getting
rid of all Hong Kong?' I enjoyed this outing.

                                                    Sunday, 14th March

To tea yesterday with Tamara Talbot Rice,§ whom I imagined to be
dead until Coote¶ told me otherwise yesterday. Stopped on way at Coln
St Denis church, which for a wonder was open. And a lovely Cotswold

---

* Director of companies (b. 1912); High Sheriff of Berkshire, 1968.
† Architectural historian (1913–84) of Barnsley House nr Cirencester; m. 1939 Rosemary
Sandilands (1918–2001), garden designer and co-editor of books on gardening with
A.L.-M.
‡ Randal Plunkett, 19th Baron of Dunsany (1906–99).
§ Tamara Abelson (d. 1993: see entry for 5 October); translator and writer on Russian
subjects (sometime fellow Byzantine scholar of J.L.-M's friend Robert Byron); m. 1927
David Talbot Rice.
¶ Lady Dorothy Lygon (1912–2002), yst dau. of 7th Earl Beauchamp; m. 1985 (as his 2nd
wife) Robert Heber-Percy (1912–87) of Faringdon House, Oxfordshire.

church it is, situated on grass in middle of tiny village. Not a single
modern gravestone, and those great table tombs. By north door a pair
in design and carving, yet a hundred years between them; one dated
1760, the other 1860; same carved panel and convex top, suggesting that
grandson or even great-grandson of original mason repeated this faultless classical design. Norman tower in central position; interior white
plastered walls; decent nineteenth-century grey oak pews. Mural
plaque dated 1631, beginning, 'Here lyes my body fast inclosed within
this watery ground/ But my precious soul in it cannot be found'.
Another to John Bridges, d. 1679 (can't be a relation, says A.).[*] And on
war memorial, 'Live thou for England, We for England died'. Beautiful,
unspoilt, cared-for church. Churches should be places for, if not rejoicing, happy memories or reminders of family piety, instead of misery and
gloom. Eardley[†] hated them for they reeked of death, he said.

Tamara lives in last cottage of a row in Calcot, hamlet one mile from
Coln St Denis. As she says ruefully, it is in lovely picture postcard
country but totally isolated for her who can no longer drive and is
crippled with arthritis. Charming son and daughter-in-law received
me and gave me delicious tea. Tamara talked non-stop and I could tell
by their silent, dead-pan faces that they were bored to death by her
verbosity, yet respectful and clearly fond. She talked to me of Russia
today where conditions are appalling, far worse than under Communist regime when people at least had jobs of sorts and enough to eat.
Her friend the director of The Hermitage, person of international
repute, has to live in one room of a flat inhabited by four families.
Worst affliction of all the wild children who hold citizens to ransom,
descending in hordes to mug and rob. Police powerless to intervene.

Monday, 15th March

Sir John Acland[‡] came to see me in Bath. Wanted to discover motives
of his father Sir Richard in making over to N.T. all the family estates

---

[*] Alvilde was *née* Bridges (her father, Lieut-Gen. Sir Thomas Bridges, being a nephew
of the Poet Laureate Robert Bridges).
[†] Eardley Knollys (1902–91); painter; close friend of J.L.-M. from 1941, when they
became colleagues on the staff of the N.T.
[‡] Sir John Acland, 16th Bt (b. 1939); er s. of Sir Richard Acland, 15th Bt (1906–92),
eccentric landowner of radical political views who donated his estates in Devon and
Somerset to the N.T.

in 1943, on which the archives say little. I was aware of the negotiations at the time but had little part in them as Killerton [Devon] was not then considered a historic house. Sir John a nice, friendly man with great feeling for his family's territorial associations, of which his father had none. Sir Richard was a fanatical idealist, founder of Common Wealth Party.* Would never communicate with son, who at the time of the gift was a small child. Sir John is writing a book about his parents, and read me the introduction, very good I thought. He has not inherited one acre of the 16,000 which once belonged to his father, but has no resentment of N.T., with whom he gets on happily. Lives rent-free in beautiful dower house. Clearly has to get rid of the chip through writing about it. I cautioned him not to become neurotically obsessed with grievance.

Saturday, 20th March

Motored to tea with Charles Stuart-Menteth† at Hiram [Winterbotham]'s‡ old house in Woodchester [near Stroud]. I have always been fascinated by my great-aunt Jane Stuart-Menteth, married to Sir James who was born before Marie Antoinette's execution. She was a great patron of my mother and siblings when they were orphan children. My host, on the one occasion I met him, told me he had a photograph of Aunt Jane, so twenty years later I have written asking to see it. Charming 1740s house which in Hiram's day was grubby but full of character. Today, archetypal *House and Garden*. Was seated in deep sofa and given huge cup of milky tea by agreeable wife, with crumbly scone, jam and hard butter. Difficulties of eating genteelly immense. He said, 'I fear you are here on false pretences. Having taken the photograph of Aunt Jane out of its frame, I find it is not of her but a previous dowager.' A mist descended before my eyes, like those London fogs which permeated Logan Pearsall Smith's§ drawing room

---

* He was elected as Liberal MP for North Devon in 1935, resigned Liberal whip to found Common Wealth Party in 1941, and sat as Labour MP for Gravesend from 1947 to 1955.
† Yr s. (b. 1928) of Sir William Stuart-Menteth, 5th Bt; m. 1963 Priscilla Newman; his great-grandfather, Sir James Stuart-Menteth, 2nd Bt (1792–1870), had m. 1846 Jane Bailey (d. 1905), dau. of J.L.-M's great-grandfather Sir Joseph Bailey, 1st Bt (1783–1858).
‡ Textile manufacturer, gardener and Cotswolds social figure, who lived at Woodchester House with his ex-guardsman servant.
§ American writer and bibliophile (1865–1946), whom J.L.-M. (as described in his early diaries) knew in London during his last years.

in St Leonard's Terrace. 'Never mind,' I said. 'Of no importance whatever. You must forgive the foolish curiosity of an old man.' We talked
agreeably of other things, while the elusive Aunt Jane again receded
into limbo.*

We dined with David and Caroline[†] alone, as of old. Cosy dinner,
in so far as one is ever truly cosy with David. He told me he was about
to sell the Lower Woods to the Nature Preservation People to raise a
final £800,000 for death duties. They will keep it sacrosant as 800 acres
of primaeval forest, and he will be spared annual maintenance costs of
£20,000. He has a grievance against the Export of Works of Art
Committee which kept him waiting three years before allowing him
to sell the Badminton Cabinet, during which time he had to pay
heavy interest on the money he owed the Treasury. He is also strongly
critical of the local planning authorities for insisting that he put vast
picture windows into the barns which he converts into little gents'
residences, in place of the original doors for hay wagons. The truth is
that these barn conversions are seldom successful, though I suppose it
is a little better than pulling them down.

Monday, 22nd March

First day of spring. A bitter wind and some rain. Freda[‡] came in the
morning, and we drove with her to luncheon party given by Coote
[Heber-Percy] in her nasty little house [in Faringdon, Oxfordshire].
But lovely old friends – Billa [Harrod] from Norfolk;[§] the Johnstons;
J. Craxton[¶] wearing moustache, the essential disguise today of what
everyone knows and accepts. Chrissy Gibbs,[**] very intelligent and
delightful, talked of Bruce Chatwin, whom he considered almost a
genius, but not beautiful with his unfinished, adolescent face. Bruce
went mad towards the end for, earning some money at last from book

---

* See entry for 20 April 1995.
[†] David Somerset, 11th Duke of Beaufort (b. 1928); owner of Badminton estate; m. 1st
1950 Lady Caroline Thynne (1928–95), dau. of 6th Marquess of Bath, 2nd 2000 Miranda
Morley.
[‡] Freda Bernstein (b. 1923); m. 1946 Sir Lennox Berkeley, composer (1903–89).
[§] Wilhelmine Cresswell (1911–2005); Norfolk conservationist; m. 1938 Sir Roy Harrod,
economist (1900–79).
[¶] John Craxton (b. 1922; RA, 1993); painter and designer.
[**] Christopher Gibbs (b. 1938); antique dealer and collector, member of N.T. commit-
tees.

sales, he imagined he was rolling, and spent extravagantly. Coote in butcher's apron dispensing good food.

At home with Freda in the evening we watched Michael Berkeley* presenting Britten's *War Requiem*. Michael very handsome, just like his mother twenty years ago, in command, bestowing attractively gracious smile from time to time. He is a splendid success.

Tuesday, 23rd March

Geoffrey Houghton-Brown's nephew Dr Newton telephoned that G. had left me a small picture in his will and asked me to collect it today when other legatees also assembling at 29 Thurloe Square. London rather jittery after Warrington bombing.† My picture a village scene at Vignolles by Jean Hugo,‡ very nice to have.

Richmond Herald§ lunched with me at Brooks's. He praised my letter in the *Sunday Telegraph* about the Bishop of Gloucester, whom together with his Truro brother he has known all his life, the brother bishops being old friends of his parents.¶ Is very upset by the scandal.

Thursday, 25th March

Have received numerous letters approving of my letter about the poor Bishop, and not all from queers either.

This evening, walking through the arches of the House, and round the purlieus of the garden within the Park, I noted chestnuts in tight bud, about to burst. As I returned, facing the setting sun, I noticed small patches of powdery grey-blue on the ground, almost the colour of the Queen Mother's hats. It was dead beech leaves from last year – the sort of speckle an Impressionist painter would have made hay with.

---

* Composer and broadcaster (b. 1948); er s. of Sir Lennox and Freda *née* Bernstein.
† An IRA bomb in a packed shopping centre that morning had claimed the lives of two children.
‡ French artist (1894–1984).
§ Patric Dickinson (b. 1950); Richmond Herald of Arms from 1989.
¶ Peter John Ball (b. 1932), Bishop of Gloucester from 1992 (and twin brother of Michael Thomas Ball, Bishop of Truro, 1990–97), had been obliged to resign his see after suggestions that he had once shown excessive interest in a young novice monk.

Friday, 26th March

Looking from my back window in Bath I can see the lovely sight of the neighbours' magnolia with its snow-white buds spread against our large, leafless copper beech. Such beauty of nature is not, as flower-lovers like to suppose, for human benefit, but a natural act of breeding and survival. Nature never intends aesthetic effects. Today's paper shows the first ever close-up photograph of the planet Venus, a kind of etched map of burnt crimson which has presumably been exhibiting its beauty to no one for billions of years. Odd.

Reading Sachie [Sitwell]'s life of Liszt,[*] who in the 1840s was mobbed in every capital of Europe. Sometimes a grand piano would be trundled into railway stations so he could perform to a crowd of admirers while waiting for a change of train. Even Liszt with his vanity and love of theatre eventually found this too much and had to call it off.

Saturday, 27th March

We lunch with Deedee Saunders[†] at Easton Grey [near Malmesbury, Wiltshire] for presumably the last time. She has already sold it for £3 million. Fine situation above little valley and village buried amidst trees. The house not really good. Entrance front so-so. Much good-taste alteration this century. Rooms faked up pleasantly. Pomposo staircase like that of London palace. The corner room we are received in is hung with large framed engravings of Panini. Ten or twelve persons assembled at long dining table while the public, come to see spectacular display of daffodils in the garden, flatten their noses against the window panes. I sit between Mollie Norwich and an ancient American lady, one of several present who travel ceaselessly around the world to stay in identical overheated hotels. Also weird old man who lives in Rome and knew many of my deceased friends like John Leslie[‡] and D'Arcy Osborne.[§] A rather gruesome occasion.

We dined alone with David [Beaufort], a rare and agreeable event.

---

[*] Hungarian composer and virtuoso (1811–86).
[†] American ex-wife of Peter Saunders, clothing manufacturer and cultivator of daffodils.
[‡] Sir John Leslie, 4th Bt (b. 1916 and not yet deceased), of Castle Leslie, Co. Monaghan; Roman Catholic Irish squire, once resident in Rome and a collector of Italian pictures and furniture.
[§] Francis D'Arcy Godolphin Osborne (1884–1964); diplomatist, British Minister to the Holy See, 1936–47; s. 1963 as 12th and last Duke of Leeds.

He says he is obliged to resurface the whole north front of the House, pointing out what I should have observed, that it is stuccoed, not of stone. Took me out to show me after dinner. Still, I wonder whether the central Old Somerset House portion with giant pilasters is not of stone. Strange that the seventeenth century should have faced rubble. He deplored that he had no friends in the near neighbourhood save, he was good enough to say, us. We did have a few who are dead. Very enjoyable evening. He is a sane, shrewd man, with a clear brain, and clearly devoted to the place.

Sunday, 28th March

We lunch with the Salmonds at Didmarton. They too are on the market, and I shall be sorry to lose them. Today I fancied they were friends and not acquaintances. He is very retiring, taciturn, sensitive, reclusive. Caryl Waterpark* who was present has recently retired from mysterious work with the RAF. Recently attended a conference in Moscow at which the Russian generals got so drunk that one of them tried to step out of an aeroplane in flight. Says the condition of that country more appalling than we can realise, people's incomes reduced by inflation to barest level of subsistence. At luncheon today, as yesterday, I felt very dotty. Have written to Nigel [Nicolson]† declining to unveil plaque to his parents in May. Could not explain the reason, which is dysphasia of a senile sort.

We got back to entertain Nick and Alice [Robinson] and little Matthew aged two and a half. A smiling, responsive child, who smiles when one smiles, sings nursery rhymes, gallops around the lawn, merry and bright. Yet two hours was enough.

Thursday, 1st April

I have received a letter from Ambrose Congreve's nonagenarian wife Marjory which amuses me no end. She claims to be a fan of mine,

---

* Caryl Cavendish, 7th Baron Waterpark (b. 1926); half-brother of A.L.-M's intimate friend Rory Cameron (1914–85); director of aviation companies; m. 1951 Daniele Girche.
† Soldier, politician, writer and publisher (1917–2004); yr son of Harold Nicolson (1886–1968) and Vita Sackville-West (1892–1962); co-founder of Weidenfeld & Nicolson; author of a book about his parents, *Portrait of a Marriage* (1973); inherited Sissinghurst Castle from his mother, and donated it to N.T.; invited J.L.-M. (1976) to write his father's biography.

and got him to buy her a complete set of my books from Heywood Hill, and then ask me to luncheon at Warwick House. Now she writes that she particularly loves my description of walks in Hungary. I have never walked in Hungary or written about it. She is confusing me with Paddy Leigh Fermor.*

Friday, 2nd April

Desmond [Shawe-Taylor]† was to lunch with us. When he had not arrived by two o'clock I rang up Long Crichel. Housekeeper said he had left at twelve, having meant to leave at eleven but fiddled around for an hour. 'I don't know what he does,' she added. He arrived at 2.45, having lost his way several times. He is much aged, and we suspect has had a small stroke on his left side. Holds his left hand as though it is fairly useless. Very red in the face, deaf and curiously dense for so clever a man. I escorted him back to the motorway when he left to stay with Charles Fletcher-Cooke.‡ He was extremely vague about the route, which we went over again and again on the map. Two hours later, Charles F.-C. telephoned to ask if D. had left us. Very sad.

Monday, 5th April

Tall, swarthier than I had imagined but very handsome, with grey hair, is Nicholas Shakespeare§ who came to see me in Bath this morning. Has immense charm. Face reminds me of Mary Keen and Patrick O'Donovan,¶ round, constantly breaking into smiles. Was at Winchester and Cambridge with Nick Robinson, whom he claims as his best friend. He came to talk about Bruce Chatwin whose biography he is to write.** Wanted to know how Bruce was regarded as a

---

* Patrick Leigh Fermor (b. 1915; ktd 2004); writer, living in Greece; m. 1968 (as her 2nd husband) Hon. Joan Eyres-Monsell, photographer (1912–2003).
† Music critic (1907–95); co-tenant of Long Crichel, Dorset.
‡ Sir Charles Fletcher-Cooke (1914–2001); barrister and longstanding Conservative MP, obliged to resign as a junior Home Office minister in 1963 owing to a minor scandal.
§ Nicholas Shakespeare (b. 1957); writer; successively literary editor of *The Times*, *Daily News*, and *Telegraph* (*Daily* and *Sunday*), 1985–91; about to publish his novel *The High Flyer* (Harvill Press).
¶ Charismatic journalist (d. 1981) who was J.L.-M's fellow officer in the Irish Guards, 1940–1.
** Published by Harvill Press in 1999.

neighbour. Anyway we talked for hours and he shared boiled eggs with me. Very easy and delightful. His second novel about to appear, the first having won awards. Very clever young man of thirty-five, who has already been literary editor of *Telegraph*, both *Daily* and *Sunday*, which almost killed him. Told me that Bruce's books, here, in America and in translation, now sell several million copies a year. Almost unbelievable. Why? It is a Byronic success story – on the one hand Bruce's extreme good looks, his comparatively early and as it were romantic death from Aids, on the other his sense of publicity and his outrageous behaviour. N.S. knew Bruce towards the end when he was a wraith, yet with burning eyes that still set people alight. N.S. himself has no 'artistic'* inclinations but takes them in his stride. Thinks Bruce a very good writer, and that there are few such about (Paddy Leigh Fermor not one of them, too contrived with his purple prose). But I wonder if Bruce is not a flash in the pan.

Friday, 9th April

Listened on radio yesterday to yachtsmen giving hair-raising accounts of experiences crossing the oceans single-handed, braving fifty-foot waves, icebergs, thunder and lightning, winds of 200 m.p.h., flooding of decks, terrible tossing, near-capsizing, and extreme loneliness. By the end of the programme I felt I had just landed at Southampton after undergoing these experiences myself. Yet all of them said they loved it in retrospect, and willingly returned to the lonely terrors of the ocean. Then this morning a man called Noel spoke of a jump from an aircraft when his parachute failed to open and his fall was broken by a large tree. He recounted every stage of the fall from seven thousand to two hundred feet, during which he was conscious the whole time and concentrated his thoughts on the past, his family, and the fatal impact that seemed imminent. Broke every bone in his body, was in intensive care for weeks and almost died. Six months later repeated jump at same site.

Igor† has come for Easter weekend. He is tall, with a good figure and Christ-like good looks, but gormless. Keeps asking frivolous

---

* Euphemism for 'homosexual' employed sarcastically by J.L.-M., his philistine father having used the word to imply effeminacy and 'unnatural vice'.
† J.L.-M's step-grandson Igor Luke (b. 1965), o. s. of Hon. Clarissa Chaplin and Michael Luke.

questions such as 'Who was the Countess of X's grandmother?' A. replies, 'You who wish to be so correct should not refer to Lady X as Countess.' He is helpful in the house, and guileless and good, but anyone more boring could not easily be conjured up by a novelist.

Sunday, 11th April

We lunched, taking Igor, with John Julius [Norwich] and Mollie. On my left sat a girl looking just like J.J's daugher Artemis,* with same governessy air, though she assured me she was no relation of J.J., just a goddaughter. It turns out she is J.J's illegitimate daughter, but whether she is aware of the fact I don't know.† I remember it being said that her mother would push the pram past the Norwiches' house in Little Venice just to annoy J.J's then wife Anne.

Monday, 12th April

We had a luncheon party for the Bank Holiday, quite an effort for A. but quite a success too. Michael and Isobel Briggs and the Peter Levis.‡ The poor Briggses have lost immense sums at Lloyd's, so Michael told A. Peter L. charmed A., and signed a copy of his excellent *Tennyson*. It is said to be selling a thousand copies a week, which is splendid for them. She is full of chat and fun.

Wednesday, 14th April

The Reverend Prebendary John Foster,§ with whom we lunched, told us that he wished Freda [Berkeley] would remove Lennox's ashes from under the altar of his church at Paddington Green. Once a year the altar has to be shifted and the Rev. is obliged to shunt said ashes around. We suggest that they ought to repose in the Berkeley

---

* Hon. Alice (Artemis) Cooper (b. 1953); dau. of 2nd Viscount Norwich and his 1st wife Anne Clifford; writer.
† Allegra Huston (b. 1964); dau. of Enrica 'Ricky' Soma (1932–69), ballet dancer, who m. 1950 (as his 4th wife) John Huston (1906–87), film director.
‡ Peter Levi (1931–2003); Jesuit priest (to 1977), Oxford classics don, archaeologist, writer and poet; Professor of Poetry at Oxford, 1984–9; m. 1977 Deirdre *née* Craig, widow of Cyril Connolly.
§ Vicar of St Mary's, Paddington Green, 1969–94 (b. 1929); received into Roman Catholic Church, 1994, and ordained as RC priest, 1996 (living and working in Bath).

Chapel at Berkeley Castle, for which Lennox had such strong ancestral feelings.*

Saturday, 17th April

I find my morning routine exhausting. Having taken A. her breakfast,
made and eaten my own, washed up, and made the beds with Peggy
(except for Sundays when I do them alone), I am worn out before
tackling letters or diary editing.† Also, wearing thick brown shoes with
leather soles tires me greatly; I now need light shoes with springy
crepe soles. Twenty years ago the idea of worrying about the weight
of my shoes would have made me hoot with laughter. Also I try to
save myself journeys in this minute house, tending to postpone fetching a tool from the outside shed until I also have to bring in some fire-
lighting paper – except that I do not remember, and end up making
two journeys anyway. My memory is so poor that I put objects – the
book I am reading, A's bedside bottle of Perrier – on the lower steps
of the staircase so as not to forget them when I next go upstairs.

Sunday, 18th April

Humphrey Stone‡ to luncheon, bringing daughter Emily§ and delicious food cooked by wife Solveig. Daughter aged seventeen, doing
thesis on monumental portrait sculpture in England. Very bright,
sweet and well-mannered, pretty with makings of a developed beauty.
Was surprised that she agreed passionately with her father about the
traditional C. of E. ritual, and undesirability of women priests. We
examined the monuments in the church afterwards.

Friday, 23rd April

Clarissa [Luke] came for the weekend, so I went to stay with Myles
[Hildyard] at Flintham. Took train from Gloucester to Nottingham

---

* Lennox was a grandson of the 7th Earl Berkeley, but owing to his father's illegitimacy
was unable to inherit the earldom, which became extinct on the death of the 8th Earl in
1942, Berkeley Castle and its estate passing to a remote cousin.
† J.L.-M. was then editing his diaries for 1953–4 and 1971–2, published by John Murray
in 1994 as *A Mingled Measure*.
‡ Typographical designer (b. 1942); m. 1968 Solveig Atcheson.
§ Art history student (b. 1975); m. 2003 Bruno Shovelton.

where Myles met me. David Rowbotham cooks wonderfully and has decorated every room with his own hands. House could not be more comfortable. I had my usual Victorian room on north-west corner, walls plastered with lovely Richmond-style ladies from Queen Victoria's Court. At dinner, David expressed strong objections to entertaining adulterous couples, meaning married men with their male lovers. 'I won't stand for it,' he said, to Myles's amusement.

Saturday, 24th April

In the morning, Myles drove me to Newstead [Abbey]. Walked along lake and round gardens, beautifully maintained, as is house. Walked down yew tunnel beside stew pond where Byron bathed. Heard first cuckoo this year, surprisingly early. A hasty look over house. Byron's bed which he had at Cambridge, with coronets at corners. Page's room alongside, for Rushton and then presumably Fletcher.* I was impressed with the way Notts County Council run this place.

In the afternoon we went to Thrumpton Hall, last visited with Hugh Euston† in 1950s. Received by George Seymour,‡ very friendly, extremely correct, snobbish, who took me round and told me about his problems with this very interesting house. I had forgotten the marvellous 1660s staircase, which has now been stripped of dark varnish to show the variety of woods used – fruit, lime and elm. A really fine construction. Saloon of same date, he thinks by Webb§ but no evidence, panelled and painted dark pink. Good furniture and pictures, notably full-length Lely¶ of Duchess of Newcastle wearing feathered hat. Fireplace of local alabaster. In the library we were joined for drinks by Mrs, aunt of Millie Acloque,** nice rugged lady resembling

---

* William Fletcher and Robert Rushton, Newstead boys who became personal servants to the poet George Gordon, 6th Baron Byron (1788–1824).

† Hugh FitzRoy, 11th Duke of Grafton (b. 1919); Chairman of Society for the Protection of Ancient Buildings; m. 1946 Fortune Smith, Mistress of the Robes to HM The Queen from 1967; in the 1950s, as Earl of Euston, he had been N.T. Historic Buildings Representative for East of England.

‡ George FitzRoy Seymour (1923–94); kinsman of Marquess of Hertford and cousin of 11th Duke of Grafton; a JP, DL and sometime High Sheriff of Nottinghamshire; m. 1946 Hon. Rosemary Scott-Ellis, dau. of 8th Baron Howard de Walden.

§ John Webb (1611–72); architect, assistant to Inigo Jones.

¶ Sir Peter Lely (1618–80); Dutch-born portrait artist.

** Hon. Camilla Scott-Ellis (b. 1947), yst dau. and co-heiress of 9th Baron Howard de Walden; m. 1971 Guy Acloque. They had purchased Alderley Grange from A.L.-M. in 1974.

Violet Powell* but without her intellect, and a strange yob-like bruiser who sat mute and gazing into space. Myles disclosed that he is the 'friend' with whom G.S. rides pillion all over the country on an enormous motor bike − *very* strange.

Sunday, 25th April

Myles drove me to Melbourne [Hall, Derbyshire] to see the garden. To our amazement we were the only visitors, though the village full of Sunday crowds. Myles fascinated by the almost invisible wires attached to statuary for alarm purposes, he having suffered several thefts and injuries to his. Statues looked pretty poor however and I wondered if they were substitutes to mislead robbers. Garden well run. Said to have been influenced by Versailles. Then a hurried visit to Sir Robert Shirley's† chapel, but too late for entry, and a walk in grounds of Staunton Harold [Leicestershire], which looks as though a Cheshire Home has vacated.‡

Saturday, 1st May

Though A. is poorly again, she insisted on preparing lunch for two understanding old friends, Patricia Hambleden§ and Chrissy Gibbs. Patricia much changed, face puffy and veined from cortisone, but cheerful. Says she feels embarrassed that her mistress [Queen Elizabeth The Queen Mother], several years her senior, feels no fatigue. Does she ever, I asked? No, never. Does she ever snub people? Never in words; but she can put down with the sweetest smile. Never loses her temper on any occasion.

Sunday, 2nd May

Lunching at the House today, Margaret-Anne [Stuart]¶ said she had been asked to a luncheon where Rupert Murdoch was also to be a

---

* Lady Violet Pakenham (1912–2002), dau. of 5th Earl of Longford; m. 1934 Anthony Powell, novelist (1905–2000).
† English traveller and adventurer (1581–1627).
‡ It had − though by 2004 the house was being restored as a residence by the Blount family.
§ Lady Patricia Herbert (1904–94), dau. of 15th Earl of Pembroke; m. 1928 3rd Viscount Hambleden; Lady-in-Waiting to HM Queen Elizabeth from 1937.
¶ Margaret-Anne Du Cane; interior decorator; m. 1979 as his 3rd wife David Stuart, 2nd Viscount Stuart of Findhorn.

guest. She was going merely in order to announce that she would not sit down at the same table with him, and then turn on her heel. I sat next to Josephine Loewenstein,[*] who said that Rupert was spending a week at Lourdes in his capacity as Chancellor of the Order of Malta, pushing the wheelchairs of the disabled and giving them comfort and refreshments. She said they were both in despair about their son Konrad,[†] who with all his gifts and intelligence, double firsts, call to the bar, piano playing attainments, etc., does nothing but scribble the beginnings of a play which will never be taken. At this the daughter Rosa[‡] expostulated with her mother, saying she was sure Konrad would find his feet and eventually write a famous book. The commendable loyalty of a sister. But will he? Cursed with too much money, I said.

Wednesday, 5th May

To London for the day. It was with some misgivings that I delivered two hefty notebooks of my diaries to John Murray. Either they will reject them, or I shall regret their publication. Mark Amory[§] and Hugh Massingberd[¶] lunched at Brooks's. M.A. very agreeable and jolly. Still struggling with biography of Gerald Berners,[**] who he suspects enjoyed being ill-treated by that brute Heber-Percy.[††] Hugh now admits that what remains of the country house regime is doomed. Says no house can be maintained with an estate of less than 10,000 acres, of which a mere score have survived.

---

[*] Prince Rupert zu Loewenstein-Wertheim-Freudenberg (b. 1930); financial adviser; m. 1957 Josephine Lowry-Corry; formerly neighbours of the L.-Ms at Biddestone Manor, they now lived in Richmond, Surrey.

[†] Prince Konrad (b. 1958).

[‡] Princess Maria Theodora (b. 1966).

[§] Writer and journalist (b. 1941); longtime literary editor of *Spectator*.

[¶] Hugh Montgomery-Massingberd (b. 1946); writer, journalist, publisher, genealogist, and author (2002) of a play – *Ancestral Voices* – based on the diaries of J.L.-M. (which by the end of 2004 had been running as a touring production for more than two years); then Obituaries Editor of the *Daily Telegraph*, where he created the modern, anecdotal style of newspaper obituary.

[**] Gerald Tyrwhitt-Wilson, 14th Baron Berners (1883–1950); composer, writer and aesthete, whose biography by Mark Amory, *The Last Eccentric*, appeared in 1998.

[††] The handsome but unstable Robert Heber-Percy (1912–87), known as 'the Mad Boy', Berners' great love who inherited his property.

Thursday, 6th May

While I was breakfasting in the kitchen, the front door rang and Tom Gibson* asked if I would witness a document. This turned out to be his formal resignation of his incumbency, to take effect from August. I knew he was to retire in a year or two, but this nevertheless came as a shock. He and Gloria have become real friends and will be sorely missed. Indeed shall we have a vicar at all, or a peripatetic clergyman from Wotton to serve our parish? Tom said he would be seventy in August and thought it sensible to retire while he had moderately good health. Has bought a house in Lansdown Place West. They will spend four months of the year in South Africa, and one month of each autumn at Lake Como.† We feel deserted.

Misha,‡ with whom I had a hasty cup of tea yesterday, went to Newbury to hear Enoch Powell§ speak in support of a friend of M. who is standing in the by-election there as an opponent of the Maastricht Treaty.¶ Powell, who has Parkinson's Disease, struggled to the platform looking gaunt, wasted, half-alive. Then spoke with burning passion for twenty minutes against the surrender of British independence, spellbinding his audience. Never had M. witnessed such a gripping display of oratory. Then Powell subsided, almost collapsed, and was led away. It was probably his last appearance on the political scene, and worth recording in history.

---

* Revd Thomas Gibson (b. 1923); Vicar of Badminton, 1974–93.

† Where he held the Anglican chaplaincy.

‡ Michael Bloch.

§ J. Enoch Powell (1912–98); writer, classical scholar and politician, known for his brilliant oratory, his opposition to Commonwealth immigration and to British membership of the European Union, and his support for Ulster Unionism; Conservative MP for Wolverhampton SW, 1950–74, Ulster Unionist MP for South Down, 1974–92; m. 1952 Margaret Wilson.

¶ Dr Alan Sked (b. 1948); writer and LSE history lecturer. He stood at the by-election on behalf of the Anti-Federalist League, of which he was founder and leader. (It later changed its name to the UK Independence Party, and he resigned from it after the 1997 general election.) The 600 votes Sked won at Newbury made little difference to the result: the seat was captured from the Conservatives by the Liberal Democrats with a majority of some 20,000. For J.L.-M's own views on the Maastricht Treaty (which was signed in February 1992 and created the European Union), see entry for 27 May 1993.

Monday, 10th May

This morning I was surprised to receive a letter from Grant [McIntyre], who has already read my diaries and is enthusiastic about them.

Thursday, 13th May

Desmond Briggs* lunched with me in Bath. Has been on holiday in some perfect little inn in Devon with Simon Raven,† his oldest friend. On their first night, they were given a table next to an old couple. Next day at luncheon, Desmond said, 'I got the head waiter to give us a table away from that couple.' Why, asked Raven. 'Because the noise of their false teeth when eating was maddening.' It then transpired that the noise came from Raven's teeth.

Saturday, 15th May

I motored A. to a garden centre near mouth of the Avon. A jolly lady attended to us. A. said to me brusquely, 'Just carry that pot, Jim.' The lady said, 'Poor old Jim. You might say "please".' Then, when we left, 'Bye bye, old Jim.'

The L.-Ms enjoyed a week's holiday at La Fourchette, Mick Jagger's‡ house in Amboise, Indre-et-Loire, whose garden A.L.-M. had designed in the 1980s.

Wednesday, 19th May

I accompany A. to La Fourchette, her first visit for two years. The incomparable Jim Honey§ our guide. We flew from Bristol and were given VIP treatment. Arnaud, Jagger's agent, met us at Paris airport and motored us. Frightful traffic, it being the eve of Ascension Day which is a public holiday. By nightfall we had got no further than Chartres, where we stopped for an excellent dinner. We resumed

---

* Publisher (1931–2002); novelist (as Rosamond Fitzroy); a JP for Wiltshire. He and his partner Ian Dixon (b. 1946) were solicitous friends to both L.-Ms.
† Novelist (1928–2001), who drew heavily in his writings from his own devil-may-care early life; Desmond Briggs was the editor of his increasingly careless work.
‡ Michael Philip 'Mick' Jagger (b. 1943); singer and songwriter, co-founder of the Rolling Stones, 1962; m. (2nd) 1990 Jerry Hall.
§ A.L.-M's partner in her garden designing activities.

journey at 11 p.m. and arrived in torrential rain at 1 a.m. A. found the journey a struggle, but managed gallantly. Jim H. marvellous with her, gentle, patient and affectionate. Clever without being educated, admits to never reading a book.

Thursday, 20th May

We recover from journey. Jaggers not in residence, which is a relief. A. given room on ground floor beneath mine. This *manoir* is enchanting. Mick J. loves phantasy with a touch of savagery – hence African masks, spears, grimacing Indian faces, a grinning skull with horns painted. Baroque mirrors, clouded glass. In the upstairs drawing room, next to my bedroom door, a canvas of George IV in Coronation robes with his retinue, including the Bachelor Duke.* Strange coincidence. I hear the cuckoo, first time since Newstead. It takes Byron or Mick Jagger to evoke this magic sound. Rains all day

Friday, 21st May

I am being very languid. Lie on bed all day reading *Anna Karenina* and dozing off between whiles. We eat deliciously in restaurants. French food as good as ever, only the formerly ubiquitous soup no longer obtainable.

Saturday, 22nd May

We motor to see the princes Philippe-Maurice and Louis-Albert de Broglie, younger brothers of the duc de Broglie† and would-be clients of A. and Jim H. They have bought La Bourdaiserie on edge of forest at Montlouis-sur-Loire and are making it into a superior residential hotel. Built 1830s in François Premier style, and like all imitations handsomer than the original style. Attractive embattled moat, now dry, affords low-ground walk. Pleasure grounds not at present attractive. Pouffes of box gone to seed. Vast walled garden with nothing to see.

---

* William George Spencer Cavendish, 6th Duke of Devonshire (1790–1858); Whig statesman and art collector, whose biography by J.L.-M., written at the behest of Debo Devonshire, had been published by John Murray in 1991.
† Victor-François, duc de Broglie (b. 1949); his brothers Philippe-Maurice (b. 1960) and Louis-Albert (b. 1963).

Ugly water-tower and windmill at far end. Yet paying visitors galore, looking bewildered. One of the young princes pretty, the other ugly – beauty and the beast.

Then to the Giscard d'Estaings* to see how the garden A. created for them is faring. Madame receives us in jeans; embraces A.; says they have just returned from China. Nice, short lady, resembling a miniature Mary Downer.† *Un peu boutonné*. Very pretty enclosure like monks' cloister garth against old abbey ruin, contrived by A. Whole place too trim for words – armed and uniformed sentry at gate; no blade of grass out of the true. The house is trim and classical *c.* 1850, later wings demolished by them. She shows us inside church when the ex-President enters. Affable. Proffers a half-shake, fingers only. Tall, bald, stooping, hollow-chested, a bit pot-bellied. Very affable. Says he saw nothing from Russian plane but the Gobi Desert. Excuses himself in order to walk the dog.

In the evening the elder of the two princes – Beastie – comes to La Fourchette to see the garden. Admires. Then drives off to dine with an English duke a hundred miles away. A. bets the princes do not come up to scratch.

Monday, 24th May

The Giscard d'Estaings came to see the garden this evening. An incident occurred of the sort which upsets me unduly these days. Before they arrived, the tiresome Arnaud turned up and announced that he had invited his parents to meet the Giscards and had arranged wine glasses on the terrace table. We were appalled by his insensitivity and cheek, and had to tell him this was not on. We had invited the Giscards who would be cross to find intruders. As if the Queen Mother had asked to see our garden at home, and arrived to find the Vicar and family, self-invited. The Giscards came, duly admired, and had tea with us in the little breakfast room with 'Tiepolo' wallpaper. He talked of Mrs Thatcher,‡ whose first years as P.M. coincided with his last as

---

* Valéry Giscard d'Estaing (b. 1926); President of France, 1974–81; m. 1952 Anne-Aymone de Brantes.

† Mary Gosse (b. 1925); m. 1947 Sir Alexander Downer (1910–81), Australian High Commissioner in London, 1964–72 (both families being known to A.L.-M. from the 1920s, when her father had been Governor of South Australia).

‡ Margaret Roberts (b. 1925); m. 1951 (as his 2nd wife) Denis Thatcher (later 1st Bt; d. 2003); Conservative Prime Minister, 1979–90; cr. life peer, 1992.

President. Was maddened by her dictatorial manner even then. Thought Callaghan* a decent fellow; but Wilson† a dreadful crook, who once pulled a fast one at a European summit in Dublin, when he announced to the press that Giscard had given way to his views, whereas it was in fact the other way round. President very handsome, splendid profile, aquiline features. Has fine manners of the old school like Charles de Noailles.‡ A. said he kissed her hand the right way, did not brush it against his cheek but just touched it with his lips. Well dressed *à l'anglaise*, jacket and tie, initials embroidered on shirt. In fact has considerable charm.

They spoke of Beauty and Beastie, who are cousins of Madame. G. said their father, the late duke,§ married a supposed heiress who finally inherited nothing. But an unknown elderly lady wrote out of the blue offering to make him her heir. Six months later she died and he inherited her fortune. He was murdered mysteriously, no one knows why, though the hired assassins were caught and convicted. G. added that all three sons – Beauty, Beastie and present duke – were the non-marrying sort, so the dukedom seems doomed to extinction.

They returned on the 25th.

Thursday, 27th May

In so far as I can understand the implications, I am bitterly opposed to the bloody Maastricht Treaty.¶ I foresee the European Community becoming like the Soviet Republics, governed by a distant, unknown, unseen force of rulers. It will produce lack of competition, lack of will to work, corruption, inefficiency, disunity and anarchy. Then we shall have a reaction in the form of tribalism, such as we now see in the former Soviet Union and the Balkans and every African nation state.

---

* James Callaghan (1912–2005); Labour Prime Minister, 1976–9; cr. life peer, 1987.
† Harold Wilson (1916–93); Labour Prime Minister, 1964–70 and 1974–76; cr. life peer, 1983.
‡ Charles, Vicomte de Noailles (1891–1981); patron of arts, arbiter of taste and manners; m. 1923 Marie-Laure Bischoffsheim (1902–70).
§ Prince Jean de Broglie (1921–76), who in fact died before he could inherit the dukedom.
¶ Signed 7 February 1992; ratified by UK Parliament after a long series of narrow votes between May 1992 and November 1994.

Saturday, 29th May

The bombing of the Uffizi[*] is the ultimate act of barbarism. The fact that such evil deeds can be committed makes me not wish to keep alive. No doubt we shall next hear of a bomb at St Mark's, Venice, and St Peter's, Rome. What can the motives be?

Monday, 31st May

I have written to young Winston Churchill[†] congratulating him on his remarks about immigration, saying that I was sure 80 per cent of the country agreed with him, though only 10 per cent had the guts to say so.

Tuesday, 1st June

Freda [Berkeley] tells A. that Yvonne Hamilton[‡] is dead. She (Yvonne) was invited to dine with Magouche[§] on Saturday but declined, with the rather odd excuse that she was going to have 'a heavenly banquet' with her deceased Jamie. On Sunday morning her maid found her dead in her bed, hands crossed over breast, a smile on her lips. She had prepared an uneaten supper, laid the table and decorated it beautifully. An overdose, presumably. Poor Yvonne, she was not ill but just old, lonely, and missing Jamie whom she adored. She was silly, but always kind, jolly and flirtatious. Loved entertaining her friends and the great and good.

Wednesday, 2nd June

To London for the day. Went first to National Trust office to look through Rudding Park file. Then Richard Shone[¶] lunched with me.

---

[*] A car bomb outside the Uffizi Gallery in Florence had killed five and injured thirty-seven as well as damaging important works of art. The atrocity turned out to be part of a Mafia plot to destabilise the Italian Government, for which fourteen people were tried and convicted in 1998.

[†] Winston Spencer Churchill (b. 1940); grandson of Sir Winston Churchill; Conservative MP, 1970–97, failing to achieve government office owing to his outspoken views and colourful private life.

[‡] Countess Yvonne Pallavicino; m. 1940 (as his 2nd wife) Hamish ('Jamie') Hamilton, publisher (he d. 1988).

[§] Jean Magruder (b. 1921); American-born social figure; m. 1st Arshile Gorky, Armenian artist (who coined the name 'Magouche'), 2nd Jack Phillips, 3rd Xan Fielding.

[¶] Art historian (b. 1949); associate editor (later editor), *Burlington Magazine*, from 1979.

He urged me to write a contemporary version of Aubrey's *Brief Lives*.[*]
Then to exhibition of Derry [Moore]'s portraits. Splendid one of
Fanny Partridge[†] with her striated countenance so full of character.
Then to London Library, where I cannot cope with the new catalogue
on a screen. Walked in pouring rain to Heywood Hill, where John
[Saumarez Smith][‡] presented me with a dark blue tie embroidered
with H.H. and outline of a book, designed by Andrew [Devonshire].[§]
Extraordinary idea. To be bestowed on the shop's longest and loyalest
customers, of which I am considered one.

Richard told me that Michael De-la-Noy[¶] wrote a horrid article in
the *Independent* on Vita [Sackville-West], whom he chose as his most
hated historical figure. R. asked me who my most hated living figure
was. I couldn't decide on the spur of the moment, though I said I
would have plumped for Lord Beaverbrook[**] were he still alive.
Richard said his was Mother Teresa.[††] I almost agreed, though I can't
actually hate her. She has certainly done much harm by denouncing
abortion and all forms of birth control as evil.

Thursday, 3rd June

J.K.-B. angelically motored down to lunch with me in Bath. I warm
to him much after I have purged my irritation at his self-deprecatory
manner. He told me that his family were coy about acknowledging
their descent from John Bunyan,[‡‡] whom they despised for his puri-
tanism.[§§] I made him follow me home to Badminton to see the garden

---

[*] Collection of notes and anecdotes about contemporaries collected by John Aubrey
(1626–97).

[†] Frances Marshall (1900–2004); painter, critic and diarist, survivor of Bloomsbury
Group; m. 1933 Ralph Partridge (d. 1960).

[‡] Managing director of Heywood Hill Ltd, booksellers in Curzon Street.

[§] The Duke had become the bookshop's majority shareholder in 1991.

[¶] Michael De-la-Noy (*né* Michael Delaney Walker); writer (1934–2002), whom J.L.-M.
had helped, during the late 1980s, to write a biography of Eddy Sackville-West, 5th Baron
Sackville (1901–65), cousin of Vita Sackville-West.

[**] Max Aitken, 1st Baron Beaverbrook (1879–1964); Canadian-born Conservative politician and newspaper owner.

[††] Albanian nun who worked among the poor of India (1910–97).

[‡‡] Writer and preacher (1628–88); author of *A Pilgrim's Progress*.

[§§] John Kenworthy-Browne's grandfather had been an Anglican clergyman, his father a
convert to Roman Catholicism.

and meet A. in the kitchen over a cup of tea. A success, I felt sure. He said the right things, and was good with her. When he left I walked in Vicarage Fields, impelled there by the sound of the cuckoo, so late in the season. Indeed heard two, one echoing the other. How my heart turns over and over. Fields awash with golden buttercups in waves, on an ocean of greenest grass.

Saturday, 5th June

A hot summer day. We drove to luncheon with Simon.* Ghastly journey, stuck in queues of traffic. On arrival found Simon and family drinking beside a new pool with fountains and rockery, like a ye-olde comfort station built in the 1930s on the Great West Road. But very kind welcome, and excellent luncheon, and jollity. Object of visit was silver forks and spoons, etc., which I brought for Simon to choose from. This they did and I am glad they will have these things which have long lain in our attic. I made a tentative condition that, were we to be burgled of our own silver, they would let us have some of it back on loan. Exquisite view of the Abberley Hills from their lawn.

Tuesday, 8th June

Very hot days we are having. A. who used to relish the heat now suffers from it owing to her heart. When I get home I sit in the shade and read. Today front doorbell rings. An unemployed youngish man with sandy moustache selling dishcloths and the like. I would not buy, but offered him money. He refused, for which I respect him, though with a pang of guilt for not being unemployed myself.

Sir John Acland has discovered an old letter of mine about the long-drawn negotiatiations between his father and the National Trust, which I describe as 'fraught with Sir Richard's protestations that everything should belong to everybody and nothing to anybody'. Which was true, I remember.

---

* J.L.-M's nephew Simon Lees-Milne (b. 1939), o. c. of his brother Dick and Elaine *née* Brigstocke; m. 1st 1962–74 Jane Alford, 2nd 1976 Patricia Derrick.

Sunday, 13th June

Yesterday we lunched at Hodges* with Charlie and Amanda Hornby.†
Much talk of his grandmother Eny‡ of whom he was fond. She
started by leaving Hodges to him, then thought he had become a
gambler and left it to someone else, then changed her mind and left
it to him again. Unfortunately they have been badly hit at Lloyd's and
may have to sell. For the moment they are selling paintings.

Today Michael and Isobel Briggs lunched with us. Michael said
that Alan Clark,§ who is one of his best friends, has been taken aback
by all the publicity attending the publication of his diaries. His wife
is upset and may leave him. Michael and Isabel also hit at Lloyd's.
M. says he has forfeited more than he ever got out of it, and I. has
lost all the money she made from *The Shooting Party*.¶ When they
left, we agreed how enormously we liked them both. I said, 'I could
live with Isobel.' A. said it was the first time I had ever said that of
anyone.

Thursday, 17th June

To London for the night. Bruce Hunter lunched at Brooks's. Hopes
soon to have an American publisher for *Venetian Evenings*.** Assures
me there is no problem with publishing my new volume of diaries as
I retain the copyright, though we might inform Yale, who own the
original manuscript,†† out of politeness.

---

* Converted fifteenth-century columbarium near Tetbury, Gloucestershire, with a
famous garden.

† Charles Hornby (b. 1939); second son of Michael Hornby and Nicolette *née* Ward of
Pusey House, Faringdon, Oxfordshire.

‡ Baroness Irene de Brienen (1883–1974); Dutch-born maternal grandmother of Charles
Hornby; m. (2nd) Admiral The Hon. Arthur Strutt.

§ Writer and politician (1931–99), who had (temporarily as it turned out) retired from
politics at 1992 general election, and whose diaries of his years (1983–91) as a government minister, *In Power*, also revealing much about his promiscuous private life, had just
caused a sensation on their publication.

¶ Novel by Isobel Colegate set on eve of First World War, published in 1980 and turned
into a fashionable film in 1985.

** Book in which J.L.-M. describes his favourite monuments in Venice, published by
Collins in 1988.

†† Many of J.L.-M's papers had been sold to the Beinecke Library at Yale in 1991.

At 5.45 to Annual Meeting of Royal Society of Literature. Freda came as my guest for award-giving by current President Roy Jenkins.* He is very dextrous and delightful on an occasion like this. In speaking he dances like a bear, making funny little gestures with his hands like Punch and Judy. When we left he rushed after us to have a word. He confirmed that his wife Jennifer was waiting until she reached a certain phase of her National Trust history before seeing me.

Freda gave me an excellent dinner at Hereford Mansions, in her roomy and desirable flat high up in a nice Edwardian block. When we had finished her friend Father Michael Hollings† came in and helped himself to whisky. Has lately been escorting Mother Teresa round his parish. She said to him, 'I am so glad you can see Jesus in me.' To my surprise, Father M. suggested that, in leaving the Roman Catholic Church, I was acting according to God's will. Somehow I feel I have not done any such thing. In the prevailing evil of the world he also sees God's mysterious hand. I quite liked him, though he is not my idea of what a priest ought to be.

Friday, 18th June

Had a bad night at Brooks's owing to the noise of traffic in St James's Street. Derry was to have had breakfast with me but evidently forgot. Ludovic Kennedy‡ came and sat at next table. We said good morning politely, then did not exchange another word, in accordance with the civilised Brooks's tradition. He had with him a black cane with silver hilt. I don't see why I should be shy of mine, which darling A. finds embarrassing.

---

* Roy Harris Jenkins (1920–2003); Labour politician, 1945–76; President of European Commission, 1977–81; co-founder and leader of Social Democrat Party, 1981–3; cr. life peer as Baron Jenkins of Hillhead, 1987; m. 1945 Jennifer Morris (b. 1921; DBE 1985; Chairman of N.T., 1986–90, and then writing a history of that organisation, which appeared in 1994).
† Michael Richard Hollings (1921–97); fought with Coldstream Guards in North Africa and Italy, 1942–5, being awarded MC; ordained RC priest, 1950; a chaplain, Westminster Cathedral, 1954–8; Chaplain, Oxford University, 1959–70; Parish Priest, St Mary of the Angels, Bayswater, 1978–97.
‡ Broadcaster, politician and humanitarian campaigner (b. 1919; ktd 1994); m. 1950 Moira Shearer, ballerina.

Saturday, 19th June

I motor to Coughton [Court, Warwickshire] to lunch with Ann Twickel* in her Colt house where once I lunched with her uncle Geoffrey Throckmorton soon after it was built in the early 1950s. She looks very like her mother old Lady Throckmorton. I arrived early and we started chatting about old times, her mother, the troubles since Sir Robert's death, the behaviour of her niece who booted out the widow, Isabel, telling her never to darken the doors of Coughton again.† Then there appeared Monsignor [Alfred] Gilbey,‡ staying upstairs. He is ninety-two, very bent, garrulous, full of good anecdotes though difficult to hear. He mumbles rapidly through clenched black teeth, his old head bent into his chest. Beautifully dressed, clean black soutane, wide purple sash, buckled shoes. He asked if he might put a personal question to me. I feared he was going to refer to my lapse from the true faith. But all he asked was whether, in my personal experience, I had ever come across an authentic case of Queen Mary demanding to be given an antique from someone she was visiting. I hadn't. He is of course a true Tridentine, unlike Father Michael Hollings. At the time of Vatican Council II, Cardinal Heenan§ said to Gilbey, 'In jettisoning the Latin Mass we are losing more than a language.' The Monsignor says his life is now totally dedicated to pleasure. Well, if it can't be at ninety-two, when can it be? He says he is enjoying the happiest possible old age. The others at luncheon were Maureen Fellowes,¶ her blimpish husband, and her Dormer daughter who is editing the correspondence of her ancestress

---

* Ann Throckmorton (b. 1911); m. 1939 Baron Ludwig von Twickel of Bavaria (died of wounds, 1945); Dame of Honour and Devotion of Sovereign Order of Malta.

† Ann was the sister of Sir Robert Throckmorton, 11th Bt, of Coughton (1908–89). He inherited the baronetcy in 1927 from their grandfather, their father having been killed in action, 1916. 'Old Lady Throckmorton' was their formidable mother (much admired by J.L.-M.), Lilian *née* Brooke, granted the right to use the style of a baronet's widow: she ruled Coughton until her death in 1955, and was responsible for its donation to the N.T. Their uncle, Geoffrey Throckmorton (1883–1971), was Clerk to the Journals in the House of Commons, 1940–8. 'The widow', Lady Isabel, dau. of 9th Duke of Rutland, was Sir Robert's 2nd wife.

‡ The Rt Revd Monsignor Alfred Gilbey (1901–98); Roman Catholic Chaplain to Cambridge University, 1932–65; resident at Traveller's Club, Pall Mall.

§ John Carmel Heenan (1905–75); Cardinal Archbishop of Westminster, 1963–75.

¶ Lady Maureen Noel (b. 1917), o. dau. of 4th Earl of Gainsborough; m. 1st 1944 15th Baron Dormer (by whom she had two daughters), 2nd 1982 Peregrine Fellowes (1912–99).

Bess, wife of the 5th Duke of Devonshire.* Grace before luncheon, all these Catholics crossing themselves. Talk of Knights of Malta, of which Mr Fellowes is one. Maureen, whom I thought pretty when I used to see her at Batsford before the war, is now a dumpy old lady who talks too much. Reminded me that her mother was Peruvian, so she speaks Spanish as well as English. Says the Noels are related to most of the great Catholic families of Europe. Exclusivity washes over them.

Monday, 21st June

In last night's dream I was with Richard Shone beside a castle on a Claude-like lake. The scene beautiful but tempestuous. The knowledge that I was capable of writing a great book surged over me. I wanted Richard to be aware of my capabilities. I fear this derives from a feeling that lately assails me that I shall never write a book again, good or bad. An ambition out of reach and attainment.

Patric Dickinson called on me in Bath, having invited me out to luncheon. In the end we went to the corner shop and bought a pie and slice of cheesecake each, and picnicked in the flat. Could barely hear a word he uttered. He does not finish sentences, and looks down to the floor. Otherwise clever and keen. Told me of further minor scandals in College of Arms, to do with fabricating false lineages.

Sunday, 27th June

To Chatsworth for weekend, driving there rather a strain. Staying were Mark Amory and wife Charlotte, both high-powered. He is nice and friendly and speaks like a Cecil, voice turning up into a scream. She is the daughter of Evelyn Joll of Agnew's, and manages hospitals for NHS. When we were introduced, she said how much she liked my novels; I told her she was the first person ever to have told me that. Also Robert Kee† and wife Kate Trevelyan, he abounding in charm, she sweet and attentive and half his age.

Debo has been appointed to a committee of three to advise on

---

* William Cavendish, 5th Duke of Devonshire (1748–1811); m. (2nd) Lady Elizabeth Foster (1759–1824), dau. of 4th Earl of Bristol.
† Writer and broadcaster (b. 1919); m. (3rd) 1990 Hon. Catherine Trevelyan.

opening Buckingham Palace to the public.* Says the Prince of Wales has long advocated public admission, and the Queen was won over even before the press started their campaign. Every consideration to be given to visitors – to be admitted by front door and there relieved of coats and brollies, returned to them at garden entrance when they leave. Debo says the Prince *never* referred to his matrimonial troubles before the separation [December 1992], but now does so. Trouble lies in fact that the Queen, Prince Philip and P. of W. all find it very difficult to talk to each other. Debo devoted to the Prince, who needs protection.

On Sunday both the Kees and the Amorys were in church to hear Beddoes the Vicar give his sermon on how God is in all things around us. Told us that, the previous night, strolling in the churchyard, he had stroked the head of a hen pheasant sitting on her nest. Afterwards I walked in the garden and sat on a bench. A cock pheasant came up to me and stroked my foot with his head, a thing that has never happened to me before. Observed that the trees in the park were squatting on their midday midsummer shadows like great black cushions.

Monday, 28th June

After a hot drive, we returned from Chatsworth in early afternoon, and had hardly got in when Bamber [Gascoigne] telephoned asking if they could come to tea. We were delighted to see them. Bamber losing hair and plumper, but still forever smiling. Christina somewhat haggard through still beautiful, resembling the later Virginia Woolf. Bamber gleefully unfolded a long and wide proof sheet of his Encyclopaedia of Britain, by which I was much impressed. He told me that Ann Gascoigne,[†] his cousin-by-marriage who is Bill Harcourt's daughter, inherited a collection of unknown miniatures which a friend visiting Stanton Harcourt identified as being by Nicholas Hilliard.[‡] These Hilliards known to have belonged to Robert Walpole,[§] who gave them to the Lord Harcourt of the

---

* The money raised from entrance fees was to be used towards the restoration of Windsor Castle, seriously damaged by fire the previous December.
† Hon. Ann Harcourt (b. 1932); er dau. of William, 2nd Viscount Harcourt (1908–79), Eton and Oxford contemporary of J.L.-M.; m. 1954 Crispin Gascoigne, o. s. of Bamber's uncle Major-General Sir Julian Gascoigne.
‡ Nicholas Hilliard (1547–1617); English miniaturist.
§ Statesman (1676–1745); the first 'Prime Minister', 1721–42; cr. Earl of Orford, 1742.

1730s,* since when they had lain there unrecognised. Mrs Gascoigne offered them to Roy Strong† for his exhibition, to get the reply that he was too busy to come and look at them, and that *everyone* these days seemed to think their miniatures were by Hilliard. They now have to be kept under lock and key.‡

Wednesday, 30th June

The [Tom] Gibsons, soon to be my neighbours in Bath at the end of the row, called to see the library. They will be dreadfully missed at Badminton. I have already inherited the chore of bestowing a daily paper on Daffers [Fielding];§ she is very welcome to it, but it is one more task to remember, come wind and wet. On the verge of seventy, Tom Gibson is a very handsome figure, with his neatly trimmed, snow-white beard. Wearing full canonicals as he dares, he looks splendid at the altar. Will I predict become R.C.¶

Friday, 2nd July

We visit Miranda [Morley]'s pretty garden this evening. David [Beaufort] present, and it was odd how he speaks of 'we'. We planned this border; we think so-and-so. Then looking at his watch he dons shirt over his naked torso, and says 'I' – not we – 'must be off'.

Saturday, 3rd July

Moira Shearer todays inveighs vitriolically against autobiographers and diarists exhibiting their squalid opinions and behaviour. She mentions several by name, but mercifully not me. And here am I about to publish more diaries, about the wisdom of which I have grave doubts.

---

* Simon Harcourt, 1st Earl Harcourt (1714–77); soldier and statesman, Lord-Lieutenant of Ireland, 1772–7; ancestor of 'Bill' Harcourt through female line.
† Sir Roy Strong (b. 1935); Director, Victoria & Albert Museum, 1974–87; writer and broadcaster.
‡ Despite these precautions, many of them were stolen in an audacious robbery some years later.
§ Hon. Daphne Vivian (1904–97); novelist, mother of Caroline, Duchess of Beaufort; m. 1st 1926 6th Marquess of Bath, 2nd 1953 Xan Fielding; eccentric resident of Badminton estate.
¶ He thought about it, but did not.

Meanwhile Nick [Robinson] suggests I write a ghost story to be published as what he calls a 'chap' book – a beautifully produced little
pamphlet with woodcuts. On thinking it over in bed, I decide I might
be able to write a story about a man haunted by himself in the future,
not by his present or past self.*

Sunday, 4th July

In bed last night, I listened to a fascinating programme about the
pianist Mieczyslaw Horszowski,† who gave his *début* in 1902 and died
two months ago aged a hundred and one. As a young man he knew a
woman who had been a friend of Mozart's son. After a long decline,
he got married at eighty and came out of his shell. A beautiful recording of him playing Schumann three years ago, when he was ninety-
eight. An extraordinary link with the past.

A. and I went to one of Alex [Moulton]'s luncheons at The Hall,
Bradford-on-Avon. Fourteen people, his niece Dione acting as
hostess. She complained to me that Alex was laying down tiresome
conditions to her son Julian whom he had nominated as his heir.
Would I intervene? I was guarded, not wishing to get involved and
never having met the boy. She says that, for an intelligent man, Alex
is maddeningly dictatorial, though she is clearly devoted to him. No
one there we knew, except for Anne Cowdray‡ and the Michael
Briggses. A stiff affair, and we left as soon as luncheon was over.

Monday, 5th July

Mark Leather who has succeeded John Leigh at Rathbone's§ motored
from Cheshire to see me in Bath. I told him what he presumably
already knew, that I was totally ignorant of all financial matters and
was absolutely in his hands. He believes that the great economic
opportunities of the future will be in China, as the Chinese work hard

---

* This was the origin of *Ruthenshaw*, a beautifully printed but unsatisfactory short story
published by Robinson in the autumn of 1994, illustrated with wood engravings by Ian
Stephen.
† Polish pianist (1892–1993).
‡ Lady Anne Bridgeman (b. 1913), yr dau. of 5th Earl of Bradford; m. 1939 (diss. 1950)
John Pearson, 3rd Viscount Cowdray (1910–95).
§ Liverpool firm which managed J.L.-M's investments.

and have been liberated economically by Mao's successor Deng.* Told me his mother was a Casson, and Sybil Thorndike's husband Lewis† his uncle.

Then Polly Lansdowne‡ took me for lunch to Royal Crescent Hotel. Charming woman, daughter of David Eccles§ and grand-daughter of Lord Dawson of Penn,¶ who attended George V on his deathbed, and has been unjustly accused (she claims) of killing him. Purpose of meeting was to talk of the film she is researching for Channel 4 on the House of Windsor.** Chief backer an American who won't allow it to be hostile to the monarchy. She told me how she worked at the Courtauld under Anthony Blunt.†† Greatly admired him as an art historian, but otherwise did not like him. Thinks he may have tried to enlist her into spydom, she then being the daughter of a Minister of the Crown. When Anthony was disgraced, she wrote to him out of pity. He instantly replied asking her to visit; but she would not go. Quite right.

When I got home, Michael Mosley‡‡ called to see the garden. Was most complimentary, but to A's disappointment did not talk garden language or question her. Rather old-fashioned, like many civilised bachelors I have known. Good manners and good company. Told amusing stories of Aunt Baba§§ and her inability to

---

* Deng Xiaoping (1904–97); *de facto* ruler of People's Republic of China from 1976 until his death.

† Sir Lewis Casson, actor (1875–1969); m. 1908 Dame Sybil Thorndike, actress (1882–1976).

‡ Hon. Polly Eccles (b. 1937); m. (2nd) 1969 (diss. 1978) 8th Marquess of Lansdowne (b. 1912).

§ David, 1st Viscount Eccles (1904–99); Conservative politician; m. 1st 1928 Hon. Sybil Dawson (d. 1977), dau. of Viscount Dawson of Penn, 2nd 1984 Mary Hyde.

¶ Bertrand Dawson (1864–1945; cr. Viscount Dawson of Penn, 1936); royal physician and medical statesman, who issued the famous bulletin from George V's deathbed in 1936 that 'the King's life is drawing peacefully towards its close', whereas in fact Dawson was about to terminate the sovereign's existence with a shot of heroin in the jugular.

** *The Windsors: A Dynasty Revealed*, narrated by Janet Suzman and first broadcast in 1994.

†† Art historian (1907–83); Surveyor of the Royal Pictures, 1945–72; revealed in 1979 to have been a Soviet agent during and after the Second World War, and officially disgraced.

‡‡ Hon. Michael Mosley (b. 1932); yr s. of Sir Oswald Mosley by his 1st wife Lady Cynthia Curzon.

§§ Lady Alexandra Curzon (1904–95); dau. of Marquess Curzon of Kedleston; m. 1925 Major E. D. ('Fruity') Metcalfe (d. 1957).

cope without servants. I was surprised to see an old man, as he seemed young when we met last.* Mouth suggests his grandfather Lord Curzon.†

Tuesday, 6th July

On Radio 3 I heard recordings of the last castrato, Alessandro Moreschi,‡ singing in St Peter's in 1902 and 1904 from the canticles of the Mass and from Rossini. A ghastly, ghostly voice with unnatural shriek of high notes turning into a yodel. Low notes occasionally lovely, though eerie. Unfortunately I missed the introductory talk, which gave the date at which the castration of choirboys ceased to be allowed. How Sachie [Sitwell] would have relished it.

Wednesday, 7th July

Tony Mitchell§ motored me to Montacute [House] and Forde Abbey.¶ The first vastly improved since my day, beautifully kept and full of rare things. Most friendly welcome from nice custodian and wife. Then to Forde in its hollow, where we were received by the present owner Mark Roper,** with whose grandmother I stayed in 1937. Appalling mass of cars and charabancs filling the field on east front, wearing down the grass and disgorging Women's Institute dames with white crimped hair and legs awry. Mark Roper began by saying that private owners arranged openings much better than the N.T., which is clearly not the case here. Then he accused the Trust of 'doing him down' by enticing more people to Montacute, which is hardly fair. Then we went round the house. It is strange that this ancient house should be so magical, for it is an architectural

---

* See *Beneath a Waning Moon*, 10 May 1986.
† George Nathaniel Curzon, 1st and last Marquess Curzon of Kedleston (1859–1925); statesman; Viceroy of India, 1898–1904, Foreign Secretary, 1919–24.
‡ Italian castrato singer (1858–1922) who spent most of his career in choir of Sistine Chapel, Rome.
§ Anthony Mitchell (b. 1931); N.T. Historic Buildings Representative 1965–96 (for West of England Region, 1981–96); m. 1972 Brigitte de Soye.
¶ Two properties in Somerset; the first bequeathed to the N.T. by Lord Curzon in the 1920s, the second belonging to the Roper family.
** Owner of Forde estate (b. 1935); High Sheriff of Dorset, 1984; m. 1967 Elizabeth Bagot.

muddle. The inanity of Mr Prideaux* sticking on a frontispiece to the Abbot's Perpendicular tower so as to obscure the side of it. But his Mannerist additions fascinating, and the Saloon a truly great room with the Raphael cartoon tapestries for which it was probably made in the 1650s. Abbot Chard's† cloisters of butter-coloured stone very handsome. Some Early English arcature revealed behind it, noble in itself. Since the Reformation, this immense and important house has never been in the ownership of a noble family, only of squires. (The Ropers are in fact a mid Victorian commercial family, though the current *châtelaine*, whom we did not see, is a Bagot of Levens.)

Wednesday, 14th July

A., who is giving a party at Newark, failed to get an answer from Burnet [Pavitt].‡ So I rang Virginia Surtees,§ who told me he was in King Edward VII Hospital after a fall. Over weekend he had his sister to dine with him. He was escorting her downstairs when he fell from mid-landing to bottom. He could not get up and she could not lift him, so she left him on the tile floor all night while she returned to his flat and slept in his bed, not liking to disturb the doctor in the middle of the night. I believe she is a bit cracked. The following morning he was taken to hospital suffering from shock, cold and great discomfort. Poor Burnet.

Thursday, 15th July

A young journalist from *Le Figaro* came yesterday to interview A. and photograph her and the garden. He was fascinated by the pictures and furniture, and thrilled to learn she had known Marie-Blanche de Polignac, Princess Winnie [de Polignac],¶ Stravinsky**

---

* Sir Edmund Prideaux; Attorney-General under Oliver Cromwell.
† Thomas Chard; Abbot of Forde (a Cistercian foundation) prior to Dissolution of the Monasteries (1539).
‡ Businessman with musical interests (1908–2002); sometime Trustee of Royal Opera House; friend of J.L.-M. since 1948.
§ Virginia Bell (b. 1917); adopted mother's name of Surtees; writer on the Pre-Raphaelites and other subjects.
¶ Winaretta Singer (1865–1943), heiress to sewing machine fortune; m. (2nd) Prince Edmond de Polignac; patroness of artists and composers; close friend during her last years of A.L.-M., then married to the aspiring composer Anthony Chaplin (later 3rd Viscount).
** Igor Stravinsky (1882–1971); Russian composer.

and Poulenc.* Now what Englishman penetrating a little house in a remote French village would have been interested in, say, Lady Ripon,† Malcolm Sargent,‡ Lennox Berkeley and John Banting?§

Tuesday, 20th July

Driving to Bath, I heard on Radio 3 that mothers will soon be able to determine whether the foetus in the womb is likely to be homosexual, moronic, epileptic or suffering from other disorders. Ought they to have the right to abort? All those interviewed with moronic or disabled children speak of the pleasure such offspring bring to them. But they are not only no pleasure to society in general, but an embarrassment and a hindrance as well as an expense to the taxpayer. Ought one to be encouraged to produce children who are half-witted etc. in a world which is already overpopulated with the sane and sound?

Wednesday, 21st July

I find Fanny Partridge's diary¶ riveting, especially as I knew most of those she consorted with. Many references to Eardley [Knollys], who I think comes out best among her friends of the 1960s. She is a very good writer, and I take heed of her comment on Lady Cynthia Asquith's diaries** that she made the mistake of feeling she had to write something every day, and described events rather than her responses to them. But the more I read the less I care for Fanny. Her prejudices come through like vitriol – anti-God, anti-royalty, anti-upper class (though I sympathise with her contempt for the idle, vain

---

* Francis Poulenc (1899–1963); French composer.
† Lady Constance Herbert (d. 1917); m. (2nd) 1885 Earl de Grey, later 2nd Marquess of Ripon (1852–1923); patroness of Royal Opera House, Covent Garden.
‡ Sir Malcolm Sargent (1895–1967); English conductor.
§ English artist (1901–72).
¶ *Other People: Diaries, 1963–1966* (Harper Collins, 1993).
** Lady Cynthia Charteris (1887–1960); dau. of 9th Earl of Wemyss and March; m. 1910 Hon. Herbert Asquith (1881–1947), yr s. of Prime Minister H. H. Asquith; writer, especially of children's stories; her diaries, covering the Great War, were published in 1969.

and snobbish like Helen Dashwood).* We were amused to read how much she disliked staying with us at Alderley.†

I remember Ted Lister‡ saying that artists had no taste. 'Just look at their houses – and their clothes.' The same can be said of Bloomsbury. Their houses were dingy, sparse and puritanical. Le Souco, Madame Bussy's§ house, reverberated with the emptiness of the rooms. Curtains never reached the ground; mingy little rugs on uncarpeted floor; ugly fabrics. Clothes both male and female dreary beyond belief. They had dogmatic theories about architecture and painting, but otherwise little aesthetic sense.

Thursday, 22nd July

Grant McIntyre telephoned to announce that Jock Murray¶ had died this afternoon, of cancer. Was clearly upset and could barely speak, for Jock was greatly loved in the office. He was always jolly, sometimes too much the schoolboy, but generous and kind. A marvellous inheritor of a glorious tradition going back to 1768.** He was the lynchpin which kept together that splendid generation of John Betjeman,†† Osbert Lancaster,‡‡ Peter Quennell,§§ K. Clark,¶¶ Paddy Leigh Fermor. I remember him at Eton, where he was one year my junior,

---

* Helen Eaton (d. 1989); m. 1922 Sir John Dashwood, 10th Bt (1896–1966); châtelaine of West Wycombe Park, Buckinghamshire, wartime headquarters of N.T., whose foibles J.L.-M. had (to her indignation) described in his wartime diaries.

† While staying with the L.-Ms in November 1965, Mrs Partridge admitted to 'feeling anxious about this visit', and concluded that she was 'subtly aware of alien values', finding everything 'just a little too conventional and safe'.

‡ Edward Graham Lister (1873–1956); diplomatist and art collector; bachelor admirer of J.L.-M., to whom he planned to leave Westwood Manor, Wiltshire, though on J.L.-M's marriage in 1951 he changed his will and bequeathed it instead to N.T. (see entry for 28 August 1994).

§ Dorothy Strachey (1866–1960); artist and writer, elder sister of Lytton Strachey (1880–1932); m. 1903 Simon Bussy, French artist (1870–1954); they lived at Roquebrune, where they knew the L.-Ms; she translated the works of André Gide into English.

¶ John Murray VI (1909–93), head of publishing firm; J.L.-M's publisher from 1990.

** The tradition came to an end in 2002 when his son sold the firm to Hodder Headline.

†† Sir John Betjeman (1906–84); poet, broadcaster and writer on architecture; Poet Laureate, 1972–84.

‡‡ Sir Osbert Lancaster (1908–86); cartoonist, humorist and dandy.

§§ Sir Peter Quennell (1905–94); writer, editor and journalist.

¶¶ Sir Kenneth Clark (1903–83); art historian; Surveyor of the King's Pictures, 1934–44; cr. life peer, 1969; father of Alan Clark, politician and diarist.

with longish fair hair all over the place, expressive mouth, wide eyes, and that jocular manner which never left him. A dear and good man, shrewd too. My greatest pride is to have been included among his authors in a humble way.

Monday, 26th July

Dined last night at the House. Beits staying, Alfred shaky on legs and Clementine enormous in unfortunate short frock and tight belt. A pleasure to see them. They talked about the burgled pictures from Russborough.* One recovered from a rascally dealer in Turkey, another found in electrician's van in a North London park, a third behind sofa in suburban house. On the whole, no one will risk buying them, so they pass from one nefarious hand to another. The police know the Dublin godfather who masterminded the raid, though difficult to pin anything on him as he never touches the pictures himself. Clem fears for the Goya and the Vermeer, which are of such international fame that it may be impossible to dispose of them except by destroying them. Clem talked to David's fortyish Israeli friend Fuhrer about the risks they run as multi[millionaire]s. Clem said, 'I have instructed my solicitors on no account to pay a ransom if I am kidnapped.' F. replied, 'My father says that nothing will induce him to redeem me if I am taken.' I thought there were some consolations to not being a multi.

Thursday, 29th July

To London for day. J.K.-B. lunched and told me that Andrew Devonshire had been robbed of £1,000 by a man who accosted him outside the bank. Visited Burnet in the nice, clean, welcoming King Edward VII Hospital. In good heart after extraction of gall bladder. Telephone never stopped ringing while I was there. To Burne-Jones†

---

* In a burglary of 1986 masterminded by the Dublin godfather Martin Cahill (who was to be murdered by the IRA in 1994), eighteen famous paintings had been stolen from Russborough House, the Beits' seat in County Wicklow. All but three were recovered down the years in various parts of the world – in some cases to disappear again in another burglary in 2001 (by which time the collection had been presented to the Irish nation).

† Sir Edward Burne-Jones (1833–98); Pre-Raphaelite artist.

exhibition in Ryder Street. On the whole I prefer his portrait drawings to the oils. There is too much milk and sugar – or armpits and
eau-de-Cologne, as Robert Byron[*] used to put it.

Tuesday, 3rd August

I drive myself to lunch with Roy Jenkinses at East Hendred. A nice,
simple old house, Georgianised with sash windows, the whole
painted white. Forecourt at rear with impressive sloping-roofed barn,
recently thatched. Arrive at noon in order to answer her questions on
early days and personalities of N.T. for the history she is writing,
to appear in forthcoming centenary year. She asked about David
Crawford,[†] Oliver Esher,[‡] Jack Rathbone,[§] Robin Fedden.[¶] My word
she is a clever woman, and sees the point of everything. About
Robin, she said, 'He had an eye. In his job expertise was not necessary, the eye all-important.' Deplores what museum people can do to
houses with their pedantic knowledge. Agrees with me that Hanbury
[Hall, Worcestershire] overdone; praises Hatchlands [Surrey]. Said
Osterley [Middlesex] so awful under V&A that it pained her to visit
it. She has the nicest face, and such good manners. Wearing handsome jersey with pink-and-white stripes. Strange how I disliked the
Jenkinses before I really knew them. I remember that, when he was
elected to Brooks's, I almost felt the club had been penetrated by
the KGB.

Roy has become a dear old duffer – almost. Sits enormous, and
gobbles his food. Has trick of waving left hand in a clutching motion
to emphasise his talk, which flows. Full of gossip and pleasantry. I
asked him to explain the currency crisis. He did so, but in such
Copper talk that I understood little. Said that, whereas when he was
Chancellor speculators were responsible for 20 per cent of currency
fluctuations, now it is 80 per cent owing to speed of communication

---

[*] Travel writer, Byzantinist, architectural conservationist and aesthete (1905–41).
[†] David Lindsay, 28th Earl of Crawford and 11th Earl of Balcarres (1900–75); Chairman
of N.T., 1945–65.
[‡] Oliver Brett, 3rd Viscount Esher (1881–1963); Chairman of Country Houses (later
Historic Buildings) Committee, N.T., 1936–62, and thus J.L.-M's immediate boss.
[§] John Francis Warre Rathbone (1909–95); Secretary of N.T., 1949–68.
[¶] Writer and mountaineer (1909–77); J.L.-M's successor (1951–68) as Historic Buildings
Secretary of N.T.

between international banks. Deplorable, but no law could stop it. We talked of houses we both liked, Compton Beauchamp [House, Berkshire] among them. Roy now working on life of Mr Gladstone.* Says he is not so sure that G's motives over fallen women quite so innocent as formerly made out. Certainly he suffered much from guilt.

Jennifer J. told me some interesting things – that Francis Dashwood[†] sold the pictures at West Wycombe which he disliked, notably Baroque Grand Tour ones, without warning the Trust, for fear they would buy them and keep them where they hung; that Charles Faringdon,[‡] for all his laughter and bonhomie, was one of the most difficult of the donors' heirs; that John Smith's[§] opinions at Committee Meetings were always as violent as they were unpredictable; that Lord Crawford protected Jack Rathbone even after his breakdown. But when she told me, looking me straight in the eye, that she had been reading correspondence between Crawford, Esher and Jack about staff problems, I trembled to think what she must have read about me.

Thursday, 5th August

Like so many, A. is gripped by Alan Clark's diaries. While admitting that his style is vivacious and his descriptions arresting, I am not sure. Too many acronyms, initials, and filthy words used as adjectives. On the whole I find him difficult to like, despite some endearing characteristics – love of animals and country churches, and loyalty to 'the Lady', as he calls Mrs Thatcher.

J.L.-M. does not mention his eighty-fifth birthday on 6 August, which was the occasion of tributes to him in the press.

---

* Jenkins's magisterial biography of the Grand Old Man appeared in 1995.
[†] Sir Francis Dashwood, 11th Bt (1925–2000); of West Wycombe Park, Buckinghamshire (donated by father to N.T.).
[‡] Charles Henderson, 3rd Baron Faringdon (b. 1937); of Buscot House, Faringdon, Oxfordshire (donated by uncle to N.T.) and Barnsley Park, Cirencester, Gloucestershire; m. 1959 Sarah Askew.
[§] Sir John Smith (b. 1923; ktd 1988); banker; MP (C) Cities of London and Westminster, 1965–70; Deputy Chairman of N.T., 1980–5; founder of Landmark Trust.

Wednesday, 11th August

On the way to Bath this morning, I listened to two Privy Counsellors on Radio 4. First Cecil Parkinson,* 'on the psychiatrist's couch'. Unburdening himself with claims that he is a private and unambitious sort of person. Very plausible unless you see through him, as I do. Has a good, rich voice until the 'eows' tumble out. A bounder and a man of little depth. Denies sexual attraction to Mrs Thatcher. Why should he feel this necessary? Then comes Wedgwood Benn† for a reading of his 'confidential' tapes, with maddening clanging as of unlocking of strongroom each time he delivers a statement. Likewise disingenuous and boastful. Even if these MPs start off with noble ideals, they are soon taken over by the game of politics. The House of Commons is so densely haunted with dishonourable motivation that you can cut it with an axe. All that counts is getting the better of your neighbour, at whatever sacrifice of loyalty or principle. At least Alan Clark is honest, if not honourable.

Monday, 16th August

A weekend of revelry. On Saturday we had a party of some thirty at Newark Park for A's [eighty-fourth] birthday. What old Bob Parsons has done for this house is miraculous. The view from front door into dining room through French windows to wide panorama of trees and hills beyond is wonderfully theatrical, and did not exist twenty years ago. On Sunday, we lunched with Hart-Davises‡ at Owlpen Farm. Very enjoyable, Peter Levis the other guests. Today, Monday, we lunched with Hardy Amies at Langford. Guests of honour were Prince Henry of Hesse§ and his friend, a jolly Neapolitan count; both live in

---

* Conservative politician (b. 1931); said to be a favourite of Margaret Thatcher, who appointed him to a succession of cabinet posts; as Party Chairman, was credited with the Conservative success in 1983 general election, but was obliged to resign from the Government soon afterwards owing to a scandal in his private life; cr. life peer, 1992.

† Anthony Wedgwood Benn (b. 1925); charismatic Labour politician; eldest surviving son of 1st Viscount Stansgate (on succeeding whom in 1960 he waged a campaign to return to the House of Commons, resulting in legislation to allow disclaimer of peerages); became a radical left-winger in favour of nationalisation of British industry, but nevertheless held office throughout the Wilson and Callaghan Governments.

‡ Duff Hart-Davis (b. 1936); writer; son of J.L.-M's schoolfriend Sir Rupert Hart-Davis (1907–99), writer and publisher; m. 1961 Phyllida Barstow.

§ HRH Prince Henry of Hesse (b. 1927); 2nd s. of Prince Philip of Hesse and Princess Mafalda of Italy; artist.

Rome. Prince, dapper little man with long thin nose and delicate features, born 1927, gave me copy of his recently published memoirs in Italian. He is a great-grandson of Queen Victoria, grandson of King Victor Emmanuel of Italy, nephew of King Leopold of the Belgians. Told me his mother, Princess Mafalda of Italy, was carted off to a German concentration camp when he was sixteen, and murdered. Poor Hardy very bent. He was called to the telephone while we were drinking coffee in the garden, and came back radiant. 'The Queen', he announced, 'has ordered two more dresses and a coat.' Fanny Partridge would be contemptuous. Hardy's colleague Ken is a bit of a mystery. Remains in the background, receives no credit or acknowledgement from H., and submits to his bossiness with a faintly amused expression. Yet not at all subservient, and even cleverer than H., I feel.

Wednesday, 18th August

Selina [Hastings]* lunching here talked of the anger and impatience of her publisher Sinclair-Stevenson,† hardly surprising as she has dallied for years over her Evelyn Waugh‡ biography. He told her that if she did not deliver in two months, the whole thing was off, and banged down the telephone. Selina said that Hugo Vickers,§ whom she went to visit, surrounds himself with life size models of every member of the Royal Family which he dresses in different robes and uniforms according to fancy, and also has enormous press-cutting albums on them all.

Saturday, 21st August

Our long-planned and much-anticipated visit to Madresfield [Court near Malvern, Worcestershire]. Many years since I was last here in 1948, when Elmley¶ was toying with the N.T. What a lugubrious

---

* Lady Selina Hastings (b. 1945); dau. of 15th Earl of Huntingdon; writer.
† Christopher Sinclair-Stevenson (b. 1939); then a publisher, subsequently a literary agent.
‡ Novelist (1903–66), whose biography by Selina Hastings was published by Sinclair-Stevenson in 1994.
§ Writer (b. 1951).
¶ William Lygon, 8th and last Earl Beauchamp (1903–79), who continued to be widely known by his courtesy title of Viscount Elmley after succeeding his father to the earldom and the ownership of Madresfield in 1938; m. 1936 Else 'Mona' de la Cour (1895–1989).

house, wrecked by Hardwick* and Co. from mid nineteenth century to early twentieth. Pitch dark entrance. One feels one's way to the tunnel-like library, at the end of which a window looks out over the garden. I could not even see the famous carved shelf-ends by Ashbee† and other Chipping Campden craftsmen. Wonderful books. Indeed, wonderful treasures of every description; miniatures everywhere, exposed to sunlight; a case of forty drawers packed with Hilliards, Olivers, Englehearts; vitrines of rare snuff boxes in dozens. The great dining-room with high-timbered ceiling and huge fat Gothic windows by Hardwick is splendid. So is the hall with staircase and gallery balustrading of crystal uprights. All ebonised by 'Boom',‡ who haunts the place. Formidable full-lengths hanging everywhere. The Lygons must have collected for generations. Among all this dear Rosalind,§ looking exhausted, her Pre-Raphaelite face so beautiful. She could never have tackled it without Charlie. I don't think I could have faced it in her position, but applaud her family piety. Madresfield has been handed down in direct or indirect line since the 1300s, and has belonged to the Lygons since the 1500s.

Wednesday, 25th August

To London for day. Train late both directions, as usual nowadays. Misha lunches with me at Cavalry Club, Piccadilly. This luncheon has become an annual event. We examine the portraits of incredibly fierce, pompous, stupid generals. I go to Parkin Gallery and buy for £175 a tiny painting of Sussex Downs seen from the sea under a storm-brewing sky, by unknown female named Malcolmson.

Why does our country cut down on defence considering the parlous state of the world – war in Bosnia, Ethiopia, Nigeria; terrorism everywhere; the menace of Saddam,¶ and hostile Iran; Russia

---

* Philip Hardwick (1792–1870); architect.

† C. R. Ashbee (1863–1942); architect and designer in the Arts & Crafts tradition.

‡ Family nickname of William Lygon, 7th Earl Beauchamp (1872–1938), Liberal statesman, who lived at Madresfield until, in 1931, he was obliged to resign his public offices and move abroad owing to scandal (see entry for 23 December 1994).

§ Rosalind Lygon (b. 1946); granddau. of 7th Earl Beauchamp; m. 2nd 1984 (diss. 1999) Hon. Sir Charles Morrison (1932–2005), yr s. of 1st Baron Margadale, MP for Devizes, 1964–92; in 1992, following death of widow of 8th Earl, she had become the châtelaine of her 'native seat' (see *Ceaseless Turmoil*, 21 May and 31 August 1992).

¶ Saddam Hussein (b. 1937); Iraqi dictator, 1979–2004.

corrupt, anarchic and tottering? And why do we open the Channel Tunnel* for the influx here to be made easier? So long as we remain an island, we can shut ourselves in and contain ourselves against the plague and terrorism of hostile foreigners. O the future!

Monday, 30th August

Freda staying for weekend. Today we had a farewell luncheon for the Gibsons, to whom I presented a copy of *Images of Bath*.† We are so sorry they are leaving. Gloria imparted the dreadful news that the corner shop below Lansdown Crescent is closing. This means we must think twice about retiring to our flat there, if in order to obtain basic foodstuffs we must descend to the town and re-ascend.

Freda told us the following rather eerie story. She has a portable telephone, and the other evening was talking on it to a friend. Tony Scotland‡ was in a room at the other end of her flat, listening to the radio. Suddenly he heard the conversation of Freda and her friend relayed from the set. He rushed to a friend's flat on the floor below, turned on the wireless and again heard Freda's conversation. F. much put out.

Wednesday, 1st September

Dicky Buckle§ called and we lunched at the posh Royal Crescent Hotel. Since I drink nothing, my half-share of the bill was fairly big. Hadn't seen Dicky for years. No longer the bright young man. Now a dear old paunchy, red-faced buffer, though has all his wits. Talked of Juliet Duff¶ and Simon Fleet.** He was extremely fond of the latter

---

* The rail service through the Tunnel opened in the summer of 1994 and revolutionised cross-Channel communications, though J.L.-M. was correct in predicting implications for illegal immigration into the UK (see also entry for 6 September 1995).
† Illustrated book by J.L.-M., published by Bamber Gascoigne in 1982.
‡ Writer, broadcaster and journalist (b. 1945); on staff of BBC Radio, 1970–91; lived in Hampshire with Julian Berkeley (b. 1951), 2nd son of Sir Lennox and Freda née Bernstein, musician and founder of Berkeleyguard Automatic Security Systems.
§ Richard Buckle (1916–2003); ballet critic, writer and exhibition designer.
¶ Lady Juliet Lowther (1881–1965); o. c. of 4th Earl of Lonsdale; m. 1903 Sir Robert Duff, 2nd Bt; mother of J.L.-M's friend Sir Michael Duff, 3rd Bt (1907–80).
** Actor, theatrical designer and saleroom correspondent of the *Observer* (1913–66); friend of Harold Nicolson, and admirer of formidable women such as Lady Juliet Duff and the ballet designer Sophie Fedorovich (from whom he inherited a house in Chelsea).

and feels responsible for his death, though Simon in fact fell down the stairs of his London maisonette when drunk and doped. We gossiped about old times, old faces, old ghosts. The truth is I don't much want to see old friends.

Thursday, 2nd September

Whereas today I enjoyed meeting Louisa Young,* K[athleen] Kennet's† granddaughter who is writing her life.‡ A very good subject, for she knew everyone of her time. She kept a diary from her first meeting with Scott until her death, and kept letters from T. E. Lawrence,§ Barrie,¶ Asquith,** etc. Louisa a very pretty girl, aged thirty-four with long blonde hair down to her waist. Nice voice. Loves K. whom she never knew. We ate boiled eggs and nectarines. She told me she had a daughter by a coal-black Ghanaian (out of wedlock, of course). Asked what I thought K. would have thought. I said that such a thing rarely happened in her day. At first she would have been shocked, but she would quickly have accepted the situation and reconciled herself completely, for she was essentially unconventional herself. I asked boldly, 'What colour is your daughter?' She replied, 'A lovely mahogany', pointing to the veneered arms of my William and Adelaide sofa. When Louisa left I said, 'I am going to give you a kiss because you are the granddaughter of that darling woman.' It must have been a horrid shock for her to be touched by the dead and pitted face of an ancient man, but she said, 'It almost makes me want to cry.'

Saturday, 4th September

I go by train to Chatsworth. Am given the red velvet bedroom, a mark of honour. Country Fair taking place in the park, in a piercing north wind. The Parker Bowleses and their two children staying – girl

---

* Hon. Louisa Young (b. 1959); yst dau. of Wayland Young, 2nd Baron Kennet.
† Kathleeen Bruce (1878–1947); sculptor; m. 1st 1908 Captain Robert Scott 'of the Antarctic' (d. 1912), 2nd Edward Hilton Young (1879–1960), Liberal politician, cr. Baron Kennet, 1935. In the 1930s, J.L.-M. had been a protégé of this tempestuous woman; he wrote her obituary for *The Times*, and an essay on her in *Fourteen Friends* (1996).
‡ J.L.-M. had already been visited on 20 August 1987 (see *Beneath a Waning Moon*) by Louisa's second cousin Alexandra Allerhand, then working on the biography.
§ T. E. Lawrence (1888–1935); soldier, writer and archaeologist; 'Lawrence of Arabia'.
¶ Sir James Barrie (1860–1937); novelist and playwright, creator of Peter Pan.
** Herbert Henry Asquith (1852–1928); Liberal Prime Minister, 1908–16; cr. Earl of Oxford and Asquith, 1925.

fifteen; boy eighteen, just left Eton, about to go to Oxford, intelligent and literary. I like Camilla, though she is not beautiful, and has lost her gaiety and sparkle. Doubtless worn by tribulations undergone. Women spit at her in supermarkets; cameramen snoop at her at the Fair. Walks with bowed head, and has trained her fluffy hair to cover her cheeks.

On the second day, Feeble[*] lunches. Tells me she means to destroy John Betjeman's letters to her, which she considers of little interest. I strongly counsel her not to do so. She insists they are dull. Yet Candida[†] has received nearly £300,000 for the rights to her father's letters which she is editing.

Andrew [Devonshire] says that two things have done a great disservice to this country. First, the reversal of several convictions of IRA members, a blow to the reputation of British justice. Secondly the Camillagate affair, which has seriously undermined the monarchy. Andrew certain that P. of W. won't succeed to the throne. Doesn't mind himself; claims to be a republican. Not too pleased when I said, 'You wouldn't like to be called Citizen Cavendish, surely?' Retorted that he knew of no republics in which dukes could not still call themselves dukes.

Friday, 10th September

David Westmorland has at last died. This can only be good news for all. Poor Jane was faced with the decision whether to amputate his gangrenous foot, and refused. He is to be buried at Badminton on Tuesday, guardsmen coming by helicopter to carry the corpse. I have been re-reading Julian Fane's[‡] little memoir of their mother, Diana It is sensitive and well-planned, but doesn't whitewash her.

---

[*] Lady Elizabeth Cavendish (b. 1926); sister of Andrew, 11th Duke of Devonshire; Lady-in-Waiting to HRH Princess Margaret; close friend of Sir John Betjeman during his later years.

[†] Candida Betjeman (b. 1942), o. dau. of Sir John Betjeman; m. 1963 Rupert Lycett Green, owner of Blades, fashionable tailors. Her two-volume edition of her father's letters appeared in April 1994 and October 1995.

[‡] Hon. Julian Fane (b. 1927); yr s. of 14th Earl of Westmorland (and of J.L.-M's friend Diana, Countess of W., *née* Lister [d. 1983]); writer; m. 1976 Gillian Swire.

Saturday, 11th September

Before I open my letters in the morning, some instinct seems to tell me which will interest and which will bore me. Of course, all circulars and bills bore me. But the handwritten address on the envelope, even when I don't recognise the hand, always seems to reveal whether I shall read the letter with pleasure or the reverse. Even a typed envelope somehow discloses.

Tuesday, 14th September

This afternoon we attended David Westmorland's funeral in the big church here. Packed with friends, all 'gratin' with a sprinkling of nice village folk in the side aisles. We were put at the rear of the nave. I took against the posh lot, women with eyes roving round to see who was there and watch the Prince of Wales, who came on the stroke and marched at the head of the queue.

Tuesday, 21st September

To London, where Jamie Fergusson* lunched with me at Brooks's. He told me that the future of the *Independent* was not secure and he often got fed up with obituarising. We ran into Stuart Preston† who latched on to us, so I had little opportunity of talking to my strange, elusive, deep, rather sad Fergusson cousin. Stuart's appearance is frankly frightening – drooping mouth, baggy eyes, purple skin. He seldom smiles, but when he does, it remarkably brings back the charm he once had. When it came to settling, he, a member like myself, allowed me to pay for him without batting an eyelid. I am always terrified of being thought the meanie that I am, so I gaily paid for him and he just as gaily accepted.

Sunday, 26th September

This evening I motored A. past Didmarton to Oldbury. Got out and admired the front of the manor house, Caroline on older centuries. Down-at-heel, yet clearly lived in by rich farmers, if not gentry. The

---

* Antiquarian bookseller (b. 1953) and founding Obituaries Editor of the *Independent*, whose father was a second cousin of J.L.-M.
† American bibliophile, resident in Paris (1915–2005); friend of J.L.-M. since 1938.

pretty church tower now redundant and falling to decay. Graveyard overgrown, nice old tombs awry and choked with thistles. Old barn converted into some sort of machinery shed. Yard concreted. Trees and hedges deracinated. The whole complex a terrible illustration of what has happened to England, the beautiful squire's England ravaged by greed and indifference. Then on to Sherston church, a very different case. If anything a bit too tarted, for this is a swanky village. I admired the double wooden gate of the porch. Very pretty carved uprights and Gothick head, might be Jacobean if it could have lasted the weather so long. By the door inside a curious white porcelain crucifix plaque on wall with inscription alongside saying it was given by an Italian soldier in gratitude for the kindness shown him by the inhabitants of Sherston when he was a prisoner of war.

Thursday, 30th September

A terrible day of incessant rain. We decided we couldn't go to Tanis [Guinness]'s[*] funeral at Hungerford. We dined at the House, only Daph[ne Fielding] there apart from David and Caroline. We talked of Nancy [Mitford]'s letters,[†] Daph much upset by a remark in a letter to Debo that she, Daph, was a bitch. Jealousy over the Colonel,[‡] of course. As though it matters now. David said that posterity should never judge people by their correspondence, as what they wrote one day was often the opposite of what they thought the next. We agreed that no biographer's words about a dead person they had never met could be of much value. At least I think we did.

Tuesday, 5th October

We both attended the funeral of Gladys Guinness[§] in Badminton church this afternoon. I did not want to go, for G.G. never meant

---

[*] Yr dau. (1906–93) of Benjamin Guinness of New York (and sister of Loel Guinness, MP for Bath, 1931–45); m. 1st 1931–5 Hon. William Montagu, 2nd 1937–51 Howard Dietz, 3rd 1951 Edward Phillips.

[†] *Love from Nancy: The Letters of Nancy Mitford*, ed. Charlotte Mosley, Hodder, 1993

[‡] Colonel Gaston Palewski (1901–84); principal wartime aide of General de Gaulle; a notorious philanderer, unhappily loved by Nancy Mitford; m. 1969 Violette de Talleyrand-Périgord.

[§] On 3 February 1980 (*Deep Romantic Chasm*), J.L.-M. related how this formerly 'nice, dull' resident of Badminton village had got drunk and attacked her husband with a knife.

anything to me. But A. insisted that, as villagers, we must. I *had* wanted to go to Tamara Talbot Rice's at Coln Rogers yesterday, but was prevented by A. having an appointment with her nose and throat specialist in Bath. We had the Gibsons to lunch before the funeral, which Tom was conducting. They told us that Gladys had left nothing but her old clothes to her niece, to spite her sister Diana whom she apparently always resented.

The Field telephoned asking me to write an article on Tresco Island.* I rashly accepted on two conditions, that the Dorrien-Smith owners have no objection, and that *The Field* organises and pays for the whole expedition. It necessitates two nights away from A., who encourages me to accept. It will take me out of myself.

Sunday, 10th October

Read terrifying article about genetic engineering. A Pandora's Box. No one knows what it will do to humans or animals. They have begun to impregnate pigs to produce more bacon, and battery hens to produce more eggs, with the result that they become so fat and heavy that their legs can no longer sustain them.

Sunday, 17th October

The [Roy] Jenkinses and the Hart-Davises lunched. Quite a success. A. produced the best possible food and claret for Roy, who drank gallons and then drove off in a huge car, very flushed. Tomorrow he flies to Vienna to make a speech at some important dinner, and from there takes train to Warsaw to do the same there. How he has the energy I can't conceive. Jennifer asked me several more questions about the N.T. for her book, which she is sending me to read in proof. After luncheon we took them to the House, where Caroline showed us round. I said to Jennifer, 'I suppose the N.T. would accept, if offered?' 'They could hardly do otherwise,' she replied with a smile. We talked of the magic of houses. She said Hardwick [Hall, Derbyshire] managed to preserve it, despite the large numbers, but Knole [Kent] only just. I said that Badminton still had it, perhaps

---

* Second largest of the Scilly Isles, famous for its ruined Benedictine abbey and the sub-tropical gardens cultivated by the Dorrien-Smith family, who have leased the island from the Crown since 1834: see entries for 27–29 October 1993.

because it was not open to the public. She nodded agreement. I find her infinitely sympathetic. She gave me an embrace when they left.

Tuesday, 19th October

To London for the day. Lunched upstairs at Brooks's, where Reresby [Sitwell]* sat opposite me. I said how much I welcomed the obituaries of Gertrude† in *The Times* and *Telegraph*. He said, stiffly, 'She hardly deserved them. She was a terrible liar and mischief maker.' Then I said, 'I hope you approved of Sarah Bradford's biography.' He said testily, 'How would you like to read about your parents' squalid little affairs?' Went to Burnet's flat. He has read the MS of my new diaries, usefully correcting errors and misspellings, and querying a few indiscretions and distasteful references, pointing out that I have used the word 'penis' several times. I am grateful to him. Then to Matthew Carr's‡ exhibition at Wildenstein's. All charcoal drawings, mostly of male and female blacks, very forcible and slightly sinister like himself. A contrast to Eliot Hodgkin's§ eighteen neat little paintings of fruits and cabbages, priced at £5,000 and upwards.

Wednesday, 20th October

Motored to Oxford to meet the President of Magdalen, Anthony Smith,¶ whom I at first confused with man of same name who is the son of Hubert Smith.** I had written offering my Buckler†† engraving of Magdalen Tower which belonged to Uncle Robert.‡‡ As I have inscribed on the back, it hung on his wall at Magdalen in 1901, and

---

* Sir Reresby Sitwell, 7th Bt (b. 1927); er s. of Sir Sacheverell Sitwell; inherited Renishaw, Derbyshire, from his uncle Sir Osbert, 5th Bt (d. 1969); m. 1952 Penelope Forbes.
† Gertrude Cooper (1908–93); housekeeper to the Sacheverell Sitwells for sixty years (originally lady's maid to Georgia Sitwell); m. Bernard Stevenson (her employers' manservant).
‡ Artist; m. 1988 Lady Anne Somerset (b. 1955), only dau. of 11th Duke of Beaufort.
§ English artist (1905–87).
¶ BBC TV Current Affairs producer (b. 1938); President of Magdalen College, Oxford from 1988.
** Sometime Chief Agent of N.T., whose son Anthony (b. 1926) was a writer and broadcaster.
†† J. C. Buckler (1793–1894); engraver of architectural views.
‡‡ Robert Bailey (1882–1917); only brother of J.L.-M's mother; a Magdalen undergraduate (whose popularity there later eased J.L.-M's admission); a clerk to the House of Commons, who devoted his spare time to boys' clubs and other good works; killed in action; a great hero to J.L.-M.

mine in 1931. Smith said, 'You may rest happy that it will be preserved
here forever.' He kindly gave me several hours of his time, showing me
round the college. In the ante-chapel, I saw the contemporary copy,
recently acquired, of Leonardo's *Last Supper*. Gazing at the memorial
tablets, I asked, 'What does *praesens* mean?' 'President,' he whispered
politely. He must think me very ignorant. At luncheon in the fellows'
canteen, the literature don sitting opposite asked who my history tutor
was in 1928. I had to confess I no longer had the slightest clue.* We
went into the library, lately redecorated with Pompeian red ceiling by
David Mlinaric.† Was shown Wolsey's‡ beautifully hand-painted
lectionary, his initials on every page. And a twelfth-century Book of
Hours with splendid illuminations, said to be the earliest known book.
Also Byron's *Lamia*, signed 'from the author'. Splendid gothic tapestry
panels in President's Lodge, given by William of Wykeham.§ President
very keen on Bruce Chatwin, talking of his impressive power of
empathy. 'He has taught me things.' I parted with the engraving
without a pang, feeling sure Uncle Robert would have approved.

Spent rest of day wandering about Oxford in glorious sunshine, no
breath of wind. Ideal conditions. Tourist season over. How could I
have ignored the architecture of this superb city when I was here?
Every house in Longwall a delight, save the disgraceful horizontal
addition to New College overlooking Magdalen Park. How could it
have been allowed? I had a lovely day, and blessed God that I still have
the use of my legs and eyes – just.

Thursday, 21st October

Am reading Elspeth [Huxley]'s¶ *Peter Scott*,** a very good biography. I
see he was awarded the MBE for gallantry. How right I was to refuse

---

* Head of History at Magdalen at the time was the mediaevalist Bruce McFarlane.
† Interior decorator (b. 1939).
‡ Cardinal Thomas Wolsey (?1475–1530); principal counsellor to King Henry VIII until
his disgrace in 1529.
§ Bishop and statesman (1324–1404), who endowed Winchester School and founded
New College, Oxford.
¶ Elspeth Grant (1907–94); m. 1931 Gervas Huxley (d. 1971); writer.
** Sir Peter Scott (1909–89); o. c. of 'Scott of the Antarctic' and Kathleen *née* Bruce (later
Baroness Kennet); sportsman, artist, naval officer, naturalist and writer; m. 1st 1942–51
Elizabeth Jane Howard, 2nd 1951 Philippa Talbot-Ponsonby. J.L.-M. (who knew him
through his mother, and never found him sympathetic) had visited him at Slimbridge
shortly before his death (see *Beneath a Waning Moon*, 12 December 1987).

the CBE,* when the heroism of my contemporary was rewarded with a mere 'M'. The reviewers criticise Elspeth for not disclosing anything of the man. True; but there was little beneath the skin. A great conservationist notwithstanding.

Sunday, 24th October

We lunch at Barnsley [Park] with the Faringdons, a large party. Charles extremely friendly, his uproarious laughter due to shyness presumably. He dragged me out of the library window to show me the way in which Nash made the windows of the conservatory disappear so that in summer it looks like the Parthenon, windows folding back like closed butterfly wings. An astonishing construction, with the steel roundel frames in the end pediments. Such a beautiful house, probably the finest Baroque in Britain. I sat next to Sarah F., one of the great beauties of our time. Not very bright, I suspect. On my other side Penelope Sitwell, who asked if it was true that I had been asked to write Sachie's life. I explained that Jock Murray had asked me to do a 'brief life', but I had declined.† She said that Sachie and Georgia were both monsters. 'Sachie?' I asked. She replied that he was as bad as she, with his evil face. Well, that was pretty plain speaking.

I enjoyed my visit to Barnsley very much. A rare survival of civilised existence – agreeable guests, delicious food, every sign of taste without luxury. A butler in attendance, and ladies waiting. This is what lefties despise and resent, and what academe has always relished – i.e., living at the expense of the bloated rich. It is the best thing which England has shown to the world.

Tuesday, 26th October

To London for Jock Murray's memorial service in St James's Church. Packed. Sat in the gallery, so heard not a word. Paddy [Leigh Fermor]'s address lost on me. But the crowd of living friends impressive. Jock was truly loved. As I emerged, Ian Anstruther‡ said to me, 'You are

---

* J.L.-M. had been offered this honour the previous year and immediately declined it (see *Ceaseless Turmoil*, 18 and 30 November 1992). He confided to his diary, however, that he 'coveted' the CH awarded to Scott.
† See *Ceaseless Turmoil*, 8 November 1989 and 17 January 1990.
‡ Old Etonian writer (b. 1922), dealing with personalities of the Victorian age.

the last of the men of letters.' Nonsense, I replied, thinking of Peter Quennell. Went to the reception at No. 50 [Albemarle Street], packed like the church. Stayed but twenty minutes, talking to Grant [McIntyre] and Gail [Pirkis].* And to Junie Hutchinson[†] and Christian Esher.[‡] These lovely friends only met at scrums where contact can't be resumed.

In the train, I thought how curious it was that I, as an old eunuch, am now totally heterosexual. I am drawn exclusively to the mystique of the female persona, whereas the male physique revolts me and the male persona has little allure. I suppose that, by a tilt of the scales, a nudge from the tip of an angel's wing, I would have been wholly 'normal' from adolescence onwards. Perhaps it is just as well that this was not the case, as I would probably have been a nasty, intolerant, anti-queer young fogey.

Wednesday, 27th October

To Tresco today. Train from [Bristol] Temple Meads, change Newton Abbot, taxi from Penzance station to Heliport. Frighteningly old, ramshackle helicopter, rattling its twenty-minute way to Tresco. Flew over toe of Land's End, even today crammed with parked traffic. Tiny patchwork fields of Cornwall. Descend in front of and below the Abbey. Received by open truck. We sit jaunty-car fashion, and jog down very narrow track to Old Grimsby, consisting of Victorian church and some five cottages, to Island Hotel. Grand luxe, double bedroom descending two steps to sitting room but all of a piece. Spacious cupboards and bathroom. Vast sofa and huge picture window.

After tea-bag in bedroom, wander towards northern extremity of this two and three-quarter miles long island. Path of fine silver sand, then a moor of bracken and heather on miniature scale. Sort of dorsal ridge on left covered with ponticum rhododendrons. Then narrow-

---

* Managing Editor, John Murray, 1987–2003 (b. 1957); founding editor (2004) of *Slightly Foxed: The Real Reader's Quarterly*; mother of Max Pirkis, teenage film actor.

[†] June Capel; dau. of J.L.-M's friend Diana, Countess of Westmorland by an earlier marriage; m. 1st Franz Osborn, 2nd Jeremy Hutchinson, QC (cr. life peer, 1978).

[‡] Christian Pike, artist; m. 1935 Lionel Brett, architect (1913–2004), who s. father, Oliver, 3rd Viscount Esher (J.L.-M's boss and mentor at N.T.), as 4th Viscount, 1963, and later invited J.L.-M. to write the biography of his grandfather, Reginald, 2nd Viscount (published by Sidgwick & Jackson in 1986 as *The Enigmatic Edwardian*).

est cow-track to cliffs, weird and rather frightening in twilight, deserted, no habitation.

Rows of bicycles outside hotel, used by young and old. No motorised transport except for 'hotel bus' and a few electric buggies. Cottages either natural granite or whitewashed. Somehow no feeling of claustrophobia in this minute kingdom. Delicious dinner, with crab caught today off Bryher.*

Thursday, 28th October

Blustery grey day with drizzle. On waking and looking through window I saw a thrush within two feet of me, paying no heed. Indeed, thrushes and blackbirds even perch on one's shoe on this island. The charming head gardener, Mike Nelhams, rather like Nick Lambourne,[†] arranges for me to be conducted round the garden. Very intelligent and affable. Garden in terraces, well laid out, straight paths. Unique in the world – things grow here that can't even in the Canaries and Azores. No moles, no snakes, few predators. No hills higher than 150 feet. One hundred and fifty inhabitants. Bad weather passes overhead to land on Cornish and Devon higher hills. But gales prevalent. Sir Cloudesley Shovell[‡] wrecked here in 1707 with all his two thousand men. Famous disaster.

In the afternoon an elderly gentleman, Roy Cooper, calls on me at the hotel and narrates so much irrelevant island history that I am obliged to stop him. I say I must go out while still daylight and see more of the island. So walk to the Abbey and back, making a good assessment. The Dorrien-Smiths not in residence, contrary to what I was told, so I got no entry to the Abbey.

Friday, 29th October

Return home. Two hours in Penzance to wander round the town. Note aprons of windows of Regency houses make in sunlight a pencilled shadow. Lloyd's Bank so attenuated classical (Ionic) as to look absurd. Gothic house dated 1823 at end of Leskinnick Street has most

---

* Neighbouring island.
† Formerly head gardener at Badminton; now working in South of France (see entries for 9 and 18 March 1995).
‡ English admiral (1650–1707).

intricate windows, the pointed arches of which still have the original panes. How have they survived? A similar cottage tacked behind.

In the train, I was shocked on opening *The Times* to be confronted by Peter Quennell's obituary. Peter of whom I saw so much before I married, and whom I regarded as the arch-stylist of English prose. Peter, with his coat-hanger shoulders, his blue Homburg and long overcoat, which caused him to resemble (as the obituarist puts it) a cross between a rake and a Calvinist minister. Thus another old friend leaves my faltering mind, until I read the announcement of the memorial service.

Sunday, 31st October

We lunch at Moorwood [near Cirencester, Gloucestershire], as Susy tells me to spell it. Main purpose of visit to enable A. to advise on the garden. The Henrys* have much improved the place, and 'returned' it to a very decent late Regency small squire's house, full of good things and pictures. S. has to tread carefully because Henry is sentimental about the 'improvements' his mother carried out; and Prue† had minimal taste. I am impressed at how S. is managing to run a largish house for these days, with only the ancient Olive to help. Apart from housekeeping and taking the children to daily schools, she sits on environmental committees.

Tuesday, 2nd November

Am struggling with my article on Tresco for *The Field*, concerned that it should be good enough to justify the expense of my visit. At two o'clock, Anthony Chandor and wife Maryanne Bankes‡ called to see library. They were appreciative and observant, commenting on books and objects – something which dear Nick [Robinson] has never done, but then he is totally non-visual.

As I left the house this morning, the telephone rang. A. having

---

* Henry Robinson (b. 1953) of Moorwood House nr Cirencester; eldest of the three Robinson brothers; farmer; m. 1984 Susan Faulkner.
† Hon. Prudence Arthur (1932–76); dau. of J.L.-M's sister Audrey by her 1st marriage to Hon. Matthew Arthur, later 3rd Baron Glenarthur; m. 1953 Major Edwin Robinson of Moorwood House (d. 1985); mother of the Robinson brothers.
‡ Anthony Chandor (b. 1932); m. 1958 Maryanne Bankes (b. 1934); Bath booksellers.

gone to London for the day, I answered. Margaret-Anne [Stuart] spoke. I guessed the reason. Loelia [Lindsay]* died last night. M.-A. was with her. Said she was very restless at the end, and plucked at the sheets as the dying are said to do. She was ninety-one and it was a release, etc. Added that Loelia had expressed a desire that I should write her obituary. I telephoned Jamie [Fergusson] who read back to me the obit. I had written some years ago. We added a line or two about her book.† Death is scampering upon us, one friend after another.

Saturday, 6th November

Marilyn Quennell‡ telephoned, affected to a degree beyond bearing, to talk of poor old Peter's death and memorial service. Wants me to be one of six readers of two-minute addresses. Now, how can one speak about a loved one in two minutes? But I felt I had to consent.

Monday, 8th November

To London to attend two exhibitions of drawings. First Getty collection at Burlington House. Leonardo, Michelangelo, Rembrandt, the lot. Then to British Museum for Chatsworth drawings, even more impressive. One can't take in more than a dozen, really. And yet I whizz through, for I shan't come again. Lunch at Brooks's, where Angus Stirling§ and Martin Drury¶ join my table, rejoicing that the hunting issue has been postponed until next year. Then I walk to National Gallery to look at the Wilton Diptych, displayed with X-rays to illustrate the artist's alterations, the foundation of his paints and even the gesso treatment of the ground wood. J.K.-B. comes to dine. I give him my original edition of Palladio, 1573. Hope he is pleased.

---

* Hon. Loelia Ponsonby (1902–93); dau. of 1st Baron Sysonby; m. 1st (1930–47) 2nd Duke of Westminster ('Bendor'), 2nd 1969 Sir Martin Lindsay of Dowhill, 1st Bt (1905–81).
† *Cocktails and Laughter* (ed. Hugo Vickers, Hamish Hamilton, 1983); described by J.L.-M. on its appearance (*Holy Dread*, 5 November 1983) as 'a dreadful affair'.
‡ Marilyn Peek (*née* Kern; b. 1928); m. 1967 (Sir) Peter Quennell as the last of his five wives.
§ Director-General of N.T., 1983–95 (b. 1933; ktd 1994).
¶ Historic Buildings Secretary (1981–95), subsequently Director-General, of N.T. (b. 1938).

Tuesday, 9th November

At 9.30 I join Hardy Amies in Wilton Row, who gives me a lift to Loelia's funeral at Send. A very smart affair. The church, which I remember as rather gloomy, now illuminated from all sides with arc lamps. Perfectly horrid; roof with flimsy renewed timbers rendered naked by the excessive light. A beautiful needlework panel suspended from lectern, worked by Loelia. Greeted by several friends so aged I did not recognise them. The Camroses,* both looking a million. Then a restaurant luncheon in Ripley, organised by Margaret-Anne and the nice niece Caroline Ponsonby.† I am to be given a pretty walking-stick of Loelia's. Good address given by Francis Sitwell, but too much about the Westminster marriage and not enough about the Lindsay. The Lindsay family there in strength, but not a single Grosvenor.

Saturday, 13th November

Alvilde said to David [Beaufort] at dinner, 'When I first met you I was so terrified that I wrote notes beforehand on what to talk about.' He said that he was equally alarmed by the prospect of meeting her, having heard she was so grumpy and formidable. 'But I adore you now,' he said.

David told us that he knew a man who was born totally blind. Recently he had an operation which enabled him to see. At first he was appalled to see how hideous human beings were. Horses, on the other hand, he found exquisitely beautiful. He was also shocked to discover that cars and buses got larger as they got nearer, while railway lines became closer as they receded into the distance. I had never thought of this aspect, so much do we take such things for granted.

Monday, 15th November

Clarissa [Luke] and Billy‡ came to see the downstairs flat in Bath, the tenant having given notice. I agree with A. that we must let them have it, yet regard the prospect with foreboding.

---

* John Seymour Berry, 2nd Viscount Camrose (1909–94); m. 1986 Hon. Joan Yarde-Buller, dau. of 3rd Baron Churston, formerly wife of Loel Guinness and Prince Aly Khan.
† Hon. Caroline Ponsonby (b. 1938); dau. of 2nd Baron Sysonby.
‡ Clarissa's boyfriend, regarded by J.L.-M. as 'a decent fellow, extremely good-looking and stupid' (*Ceaseless Turmoil*, 3 April 1991).

I have been re-reading Richard Rumbold's* *My Father's Son* [1958]. A beautiful writer, who possessed, as Harold and Vita put it, 'that small flame'. He showed great courage and daredevilry in the air. Combined extraordinary sensitivity with maddening innocence. Wanted the simplest things explained to him − like how to behave in society. Also maddening was his obsession with himself and his ills, and absence of humour. 'Harold says I ought to make more jokes. Must make up some.'

Tuesday, 30th November

I lunched with the Gibsons in their posh new flat in Lansdown Place West. Just as I expected, only more so. Fresh and opulent, lovely new fitted carpets, spotlights in ceiling, dining room deep red, drawing room yellow stipple. Conventional furniture, family pictures, and lampshades like mine, pleated in stripes. Present were nice solicitor and wife. A rather tiring occasion, but the Gs so pleased and happy. Gloria told us they had received an invitation to some church occasion addressed to 'The Revd T. Gibson and partner'. Furious, she complained to the Archdeacon that they had been married thirty-five years, producing four children in wedlock. The Archdeacon replied casually that she should live with the times, and not be so stuffy.

Thursday, 2nd December

Hugh Massingberd, who after a hasty dinner at Brooks's took me to see the beautiful film of the Japanese man's† novel *The Remains of the Day*, told me that he had not yet got over a damning letter from Duff Hart-Davis about what Hugh had intended to be a rave article on Owlpen Manor. It almost made him hand in his resignation from the *Telegraph*, so much did it make him feel a failure as a journalist. I told him he was too sensitive. He said that his wife Caroline‡ was thinking of joining Mother Teresa in Calcutta, and he was wondering whether to do so too. What did I think? I thought it would only be a good

---

* Intimate of Harold Nicolson who committed suicide in 1961.
† Kazuo Ishiguro (b. 1954).
‡ Caroline Ripley (b. 1947); er dau. of Sir Hugh Ripley, 4th Bt (1916–2003); fashion model; m. 1983 Hugh Massingberd as his 2nd wife.

move provided they both dispensed condoms on the streets of Calcutta along with solace.

Friday, 3rd December

A. asked me which among my dead friends I would most like to spend an evening with, were I allowed the privilege. Tom Mitford?* No, I said, not Tom, for I last saw him half a century ago, and I, a different person to the J.L.-M. of 1943, would not know what to say to him.

Tuesday, 14th December

Today the name of a maniac called Zhirinovsky† has dawned upon an unsuspecting world. Promises to be as dangerous and loathsome as Hitler. Worse, if his quoted pronouncements were made in seriousness. Not much prospect of world peace if this clown–maniac gets power.

Saturday, 18th December

We lunch with Woman. Only ourselves, but a spread fit for three crowned heads – roast chicken ('Jimbo, just lift the chicken out of the oven'), gravy, bread sauce, veg., potatoes, stewed apples and mince pies. Woman hobbling on two sticks and as deaf as a post. Says that on opening the *Telegraph* she first looks at Matt's cartoon, then financial pages to check her 'portfolio'. She persecutes her stockbroker in Marlborough several times a week, hoping he is out and will have to ring her back. I pointed out that he probably charges for the calls, which had not occurred to her.

---

* Hon. Thomas Mitford (1909–45); only brother of the Mitford sisters, whom J.L.-M. loved at Eton.
† Vladimir Volfovich Zhirinovsky (b. 1946); Russian lawyer and politician of ultra-nationalist views and outrageous statements (e.g., that he would risk nuclear war with the USA to recover Alaska), whose so-called Liberal Democratic Party captured almost a quarter of the vote in parliamentary elections of December 1993, but was little heard of a decade later.

Sunday, 19th December

At tea, Madeau Stewart* rang to say that Alice Fairfax-Lucy† died this morning. She said that Edmund‡ did not want me to get a shock when I saw it in the paper. But it would not have been much of a shock, for I expect all my contemporaries to die, especially those whom I have not seen for years because they are frail or dotty. Dear Alice, she and Brian were angels to me at Charlecote, so kind and hospitable, and such fun too. There will be a memorial service which I shall try to attend.

Wednesday, 22nd December

Though feeling awful, I went to London today to lunch with Marilyn Quennell, who had asked me and others to discuss Peter's memorial service. Ghastly Underground journey to Chalk Farm, changing several times. The house where Peter spent his last years with his last wife is in a Victorian cul-de-sac, ugly and claustrophobic. Ushered downstairs to basement dining room. Out of the dark loomed ex-Belgian Ambassador, nice artist neighbour called Tim Jaques,§ and Stephen Spender.¶ An air of desperation. Marilyn presiding at round table, coming and going. Quite clear she was already drunk. Very argumentative and affected, acting the great lady like Anne Rosse** used to do, but worse.

Stephen, looking huge and benign, was very friendly and volunteered to sit next to me. We talked of Sunday shopping,†† I remarking that it was presumably convenient for the daily workers. 'That', said S. laughing, 'is the first democratic sentiment I have heard you

---

* Miss Madeau Stewart; cousin of Mitford sisters.
† Hon. Alice Buchan (1908–93), dau. of 1st Baron Tweedsmuir (the novelist John Buchan); m. 1933 Brian Cameron-Ramsay-Fairfax-Lucy, later 5th Bt (1898–1974), whose father had bequeathed Charlecote Park, Warwickshire to N.T.
‡ Sir Edmund Fairfax-Lucy, 6th Bt (b. 1945); artist; life tenant of Charlecote Park; m. 1st 1974 Sylvia Ogden, 2nd 1986 Lady Lucinda Lambton.
§ Illustrator and typographical designer (b. 1933); stalwart of Omar Khayyam Dining Club.
¶ Sir Stephen Spender (1909–95); poet; m. 1941 Natasha Litvin.
** Anne Messel (1902–92); m. (2nd) 1935 Michael Parsons, 6th Earl of Rosse (1906–79).
†† A law permitting the general opening of shops on Sunday finally took effect from August 1994.

utter.' Marilyn asked why Peter gave up writing poetry when he was a good poet. S. said that P. did not have the calling. M. maintained it was because he recognised that his poetry was unfashionable. He ought to have ignored his contemporaries, and persisted instead of 'indulging in the fleshpots'. 'No harm in that,' said S. I agreed with M. that if P. was a true poet he should not have been affected by silly fashion. Mentioned Hopkins.* S. said the trouble was that poets wanted passionately to write whereas few wanted to read what they had written.

S. enjoys being a knight. Owes it to Isaiah Berlin,† his long-time protector, who has the ear of all who matter, the Crown, Number Ten. S. doesn't mind the prospect of dying, though worries about how Natasha will be looked after. Also fears there will be many books and articles about him, disclosing his love affairs – 'not that you will be in that category,' he added. Admits he suffers much from guilt about the past. He has a new volume of poems coming out in February, and said that the period between advance copies and publication was like that between a death and a funeral. I was touched by his niceness to me. We asked each other why we had not in our long lives seen more of each other. I said I wished we had been friends at Oxford, when I was in need of friends. I thought, but did not say, that he might have rendered me less right-wing, I him less left. Who knows?

By this time, Marilyn had disappeared. When I looked for her to say goodbye she was supine on a sofa, mouth open.

Friday, 24th December

Edmund Fairfax-Lucy telephoned. I knew at once what he wanted. Would I write something to read at Alice's memorial service on 15 January? I said yes, and now regret. Even worse than Peter Q.; for what am I to say? I can't get out of the writing now, but may rat on the reading.

Saturday, 25th December

Luncheon at the House, sitting next to Daph[ne Fielding]. She is not senile but very deaf, and only seems to take in what one does not intend her to hear.

---

* The poetry of Gerard Manley Hopkins (1844–89) was unknown to the world until a selection of it was published by Robert Bridges in 1918, almost thirty years after his death.
† Sir Isaiah Berlin (1909–97); Russian-born Oxford philosopher and historian of ideas.

Wednesday, 29th December

Lunch with Eeleses* at Holwell Farm. A nice mixed brew, Adrian's partner Colin Anson staying. He told me that his Arbuthnot forebear, attending a public dinner in Edinburgh for George IV, was told by the King in his cups, 'Arise, Sir William'. The new Sir William didn't know whether he was to be a knight or a baronet. Nor, apparently, did the King. However, Sir W. assumed the latter dignity; and so the baronetcy survives.

---

* Adrian Eeles; dealer in prints; lived with wife in Ozleworth Valley.

1994

Saturday, 1st January

Richard Robinson[*] lunched with us. He is still very youthful in complexion, and A. noticed that his slender hands were beautiful. Told us he intended to devote his leisure to a venture in aid of the 'Chernobyl children' now being born eight years after the leakage[†] – babies with no hands or arms, twisted, mad. While my own wish is to prevent babies being born, I can find no flaw in this nice, deserving youth, who will, I fancy, one day be made a knight. He embraced me affectionately on parting.

Sunday, 2nd January

Delicious luncheon with Peter Levis at Prospect Cottage, Frampton-on-Severn. Matthew,[‡] Cyril's son by Deirdre, is astonishingly handsome – slight with a faun-like figure, wavy longish fair hair like a Renaissance prince. Says little, but misses nothing, and Peter says he is very clever. He went for an interview to College of Arms, but was disappointed to discover there was virtually no pay.

Tuesday, 4th January

Madeau Stewart tells me that Alice Lucy's little house at Burford has been raided and all treasures taken except for books, the buggers doubtless being illiterate. The moral being that one should not, after death and before burial, leave one's house unattended. They can't be so illiterate as not to be able to read the funeral announcements.

While reading James Agate's[§] immensely clever *Ego 9* I nodded off for a split second. During this flick of an eyelash I suddenly felt

---

[*] Youngest of J.L.-M's three Robinson great-nephews (b. 1957); merchant banker.

[†] The explosion of the Ukrainian nuclear reactor had occurred on 26 April 1986; the Chernobyl Children's Project was founded by Adi Roche in 1990.

[‡] Matthew Connolly (b. 1970); genealogist; ed. *The Selected Works of Cyril Connolly* (2002).

[§] Theatre critic (1877–1947).

desperately lonely without Mama and Papa and wondered how I could get through life without them. Then I remembered that I had not been wholly foresaken, as A. was still with me. The relief was so great that I actually cried. Now I ask myself sadly, how long shall I have A. for? How long shall we remain united?

Saturday, 8th January

I am thinking of writing to Mr Major* to tell him that he can't both go 'back to basics' and have 'a classless society'.[†] For basic politeness and civilised behaviour are the attributes of a gentleman, nurtured in country houses and on the playing fields of Eton. Outside such sanctuaries of good breeding, brutishness and vulgarity flourish. Which is why few things are more distressing than to see aristocrats behaving like louts and swine.

Tuesday, 11th January

Peter Quennell's memorial service at St James's, Piccadilly. When my turn came I cast asunder all nerves and read my piece.[‡] I looked up from time to time but did not focus for fear of spotting a face I knew. I think it went all right. Roy Jenkins came up afterwards to congratulate, as did George Weidenfeld,[§] so presumably I did not disgrace myself. But the agony before the event is even greater than the relief when it is over. Stephen Spender, who was also due to read an address, failed to turn up or even send Marilyn a message.

Sunday, 16th January

Tony Lambton[¶] blows in at midday. He has beautiful manners, and is charming without having charm, but makes me uneasy. Is full of hates

---

* John Major (b. 1943; KG 2005); Conservative Prime Minister, 1990–7.
† Recent slogans of the Major Government – which predictably resulted in the tabloid press launching a campaign to expose 'sleaze', both financial and sexual, among Conservative MPs.
‡ In his eulogy, J.L.-M. remarked that he was probably the only person to have known all of Quennell's five wives.
§ Austrian-born publisher (b. 1919); co-founder with Nigel Nicolson of Weidenfeld & Nicolson, 1948; cr. life peer, 1976.
¶ Antony Lambton (b. 1922); s. father as 6th Earl of Durham, 1970, and disclaimed peerages but continued to use courtesy title Viscount Lambton; MP (C) Berwick-on-Tweed 1951–73, resigning seat and office in Conservative Government following 'the call girl affair' of 1973.

and dislikes, and one has to avoid seeming to agree with him. Also mischievous. He notices everything, which I like. Praises my little room where we sat, and asks about the pictures. What is that house? My grandmother's. What was her name? He presses us both to stay with him in Italy, but I don't think either of us could stand the strain.

Sunday, 23rd January

In the afternoon I walk to Worcester Lodge, an hour and a half. Not bad, considering my legs are now feeble. A fine afternoon with sun, with heralding of spring and definite whispering of Siren songs. Even at eighty-five I am disturbed, wanting to be off. In the garden a few aconites and snowdrops already out; and the goldfish, who should be hibernating at the bottom of the pool, are darting about.

Tuesday, 25th January

M. telephones to say Maître Blum* has died, aged ninety-five. He minds, naturally, yet is not bereft because for the past three years she has been out of the land of the conversing. I have read his excellent obituary in the *Telegraph*. He told me the *Daily Mail* also telephoned asking for an article on her. He agreed, on condition that no alterations were made to his copy. When they received it, they complained that it contained no scandal. M. assured them that no scandal was associated with the Maître.

Saturday, 29th January

Woman brought Diana [Mosley] to luncheon. Diana very thin and deaf. Is distressed by an article on her in *Mail on Sunday* by Brian Masters,† with ravishingly beautiful photograph. When she left I read it with care, and don't think he meant to be unkind at all. He allowed Diana to speak for herself. All that is objectionable are the captions, highlighting that she is still hated throughout the world after fifty years, etc. I have written to tell her what I think.

---

* See notes to 11 February 1993.
† Writer (b. 1939), celebrated for psychological studies of serial murderers.

Sunday, 30th January

Dreadful luncheon at Newark, twenty-four of the county. Why do Bob and Michael do it? On my right Brenda Tomlinson,[*] not county but classless. She talked of her journeys round the world with Charles, who is in demand everywhere to read his poetry, and never travels without her. She said that Andrew Barrow,[†] whom she met for the first time last week, asked her what she thought about love. Of course, I said, you replied that you knew nothing about it. Oh, she replied, but I think I do. Nicholas Shakespeare is to spend a day with them to talk about Bruce [Chatwin]. I said she must tell all. Brenda said, 'How could I possibly disclose what he said behind Elizabeth's back?' I said that Bruce had become a public figure of absorbing interest, as he had always wanted to be, and that she would do no good by denying his biographer, a very intelligent man and good writer, all she knew.

Saturday, 5th February

Lying in bed this morning later than is my wont, I decide that I feel worse in bed than out of it. In bed I seek tranquillity – but find worrying dreams, restless waking, a quickening of the heartbeat and consequent breathlessness.

Thursday, 10th February

With some foreboding, we set out for Agadir. Horrid journey, changing planes at Casablanca. Reach Al-Medina Palace Hotel at eleven, having left home at 1.30. David [Herbert][‡] has booked ambassadorial suite for us, next to his own room. Far too large, miles to walk to bathroom. But charming décor – tiled floor, blue woodwork, blue panes in windows, Moorish beds. Agadir totally rebuilt since earthquake,[§] but smart part where we are in good taste, with no tall buildings. Lovely sun, and temperature perfect. Cool at nights.

During our visit, Ramadan starts, and dottiness ensues among

---

[*] Charles Tomlinson (b. 1927); poet living in Ozleworth Valley; m. 1948 Brenda Raybould.
[†] Writer and journalist (b. 1945); yr brother of Julian Barrow, artist; m. (2nd) 2000 Hon. Annabel Freyberg, dau. of 2nd Baron Freyberg.
[‡] Hon. David Herbert (1908–95); yr s. of 15th Earl of Pembroke.
[§] An earthquake on 29 February 1960 had flattened the city and killed more than 15,000.

Muslim inhabitants. I walk on beach, which is like Blackpool today. The young kicking footballs, doing physical jerks and acrobatics, messing about on motor-bikes. But no one nasty to me. Observe camels, so savage and haughty in their expressions yet, like all animals in human bondage, poignant.

David much aged. Enormous nose; toothless. Wears fanciful clothes, and fez-like hats adorned with gold braid; hands covered with enormous rings like pylons. All part of his endearing persona. He is thrilled that National Portrait Gallery have commissioned a picture of him as an eccentric English milord. He alternates between bouts of depression and enjoyment of stories of yore – how Vita approved of Harold's love for him, but begged H. not to change him from the humming-bird he was; how Tallulah Bankhead,* when one of her lovers left her at midnight for bed, said to him, 'If I'm not back by five, just begin on your own.'

On Shrove Tuesday, we were joined by Peter and Kate Townend.† She bright and sympathetic, with look of her mother Patricia Hambleden; he handsome and intelligent, with deep rich voice, but a heavy drinker, a sort of buccaneering, Paddy Leigh Fermor type. He was very good with David. I became fond of him.

We return on the 18th, both feeling better for it. I have managed to rough out an article for *The Field* on roofs, and read three books.

Thursday, 3rd March

So Harold Acton‡ has now gone. What do I feel? Nothing much. It was high time for him. Papers full of praise, all obituaries laudatory and favourable. He is another example of a man remarkable not for what he has left behind but what he made himself into. Sad that the lovely Pietra garden will no longer be for private delight. The house always struck me as horribly melancholy. Edwardian of course, with the sort of Italian paintings and Renaissance treasures which leave no room for future ages. Bedroom so cluttered that it was rash to unpack for likelihood of losing one's things among the junk. I did not quite

---

* American actress (1902–68), who lived and worked in England, 1924–30, causing concern to the Home Office which regarded her as a corrupter of British youth.
† Hon. Katharine Smith (b. 1933), dau. of 3rd Viscount Hambleden; David Herbert's niece; m. (2nd) 1973 Peter Townend.
‡ Sir Harold Acton (1904–94); writer and aesthete; owner of Villa La Pietra, Florence.

belong to his generation; there was four years' difference between us, which when we were young was considerable. He was wonderful to be with, wonderful. That unique voice, with inflexions more Italian than English. His grandfather's origins wrapped in mists. Once, during the war, we dined together and strolled back to Eaton Place where he was staying in the Rosses' little house in their absence. H. in uniform, an odd spectacle. He persuaded me to stay and go to bed with him. I agreed, but it meant nothing to me. Next morning he rebuked me for icy-cold unresponsiveness, and I don't think he ever quite forgave me. People who have been rejected – or worse still, who have been accepted and then treated with indifference – harbour lasting resentment, and hurt. Harold's appearance never changed since I first met him at McNeile's House [at Eton] in 1921, when he was a senior boy and I a new boy. He seemed bald even then. A sort of Horace Mann,* to be remembered for his erudition, intelligence and sparkling conversation.

Friday, 11th March

To London to attend Heywood Hill's first 'literary luncheon', given at Pratt's† by Andrew Devonshire and John Saumarez Smith. The cosiness of Pratt's, mid Victorian interior, stuffed birds, antlered heads, engravings of 1850s worthies in maplewood and ebony frames under carved coronets. Asked by Fanny Partridge how one qualified for membership, Andrew said mischievously, 'Well, the Brigade of Guards, a respectable public school, and a passable family used to be *de rigueur*, this is sometimes now relaxed, but whenever it is we are apt to get cads.' I had hoped to see Candida [Lycett Green], but she chucked and in her place the Sergeant‡ from Paris roped in, most willingly. He sat on my left and Andrew on my right. Andrew a very good host, in genial mood. Said he was addicted to the news, watched it several times a day. The Robert Kees, Michael Briggses and Fanny the other guests.

From Pratt's I walked up the road to Murray's and was received

---

* Sir Horace Mann, 1st Bt (1701–86); British envoy to the Court of Florence, whose main duty was to keep an eye on 'Bonnie Prince Charlie' there; friend and correspondent of Horace Walpole.
† Club off St James's Street, owned by Duke of Devonshire.
‡ Stuart Preston.

by Grant and Gail in the grand Byron room. Gail has finished editing my new diaries, making few alterations and some good suggestions. We discussed the jacket. Walked on to Waddington Gallery, Clifford Street, to see John Lessore* exhibition. Swirling dancers in motion, very Impressionistic, misty grey light. Then to Modigliani† exhibition at Burlington House. Far too many, and I could only look at a few. Exceptional economy of line to yield three-dimensional effect.

Saturday, 12th March

Our long-planned luncheon with the Roy Jenkinses. Other guests Roland Philipps,‡ son of Mollie Norwich and grandson of Ros[amond Lehmann], a publisher and a friendly fellow, and wife, literary agent. Also Clarissa Avon,§ who retains a splendid slim figure whereas her face is a cobweb of creases making her look far older than her seventy-three years. She reminded me that she had known me since she was six. Jennifer is my idea of the perfect wife. Her history of the N.T.,¶ which I have now read in proof, is a magisterial tome. It is very nice to me – or rather about me.

Tuesday, 15th March

To London, object of visit to attend Prince Charles's party to launch *Perspectives.*** A. said I must go, it would be rude not to, and besides one must support a good cause. Forgot what time expected, so chose 6.30. Walked from Brooks's down to St James's Palace. On entry,

---

* British artist (b. 1939); nephew of Walter Sickert.
† Amedeo Modigliani (1884–1920); Italian-born Paris artist.
‡ Hon. Roland Philipps (b. 1962); yr s. of 3rd Baron Milford and Hon. Mary ('Mollie') Makins (who m. [2nd] 2nd Viscount Norwich); publishing director of Macmillan (later Managing Director of John Murray and publisher of this volume); m. 1991 Felicity Rubinstein (b. 1958), literary agent.
§ Clarissa Churchill (b. 1920); niece of Sir Winston and sister of J.L.-M's friend J. G. ('Johnnie') Churchill (1909–92); m. 1953 Sir Anthony Eden, Prime Minister 1955–7, cr. Earl of Avon, 1957.
¶ Jennifer Jenkins and Patrick James, *From Acorn to Oak Tree: The Growth of the National Trust* (Macmillan, 1994).
** Unsuccessful architecture magazine supported by the Prince, published from 1994 to 1998.

found Palace curiously deserted. Didn't want to arrive first so, having passed through downstairs gallery and surrendered overcoat and brolly, I sat on a scarlet bench and waited. A nice lady approached and asked if I was feeling unwell. I assured her not, but did not like to explain why I was waiting. She insisted on accompanying me upstairs, lending an arm which I didn't need. Directed me through two rooms overlooking Friary Court towards a large drawing room literally *jammed* with people. She explained that over five hundred had already come. I couldn't even get beyond the entrance door. Eileen Harris saw me and came up to talk, but I couldn't hear a single word. I stood for a few minutes, doubtless looking like a dazed rabbit, then retreated and left. I think the stairs are those in double flight illustrated in Pyne.[*] The two approaching galleries dull, one with Tudor fireplace; red walls, furniture against walls, dull portraits. No opportunity to poke around. When I telephoned A. before dinner, she was furious with me for not arriving promptly at the decreed hour of six.

Wednesday, 16th March

Today, after going to Claude exhibition at National Gallery – ravishing – I called on Nick [Robinson] at his charming flat in Shepherd Street which used to be his office. Hung with good watercolours collected by his father. We were joined by his friend Emma Foale,[†] wife of eminent surgeon, niece of my old friend Archie Gordon[‡] and great-niece of old Mrs Pleydell-Bouverie.[§] We lunched at Italian restaurant and discussed the ghost story Nick wants me to write.

I caught early train back to Chippenham and drove to Malmesbury to collect from Mrs Nicholls' shop the two turquoise Minton saucers I bought the other day. Didn't dare own up to A., who would have thought it an extravagance. Said nothing about it when I got home, she sitting in her usual chair drinking tea, waiting for me. There is no reason for me to feel guilty, for after all, it is my money and my pleasure. Yet I don't want to keep things from her, and be underhand. We

[*] W. H. Pyne, *Royal Residences* (3 vols, 1819).
[†] Lady Emma Gordon (b. 1953); er dau. of 6th Marquess of Aberdeen; m. 1980 Dr Rodney Foale.
[‡] Lord Archibald Gordon (1913–84); s. bro. 1974 as 5th Marquess of Aberdeen.
[§] Pre-war owner of Coleshill estate, Oxfordshire, parts of which were donated to N.T.

had a happy evening, and when I kissed her goodnight she laughed and said, 'What dreadful old crocks we are.'

Friday, 18th March

When I left for Bath this morning, I did not for some reason kiss A. goodbye as I usually do. After a good day's work, and some shopping, I got home at 4.45. Unloaded car, walked to gate, opened gate – and then I saw her in front of me, lying on the flagstones, the slippery flagstones she so dreaded, her car keys in hand. The shock appalling. 'My darling!' I called to her, scattering my things as I bent down. Felt her forehead, which was cold. Could not move her. Dashed to estate office, begging for help. They telephoned Peggy and Gerald,* who came quickly. Peggy rang for ambulance, but Gerald knew she was dead. Men came, carried her into drawing room, laid her not on sofa but on floor. I could not look at her again. Ian [Dixon] came and sweetly sat with me drinking whisky until Clarissa and Billy arrived from London. Suave undertaker came. I begged for her rings before she was taken away to mortuary chapel in Chippenham. O dear God, to see her stretched before me on the cold stone, in the rain. She had come straight from the hairdresser and looked so pretty. Sudden, I am sure – but what is 'sudden' at the time of death? And I not there to hold her hand. These days to be my hell on earth.

Thursday, 24th March

Yesterday we went, driven by Billy, whose presence has to be accepted, to the undertakers at Chippenham. I wanted to have one last look at her, if only to mitigate the guilt on my conscience at having allowed her to be swept away without a last goodbye. Funeral parlour clinically clean. Handsome, affable official received us, directed us to silent, windowless chapel. There she lay on the bier, her head uncovered. Serene she looked, and beautiful; not a line visible. At my request, Clarissa cut a few locks of her dear hair. Then I asked to be alone. In agonies of tears I kissed her brow, as hard and as cold as marble, and begged her to forgive me for being the rotten husband I was. Quickly pulled myself together.

I am inundated with letters. Mightily pleased by the obituaries of

---

* Peggy Bird, the L.-Ms' daily help, and husband.

her in *Independent* by Mary Keen and Coote [Heber-Percy], and *Telegraph* by unknown.* Not intimate, all about her horticultural expertise. Rosemary [Verey] telephoned to read out another she had written for *The Times* – wonderful and generous. I never supposed she would have any obits.

So long as I am busy, and no one commiserates, I am all right by day. Lying in bed before falling asleep is dreadful. I am irritated by Billy's presence, and have told Clarissa that both of them must leave me on Saturday. He may be well-meaning, but he is extremely dumb and boring.

Friday, 25th March

The day I have dreaded ever since it occurred to me some thirty years ago that she might die before me. We had some twenty-five to a stand-up luncheon before the funeral in Little Badminton Church. Charming vicar Ian Marchant officiated, Tom Gibson being in South Africa. He spoke sweetly of A.; and Tony Scotland read verses from Corinthians I, Chapter 15, most beautifully and professionally. Several people from the village and a handful of old friends. I had to walk out first behind her dear coffin to the hearse. Then the crematorium, which was not too harrowing. Marchant read a prayer; and the large curtains, like those at Covent Garden, silently closed. Then home. Clarissa took her descendants to Old Werretts[†] for tea, while Nick and Richard [Robinson] stayed with me and we did the Cherry Orchard walk.

Monday, 28th March

Time has somehow ceased. The evenings alone are agony, and the nights frightening. I go in and out of her bedroom. The whole house is full of coffee cups – her notes, diary, telephone book, every single thing is redolent of her.

Yesterday I lunched at Old Werretts. Before I left, Ian asked to show me something which he said was sacred to him. In his darkened bedroom was a sort of shrine, a small table with crystal vases and mini-

---

* It was by George Plumptre (see notes to 27 June 1995), the Obituaries Editor, Hugh Massingberd, being indisposed at the time (see entry for 13 October 1994).
† House of Desmond Briggs and Ian Dixon.

ature columns lit up by night lights, and a collage of photographs of the people he most loves – his family, Daphne [Fielding], and others including A. and me. All rather curious and touching. He told me that he took the wreath from the crematorium on Friday and dropped the petals one by one into the swirling river that flows through Castle Combe. I thought of Millais'* picture of Ophelia. A sweet act of friendship.

Thursday, 31st March

Last day of this terrible month. Nick and Henry [Robinson] came, bringing lunch cooked by Susy. I relish their kindness and affection but find it difficult to follow their conversation.

At four, the undertaker called. He bowed from the waist and asked solemnly if I was prepared to receive the urn, which he held out like the Archbishop offering the orb to the Queen. He added a few words, 'If I may presume on such an occasion', etc. I asked him if he was sure the ashes were A.'s. He appeared to be shocked by the question. 'Perhaps in the big cities misadventures may occur.' Laughing and crying, I carried upstairs the large, brown, nondescript plastic urn, embraced it, and put it inside the large blue-and-white bowl above my clothes cupboard. I don't find it macabre; on the contrary, a comfort to have her remains so near me while I sleep.

Sunday, 3rd April

Today at breakfast I read the most beastly article by David Cannadine† about Harold and Vita, calling them snobs. I rang Nigel to express my outrage. During Holy Communion, I thought I must reply to it. On return I drafted and redrafted letter to *The Times*, then drove to Old Werretts where Desmond despatched it to the editor on his fax machine. They then drove me to the Norwiches where we lunched. About ten, including Sue Baring‡ and the nice Levis. Then back in pouring rain to see Clarissa and Billy. They went through A.'s jewelry, spreading it out on kitchen table. She asked him what he thought of each piece. I said

---

* Sir John Everett Millais (1829–96); Pre-Raphaelite artist.
† Cambridge historian (b. 1950), then teaching in America.
‡ Hon. Susan Renwick (b. 1930), dau. of 1st Baron Renwick; m. 1955 (diss. 1984) Hon. Sir John Baring (b. 1928; succeeded 1991 as 7th Baron Ashburton).

nothing, but found it painful to watch him handling A's precious personal things. Then dinner at the House, numerous children and friends. Delicious caviare, both David and Caroline abstaining out of boredom with it. He said it was Persian, and the best in the world.

Afterwards I talked with David in the library about his houses in the village and all the trouble he has with the planning officers, who are obstructive and tasteless. I find him very sympathetic when his attention can be won.

Monday, 4th April

Motor to Caudle Green to lunch alone with dear Woman. She is pleased with the felt pull-down hat which she wore at the funeral, for which she paid thirty shillings in 1936; today it would cost £60. Nick dines, a pillar of comfort and encouragement.

Tuesday, 5th April

I visit the Harrises in their lugubrious cottage at Ashcroft. At home and without an audience, John sheds his boisterous jocularity and talks calmly and wisely. I take to her more and more. We discuss the back-slidings of the National Trust, which they say is beaten to the ground by its own bureaucracy. Terribly depressed when I get home in the evening. Home is like my own empty heart.

Wednesday, 6th April

I am haunted by my lamentable unkindness to A., particularly in two respects. First, I never tried hard enough to understand and share her love of gardening. She put plants into the earth with her own hands, nurtured them, watched them grow, and when they were blossoming, looked not merely at them but into them. Secondly, I was often horrid about her descendants, so that she was reluctant to discuss with me all the worries they caused her. I find it hard to forgive them; yet I behaved very ill.

Thursday, 7th April

I remember Jamesey [Pope-Hennessy] once said to me, when we saw a discarded tin, 'It's a sobering thought that this tin may exist long after we are dust.' And here around me are all the tins she bought, and the food in the freezer which she put there. The misery is unendurable.

A sad little ceremony this morning at Newark, attended by half a dozen National Trust people, at which Bob [Parsons], almost in tears, plants a deodar in front of the house. In a week's time he leaves for good.

Saturday, 9th April

Debo telephones after breakfast. 'It's nothing alarming,' she begins. 'Woman, staying with her friend Margaret Budd, fell on the stairs and broke both her legs. She's being operated on at the London Hospital.' At eighty-seven, what chance is there of recovery?

Tony Lambton telephones asking me to stay with them in Tuscany, and Michael Mallon* writes that John Pope-Hennessy† wants me to stay in Florence. Rather flattering to be invited by the two men who frighten me most in the world.

Sunday, 10th April

Listened to John Gielgud on the wireless playing King Lear. I followed Act One with my open Shakespeare, losing thread from time to time as they took liberties with the text. Excellent and moving though John was, I couldn't listen to more owing to the tremendous and unrelenting melodrama, with so much shouting and passion and those intermittent trumpets. In future I shall just have to read Shakespeare to myself; I can no longer see him on stage or even listen to him on the radio.

Tuesday, 12th April

To London. After giving Misha luncheon at Brooks's, and seeing Goya exhibition at Burlington House, I was collected by the Loewensteins' chauffeur who drove me to Petersham Lodge [Richmond], where I stayed the night with Josephine. Rupert was in Germany, visiting the

---

* American art history student (b. 1960); personal assistant to Sir John Pope-Hennessy.
† Sir John Pope-Hennessy (1913–94); elder brother of James P.-H.; art historian and museum director, latterly Chairman of Department of European Paintings at Metropolitan Museum, New York, 1977–86.

head of his family. Like being summoned to headmaster's study, says J.; the family do not quite approve of him owing to his Jewish connections and making his money from the Rolling Stones. This house very posh, but pretty and extremely comfortable. Good dinner, at which the conversation flowed. She is a dear soul.

Wednesday, 13th April

Driven by the Loewensteins' chauffeur, I join a group of the Textiles Conservation Centre (of which I am patron) to visit Ham [House, Surrey] and Osterley [Park, Middlesex]. Ham still magical, all rooms suitably shrouded. All seventeenth-century fabrics and furniture still in place from original inventories made during reign of Charles II. Osterley, on the other hand, disappointing. It is stark, furniture around the walls, nothing in centre, few carpets. The library ceiling, walls, dado and bookshelves all dead white. At least John Fowler would have had shades of white. The looking glasses far too flimsy. My taste for Adam tinsel and clinkclankery has abated.

When the chauffeur called for me at five, he told me there was a message for me to ring the Duchess of Devonshire. Which I did on the carphone. Pam. Dead from a sudden clot. I was too moved to speak to Debo, who was herself dreadfully grieved. She asked if I might write an obituary for the *Telegraph*. I decided I must, and sketched it out on the train home. Darling Woman, whom I have known and loved since I was fourteen.

Monday, 18th April

I motor to Swinbrook for Woman's funeral. I pick whatever flowers in the garden are out, which Peggy ties up in some mauve paper and ribbons, and insert note to Darling and Wonderful Woman from her devoted Jimble. Woman's coffin unvarnished, in natural wood, as she wanted. She is buried away from Nancy's and Unity's plots by desire of the vicar, afraid of too many sightseers crowding around a Mitford enclave.

Wednesday, 20th April

Consternation. The lead bird-bath, prettily decorated along the rim, maybe eighteenth-century and beloved by A., has been stolen.

Nothing is safe. Doe Bowlby* was telling me that their house was burgled on three successive nights while they were sleeping upstairs.

My *Times* letter about Harold and Vita has had a favourable reception. People mention it with approval or write to congratulate. It has prompted others to write to *The Times* about the simple kindness they received from Vita at Sissinghurst.

Tuesday, 26th April

Jeremy Fry† telephones, back from southern India where he is building a house. Commiserates about A. and says how much he admired and loved her. Jeremy can be very touching. Told me to withdraw into myself. This is indeed what I would like to do, but I get caught up in events. Now Debo has written to beg me – 'beg' is her angelic word – to join the family celebrations the week after next for tercentenary of Devonshire dukedom.

Thursday, 28th April

Saintly Richard [Robinson] motors me to Heathrow and sees me through the barrier. I go to stay with Anna-Maria [Cicogna]‡ in the Casetta, Venice. She has had a growth removed from her nose, and is philosophical and brave. Nino, the elderly butler, is a real gent. In ushering me in to dinner he made a formal little speech, saying how sad he was about the death of A., a *donna brava*. I murmured something about *molto dolore*, and felt warmly towards this splendid man. Hearing Anna-Maria talk in animated Italian with her architect friend Riccardo, about the Balkan situation and Italian corruption, it struck me that Italians treat the physical act of talking, with its cadences, mimicry, emphasis, gestures and grimaces, as a form of art.

Friday, 29th April

With no immediate worries on top of me, I have the best sleep in ages. Take traghetto to S. Siglio. Cash cheques at bank. Walk to Palazzo

---

* Dora Allen; m. 1930 Sir Anthony Bowlby, 2nd Bt, of the Old Rectory, Ozleworth, Glos.
† Inventor and businessman (1924–2005); m. 1955 (diss. 1967) Camilla Grinling.
‡ Anna-Maria (b. 1913), dau. of Count Giovanni Volpi (Mussolini's finance minister); m. 1932 Count Cesare Cicogna Mozzoni; prominent resident and hostess of Venice.

Grassi. Long queues of yelling *gruppi*, Venice bursting with the young
of the whole world. Noise like monkey house at zoo. Exhibition of
Renaissance architecture from Brunelleschi to Michelangelo superbly
shown, if too large. Fight my way round. How A. would have hated
all the architectural drawings and plans. I find my painting [of St
Peter's, Rome] splendidly hung on wall by itself, and surface cleaned
so the gold highlights visible for first time. I feel proud. The ropes
rather too close, making me apprehensive of the pointing fingers of
admirers. Other treasures Urbino painting of Ideal City, the San
Bernardina Miracles, and lovely panel of building of a house with
craftsmen at their various jobs.

At luncheon – delicious melon and risotto – A.-M. talks of
B[ernard] B[erenson]* whom she loved. I saunter round the block
afterwards. Water lapping the stone pavement of Zattere; melancholy
bells of Salute; rattle of motor-boats; semi–nude sunbathers on quay.
I ask myself, am I interested in Venice still? Not sure. Return to the
Casetta, so pretty, impersonal and dismal. Shades of A. and Derry
[Drogheda]. I am filled with melancholy reflections. Nothing bright
and beautiful lasts. Everything fades. Life dies. I call for tea. Even that
fills me with sadness, causing me to recall how A. thirsted for it
towards the end of the day.

A.-M. and I cross to S. Marco and walk to Palazzo Berlingieri,
enormous untouched 1830s and 40s. We are eighteen in all. During
the eternity before we descend to dinner, I wander to balcony to look
at view in fading sunlight, and see a blood-red sailing boat from
Chioggia passing across S. Giorgio. I am seated on right of hostess
Barbara Berlingieri, nice woman who adores Venice and her
husband's palazzo. He is dull, with a major's sandy moustache, talking
of his forthcoming visit to Badminton Horse Trials. On my other side,
the divine Donatella Asta. Have seldom beheld a more beautiful
woman. I thought A.-M. was never going to leave.

Saturday, 30th April

I have told A.-M. that I can't face the further cosmopolitan lunches
and dinners to which she proposes to take me. She accepts this kindly.
I loaf around Rialto area, looking for churches little known to me

---

* American art historian (1865–1959); lived at Villa I Tatti, Florence (now the Harvard
University Center for Italian Renaissance Studies).

because previously shut. They are still shut, apart from S. Giacomo di Rialto.

Sunday, 1st May

May Day, and a Sunday. Huge milling crowds everywhere. No vaporetti, which seems undemocratic. I go to Anglican Church for Holy Communion. No old friends present, not even Rose Lauritzen.[*] At luncheon, A.-M. talks of her friends the Thorneycrofts.[†] As Chairman of Conservative Party, he was Mrs Thatcher's greatest confidant. Then he was suddenly dropped like a stone. Was staying with A.-M. when envoy from Mrs T. arrived to deliver information. He took it on the chin, and has never made any comment on it to A.-M., then or since. When Peter is dead, A.-M. may ask Carla.

Monday, 2nd May

I suffer from sore throat, which I attribute to chalice yesterday morning. Over lunch, A.-M. says she has no feeling whatever for defunct husband. He left her years ago, asking for divorce. Wander in afternoon sun again. Wisteria draping walls. To San Zaccaria to see Bellini with angelic lute player, then to S. Giovanni in Bragora with its divine Cima over altar. See Santo Spirito on the Zattere for first time, just as purple-shirted priest about to shut it. He hovers politely to allow me a glance. Pitch dark inside, high ceiling, stucco panels, marble-pillared side-altars.

Tuesday, 3rd May

Last day in Venice, spent with A.-M. at Palazzo Grassi exhibition. She a surprisingly indefatigable sightseer, taking lively intelligent interest in exhibits. Her comments interesting and her knowledge of Venice considerable, she being ex-queen of this city. I find her very

---

[*] Hon. Rose Keppel (b. 1943); yr dau. of Viscount Bury, e. s. and heir of 9th Earl of Albemarle (whom he predeceased, 1968), and his 1st wife Lady Mairi Vane-Tempest-Stewart, yst dau. of 7th Marquess of Londonderry; m. Peter Lauritzen.
[†] Peter Thorneycroft (1909–94); politician, Chairman of Conservative Party, 1975–81; m. (2nd) 1949 Countess Carla Roberti, dau. of Count Malagola Cappi of Ravenna, Italy; cr. life peer, 1967.

companionable in spite of her being hedged in by social conventions. Her daughter Marina and grandson come to stay, and I meet them at dinner. Daughter must be sixty but looks extremely young. Fair hair (dyed?), chic, assertive and brusque. Grandson about twenty-five, extremely handsome bilingual Italian living and working in England. Well-dressed, with usual exquisite manners of upper-class Italians. He talked with amused disdain of the Somerset boys.*

Thursday, 12th May

By train to Chatsworth. Debo clearly preoccupied, so I retreat to my bedroom, the Red Velvet, and rest until festivities begin in park at 7.30. Incredible celebrations of ducal tercentenary on scale of Louis XIV. Huge auditorium constructed on far side of river; around it, tents and cone-like huts illuminated like a Saracen encampment. An enormous dinner tent (not for house guests dining later in Painted Hall). Mingling with invited crowd are men on stilts, men with bagpipes, jugglers, funny men, singing men with instruments. I run into people I know – Diana Scarisbrick† the jewelry expert; John and Laura Saumarez Smith; Brian Masters (staying in house), bearing deep scar across his cheek from a strange man who called at his door.

Watch pageant staged across the Derwent against architectural background, to which we are summoned by 'revolutionaries' in full-bottomed wigs bearing Orange flags. One of them approaches asking me to sign petition in favour of William of Orange, which I do laughingly, saying I feel a traitor to my Stuart allegiance. 'I've read your books,' says petitioner to me knowingly. Pageant a truly amazing spectacle, though cold so intense I fear hypothermia. All the dukes impersonated from the first down to Duke Eddie, all in correct contemporary costumes. Then fireworks such as I had never seen before – fingers of gold and corkscrew serpents weaving into the sky – accompanied by water music by Beethoven, Handel, Elgar. Then Andrew, sitting next to me, descends to riverbank to make short speech of thanks. Wild applause, everyone much moved, many in tears.

---

* Sons of 11th Duke of Beaufort and Caroline *née* Thynne: Harry, Marquess of Worcester (b. 1952; m. 1987 Tracy Ward); Lord Edward Somerset (b. 1958; m. 1982 Hon. Caroline Davidson); Lord John Somerset, photographer (b. 1964).

† New Zealand-born expert; m. Peter Scarisbrick; author of *Jewellery in Britain, 1066–1837* (Michael Russell, 1994), and organiser of jewellery exhibitions.

Back to house for dinner at 11.30. Sit next to Stoker* who talks most affectionately of his father, praising his phenomenal generosity and public spirit. Do not get to bed until two in the morning, for the first time in years.

Friday, 13th May

Paddy Leigh Fermor staying. Is seventy-nine and still handsome, but now deaf. While others motor to park this evening to see further fireworks, we stay behind and chat. He is full of anecdotes; tells how the old Duchess of Portland,† unable to find a taxi outside Claridge's, exclaimed, 'Oh well, nothing doing, I suppose I'll have to leg it.' The house literally shakes with the fireworks and the music, of which I have a wonderful behind-the-scenes view from my bedroom window. This event has involved Andrew in two years' planning. I have told him it is one of unsurpassed generosity, devoted exclusively to the enjoyment of others.

Sunday, 15th May

Church at 10.30. Dear old Mr Beddoes devotes his sermon to the munificence and goodness of Andrew and Debo, and invites congregation to applaud them like the Pope inside St Peter's. The spirit of community at Chatsworth, he says, must be unique. Then luncheon in Vicarage garden. I know no one, but chat affably to the gardeners and staff. Am then motored home to Badminton in Andrew's new Bentley, with ducal cyphers and coronets on front panels.

Wednesday, 18th May

Motored to Oxford, where I collected Derek Hill at the station. We went to an Italian restaurant where we were joined by Dr Graham Speak, Hon. Sec. of Mount Athos Society, and Bishop Kallistos, Chairman, with silky white beard and affable manner. Bishop talks with beautiful diction, every syllable enunciated. I understood every

---

* Peregrine Cavendish, Marquess of Hartington (b. 1944); son of 11th Duke of Devonshire (whom he s. as 12th Duke, 2004); m. 1967 Amanda Heywood-Lonsdale.
† Winifred Dallas-Yorke (d. 1954); m. 1889 William Cavendish-Bentinck, 6th Duke of Portland (1857–1943).

word he said, both then and later when he delivered his lecture on the
Holy Mountain. A polished performance, very gripping and nostalgic to us Athonites. He is English, of course, by the name of Ware.
Sir Steven Runciman* presided, having come from Scotland by train
without attendant or minder. Is ninety-one. A handsome man, and
very robust for his age. Has all his marbles. Is inscrutable, lofty, cold as
ice. Carriage of head noble and disdainful. Slight curve of underlip;
hooded eyes giving sidelong looks. We left together; but having met
only once before, we had little to say to each other.

Derek returned with me to Badminton to stay the night. We dined
at the House with Caroline and Brigid Salmond who was staying. I
dropped two bricks with Derek. I inadvertently referred to A. having
called his portrait of me 'the Mexican head'. And, when he asked me
where I kept his painting (which I like) of St Peter's seen through olive
trees, I couldn't remember.

Am I making a mistake in telling friends that I am going to Scotland
in search of a religious asylum in the Hebrides to retire to? My desire
to do some such thing grows stronger every day, provided the retreat
offers the minimum of comfort I am accustomed to, and the fathers
are intellectual men. I see myself spending my last days in devout
contemplation.

Wednesday, 25th May

The dreaded day of A's memorial service at St Mary's, Paddington
Green. Desmond Briggs accompanied me in the train, insisting that I
travel first class with him and shocked that I did not do so habitually.
We walked from station to St Mary's, under the flyovers. Lovely little
church. Found the Gibsons there, and Clarissa. Lovely flowers, vast
bunches of alliums and white. I sat in front bench of box pews, a sym-
phony of gold and white, with Clarissa, Freda [Berkeley], Anne Hill.†
Church full, even the galleries, which was a relief. Beautiful service.
My Bidding Prayer read by Tom Gibson, words on our splendid
service sheet printed by Mitchell of Marlborough. Both clergymen
looking handsome in full canonicals. Derry [Drogheda] read Psalm 50;

---

* Hon. Sir Steven Runciman (1903–2000); yr s. of 1st Viscount Runciman of Doxford;
Cambridge historian, specialising in Byzantine Empire and Crusades.
† Lady Anne Gathorne-Hardy (b. 1911); o. dau. of 3rd Earl of Cranbrook; engaged to
J.L.-M. in 1935–6; m. 1938 G. Heywood Hill, bookseller (he d. 1986).

then Tony Scotland read from Vita's *Garden Book*. Michael Berkeley gave the address – too anecdotal in view of Rupert Loewenstein, but I thought excellent. I did not cry, except once during hymn. Anthems by Poulenc and Mozart which A. would have loved. At the end, I walked down the aisle with a firm step and even a smile of pride on my lips, to 1980s Quinlan Terry* church hall, where plenty of excellent food and drink. The Gibsons motored me to Brooks's where I was joined for tea by J.K.-B. and George Dix† who mysteriously appeared. Nick motored me home, where we dined off smoked salmon sandwiches left over from party.

Thursday, 26th May

Extraordinary dramas concerning Igor, who failed to turn up to his grandmother's service yesterday. It seems that, as a result of a mysterious telephone call, he went to Marseilles. Hoped to be offered a job there, but was robbed on arrival of everything including money. Slept on beach for two nights, where he was bitten by a viper. Leg swelled to enormous proportions. A kind French lady took him in when he collapsed at her front door while hobbling to the British Consulate, where he had hoped to be allowed to telephone to his mother. What does it all mean?

Friday, 27th May

Terrible journey to Scotland. Gerald drove me to Bristol airport and lost his way. Minor panic. But major panic at Glasgow, where I went to the wrong station. Did not arrive at Oban until 9.20 p.m. Hotel not the one I remember, but very clean and costing only £25 a night for sandwiches, breakfast and one night's lodging.

Saturday, 28th May

Returning from breakfast, I find a note on my packed luggage: 'Dear Mr Lees-Milne, Sorry I've had to strip your bed. Haste ye back. Your Housemaid.' This could never happen in the South.

It being a Bank Holiday weekend, a long queue of tourist passengers

---

* Architect (b. 1937).
† Friend of J.L.-M. since 1945, at which time he was a US naval officer.

waiting for boat. I sit in stern, in hot sun. Cloudless view of Ben Nevis. Met at Craignure by John and Jill Horsman.* We cross in ferry to Lochaline, and motor to Drimnin where I am to stay three nights. John, who is sixty-five, is a happy man, a cross between Prince Charles and Hamish Erskine.† A rather naughty face; excellent manners; affectionate. Says he spent war in Australia, receiving excellent education at Geelong.‡ She is younger, and has two grown-up daughters by previous marriage. A strong but sweet character, who clearly adores him. After luncheon I totter in the direction of Loch Sunart, hampered by unsuitable shoes. Yellow gorse with its sweet smell in full bloom.

Sunday, 29th May

Drimnin very cold. House down-at-heel. My bedroom huge and bare with tattered carpet. Bathroom down long passage. Downstairs one large room for sitting, fire always burning in large grate under black marble overmantel. Heavenly day. Have never seen Argyll more beautiful, with vivid fresh greens and blue water.

My fellow guest one Mandy Aldridge, whose son is on canoeing jaunt round Mull, hoping to win Duke of Edinburgh medal. She accompanies me to see ruined RC chapel of house, to which I used to walk when staying at Killundine§ in 1930s. Chapel on splendid rocky promontory just over the Sound, which one can hear lapping below. Decipher gravestone of Mrs Gordon who died 1942 aged 96. Masses of bluebells, violets, primroses. Then John motors me to Killundine. House demolished 1950s and grassed over. Killundine factor and wife greet us, referring to me as 'Mr James'. After so much expectation of revived memories, the view disappoints a trifle, perhaps because trees now obscure view of Ben Mohr mountain.

Drimnin's estate covers 10,000 acres, as did Killundine's. Is on the way to nowhere. No strangers, no danger of burglars, doors left

---

* Suffolk farmers who had inherited Drimnin estate, Glenmorvern; befriended by L.-Ms during a Nile cruise in 1992 (see *Ceaseless Turmoil*, 25 February 1992).

† Hon. Hamish St Clair Erskine, MC (1909–74); yr s. of 5th Earl of Rosslyn; Eton contemporary of J.L.-M., well known for his rakish escapades.

‡ Industrial town near Melbourne, famed for its grammar school.

§ Glenmorvern estate owned from 1931 to 1936 by J.L.-M's eccentric but beloved Aunt Dorothy (*née* Heathcote-Edwards, 1884–1965), widow of his Uncle Milne (Alec Milne Lees-Milne, 1878–1931). From 1934, when he converted to Roman Catholicism, J.L.-M. attended the RC chapel at Drimnin when visiting his aunt.

unlocked. At this season, it is light from 4 a.m. to 11 p.m. In the after-noon, Jill drives me up the track along Loch Sunart, above the deserted Isle of Oronsay, rocky and wooded, where seals and pine martens proliferate. View of pink Glenborrodale Castle which so intrigued me in the days when we steamed up to it on Uncle Milne's yacht.

Monday, 30th May

Am introduced to Dolly, a Highland lassie in her seventies who has lived in Drimnin all her life. Began working for John's aunt, and remembers the Gordon dynasty. Remembers Aunt Dorothy in the 1930s, her father having been the postman and her uncle Aunt D's keeper. Remembers the excitement caused by her pipe-smoking, which as a girl she used to watch covertly from behind a bush. Remembers all the McCallum family* – Jessie the cook, Teenie the kitchenmaid, Ina the parlourmaid, Mary the housemaid, Georgie the chauffeur.

Windy and grey day. Very cold. I stay indoors reading – K. Clark's wonderful *Looking at Pictures*; Nico Henderson's[†] diaries about his contacts with the great.

Tuesday, 31st May

We leave at 8.45. In passing I merely wave to my Castle of the Dogs,[‡] without once having got to climb it. They motor me to Knock[§] beyond Salen which I can't have seen since 1930. Just as I remember it, off the narrow road, handsome whitewashed front without distinc-tion. I also remember the sturdy granite bridge over the river which flows from Loch Bà to Loch na Keal, along which Aunt D. and I watched with such merriment as Uncle Milne walked with my grand-mother and laughed at his own shyness, not knowing what to say to his own mother.

---

* Retainers of Aunt Dorothy.
† Sir Nicholas Henderson, diplomatist (b. 1919); HM Ambassador to France (1975–9) and USA (1979–82); m. 1951 Mary Barber (d. 2004).
‡ 'A pile of rubble' (as he once described it), inherited by J.L.-M. from his aunt.
§ Estate on Isle of Mull, owned by J.L.-M's Uncle Milne from 1926 until his death in 1931.

I had lovely drop scones and marmalade and coffee on boat to Oban, and got home at 10 p.m., having completed the journey in reverse.

Friday, 3rd June

Nick meets me at Marlborough and motors me to Longford Castle [near Salisbury], where we lunch with the Radnors.* We see the famous Coleshill Baby in its glass case. They say it is not made of wax but the very baby embalmed. But they do not know its history beyond hearsay, and assure me there is no written record. So Nick and I decide that I should not write the history of the Coleshill Baby but of a fictitious baby and place, which makes my task easier.

Although of great interest architecturally, with its triangular Elizabethan plan and Salvin alterations, Longford is not a nice house. Superb contents, of course – Holbein's Erasmus and Sir Thomas More, Kent-style furniture, Compagnie des Indes service from 1740s. Really another museum house like Madresfield. The rooms all Victorianised and without distinction, except for a circular sitting room, with Gothic pendant ceiling and short dark marble columns, possibly Elizabethan. Nice though to visit a country house which is still one, and not open to the public. They are alarmed by recent robberies at Abbotsford, Luton Hoo, etc. and have installed all-night floodlighting. Lord Radnor large, stout and disabled by polio. Very jolly and shrewd, laughing a good deal. She the third wife, delightful and simple; must have been pretty.

Sunday, 5th June

Lunched with Jenkinses at East Hendred. Other guests Johnnie Grimond, son of late Jo but without his cleverness or good looks, and wife, daughter of Peter Fleming.† We talked about the disadvantages of being the son of a famous man. I said that Randolph Churchill's‡ life was ruined by this circumstance, adding that, if I had had a famous

---

* Jacob Pleydell-Bouverie, 8th Earl of Radnor (b. 1927); m. (3rd) 1986 Mary Pettit.
† Hon. John Grimond (b. 1946); s. of Jo Grimond (1913–October 1993), politician, Leader of Liberal Party 1956–67, cr. life peer 1987; journalist and economist, sometime editor of *The Economist*; m. 1973 Kate, dau. of Lt-Col Peter Fleming, travel writer (1907–71), and the actress Celia Johnson (whose biography she wrote).
‡ Journalist and politician (1911–68); o. s. of Sir Winston Churchill.

father, I should undoubtedly have killed myself. Grimond replied, 'My elder brother killed himself.' She, having been brought up at Nettlebed, has known Rupert Hart-Davis from birth. I said that at Eton he was the hero both of the masters and the boys. Roy regretted having been unable to attend Alvilde's memorial service (though she sweetly came, having only met A. twice). He said he had first met A. at Ann Fleming's. 'And did you find her formidable?' I asked. 'Well,' he replied, 'I had to take the measure of her, but when I met her again, I saw the great point of her.' This pleased.

When I got home, Clementine Beit telephoned from Ireland, pleased with my obituary of Alfred in the *Independent*, but insisting it was not true that Alfred declined ever to enter the main block of the house after the burglary. I certainly never mentioned this and it must have been inserted by the editor. She added she was having a fearful time over Alfred's will, and for the moment did not have a single penny. This from the widow of one of the richest Englishmen.

Wednesday, 8th June

Spent day at county archives, Trowbridge, reading Paul Methuen's* correspondence with his wife Norah from 1919 to 1931. Did not glean much, except evidence of their great love and closeness.

Gail [Pirkis] has sent me proof of pretty jacket of my new diaries. Having almost finished page proofs, I fear the critics will wallop me for gossip and snobbery.

Billa [Harrod], to whom I said I could no longer accept invitations to meals from local friends here since I could not return their hospitality, gave a snort down the telephone. 'How can you be so middle-class? Of course, accept every one you want to go to, and don't give it a thought. After all, you are very old.'

Monday, 13th June

Go for a walk at 9.30 p.m. Still light. Turneresque sunset approaches as I walk under the bridge towards Slates, then turn off and wander

---

* Artist (1886–1974) who succeeded as 4th Baron Methuen in 1932 and devoted himself to the conservation and management of his Corsham estate in Wiltshire; m. 1915 Eleanor (Norah) Hennessy; one of the subjects of the book on departed friends on which J.L.-M. was now working (published by John Murray in 1996 as *Fourteen Friends*).

through the arboretum. Mysterious tranquillity. Weird shadows. Strong smells of summer. Delicious, because the world is my own.

I am seriously worried about approaching publication of new diaries. Am certain I have made a grave mistake. When I rebuked M. for not having stopped me when he read them in MS, he said, 'Well, I did wonder about that bit about Princess Margaret.' Why the hell didn't he say so at the time? I have in fact modified that entry slightly.* The last thing I want is to have the press spotlighting it as another jibe against royalty.

Tuesday, 14th June

Clarissa and Billy for tea. They put me in such a rage that I have to ask them to leave. C. with her henna'd hair, eyes and mouth like a clown's, silver rings on every finger, talking drivel and constantly asking Billy what he thinks – as though he can think at all – rouses the devil in me.

Thursday, 16th June

To London. On train met James Methuen-Campbell,† who had just finished his book on Denton Welch.‡ We talked of his uncle Paul M., subject of my current essay. Left corrected proofs of *A Mingled Measure* with Gail at Murray's. At Parkin Gallery, Michael Parkin showed me transparency of the splendid lifelike portrait of David Herbert commissioned for National Portrait Gallery, wearing jewelled cap and holding cigarette, by Tangerine artist David Mynors. To Royal Society of Literature, where Heinemann Prize awarded to John Hale§ for his excellent Renaissance book. Though present and seemingly happy, he was too frail to make a speech of thanks, which his wife did on his behalf. Rupert Loewenstein came as my guest, and drove me afterwards to spend night at Petersham.

---

* Very slightly indeed, so far as the present editor ('M.') can judge.

† Grandson (b. 1952) of Hon. Robert Methuen (yst bro. of Paul, 4th Baron Methuen) and Hon. Olive Campbell (only dau. of 4th Baron Blythwood); inherited Corsham estate on death of John, 6th Baron Methuen, 1994; heir presumptive to 7th Baron Methuen from 1998; writer and musicologist.

‡ Writer and artist (1915–48); his biography by James Methuen-Campbell was published in 2002.

§ *The Civilisation of Europe in the Renaissance*. (J.L.-M. had twice won this prize: in 1957 for *Roman Mornings*; and in 1982 for his biography of Harold Nicolson.)

Friday, 17th June

After leaving Loewensteins I called on Bamber and Christina
[Gascoigne] at their terrace house in Richmond. Bamber now resembles a benevolent Faust, she is still Virginia Woolf. I find his crest-of-
the-wave attitude invigorating and touching. House delightful and the
very opposite of the Loewensteins' luxurious establishment, crammed
with books from floor to ceiling. I parted from them with warmth of
heart.

Tuesday, 21st June

The longest day of the year, and probably the coldest and wettest since
the Flood. To Trowbridge, where I went through another batch of
Methuen papers. Reading through a file of Paul's correspondence
during the 1930s and 40s with the N.T., I was amazed to come across
the following sentence in a letter of mine dated 11 August 1938:
'Count Grandi [the Italian Ambassador] I hope to see on his return
from his holiday, and the Portuguese Minister I know and will make
a point of seeing after the summer.' How on earth did I come to be
acquainted with these distinguished ambassadors at the age of thirty?
I have absolutely no recollection of either.

Wednesday, 22nd June

Seeing the garden so lush and crammed with blooms, roses at their
most glorious, I feel I ought to take more of an interest in it, at least
to the extent of learning the generic name of every plant in it. Today
the Borderlines party of gardening experts came to Badminton, visiting first the House, then here. They were very appreciative, raving
about the garden and A's wonderful taste and sense of handling and
placing plants. Lady Moyra Campbell* told me she had come all the
way from Northern Ireland just for this day. They all talked to me
about A. and her reputation.

Monday, 27th June

John Jolliffe† lunches with me in Bath. I like him, but find him mys-
tifying. Can't make out what he does for a living; perhaps he doesn't

---

* Lady Moyra Hamilton (b. 1930); o. dau. of 4th Duke of Abercorn; m. 1966
Commander Peter Campbell.
† Hon. John Jolliffe (b. 1935), yr s. of 4th Baron Hylton and Lady Perdita Asquith; writer.

have to. But he always makes one understand that he is up to something. He is well-informed, eminently desirable socially, tall and handsome in a conventional way, resembling the Bachelor Duke. A decent
writer, decent at everything.

Tuesday, 28th June

I only saw a few minutes of the Prince Charles interview,* but it was
enough to make me deplore the whole exercise. This well-meaning
middle-aged man struggled to get the words out and writhed with
intellectual deficiency, wrinkling his forehead and making grimaces.
A great mistake for him to admit marital infidelity. He should have
refused to discuss such matters, whatever the pressure. I was left with
the feeling that he is not equipped to be a constitutional monarch, and
certainly not to wrestle with clever minds. And why expose himself
to twelve million viewers, complaining of his persecution by the
press?

Sunday, 3rd July

I motored to Chicheley [Hall near Newport Pagnell, Bucking-
hamshire] to stay a night with the Nuttings. Adventurous journey in
sweltering heat, almost getting lost at Milton Keynes. Large party
assembled on lawn in shirt sleeves, mostly children and grandchildren.
Asa Briggs and Lady staying.† I at first found her forbidding, she being
a high-powered lady of the St Hugh's type, versed in every subject.
He is an oldish bundle, shaggy, baggy-trousered.

   Diane [Nutting] took me for tea to the Menagerie, where Gervase
[Jackson-Stops] conducted us round his new garden, a miniature
Chiswick with a grotto and two temples, one classical, the other
rustic. Like a print by Rigaud.‡ A dear fellow, his enthusiasm very
fetching. But surrounded by a curious gang of pony-tailed, unshaven,
ill-mannered men. Gervase distributing cups of tea and laughing.

   At dinner, Briggs – who drank vast quantities of wine without

---

* By his official biographer Jonathan Dimbleby, on BBC television.
† Oxford historian (b. 1921), noted for studies of the mass media; Provost of Worcester
College, Oxford, 1976–91; Chancellor, Open University, 1978–94; m. 1955 Susan
Banwell; cr. life peer, 1976.
‡ Hyacinthe Rigaud (1659–1743); French artist.

seeming to become intoxicated, though his tongue was loosened –
spoke of his war work as a decoder at Bletchley Park [Bucking-
hamshire], into which he was drafted just after leaving his excellent
grammar school and before going to Oxford. The Germans unaware
that we were deciphering their messages. Russian allies not told;
Americans were. Briggs worked directly under Sir Stuart Menzies,
'C'.* He was interested to be told that Stuart was A's first cousin,
brought up by his mother, A's Aunt Totty,† at Westonbirt and
Dorchester House, and that most of his friends and relations regarded
him as a genial hunting man. Briggs told me that he was the first person
to know of Doenitz's‡ decision to surrender, being duty officer at the
time. Said that, although the war could be said to have been won at
Bletchley, most of his colleagues, young men of great brilliance,
received no rewards, honours or recognition for their secret work.

I was given the top floor library of 1720 to sleep in. Fashioned for
Sir John Chester,§ with secret shelves behind corner carved pilasters.
Johnny and the Briggses left immediately after early breakfast; Diane
took me for a brisk walk around garden before hurrying off herself.
A couple who are dedicated to their careers. I continued around the
canal walk designed by Bridgeman, and before leaving saw the church,
with remarkable rood screen by [Sir Ninian] Comper,¶ of 1904.

Friday, 8th July

Pangs of sadness pierce me when I come across something which A.
would have delighted to hear about. I see the eagerness on her face
when I say there is an article in this week's *Country Life* by her beloved
Fred Whitsey** on Laurie Johnston's†† gardens at Hidcote and

---

* Sir Stuart Menzies (1890–1968); chief of Secret Intelligence Service (MI6), 1939–52.
† Susannah, dau. of Arthur Wilson of Tranby Croft; m. 1st J. Graham Menzies, 2nd
Lt-Col Sir George Holford (1860–1926) of Westonbirt House nr Tetbury,
Gloucestershire.
‡ German admiral (1891–1980); nominated by Hitler to succeed him as German head of
state, 30 April 1945; ordered surrender of all German forces, 8 May.
§ Builder of the Hall in the 1720s.
¶ Sir Ninian Comper (1864–1960); architect and artist, specialising in church decoration.
** Horticultural writer (b. 1919).
†† Major Lawrence Johnston (1871–1958); Anglo-American horticulturist who created
famous gardens at Hidcote, Gloucestershire and La Serre de la Madonna, Mentone, the
former of which was donated to the N.T. in 1948 largely through the efforts of J.L.-M.

Mentone, or when I tell her what Asa Briggs thought of Stuart Menzies. And then there is her garden. Today Paul and Jane [her former gardeners] came to tea, and we walked round the garden. Jane remembered every corner and the name of every plant she put in, and Paul marvelled that the box and yew hedge had grown so high, for he planted it under her supervision. I blessed them both, and when they left, felt like crying. Now I understand why the garden meant nearly everything to her. The plants were her living children, propagated by her.

Monday, 11th July

Wonderful spell of fine weather. Desmond [Briggs] and Ian [Dixon] motored me to Longleat for Daphne Fielding's ninetieth birthday luncheon. The park looked marvellous in the sunshine, except for the masses and the funfairs and the lions. The party just what I feared. Upstairs in Alexander Bath's* new 'penthouse', as he calls it, really one end of Bishop Ken's† library. Taste in fabrics and furnishings appalling; mulberry fitted carpet, jazzy cushions, office furniture. A band playing some ghastly sort of African jungle music so loudly that we could not hear a word said. Lord Bath with grey fuzzy hair all over face down to shoulders was dressed, as was his brother Christopher,‡ as a Mexican bandit. He was jolly, and quite mad. I sat next to Debo and charming man called William Sieghart§ who has lately returned from exploring Abyssinia. Is a publisher of contemporary poetry and a magazine called *Help*. Brought tall pretty girl to whom, he confided, he was hoping to be engaged before the day was out. Noise in too-small, low-ceilinged eating room likewise appalling. Debo and I gave up. Didn't enjoy it much,

---

* Alexander Thynne, 7th Marquess of Bath (b. 1932); e. s. of Daphne Fielding and brother of Caroline, Duchess of Beaufort. Brilliant and beautiful in youth, he had become a famous English eccentric, preaching free love and naturism, founding the Wessex Regional Party, becoming a rock musician, writing curious books, and filling the Elizabethan rooms of Longleat, Wiltshire with erotic murals.
† Dr Thomas Ken (1637–1711); Bishop of Bath and Wells from 1684 (imprisoned by James II for refusal to publish Declaration of Indulgence); spent last years at Longleat as guest of Lord Weymouth.
‡ Lord Christopher Thynne (b. 1934); m. 1968 Antonia Palmer.
§ Poet, publisher, broadcaster and philanthropist (b. 1960); founder of National Poetry Day, and Action for the Homeless; m. 1996 Molly Dineen, filmmaker.

though honoured to be placed at top table with Daphne and the D[evonshire]s.

Last night listened on Radio 3 to Wilfred Thesiger talking about his life. (I wonder if Sieghart has heard of him; he hadn't of Robert Byron.) Was struck by the beauty of Wilfred's voice – deep, resonant, old-fashioned, *bien*. He was born in Abyssinia and impressed the Emperor* at the age of nine. Was devoted to the Lion of Judah and held him in high regard. Tried to explain why he so loved and respected the Marsh Arabs. Stressed their sense of honour and generosity. Then dwelt on their appalling cruelty and scalp-hunting, which negatives their good qualities it seems to me.

Thursday, 14th July

To London for the night, spending the day at Brooks's. Jack Donaldson lunched. He can't get out of a chair without a stick, and says life no longer has much purpose for him. Like me, he upholds the Anglican faith. Worries about whether there is an afterlife, but hopes for the best. Both his parents died fervently sure they would be meeting again in the presence of their Maker. His uncle Donaldson was Bishop of Salisbury and before that Bishop of Queensland. On arrival in Queensland he was greeted at the harbour by a man who introduced himself as his half-brother, his father's illegitimate son. Shook him a bit.

Then Richard Shone for tea. We talked of the Nicolson brothers. To my surprise, he said that Ben's† intellect had been superior to Nigel's. I said I had little opinion of Ben's. He said that Ben's mind might have been a small glass, but was filled with the purest water, and that Nigel had not written a good book yet. I can't subscribe to this.

Then Kenneth Rose dined, extremely friendly and affectionate. Talked of Paul Methuen and offered to send me diary extracts about him. He said that no one understood why Leslie Rowse‡ had not been given a CH and I a knighthood. I told him about my rejecting a CBE.

---

* Haile Selassie (1891–1976); Emperor of Ethiopia; fought a successful war to establish disputed claim to throne, 1930; displaced by Mussolini, 1936–41; deposed, 1975.
† Benedict Nicolson (1914–78); er s. of Harold Nicolson and Vita Sackville-West; art historian; Deputy Surveyor of King's Pictures, 1939–47, from which post he resigned to devote himself to the editorship of the *Burlington Magazine*.
‡ A. L. Rowse (1903–97); historian and Fellow of All Souls.

What would I have done with it?* Kenneth, who is very touchy himself, complained of Derek [Hill]'s touchiness. He is a Trollopian figure, a sort of super-intelligent version of Taper and Tadpole.†

Wednesday, 27th July

Having finished my essay on Paul Methuen, I thought I would visit Corsham again after all these years. Went round state rooms and gardens. All very well maintained. For all his faults, John Methuen‡ evidently cares for Corsham. Was stunned by beauty of picture gallery with rare eighteenth-century collection of paintings, Adam mirrors and furniture. All of highest quality. And Paul's thick and sumptuous carpet, which struck me as slightly faded already. James Methuen-Campbell appeared, about to visit John at Bath Clinic. Showed me how the carpet was woven in two strips, sewn together invisibly. On hearing who I was, one of the guides presented me with a catalogue, while another came up and shook me by the hand, remembering me from the old days when I was a trustee. James told me that John's recovery is unlikely; he is dying of alcoholism, and when deprived goes into a coma.

Tuesday, 2nd August

I dined at the House, just with David and Caroline alone, which I like. We ate in the library at a small table, a fire burning in the grate as the weather has suddenly turned cold. Really, I find him charming, so wise when he talks seriously, always funny in that deadpan manner. He said he hadn't the slightest idea how to judge contemporary painting. But surely you must, I said, you are the most successful gallery owner. No, he said, he didn't, but he had learnt from long experience what his clients like and want, which is another thing. David spoke amusingly about late Master.§ Once, when they were out walking

---

* See entry for 21 October 1993 and note. Rose himself was offered and accepted a CBE in 1997.
† Political operators in Disraeli's novel *Coningsby* (1844).
‡ John, 6th Baron Methuen (1925–94); nephew of Paul Methuen; Scouting enthusiast.
§ Henry Somerset, 10th Duke of Beaufort (1900–84); m. 1923 Lady Mary Cambridge (1897–87), dau. of 1st Marquess of Cambridge; leading figure of hunting world, known as 'Master' from age of eight; cousin of David Somerset (who succeeded him as 11th Duke); landlord and disapprover of J.L.-M., whose lack of interest in field sports he found incomprehensible.

together, Master suddenly said he must telephone Gundry, his co-
MFH. David happened to have the latest variety of mobile telephone
in his pocket; he extracted this, dialled Gundry's number and handed
it to Master. Master spoke, and handed it back without a word. Wasn't
going to admit that David could have something he hadn't got.

Very kind about my predicament they were. He asked me if I was
very hard up and muttered that I need not pay the rent of course.
Whereupon I had to protest, for I am not totally broke and would die
sooner than become a lame dog. He talked of Italian corruption and
said it was a hopeless situation, for it has long been axiomatic in the
Italian business world that every deal must be prefaced by slipping a
tip into an intermediary's hands. Agnelli* was an honourable man, but
would get nowhere without conforming. Yet today this is regarded
as corruption by the magistrates. David said that bribery in Italy was
stamped out by Mussolini, and after Mussolini's fall returned. Now
almost ineradicable.

Friday, 5th August

Selina [Hastings] lunched here on her way to her mother's house
which she is trying to sell. She is pleased that the *Telegraph* will serial-
ise her Evelyn Waugh. Is now going to write Rosamond [Lehmann]'s
biography. Went off with Nancy [Mitford]'s clock which A. left her,
seeming much pleased and touched.†

Saturday, 6th August

My birthday, now mentioned in both *The Times* and *Daily Telegraph*.
Cards from dear old Rupert [Hart-Davis], darling Debo, one or two
others. I made an expedition to Wickhamford,‡ stopping on the way
to see the churches at Dumbleton, Wormington and Aston Somer-
ville. Finally arrived at Wickhamford church. What a gem it is. I
looked around and decided to sit and ruminate on our old manor pew.
Forgot how uncomfortable it was, the projecting top digging into
one's back. Glad that the now pale faded red-striped bench squabs

---

* Gianni Agnelli (1921–2003); head of Fiat (founded by his grandfather), 1966–96.
† Her first major work, published in 1985, had been a biography of Nancy Mitford.
‡ Wickhamford Manor near Evesham, Worcestershire, where J.L.-M. was born in 1908,
and his parents lived until the 1940s.

survive. Then spent three hours in Manor and garden with current owners, very friendly and welcoming couple called Ryan-Bell.* Extremely proud of the place and eager for historical information. Thrilled with the few anecdotes I could dredge up from brain. I went all over the house with them, seeing Mama's oak-panelled bedroom in which I was born eighty-six years ago. At what time, they asked eagerly? The place has not been so much altered inside as I had supposed. Taste none too sound. Audrey's bedroom still has its curious beam struts; original pre-1914 bathtub with maker's name in blue still in place under taps, Rufford & Sons; same seat in downstairs lav. So much the same. I did not feel too sad, in fact pleased by their delight. A nice, decent new family. Pond covered with water lilies, which he means to eradicate. He led me to the drain where the twin Scots firs stood, and said, 'Listen!' He waited while I intently listened. Yes, the same deep, resonant, nostalgic sound, cavernous and gentle.

Monday, 8th August

John K.-B. comes to stay night. So affectionate and fond of unworthy me. After luncheon we visit Lacock [Abbey] and go round this melancholy house which is quite well kept up. Too many family pictures with no identification but some interesting new revelations, like the James I hall chairs and Queen Anne studded travelling trunks.

Tuesday, 9th August

At midday John motors me to Lydiard Tregoze [near Swindon]. The house not as perfect as I had thought on last visit. The mauve colouring, the skied chandeliers. And now the entrance hall made into a shop, the ubiquitous ghastly shop indispensable to every country house open to the public. The nice lady guardian apologises, explaining that house now run by Parks Committee of Swindon Council which has no grain of taste or knowledge of what a house of this architectural standard should look like. But it is certainly an improvement on what existed of yore. Visit church. Very interesting triptych of Sir John St John's seventeenth-century lineage. Ugly and coarse figure of Sir John under brutish canopy. But pleasing alabaster monu-

---

* Jeremy and June Ryan-Bell; owners of Wickhamford Manor since 1979.

ment to father St John between his two wives. J. leaves me after tea
to return to London. We part most affectionately.

Thursday, 11th August

At 5.30 I went to see Daph. We talked of Caroline, who is going into
Gloucester Hospital today for tests. She has jaundice and has been
feeling rotten but would not put off an engagement in Wales yesterday,
being very dutiful, and motored straight to Gloucester from Wales.
Daph thought she was suffering from gallstones.

An hour after I left Daph, she rang to say that C. had just telephoned her with bad news. She has a tumour which is inoperable.
Over my sparse dinner, I felt quite sick with sorrow and anxiety.

Friday, 12th August

Visit to Norfolk. I motor to Todenham, just under fifty miles. There
lunch with Liz Longman* who motors us to Burnham Market where
we stay three nights with Sylvia Combe.† Pretty farmhouse of flint
amid grove of weeping willows, meadow with sheep and horses in fore-
ground. Sylvia reminds me that I stayed there when I was fifty and was
miserable at being so old. House rather run-down. She said that when
Simon was alive they had four indoor servants; now one very nice
woman from the village comes for two hours twice a week. Liz complained of a dead mouse in her bedroom. Mine has two doors, neither
of which shuts, and a window which jams. I could never stay here in
winter. But what a darling Sylvia is. Extremely active, and intelligent
with prodigious memory. She is eighty-five. When I nearly sobbed in
telling of A's death, she put her arms round me and kissed me.

Saturday, 13th August

It is A's birthday today, and I am glad not to be at home. We lunch at
Raynham with Lord Townshend,‡ a widower and a charming and

---

* Lady Elizabeth Lambart (b. 1924), er dau. of Field Marshal 10th Earl of Cavan; m. 1949
Mark Longman (he d. 1972).
† Lady Sylvia Coke (b. 1909), dau. of 4th Earl of Leicester; m. 1932 Simon Combe (d.
1965); she lived at Burnham Thorpe near King's Lynn.
‡ George, 7th Marquess Townshend (b. 1916).

welcoming friend. Billa there, to whom I present the silver camel
which I bought from her years ago. Excellent roast mutton meal in
small dining room, Lord T. running to and from serving room. When
we finished, a tall, immensely distinguished housekeeper with aristo-
cratic face came to clear away. When I congratulated her, she complained that we were poor eaters. Then tour round this delightful
house. Rooms all retain their shapes and decoration unaltered, yet are
bare. A sense of bailiffs having just left with half the contents. He said
that during the war the house suffered terribly from billeted troops.
He has saved this place, which when I first saw it in 1937 was in the
shadow of death. Beautiful architecture and park.

Sunday, 14th August

Last night we went to the Pageant at Holkham [Hall, Norfolk], before
the south front. Sylvia in a state of frenzied anxiety, having contrib-
uted to the script owing to her knowledge of the Coke family. We sat
in hard chairs for two and a half hours. It was cold, but not unbear-
ably so. I wore my old hat and fur-lined jacket. Pageant a copycat
version of Chatsworth one. Very well done. Actors mime voices produced from concealed loudspeakers. Each ancestor appears in charac-
teristic guise at the most notable moment of his or her career. Old
carriages drawn by splendidly groomed horses. An ancient yellow
Daimler limousine introduced.

Today we lunched at Elsing Hall, which I last visited in April 1943.
Before we went there, Sylvia made me read account of that visit from
my diary.* I laughed so much I had to stop. Not a covetable house,
much altered mid nineteenth century. Present owners David and
Valerie Cargill. He a jolly man and knowledgeable gardener; she rather
gushing; both very kind. We lunched, enjoyably, out of doors by the
lake. The garden large and attractive, kept up entirely by them, overgrown with shrubs of all kinds. Reminded me of Keith Steadman's
garden [at Wickwar, Gloucestershire], or Hiram [Winterbotham]'s in
the old days at Woodchester.

We dined at Holkham. Sixteen to dinner in audit room. The little

---

* 'The present owners are impoverished. They have one indoor servant only. The house
is incredibly shabby, dirty and primitive . . . It is pathetic how within three years country
people, who are unable to travel, become blind to the squalor to which they have been
reduced.' (*Ancestral Voices*, 28 April 1943.)

library where we assembled is perhaps the most beautiful room in England. Lord Leicester[*] a charming man. I sat on left of Lady L., known as 'the sex kitten' and very attractive. After dinner, Sylvia, Liz and I were conducted by Lord L. round the dimly-lit state rooms. Wonderful experience. Shown Bolognese painting for which he has received £6 million from Treasury on condition that it remains *in situ* at Holkham. This an arrangement which I always advocated, and hoped might happen while I was at the N.T. This visit brought home to me the subtle secret of Holkham. It is the most purely architectural house I know. The planning, the finishing are absolute. One senses the mathematical precision of the construction, every conundrum solved to perfection. A great work of art. The result is that it is surprisingly easy to live in. Each wing is self-contained. A key-hole vista from wing to wing across the corridors and central block presents an uninterrupted sonata of Palladianism at its zenith.

Wednesday, 17th August

Yesterday I bought a book of stamps and a battery for my wireless at a local shop. I left the stamps on the counter, and could not later find the battery. No one who is not senile can imagine the shame and misery of those who are senile, any more than anyone knows what the dead are enduring in the next world, if there is one. When I saw Humphrey Whitbread[†] clambering to his seat for the pageant the other night, mouth open and drooling nonsense, my heart was wrung with pity. Whereas ten years ago I would have sneered. Poor Humphrey. He is a Coke cousin but hasn't been to Holkham since 1936. During dinner the following night he made no sense at all, and staggered off to his bedroom before the pudding.

Monday, 22nd August

Caroline telephoned to thank me for my letter which followed her home from hospital. Asked me to dine tonight, just the family.

---

[*] Edward, Viscount Coke (b. 1936); s. father, 19 June 1994, as 7th Earl of Leicester; m. (2nd) 1986 Mrs Sarah de Chair.
[†] Humphrey Whitbread (1912–2000); heir to Whitbread brewing empire; art collector, philanthropist and sometime High Sheriff of Bedfordshire; lived at Howard's House, Cardington, on estate of Southill Park, Regency house built by his ancestor Samuel Whitbread.

Greeted me warmly on arrival, saying, 'I've never felt better in my life. They have got rid of the jaundice. The consultant who examined me says there is nothing to be done, and that I might live three months or even a year.' I said, 'Are you sure it will not be three years or even more?' She was cheerful, laughing, putting on the bravest face. Is planning a trip to Java in February. Yet over all the joviality at dinner a veil of sadness hanging. David, who adores her, sat baffled. When I left, he followed me to my car, saying, 'Isn't it awful about Caroline? So sudden, almost incredible. What with Alvilde going, and now this.' I said life was ghastly on the whole. He was much moved, and so was I. He turned away, and I drove off.

Thursday, 25th August

To London for day. Walked along long underground passage from South Kensington station to V&A. Had forgotten this Victorian feat of engineering, so extraordinary and ugly. Filled with buskers and sellers of junk. Spent morning at Pugin exhibition. P's wallpapers and decorations are superbly bold and colourful; silver church vessels and copes likewise; but his spiky chairs, thrones, stools are absurdly uncomfortable even to look at, let alone sit in. To Heywood's shop. John Saumarez said that my new diaries make a good read and he has already had orders for 200; that he had read my ghost story in bed last night, and that too would sell. I know John's opinions now so well, and respect him for his honesty. To tea with Misha, who is teaching himself to draw. He made two sketches of me, not very lifelike I fear. He looked well, but is already balding. He walked with me to Paddington, carrying my paraphernalia. I was pleased to see him again, but have little desire now to see any friend for more than an hour.

Sunday, 28th August

Dearest Rupert [Hart-Davis]'s birthday. Sent him a tit-for-tat card, reminding him that he was again one year older than me.

    Diana Kendall* telephoned that John Methuen had died in Bath Clinic. No surprise. John meant nothing to me. Paul loathed him. It is believed that John has left Corsham to his nephew James Methuen-

---

* Former secretary to Paul Methuen.

Campbell as his brother Robert has no son – though Robert has now divorced his old wife and married a young woman and may produce an heir. I hope John did leave it to James.

Lunched today at Cirencester with Rory Young.[*] A radiant young craftsman full of enthusiasm, learning, experience of old buildings. A miracle-worker with stone and marble. Nice artisan house in Park Street which he has jollied up and made extremely attractive, adding bits and pieces, fireplaces inlaid with diamonds of polished Purbeck, *oeil-de-boeuf* windows on end, and so forth. Other guests Sonia Rolt, widow of Tom,[†] the great man of canals, one Peter Burman,[‡] prominent conservationist, bearded and gentle, and Judith Verity,[§] abandoned wife of Simon, with whom Rory is now living either as lover or collaborator. Long discussion over delicious farmhouse meal about whether ball moulding of doorway of Bishop's Cleeve church should be 'restored' – i.e., copied by some competent mason – allowed to rot as it is doing, or be scrapped and replaced by a modern design.

Rory told us that as a boy he called on the owner[¶] of a beautiful ancient house called Norbury in Derbyshire, an old bachelor who fell in love with Rory and would, had R. reciprocated his love, have left Norbury to him. I was reminded of Claud Phillimore[**] calling unannounced when an undergraduate on Bertie Landsberg[††] at La Malcontenta. Bertie did in fact leave the house to Claud after the death of his wife Dorothy, but it did little good to C., who couldn't afford to live in this Palladian villa. And then there was Ted Lister, who was going to leave Westwood [Manor, Wiltshire] to me until I married and he changed his will.

Reading articles in *Country Life* on Stokesay Court [Shropshire], whose contents are to be sold, I was reminded that I once wanted to

---

[*] Designer, stone-carver, conservator of historic buildings (b. 1954).

[†] L. T. C. Rolt (1910–74); short story writer, and expert on history of railways and canals.

[‡] Writer and Director of Centre for Conservation Studies, University of York (b. 1944).

[§] Judith Mills; m. 1970 Simon Verity, memorial sculptor and letterer (b. 1945).

[¶] Marcus Stapleton-Martin (1911–87); he left his house to the N.T.

[**] Architect in the classical tradition (1911–94); m. 1944 Elizabeth Dorrien-Smith of Tresco Abbey, Isles of Scilly; s. nephew as 4th Baron Phillimore, 1990.

[††] A. C. Landsberg; Brazilian owner and restorer of Palladio's Villa Malcontenta on river Brenta near Venice, built in 1569 for Foscari family (to whom Claud Phillimore eventually returned it).

write an article on this house myself. I asked Philip [Magnus],* who regretted that his wife was not keen on the idea, as her grandfather Mr Allcroft who built the house was a dreadful man without an 'h' to his name, whereas her grandmother who was a Russell came from some grand and interesting house. I expostulated that all this was totally irrelevant. I was interested in Stokesay as a late Victorian house complete with contents, all collected by one rich manufacturer. Of gloves, Philip added in horror. Yes, gloves, I said, that is the point. Of course the absurd Jewel was mightily ashamed. And yet I believe both would have liked the place to be preserved. Idiotic they were. She left millions and could have endowed the house for the N.T.; and had Philip been less of a snob, he would have insisted. For she had no mind of her own and would have done anything he wanted.

Thursday, 1st September

Belinda Cherrington from the BBC came to interview me for a programme on the N.T. A sensible woman whom I liked. She asked what I thought would happen to the Trust over the next hundred years. I speculated that it would continue to flourish but the number of properties would not increase much. She was aware of the criticisms, chiefly of bureaucracy. Then I dined with the Mitchells at Dyrham to meet Martin Drury, lately appointed Director-General. Nice man as always, with that youthful, almost adolescent look some middle-aged men preserve which causes one to wonder about their sexuality.

Friday, 2nd September

I visit Daphne [Fielding], who does not seem to take in the gravity of [her daughter] Caroline's trouble. Talks of how as a girl she hated her uncle Douglas Haig,† a martinet who was always telling her to keep a straight back, sit upright, etc. Later, Caroline telephones for a chat, so unlike her. Apologises for not being able to dine to meet Gervase, or take two N.T. groups round the House next week. Says she feels pretty

---

* Sir Philip Magnus-Allcroft, 2nd Bt (1906–88); historian; m. 1943 Jewel Allcroft of Stokesay Court.
† Field Marshal (1861–1928); cr. Earl Haig, 1919.

well none the less and often wonders if what the doctors have told her can be true. O dear God. I sit here in the kitchen, the rain pouring outside, and wonder if I can stay in Badminton if C. is going to die. The sadness of it all. And in tears I tear up the little notes of telephone numbers and appointments which A. made just before she died. Each tear (and tear) is a stab at the heart.

Saturday, 10th September

I have been at Chatsworth since Sunday. The blissful comfort and freedom. Was motored here in Andrew's new Bentley – bought from the sale of a horse, he says. Am given my favourite room, the Red Velvet, with daybed, the most comfortable in the world for reading. Country Fair in park. Wonderful spectacle of parachutists turning somersaults, flames issuing from their feet.

This morning I sat over the breakfast table until 10.30, listening to Andrew who was in one of his chatty moods. He talked of Hatfield [House, Hertfordshire], saying it was much larger than Chatsworth and the Salisburys richer.* Primogeniture means everything in that family; younger sons practically penniless. Andrew adores Brooks's and the hall there, so beautiful; but dislikes White's, full of City cads and rogues.

Philip Jebb† comes for two nights. Is very thin and frail. Beautiful, deferential manners, laughing in unwonted way at every word spoken to him. Has lung cancer, knows he is doomed. At beginning of August was given six weeks to live. The Ds devoted to him, and on his parting an almost emotional scene.

Jayne Wrightsman‡ comes for twenty-four hours. Debo and I await descent from clouds of her helicopter by the bridge. She is tiny, slight, dark with rinsed blonde hair, aquiline nose, hawk eyes, handsome, well-preserved. Is intelligent and enthusiastic, and when she sees something she dislikes – such as Freud§ paintings – says 'Oh Debo' and turns away. Unexpectedly likeable for so rich and spoilt a transatlantic lady. Is accompanied by Charles something, who is head of the

---

* The Duke's mother was a daughter of the 4th Marquess of Salisbury of Hatfield.
† Architect (1927–95); m. 1955 Lucy Pollen.
‡ Jayne Larkin; m. as his 2nd wife Charles Wrightsman, President Standard Oil of Kansas. 1932–53, art collector, Trustee of Metropolitan Museum, New York (he d. 1986).
§ Lucian Freud (b. 1922); artist, patronised by the Devonshires.

Frick.* Tells me he was educated at Cambridge, his parents impecu-
nious dons. Brought up among Huxleys and Darwins. Name-drops.
Very knowledgeable about the silver here.

Feeble brings the Runcies† to luncheon, introducing us by saying
to me, 'You know Bob Runcie?' I thought how fifty years ago pres-
entation to former Archbishop would elicit doubled-up bowing if not
hand-kissing. He very sympathetic, wearing clerical blue pullover and
no jacket. She rather plain, but sharp. Feeble talks openly with
Archbishop about her doubts. He says he is assailed by them too. I say
to Lady R., how awful for him, having to disguise these doubts from
the world. Yes, she says, but all clerics have them.

Andrew comes from visiting Lord Mayor of Sheffield and her lady
friend, the L.M. being a woman. How times have changed.

Andrew tells story about Angela Conner,‡ of whose busts he has
half a dozen on the west staircase. She made a bust of Michael Astor§
which he disliked so much that he took it on a boat and dumped it
off Eastbourne. Bust subsequently netted by fishermen who read
name of sculptress on base and sent it to her. How Michael was able
to explain the incident Andrew does not know.

Am left to myself here most of the day. Have typed out ghost story
for Nick, gone for walks, and read a book about the spy Maclean.¶
Freedom from letters, from gardeners, from the interruptions at
home, has been true bliss. Never have I had kinder friends. And the
more I know Andrew, the fonder I become. He is always interesting, if at times nerve-inducing. I am very happy here, except that I
feel inadequate in not repaying their kindness by being better
company.

Motored home, 160 miles, by the clock man.

---

* Charles Ryskamp (b. 1928); Director of Frick Collection, New York (founded by steel
and coke tycoon Henry Clay Frick [1849–1919] and still occupying his original house),
1987–97.
† Robert Runcie (1921–2000); 102nd Archbishop of Canterbury, 1980–91, known for
his exuberance, ecumenism and ideological clashes with Thatcher Government; cr. life
peer, 1991; m. 1957 Rosalind ('Lindy') Turner. J.L.-M. had encountered them six years
earlier at a London theatre (see *Ceaseless Turmoil*, 20 April 1988).
‡ Sculptress patronised by 11th Duke of Devonshire.
§ Hon. Michael Astor (1916–80); s. of 2nd Viscount Astor and Nancy *née* Langhorne;
writer and patron of artists.
¶ Diplomatist and traitor (1913–83), who fled to USSR with Guy Burgess in 1951.

Wednesday, 14th September

Gervase [Jackson-Stops] stayed last night, arriving at 8.30. Kindly brought a chicken and a pudding for our supper. He told me how the other day he saw Graham Thomas[*] at a party and went up to him with arm outstretched. The old man dashed past him without a nod of recognition, looking over his head and saying 'How-do-you-do, Duchess' to Mary Roxburghe. Gervase has a friend who has a friend who is a telephonist at Buckingham Palace. The telephonist tells G's friend that, every morning, the Queen rings up the Queen Mother. Telephonist says to Q.M., 'Good morning, Your Majesty. Her Majesty is on the line for Your Majesty.'

Thursday, 15th September

Drove to lunch with Hardy [Amies] at Langford. Party included John Bayley and his wife Iris Murdoch.[†] I.M. not easy and rather deaf I suspect, but amiable. I was amazed when she kissed me. Looks like a sad full moon longing to wane. Almost piteous, on verge of declension. He most attentive and adoring.

Sunday, 18th September

Nick the milk boy is twenty-five and has become a stout, beaming bruiser, with perpetual smile. Told me he got up every morning at 2 a.m. to start his rounds. I asked when he got to bed in the evenings. 'When I feels like it,' he said. 'And do you sleep during the day?' 'Oh, occasionally I dozes.' He is the happy ploughman.

Monday, 19th September

Had a sad dream last night – that A. said to me, 'You never write to me these days', to which I replied, 'No, perhaps it's because I see you every weekend.' Write, indeed. I talk to her and send her messages into the vacuous air, and no reply comes.

Lunched alone with Michael and Isobel [Briggs]. A heavenly

---

[*] Graham Stuart Thomas (1909–2003); adviser on gardens to N.T., 1954–74.
[†] Dame Iris Murdoch (1919–99), Oxford philosophy don and novelist; m. 1956 John Bayley (b. 1925), Professor of English at Oxford; then suffering from Alzheimer's Disease.

couple. I like being with them more than any other friends. Midford now perfection, full of lovely things, beautifully decorated by them without any professional nonsense. Of Iris Murdoch, Isobel observed that she always pauses before replying to any remark, however trite. Wonders whether she possesses the elusive thing, a sense of humour.

Tuesday, 20th September

I visit Stanway.* Lots of people, even on a weekday in September. House and grounds rather down-at-heel, and shown in a simple, happy-go-lucky, non-N.T. way which I found rather charming. But oh Lord, how dilapidated the furniture, paintings, tapestries and all. Walked up the terraces half way to the pyramid and thought the place as romantic as ever. Stood leaning against an arch, gazing at and imbibing the west front. The stone is not butter-colour, nor honey, but sunset itself. Bottom half glows like a fiery sky. I know no other building quite so alive with searing, wreathing gold. Then the top stage is silvered o'er with lichen. The combination is divine. The three pointed gables lean backwards as from the brink of chaos, but with effort hold themselves back for the aesthetic delight of a further generation or two of civilised mortals able to appreciate. I shan't go again and am pleased I did so before this season ended. This summer I have managed to visit a number of country houses in my district which are open to the public.

Sunday, 25th September

Harry Fane,† whom I met last night dining with his mother Jane Westmorland, never reads a book, but knows all about computers. He swears that books will cease to exist within thirty years and all reading will be done on computers. Already there is some kind of central information exchange which you can contact by computer for any facts – the varieties of bamboo, child welfare in Peru, anything. Within minutes, all human knowledge on the subject is sub-

---

* House in Gloucestershire owned by James Charteris, Lord Neidpath (b. 1948), only surviving s. of 12th Earl of Wemyss; a haunt of 'the Souls'.
† Hon. Harry St Clair Fane (b. 1953); yr son of 15th Earl of Westmorland; Page of Honour to HM The Queen, 1966–8; m. 1984 Tessa Forsyth-Forrest.

mitted on the computer screen. I suppose the modern equivalent of Selfridge's Information Bureau. Harry is supplied with these devices, so there is no subject in the world he cannot learn about in twenty minutes.

Tuesday, 27th September

Attended induction of our new Vicar in Badminton church at 7.30. Church crammed, rather to my surprise. I am seated next to Caroline wearing her enormous red hat. In the semi-dark I cannot see how she looks and do not like to stare. She whispers that the word 'induction' sounds like waterworks. Yes, I retort *sotto voce*, it suggests an enema. She fidgets a lot and has a tickle in her throat. We both agree the new vicar has a good voice, better than Tom's. I have never seen so many dignitaries – the Bishop and Archdeacon of Tewkesbury, Bill Llewellyn,* unmitred but with long wisps of hair down neck. A reception in the House at which Caroline presides in absence of David and the Worcesters. Rather bad of them, but they are hopeless rotters, aren't they? I chat with Bill Llewellyn about our days together at McNeile's [House, Eton]. Then, having done my duty, I slope away for home.

Wednesday, 28th September

To London for the day. Lunched with Grant [McIntyre] and Gail [Pirkis] at Caprice Restaurant, cheerful little party. Very good food of which I ate frugally. On leaving, they observed that Edwina Currie[†] and Sophia Loren[‡] had been lunching, both lost on me. Went to National Portrait Gallery to see exhibition of portrait drawings by the great of the great, such as Holman Hunt[§] by Millais, and Millais by Hunt. Then to Burlington House for Venetian eighteenth-century exhibition. The influence of Veronese on Piazzetta, Carlevaris and the Riccis is emphasised. Sparkling Venice.

---

* Rt Revd William Llewellyn (1907–2001); Vicar of Badminton, 1937–49; Bishop of Lynn, 1961–72; Eton contemporary of J.L.-M.; m. 1947 Innes Mary Dorrien-Smith of Tresco Abbey, Isles of Scilly.

† Publicity-seeking Conservative MP (b. 1946).

‡ Screen name of Sofia Scicolone (b. 1934), Italian film star.

§ William Holman Hunt (1827–1910); Pre-Raphaelite artist.

Friday, 30th September

Nice to be invited to luncheon at Corsham after twenty years. Happily James Methuen-Campbell has inherited, and moved across the way from his cottage. Ate in the dining room with the armorial ceiling. The bronzes of this room not yet brought back from strongroom. Library still under dust-sheets, all very shabby and dirty since Paul's day. Chairs messed about by labradors. Don't like the dark green paint which Paul and Norah substituted for the oak grain. James says the doors are mahogany and never should have been grained. Took me upstairs to boudoir and private bedrooms of Paul and Norah. Appalling condition of Aubusson carpets from John's dogs, the easy chairs turned into dog baskets. Full of wonderful treasures, like Calke [Abbey, Derbyshire]. James already has plans for repairs and will do well. He is something of a young fogey, but extremely affable and keen.

Wednesday, 5th October

I am finishing Fanny [Partridge]'s latest diaries,* which are of course splendid. What an intelligent woman. Her dissection of her friends' characters is always kind, but nevertheless as sharp as a surgeon's blade. Most of her Bloomsbury friends were pretty awful, Gerald Brenan,† Lionel Penrose,‡ Bunny Garnett§ and the ineffable Julia Strachey.¶ All deceiving wives and lovers. I would not say to anyone that there is something about Fanny I don't like, apart from her godlessness and leftishness, but there is a certain smugness and reluctance to acknowledge the validity of any views opposed to her own. She evidently didn't enjoy staying with us, and considered us retrograde Tories. She magnifies the silly prejudices of people she has to meet – for like all Bloomsberries she relishes the good life which the upper crust provide. Yet she makes my own diaries seem adolescent and low-brow.

---

* *Good Company: Diaries, 1967–1970.* The volume begins with a description of a tense weekend with the L.-Ms at Alderley, during which J.L.-M. had a terminal row with James Pope-Hennessy.

† English writer of works on Spanish literature and autobiographies (1894–1982).

‡ Lionel Sharples Penrose (1898–1972); Galton Professor of Eugenics, University College, London, 1943–63, and of Human Genetics 1963–5.

§ David Garnett (1892–1981); novelist and critic, whose first wife was Frances Partridge's sister.

¶ Novelist and journalist (1901–78); niece of Lytton Strachey; m. 1st Stephen Tomlin, 2nd Lawrence Gowing.

Thursday, 6th October

At John Murray's rear waiting room under glass dome, John* staggers in with boxes of my new diaries† to be signed. He says, 'I am the porter and do the humblest work.' Laughter from female staff. He is a dear fellow. Told me he was editing his father's commonplace book for publication, 'in which you will find yourself quoted'. I sign some seventy copies, my signature getting worse as I go along.

Luncheon party of Ambrose Congreve at Warwick House. Had to get policeman's permission to enter precincts after he had telephoned butler at W.H. Ambrose larger and puffier than last year, yet healthy. Introduced me to a rather horsey, youngish man, Lord Zetland.‡ Also an eminent scientist, Sir Something, and eminent Indian surgeon. Odd party. Ambrose announced to the others that I had started the N.T., and I had to put them wise. The richness of this mansion overlooking Green Park, butler waiting for tinkling of little bell for instructions, 'Burgess, be an angel and fetch the cigar piercer from my bedside table', etc. Left at three o'clock for Parkin Gallery to see excellent little exhibition of Whistler§ etchings.

Sunday, 9th October

Hugh Massingberd has given my diaries a marvellous review this morning, calling me a dear old English gentleman.

Lunched with Derry and Alexandra [Drogheda] at Combe. A jolly party, including grandparents and children who for our delectation played violins, the baby Marina with minute instrument absolutely without self-consciousness. Benjamin resembles Garrett in litheness, silkiness and charm. Little Garrett very forward and sweet. Nico [Henderson] talked of Mrs Thatcher, saying her rudeness to cabinet colleagues, especially to Howe,¶ was odious beyond words. He had experienced it himself often enough. No man would ever address

---

* John Murray VII; head of publishing firm, 1993–2002.
† *A Mingled Measure: Diaries, 1953–72.*
‡ Mark Dundas, 4th Marquess of Zetland (b. 1937), whose grandfather, 2nd Marquess, Conservative statesman, had served as Chairman of N.T., 1931–45.
§ James McNeill Whistler (1834–1903); American-born artist.
¶ Sir Geoffrey Howe (b. 1926); Conservative politician (Foreign Secretary, 1983–9), whose speech in the House of Commons after his resignation from the Government in November 1990 led to Mrs Thatcher's downfall; cr. life peer, 1992.

another man in such a way, but he feared it was in the female dispo-
sition.

Thursday, 13th October

I lunch with Hugh Massingberd at Travellers' Club. We both have an
urge to embrace on meeting, possibly a result of our never having
received embraces as children from our respective fathers. Hugh
looking well, with good complexion, and much thinner. He told me
about his heart attack. Happened over lunch, with his sixteen-year-
old son.* The boy shocked by the experience, but behaved splendidly.
Ambulance summoned in nick of time. Hugh believes he 'died' more
than once. Felt no fear, because it was as if the whole experience happening to someone else. Operation took eight hours. His concentration and memory affected, and he now finds it an effort to write. But
when restored intends to write book on the subject. His illness has
brought him closer to his wife, and they hope to go and live in
Lincolnshire.

We talked of how Tony Powell and Simon Blow† are both
obsessed with their lineage. Hugh thinks it is because they both feel
they have something to hide – the Blow ancestry, in Simon's case.
Hugh admits his own obsession may have something to do with his
mother's family being no great shakes, she being daughter of a stockbroker. Perhaps my own interest in lineage comes from my being of
yeoman stock.

I noticed that Hugh was still fairly greedy, though he assures me
that he takes far more care over *what* he eats. When the waiter tempted
him with a jug of cream, I was surprised to hear him say, 'Get thee
behind me, Jesus!' It transpired the waiter was a Spaniard and Jesus his
name. Hugh said, you should hear Monsignor Gilbey addressing him.

Sunday, 16th October

There is something rather wicked and wonderful about afternoons.
Having spent this morning first recovering from yesterday evening
when I dined with Jane Westmorland and listened to her and female
friend talking rubbish about hauntings and exorcism, then going to

---

* Luke Massingberd (b. 1977); picture editor and designer.
† Writer, former racing jockey (b. 1943).

church where we had four hymns (too much), and finally writing to
Diana [Mosley] but forgetting to deal with the fascinating contents of
her last letter about her love of Hitler, I lunched off tinned tongue and
tinned potatoes and then meant to continue with my essay on Robert
Byron, but felt so sleepy that I went to bed. Turned on Radio 3 and
listened to beautiful songs by Gounod,[*] Fauré[†] and Reynaldo Hahn,[‡]
all so evocative of Princess Winnie and the Nineties, and reminding
me of A. They inspired me to take down her bathroom photographs
and write on the backs who they were – Pavlova,[§] Fauré, Menuhin,[¶]
Lennox Berkeley and Chaliapin.[**]

In her *Spectator* column, Debo has teased me for writing in 1972
that Britain was bound to become Communist within twenty-five
years. I have written to her that some people consider the anarchy and
corruption which is now taking the place of Communism in Europe
to be even worse. Meanwhile the Booker Prize is awarded to a novelist whose characters talk in profanities, and the Nobel Prize given
to two terrorists.[††]

Thursday, 20th October

To London. Saw Sitwell Exhibition at National Portrait Gallery, very
worthwhile. The Sitwells all whinged about cruelty they suffered at
hands of their parents and at school. I think this may have been on
account of their ugliness, before adulthood brought character to their
faces. Lunched with Polly Lansdowne, nice woman, intelligent
without being intellectual, who is doing research for three-part television documentary about Winston Churchill. I think I was able to
help her with memories of Randolph and Johnnie [Churchill],
though I declined to be interviewed on film. After luncheon, I went
to *Oldie* office to be interviewed by Naim Attallah.[‡‡] Nice man, very

---

[*] Charles Gounod (1818–93); French composer.
[†] Gabriel Fauré (1845–1924); French composer.
[‡] Venezuelan-born French composer (1875–1947); lover of Marcel Proust.
[§] Anna Pavlova (1882–1931); Russian ballerina.
[¶] Violinist (1916–99); cr. life peer, 1993.
[**] Feodor Chaliapin (1873–1938); Russian bass singer.
[††] The Nobel Peace Prize had been awarded that year to Yasser Arafat and Yitzhak
Rabin; the Booker Prize to James Kelman for his novel *How Late It Was, How Late*.
[‡‡] Lebanese-born businessman (b. 1931); publisher of books and magazines (including
the *Oldie*).

Jewish-looking like John Sutro[*] and George Weidenfeld, ugly, smiling and clever. On train home read disobliging review of *A Mingled Measure* in *Private Eye*, accusing me of being a crashing snob and bore, accompanied by cartoon of me looking like an old queen. Am not unduly wounded, but can't say I like it.

Friday, 21st October

Having spent the day at Stourhead, Independent Television came to film me in Bath at five. They moved everything in the room, finally inviting me to sit enthroned in the middle of nothing. This was unnatural and made me feel uneasy. For some time they refused to begin as they detected outside noises, first someone's radio upstairs, then an ambulance outside. I pointed out they were in a city and such sounds were to be expected. They nevertheless made me stop the clock and switch off the electric fire. The presenter, Mike Hutchinson, was then recorded on his own asking a series of idiotic questions about the N.T. I was then filmed replying to these questions. Then I was asked to repeat several of the things I had said. Then the film ran out, and I had to repeat again. Then something exploded, and again I had to repeat. The result can't have been much of a success, though I liked them.

Sunday, 23rd October

Leslie Rowse writes to me that one should never say different *to*, only different *from*. I look up Fowler, who says it is pedantic to object to *to*, which has become common usage. Leslie also encloses, transcribed in his own hand, a longish eighteenth-century poem about some noble lord who had a huge member, like the Duke of Alba.[†]

Tuesday, 25th October

Bevis Hillier[‡] visits me in Bath to talk of John Betjeman. We are very friendly together, and I like him. I ask him why Selina's *Waugh* is

---

[*] Aesthete, film producer, bon vivant and founder of Oxford Railway Club (1904–85).

[†] See *A Mingled Measure*, 10 May 1953.

[‡] Writer, journalist and critic (b. 1940); sometime editor of *Connoisseur* and *The Times Saturday Review*; the three volumes of his monumental biography of Sir John Betjeman were published by John Murray in 1988, 2002 and 2004.

having such sensational success, whereas his first volume on Betjeman
didn't and he doesn't expect the second to either. He replies that it is
because of the American market. 'Waugh is just what they imagine an
Englishman to be, with his filthy manners and arrogance. Whereas
Betjeman is someone they can't understand – his Joan Hunter Dunn*
and teddy bear and underground world are to them provincial and
unintelligible.'

Thursday, 27th October

I lunched with Desmond [Briggs] and Ian [Dixon] to meet a boring
old man with white beard called Brinckman,† snobbish and donnish.
He said he spent his days and much of his money having his pedigree
worked out by College of Arms. He said, 'All of us round this table
must be descended from William the Conqueror.' 'Not me,' I
retorted. 'I haven't a drop of royal or noble blood in my veins. All my
ancestors were yeomen.' 'Oh,' he said, seeming disappointed with
me.‡

Sunday, 30th October

Weekend at Madresfield. Both Debo and I arrived at 4.30 on Friday,
just as dusk turning to dark, and roared with laughter when we discovered that we had both turned up too early, and stopped and read
in a lane outside the gates. Other guests Nico and Mary Henderson,
great fun, and full of flattering quotation from my new diaries. Also
Lady Lichfield,§ dark-haired with heavy, madonna-like features,
amiable, uninteresting. My bedroom huge, pitch-dark and icy-cold.
Walls covered with sub-fusc tapestry; huge four-poster bed. The
whole house most melancholy. Debo and I both fascinated. On

---

* Heroine of the poem *A Subaltern's Love-song*, inspired by a woman of that name whom
Betjeman met in a wartime canteen.
† Sir Theodore Brinckman, 6th Bt (b. 1932); antiquarian bookseller.
‡ Brinckman was presumably alluding to the fact that, going back thirty generations, each
one of us has approximately one thousand million ancestors: in the case of families who
have remained in one country since time immemorial, these are likely to have included
most of the reproducing individuals who were around at the time.
§ Lady Leonora Grosvenor (b. 1949); dau. of 5th Duke of Westminster; kinswoman of
Rosalind Morrison; m. 1975 (diss. 1986) Patrick Anson, 5th Earl of Lichfield, photographer (b. 1939).

Saturday night a dinner for ten in the enormous dining room, open to the roof, after which we sat in the *eau-de-nil* drawing room.

Today Charlie [Morrison] drove Debo and me to Ombersley [Court near Droitwich] to see the enormous early eighteenth-century painting of Chatsworth. It was given to the Sandyses by Sir Robert Walpole, a friend of 2nd Duke of Devonshire. Lord and Lady Sandys* very shy, courteous and welcoming. Wonderful panelled rooms. Portrait of Marchioness of Downshire, her little foot firmly set on footstool. She was the last of the Sandys who somehow managed to get herself re-created Lady Sandys [1802] and arrange for the title to go to her younger son. Behind her an *enfilade* of rooms which looks exactly the same today, only the panelling darker. Fine hall, all by Francis Smith of Warwick.† A rare, unknown house. He trotting briskly in double cutaway coat, large prominent teeth, smiling. He said it was a red letter day for him, as they rarely see anyone. He remembered attending a village fête at Wickhamford with my parents. I felt rather hurt when Debo on leaving said of my beloved Worcestershire, 'What a dreary bit of country.'

On return to Badminton, I spoke to Caroline, who visited Prince Charles at Highgrove yesterday. He sent for her but when she got there had nothing much to say. He probably knew of her trouble and wished to be friendly and sympathetic, yet did not care to broach subject, rather to her disappointment. She noticed a single place set for dinner in the dining room, and a small tray with breakfast china laid out in the pantry. Rather 'how', as Vita would say.

Monday, 31st October

Was shocked to hear of John Pope-Hennessy's death. *Daily Telegraph* telephoned with the news and asked if I would write an obit. I refused, saying they must get someone of John's calibre to do it, like a past director of National Gallery or British Museum, though I agreed to contribute a short appreciation. John had an aura of greatness. I never cared for him in the old days, finding him cold, cruel and a bit inhuman with his great learning. Yet I always admired him, and in recent years he seemed to become fond of me, perhaps because I was a link with his parents and Jamesey. I look back with a certain

---

* Richard Hill, 7th Baron Sandys (b. 1931); m. 1961 Patricia Hall.
† Architect and master builder (1672–1738).

poignant awe on this highly intellectual family, so self-congratulatory, supercilious and exclusive. Dame Una,* running her tight little literary group with Ivy† and Rose.‡ How she worshipped and protected her two sons. What would she have made of Jamesey's death? I believe John never recovered from it. How superior I used to feel they all were to me.

Tuesday, 1st November

The [Tom] Gibsons to tea. They told me that Mervyn the gamekeeper and Don the chauffeur were so sad about Caroline's illness that they felt they must do something. So they invited her to luncheon at the Didmarton pub. And they all had a whale of a time.

Friday, 4th November

I lunched with the Badenis§ at Norton. Lashings of caviare, brought by Jan from Poland. He a non-stop talker; she quiet, poised, sensitive, intelligent. A happy marriage between formerly penniless Polish aristocrat and rich heiress. As I left, he pointed with pride to his framed genealogical tree, showing his sixty-four noble quarterings. Jan went to the Palace recently for the state visit of Lech Walesa.¶ Says the Polish President is a good, deeply religious man, but an uneducated peasant, with elementary notions of how to behave. Jan is a Knight of Malta, of course, and adores it. They are looked after by a devoted Indian servant who has been with them for thirty-six years. Jan said, 'He is like a beloved dog, who does what you tell him and needs to be patted in return, which we do all the time.'

Tuesday, 8th November

Two-day visit to Downside.** Pouring with rain when I arrive, and pitch dark. The early English nineteenth-century interior is strikingly

---

* Dame Una Pope-Hennessy (1876–1949); writer; mother of John and James.
† Dame Ivy Compton-Burnett (1884–1969); novelist.
‡ Dame Rose Macaulay (1881–1958); novelist and travel writer.
§ Count Jan Badeni (1921–98); wartime Polish aviator; High Sheriff of Wiltshire, 1978–9; m. 1956 June Wilson.
¶ Polish national hero (b. 1943), who during the 1980s led the Solidarity movement which challenged the Communist regime; President of Poland, 1990–5.
** Benedictine abbey and public school near Bath.

beautiful, more so, indeed, than a real Gothic cathedral. Dom Philip Jebb* emerges from the gloom and takes me to my room in the ugly new guest wing. Room ample, clean and bare, with smell of stale tobacco and the sort of windows that don't open. Then to refectory for tea, the only meal which allows talk. Introduced to Father This and That, making monkish jokes incomprehensible to me, but friendly and extremely polite. Then I withdraw with Dom P. to talk about the things which are on my mind – my inability to communicate with A., and my worries about overpopulation, the main reason for my estrangement from Roman Catholic Church. He frowns in a smiling way, and suggests I read *Humanae Vitae*† in full.

At 6.30 Vespers in the church, which is dark, high and full of shadows. The monks process in like gigantic black crows, their hoods up, and then when they reach the altar they fling their hoods off. Chanting very impressive. Back they come with military discipline and part to left and right. Dinner at seven sharp. No talk, which suits me. Good school food – curried chicken and rice, followed by chocolate mousse. They gobble it down at incredible speed with which I cannot keep up. A finger code is used to request salt, butter, mustard, etc. A monk from pulpit reads from boring History of the York Archdiocese in Twelfth Century throughout. A little bell signals end of meal and we all process to monks' Calefactory, where we sit in groups and drink weak coffee. I am joined by a jolly priest who was a friend of Illtyd Evans‡ and tells me how much he enjoyed *Roman Mornings*.§ A bell rings for Compline. Monks return to church, and I retire at 8.45 to a fitful sleep.

On Wednesday (9th), I breakfast at guest table in refectory. Monks eat in silence, bibs tucked under chins. It pours all day without cessation, and I suffer from imprisonment feeling. Sung mass at 8.45 with billowing incense and full canonicals. No Communion for me, no longer being a registered RC. Later, Dom Philip visits me in my room. He is polite and beaming, yet I suspect does not like me much.

---

* Headmaster of Downside School, 1980–91, and Prior of Downside Abbey 1991–2001 (b. 1932); brother of architect of that name whom J.L.-M. met at Chatsworth, 10 September 1994.

† Encyclical of Pope Paul VI condemning birth control, issued 25 July 1968.

‡ Intellectual Dominican priest given to over-indulgence in food, drink and tobacco, whose death while on holiday in Greece J.L.-M. reported on 3–4 August 1972 (*A Mingled Measure*).

§ Published 1956 and awarded Heinemann Prize.

No wonder, for he knows I will not revert. I criticise *Humanae Vitae* for proposing, as an alternative to contraception, a fatuous method of having sex. It does not convince me; and he does not convince me that Catholics don't live in a world of make-believe.

A feeling of intense loneliness here. Memories of private school rise within me. The church is magnificent, but the aura not uplifting. I feel that the moment they can get away the brothers will indulge in every diversion known to man. I would certainly be driven to drink here. It is bitterly cold. Another guest, an aspirant monk (Cistercian) here to learn Latin, complained to me of the privations. Already, I thought.

Sunday, 13th November

Badminton church packed for Armistice Sunday. David read the lessons extremely well. Caroline looked much changed, but afterwards in the porch was talking animatedly to all and sundry. Before dark I went for a walk in the park. C. passed in her car, and stopped. She remarked how lonely I looked without Folly. Odd that she should have said this, for I had just been thinking of Folly, when I thought I heard the patter of her little feet beside me, only to find it was some dry oak leaves bouncing alongside. I told her I was longing to see her, and asked if she would lunch with me one day at home. She said she wanted to see me too very much, but next week was not good, as she was spending every night at Gloucester Hospital undergoing some form of treatment, and a huge party was coming for shooting. Her face was grey and puffy. Walking back I felt exceedingly sad and lonely.

Saturday, 19th November

I finish typing out my piece on Robert Byron. Peggy present, the only person whom I never mind being in the room when I am writing. In fact I like to hear her bustling about. She never interrupts me, whereas I talk to her when it suits me. I almost miss her when she is not about. She has the tact of the true lady she is.

Monday, 21st November

Michael Cyprien, who took about fifty photographs of me last week for *Perspectives*, has sent me the one he considers the best. I dread to think what the others look like. On opening it at breakfast, I gasped, confronted by what looked like a ragged doll made out of corrugated paper. Although I shave every day, I don't take in the ghastly truth that I am so decayed and hideous as to make children and animals hide in terror. I imagined myself to be a boy until I was forty, a youth until fifty, young middle-aged until seventy-five, and since then old, but not a scrunched piece of cere-cloth. I have thanked him, saying how pleased I am to be thus depicted.

Wednesday, 23rd November

To London to see the Whistlers at the Tate and Young Michelangelos at National Gallery. Too many Whistlers. He is a great, but not a very great, artist, with several different styles. In the big portraits he seems to get bored with the clothes, which become flat. I liked best the water-colours of Thames Embankment in silver and black. Michelangelo's entombment figure of Christ seems to be in levitation; his feet do not even touch the steps, and there is little sign of effort in the face of St Joseph who is supposed to be lifting him by the arms.

Thursday, 24th November

Giles Clotworthy[*] rang to say that Michael Trinick[†] died yesterday, which grieves me much. He was such a good and wonderful servant of the N.T., and did more than any man to bring about its great success in his beloved Cornwall. Giles sweetly said that Michael and I were his heroes at the N.T., sharing the same outlook. I feel sad.

Sunday, 4th December

John Kenworthy-Browne stayed the night and talked of John Pope-Hennessy. Praised his cleverness and good company, saying that alone he could be very funny. Surprising to me. But his ruthlessness and unkindness could be very shocking. When he left London, he never said goodbye to Maria, his faithful charwoman for eighteen years, or gave her a present. While tidying up Jamesey's papers, J.K.-B. found

---

[*] Former MI5 officer who joined Cornwall staff of N.T., 1983 (b. 1944).
[†] G. E. M. Trinick (1924–94); served N.T. from 1953 to 1984 as land agent, later Historic Buildings Adviser, for Cornwall (of which county he later became High Sheriff).

a letter from Harold [Nicolson] in which he wrote that John had sent Ben [Nicolson] a letter of such vituperation and contempt that Ben took to his bed for a week. J.K.-B. read my piece on Robert Byron and made some helpful suggestions.

Debo tells me that next weekend they have Senator Edward Kennedy* to stay – for family reasons, he being Kick's† brother. And Prince Charles has invited himself to stay at the same time. Awkward for the poor man, staying in the same house as an Irish republican sympathiser.

Sunday, 11th December

Xmas looms terribly, and the present giving and receiving, and the packing thereof. This morning, after church at Acton Turville (three of us only), I finish and despatch my review for *Country Life* of Gervase's exhibition of watercolours of N.T. houses, called *People and Places* after my book. Now I am asked by *The Field* to write an article on those families mentioned by Shakespeare which survive today.

Friday, 16th December

There are moments when a strange feeling comes over me in waves, and the mind simply ceases to function. It happened this evening when I was sitting by the fire, after speaking to my solicitor about the arrangements under which Clarissa might take the Bath flat. It is having to think about figures which seems to bring it about. I cannot grasp them. They have no meaning. They quite literally drive me mad. I feel as if I am whirling round in one of those revolving wheels at the circus, powerless, miserable, frightened, longing for peace or even death. Dreadful, dreadful. Then gradually it abates, and I am all right again.

---

* Youngest (b. 1932) and only surviving brother of President John F. Kennedy; Democratic senator for Massachusetts from 1962, whose career was blighted by (but survived) the 'Chappaquiddick incident' of 1969 resulting in the death of Mary Jo Kopechne.
† Kathleen A. Kennedy (1920–48), sister of the Kennedy brothers; against her family's wishes, she m. 1944 William Cavendish, Marquess of Hartington (elder brother of Andrew Devonshire), who was killed in action later that year, she herself subsequently dying in a plane crash.

Sunday, 18th December

Last night the Henry [Robinson]s dined, and were delightful. When I said I would have to retire to a home, they said I must do nothing of the sort. The flat at Moorwood has been put in apple-pie order, and is at my disposal. Under no circumstances must I go anywhere else. I was deeply touched. We also talked about the morality of destroying letters even when the writers or recipients have demanded their destruction. I told them that I wanted A's bundle of my letters to her to be destroyed unread. I haven't yet summoned the courage to read them myself, fearing they may be disagreeable letters. They were both emphatic that heirs or children are under no obligation to fulfil such wishes; it was up to the original recipients to do the destroying.

Wednesday, 21st December

Re-reading Victoria Glendinning's *Vita*,[*] I begin to see in our marriage the palest reflection of Harold's and Vita's, with all its high tragedy and farce.[†] My admiration for Vita is not what it once was, for I now see that, in the days before I knew her, she was a *femme fatale*, and not always over-scrupulous with the truth.

Thursday, 22nd December

Luncheon at the House, Derek Hill down for the day. I sat next to Caroline. The most noticeable change was in her voice, full of odd inflexions and lacking the usual sparkle. She has no self-pity whatever, says she is not going to bother with any suggested cures and will just let things take their course. When I told her that A. had left her the Apollo, she said she was touched, and would leave it in her will back to Essex House, to be kept in its place by all future tenants. She said she wanted a huge funeral with 'tents', all her friends to come. 'And you must see that David does it,' she said to me, with her familiar nudge of the elbow.

---

[*] Hon. Victoria Seebohm (b. 1937), writer and journalist; dau. of Baron Seebohm; m. 1st Professor Nigel Glendinning, 2nd Terence de Vere White, 3rd Kevin O'Sullivan; her *Vita: The Life of V. Sackville West* was published by Weidenfeld & Nicolson in 1983.
[†] J.L.-M. had had an affair with Harold in the 1930s, A.L.-M. with Vita in the 1950s; Harold and Vita acted as witnesses at the marriage of the L.-Ms in 1951.

I drove Derek to Highgrove for the night. Foggy and dark afternoon. Young policeman at gate stopped the car and asked to see under
the bonnet. Was amazed when I said that I did not know how to open
it. Eventually we were let through. Derek says I am one of those
friends he can count on the fingers of one hand. His effusive affection
embarrasses me, though I am very fond of him.

Friday, 23rd December

Driving us to Chatsworth, Coote [Heber-Percy] says that Rosalind
wants a biography of 'Boom'* – the pet name by which Coote's father
was known to his children, though they never used it to his face and
he was probably unaware of it. She thinks David Gilmour[†] may be the
man to do it, though he understandably says he cannot unless there
are papers. And Coote is pretty sure that her brother, that stick Elmley,
destroyed Lord Beauchamp's manuscript autobiography. A great
shame, for he would make a wonderful subject – the noble statesman,
Knight of the Garter, Warden of the Cinque Ports, driven abroad by
his brother-in-law, the loathsome Bendor, not even allowed back for
his wife's funeral for fear of arrest. Coote accompanied her father
from Venice on that occasion. When the boat from Havre reached
Folkestone, a friend by pre-arrangement was on the pier to signal
whether it was safe for them to land or not. He waved his arms in
negative fashion. So poor Lord B. and Coote remained on the boat
and returned to France. Then a fortnight later Lord B's favourite son
Hughie died in a motor accident. Miserable, Lord B. returned across
the Channel, no longer caring what might be done to him. In fact he
was not arrested, and remained at Madresfield for the remaining years
of his life. Greek tragedy.

    Paddy and Joan [Leigh Fermor] staying. I think he is the most
charming individual I have ever met. There is nothing he does not
know, and he has a Betjemanian sense of the ludicrous. Has the best
manners, and is touchingly modest about his achievements. Also
Dinah Bridge,[‡] *jolie laide* widow, sympathetic and sweet, and Margaret

---

* Coote's father, 7th Earl Beauchamp (1872–1938): see notes to 21 August 1993.
[†] Hon. David Gilmour (b. 1952); biographer and historian; e. s. of Baron Gilmour of
Craigmillar.
[‡] Hon. Dinah Brand (1920–98), yr dau. of 1st and last Baron Brand; m. 1st 1943 Lyttleton
Fox, 2nd 1953 Christopher Bridge.

Budd, who was Woman's devoted friend and minder. And Diana [Mosley], who told me of the infamy of Caroline Blackwood's* book, which she has seen in proof. It libelled Diana in stating that the Mosleys were imprisoned for treachery. D. sent a fax demanding that this be cut out, to which the publishers agreed. D. says the book is also vitriolic about Misha, depicted as Maître Blum's subservient accomplice in 'destroying' the Duchess of Windsor. Bosh. I have written Misha to warn.

Christmas Day, Sunday, 25th December

We all exchanged presents in the Stag Parlour in the morning, and gushed effusively. I was given a blue pullover with 'Devonshire 300' on the chest, and a small basket of whisky and wine. Then we went to church, full to the brim. Dear Mr Beddoes gave a gentle, sensitive sermon. At the end of the service, Andrew rose, and from the aisle thanked Mr B. on behalf of the congregation, saying that everyone loved him. We left emotionally charged.

Stayed up till midnight with Andrew, Paddy, and a charming young man called Alastair Morrison,† talking about the monarchy. P. and I lamented the scrapping of royal ceremonial. Andrew said he was a republican and it was time to stop all that rubbish. Paddy riposted that the Crown was about the only thing the UK still had to offer the world, now that it could not even get a Cunard ship ready in time for its cruise. At which Andrew blew up, cursing Paddy as an absentee expatriate who didn't know what he was talking about, that Britain's economy was the best in Europe, lowest unemployment, etc. In fact he was furious and rather rude. P. behaved with perfect calmness, apologising for what he had said. Then redeemed himself by adding that Debo would have made a wonderful Queen. Everybody would have adored her, with her combination of friendliness and dignity. No one would have taken liberties with her, for nobody does. He also said to me (more than once) that he wished he had kept a diary; that had

---

* Lady Caroline Blackwood (1931–96); novelist; dau. of 4th Marquess of Dufferin and Ava. Her book *The Last of the Duchess* – effectively a novel in which she omitted to change the names of the real people upon whom her story was based – appeared in 1995.
† Eldest son (b. 1958) of Hon. James Morrison (who s. 1996 as 2nd Baron Margadale); m. 1988 (as 2nd of her 3 husbands) Lady Sophie Cavendish (b. 1957), yst dau. of 11th Duke of Devonshire.

he done so it might have helped him pick up the threads he finds so attenuated and thin, so difficult for horny old fingers to feel. Yes, I said, a diary does keep the fingers flexed.

Thursday, 29th December

In today's *Times*, John Grigg* has an article entitled 'Who Deserves to be Honoured?' Gives two examples, Leslie Rowse and myself, which is kind though embarrassing, since in my case They (whoever They are) do not deserve to be chided.† As for Leslie, I don't know. He too may have rejected a bauble in the past. Meanwhile I have received a nice letter from William Waldegrave,‡ in his own hand, acknowledging my card in support of the OM for Leslie.

At Chatsworth I asked Diana outright if she had read *Ruthenshaw*, which I sent her but to which she made no acknowledgement. In that sweet manner of hers which portends candour, she replied, 'It gave me no *frisson* at all.' Which was her way of saying it was a damned bad story.

---

* Writer (1924–2001); succeeded father as 2nd Baron Altrincham 1955, but disclaimed peerage 1963; m. 1958 Patricia Campbell.
† See entry for 21 October 1993 and note.
‡ Conservative politician (b. 1946); yr s. of 12th Earl Waldegrave; then Secretary of State for Agriculture; cr. life peer as Baron Waldegrave of North Hill, 1999.

1995

Sunday, 1st January

Yesterday, Desmond and Ian gave their customary New Year's Eve luncheon at Old Werretts. But no Alvilde – and no grouse. Instead they had the Norwiches, and we ate a stew. We discussed what constituted an intellectual. I opined that John Julius must be one, as he knew the answer to every question, and had written histories of the Normans, the Byzantines and the Venetians. He insisted that he certainly wasn't. Good examples of people who were, he said, were Maurice Baring,* Freddie Ayer† and Isaiah Berlin. I suppose an intellectual is someone who thinks thoughts and pursues them. I haven't really thought a thought in fifty-five years.

Miranda [Morley] came to tea. She spoke of Prince Charles, whom she once knew quite well. He is so hostile to unwelcome advice that a friend who contradicted him was likely to be dropped and never spoken to again.

Wednesday, 4th January

The Poës‡ called on me this morning in Bath. She wanted to know what I remembered of her father, Nigel Richards,§ who in 1931 rented the first floor of a house in Upper Brook Street where I had the garret. I could only recall that he was dashing, extremely handsome, and a great one for the women. 'And for the men,' she added. Cyril Connolly¶ once wrote that he was the most beautiful male he had ever seen.

Thursday, 5th January

The article *The Field* has asked me to write on the names in Shakespeare's histories is causing me much angst, and will take me a

---

* Writer and poet (1874–1945).
† Sir Alfred Ayer (1910–89); Oxford philosopher.
‡ John Poë (b. 1922), cousin of J.L.-M.; m. (2nd) 1966 Emma Law (*née* Richards).
§ Engineer; m. 1937 Betty Fletcher Mossop; killed in action, 1944.
¶ Writer and journalist (1903–74); editor of *Horizon* (1939–50), who modelled the principal character of his novel *The Rock Pool* (1936) on Nigel Richards.

month at least. Am re-reading the plays, particularly moved by the small incidents. Deep poignancy in the gardener planting a hedge of rue on the site of Richard II's poor Queen's tears, or Richard learning that his beloved roan Barbary did not throw off Bolingbroke but carried him proudly. As for the scene in *King John* in which the young Prince Arthur is finally spared having his eyes gouged out by Hubert de Burgh, it is too harrowing to be recollected.

Monday, 9th January

When I lunched yesterday with Richard and Penny Wood* in the village – other guests Canon Barry and wife, and Mary Owen and husband – they mentioned that they had a videotape of the TV programme on the N.T., as yet unseen by me, in which I feature. After luncheon we watched it. I was horrified to see a worn-out, drooling old man, hardly able to express himself, like a very ancient bloodhound, bags under lustreless eyes. The shame of it. What they made me say was trivial, but all right.

Was interested to read an article by Martin Gayford on Anthony Blunt, about his obsession with Poussin† and identification with that painter's mysterious character. I don't think Blunt was a man of evil intentions, but rather one whose youthful ideals got the better of him. He got involved with the Communists and couldn't extract himself. Events pursued and enmeshed him. The fear of eventual exposure must have haunted him, if it did not induce the cancer which killed him.

Thursday, 12th January

Andrew and Debo took me to Grosvenor House at midday for the N.T's centenary luncheon. I was whipped away from them to sit at top table – rather flattering, and a reversal of the customary proceedings when I am in their company. I had Angus Stirling's nice wife‡ on my left and Dione Gibson§ on my right; Jacob Rothschild¶ on the right of

---

* Land agent for Badminton estate and wife.
† Nicolas Poussin (1594–1665); French artist.
‡ Armyne Morar Helen Schofield, dau. of W. G. B. Schofield and Hon. Armyne Astley, dau. of 21st Baron Hastings; m. 1959 (Sir) Angus Stirling.
§ Elizabeth Dione Pearson; m. 1945 Richard Patrick Tallentyre Gibson (1916–2003), director of companies, cr. life peer, 1975, Chairman of N.T., 1977–86.
¶ 4th Baron Rothschild (b. 1936); banker.

Lady G., National Heritage Minister* on left of Lady S. The Prince of Wales made an excellent speech. While waiting for the Prince before luncheon, I talked to William Waldegrave. He is good-looking and still youthful, but said his life was made hell by animal rights activists. He is promoting a scheme to rescue the vast collection of Horace Walpoliana[†] made by 'Lefty' Lewis[‡] for display at Strawberry Hill, which the Vincentians wish to evacuate. He knew L.L., who was a rogue. You had to count your spoons, he said, when Lefty was about.

Debo, who seldom criticises, complained that John Cornforth,[§] who had been staying at Chatsworth on some business, was very limited in his interests and only ever talked about conservation. This is true. He gives one a pitying look if one tries to change the subject from curtain tassels and Georgian wallpapers to, say, the Bosnia crisis. He was also very dismissive of the Prince of Wales, and Debo did not like that.

Wednesday, 18th January

Last night on TV I watched Attenborough's[¶] *Secret Life of Plants*. Though fascinating, science strips nature of all romance and poetry. Plants, it seems, are as sex-obsessed, ruthless and predatory as animals. Ruskin was probably the last writer to see nature properly in the old-fashioned way, before the advent of the railways. He crossed the Alps on foot as a young man. Yet he took a scientific interest in plants, as his drawings show, whereas Keats and Shelley romanticised nature, and Byron merely considered it a backdrop for the human dramas which interested him.

Friday, 20th January

After days of filthy weather, the sun has now come out, and with it that unmistakable flavour of approaching spring. Even indoors I sense it, stirring my old vitals; and I hear the Siren whispers, not voices yet.

---

* Stephen Dorrell (b. 1952).

[†] Horace Walpole (1717–97); yst son of Sir Robert Walpole; politician and writer, famed for his literary correspondence; built a 'Gothic castle' at Strawberry Hill near Richmond, Surrey.

[‡] Wilmarth Sheldon Lewis (1895–1979); collector and editor (for Yale University Press) of the letters and other writings of Horace Walpole; founder of Lewis Walpole Library at Yale.

[§] Architectural historian on staff of *Country Life* (1937–2004).

[¶] Sir David Attenborough (b. 1924); broadcaster and naturalist.

It already makes me restless and unhappy, full of regrets for the long-lost opportunities of youth.

Sunday, 22nd January

A nice review of *A Mingled Measure* by Roy Jenkins, describing my diaries as a work of art.

I have answered a letter from one Peter Stevens, who claims to be a fan of my diaries, and says he is the nephew of Audrey's late husband Tony Stevens; his father, whom he last saw in 1939, was Tony's brother. He begs me to tell him anything that I know about Tony in addition to what I wrote about him on his death.* In my letter to Mr Stevens, I have been frank about Tony, and have urged him to get in touch with Dale,† who longs to know more about her father and his origins, but may not be aware of the full story. Strange how my diaries provoke family skeletons to tumble from cupboards – such as my father's illegitimate son by the coachman's daughter.‡

I dropped a frightful brick last night, when I was motored by Miranda to dine with Julian and Serena Barrow.§ Andrew Parker Bowles was among the guests, a jolly, bouncy-puppy type of soldier, a bit of a *blagueur* and probably stupid on the whole. He made a 'macho' remark to the effect that women have no sense of the beautiful and men thrive on flattery, and looked across at me, trying to get me to agree with him. For some reason, I found myself saying that all women were in love with David Beaufort. 'Oh I say, isn't that going a bit far?' he asked, jerking an eyebrow towards Miranda sitting next to him. I jerked too, and saw Miranda's impassive face. So I added rather lamely, 'I mean, from a distance of course.' O senility!

Tuesday, 24th January

To London to see Byzantine exhibition at British Museum. Was particularly impressed by remnants of fabric, silk embroidery from

---

* See *A Mingled Measure*, 19 December 1972.
† Daughter of J.L.-M's sister Audrey (1905–90) by her 2nd marriage to Cecil ('Tony') Stevens (d. 1972); m. 1964 James Sutton, mechanical engineer, yr s. of Sir Robert Sutton, 8th Bt.
‡ See *Ceaseless Turmoil*, 9 August 1990 and notes.
§ Artist (b. 1939), whose painting graces the cover of this book; m. 1971 Serena Harington.

dresses. Amazing how little change in style over eleven centuries. Exquisite carvings in ivory, often full face. Got home in time to see that wonderful Neil MacGregor's* second TV programme on paintings in National Gallery. He possesses a diffidence and articulateness which enchants me. His manner not condescending like K [Clark]'s, nor flamboyant like John Julius's, but delightful and interesting. Excellent in describing how the Renaissance rediscovery of the ancient world and revival of Humanism must have been as disturbing to 'Gothic' Christian thinking as the moral chaos of today is to mine.

John Saumarez Smith alarmed me by saying that the short-list of the Heywood Hill 'Book to Please' prize consists of Paddy [Leigh Fermor], Robert Kee and myself – which Debo observed would cause a flutter in the Chatsworth dovecote as they are all such intimate family friends. I pray I am not the recipient. The embarrassment and fuss would probably kill me.

Saturday, 28th January

Shocked to see obituary of Father Derek Jennings,† the nice young priest I met some years ago with Anna-Maria Cicogna. Only in his forties. Very brilliant, very social, very affected and rather camp. I last saw him at a book sale at Christie's, where he was distressed at not getting a copy of Bridges' 1918 edition of Hopkins' poems, which went for £800. So I said I would leave him the copy which was given to me by Harold, and he was thrilled. Lucretia [Eeles] tells me that the Cardinal‡ visited Father Derek in hospital and prayed by his bedside while he died.

Watched horrifying episode of *The World at War* on the Jewish genocide. Felt sick, and deeply ashamed to think that such atrocities had been happening while I was alive. Then another hideous Attenborough film on the sex-life of plants. He says what I have always thought, that plants were not created for our delight, just for the eternal cycle of birth, eating, copulation, war and death.

---

* Robert Neil MacGregor (b. 1946); Director of National Gallery, 1987–2002.
† Anglican convert to Roman Catholicism (1946–95); known to his friends as 'Dazzle'; formerly on staff of English Heritage; last mentioned by J.L.-M. on 21 October 1992 (*Ceaseless Turmoil*).
‡ Basil Hume (1923–99); Cardinal Archbishop of Westminster, 1976–99.

Sunday, 29th January

Tony Powell's diaries* are very enjoyable and hard to put down. His comments are out of the ordinary, and very sharp and pointful. He is (so far) charitable about A. and me. Yet he does not emerge as sympathetic. There is a hard wooden superiority about him, a censoriousness, and immense snobbishness. Very self-centred, like most literary stars; most of the engagements he mentions are for newspaper and television interviews. Curious that he should accuse Diana Mosley of encouraging the press to refer to her as 'Lady Diana Mosley', when only at Christmas she was complaining to me about this ignorant and prevalent habit. For someone not nobly born, and indeed hailing from a frightfully unimportant family, he is remarkably obsessed with genealogy. Really very boring, and much less funny than Harold [Nicolson] on the McCrackells of Scottish antiquity. I would never mention my own forebears in such a way. When Mary Beaufort once asked about my great-great-grandfather in the Raeburn† portrait, I replied, 'He was nobody much, and if I told you it would mean nothing to you.' I can see Tony now at The Chantry, running out of the library to greet us in his blue and white striped apron, a touch of flour on his black eyebrows, announcing that his curry dish would be ready in five minutes. And over the library shelves those prim and purse-lipped ancestors like the chorus of dolls in *Petrouchka*.

Thursday, 2nd February

Yesterday, Henry [Robinson] met me at Lansdown Crescent and angelically carried all my reference books, or rather those I particularly need, into the back of his huge car. At Essex House, he carried them up to A's room, and placed them where I indicated.‡

Today, Mary Keen drove me to Cheltenham Museum, where we were given lunch and conducted round by George Breeze, the tall and handsome young director. A very good provincial museum, founded 1899. Building pretentious Edward VII Baroque, and appropriate.

---

* Anthony Powell, *Journals 1982–86* (Heinemann 1995).
† J.L.-M's great-great-grandfather, the Glasgow merchant Robert Thomson (1771–1831), had been a friend of the artist Sir Henry Raeburn (1756–1823), who painted several portraits of him.
‡ Though he only vacated his Bath library in October 1996, J.L.-M. no longer visited it daily and now did much of his writing at Badminton.

The Museum's speciality is the Arts and Crafts section, of Chipping Campden and Sapperton schools. But I liked best a joyous panorama of Dixton Manor in George I's reign, depicting peasants haymaking, merrymaking, dancing with fluttering handkerchieves.

Anne de Courcy* rang up to talk about Diana Mosley. I reminded her that, on the outbreak of war, Tom [Mosley] announced to all his beastly Fascist followers that they must now fight for King and Country. She knew about this, but said that one must not overlook the vicious anti-Semitism of his pre-war speeches. Still, I do not think he would have become a Quisling.

Sunday, 5th February

At Little Badminton church this morning, the church warden Arthur Vyner, as he handed me prayer and hymn books, whispered in my ear, 'Prince Charles is here.' Richard Wood respectfully but firmly waved me away from my accustomed pew in the left aisle, saying 'Sit between Penny and me', which I obediently did. Throughout the Communion Service, their child shouted and screamed without intermission. When the time came to receive the Sacraments, the Prince slowly advanced to the last stance at the altar rails, so as to be last to receive – my usual stance, in fact. No one else would go near him. So I thought, how silly and obsequious, and took the place next to his. At the end of the service, he talked politely to the Vicar (unknown visitor, but good) while we waited, I longing to get away.

I met Coote at Faringdon and she drove us to Heck's† house where Diana and Debo staying. Heck's brother Loyd‡ was lunching, and afterwards took us to his own house to see the pictures. I have always wanted to see the famous Wantage collection – and my word, it is something. Turners and Corots galore. Long, low house, a picturesque jumble outside with good pavilion by Claud Phillimore annexed to Lord Burlington's wing.

---

* Anne Barratt; m. 1st Michael de Courcy (d. 1953), 2nd 1959 Robert Armitage; writer and journalist, whose biography of Diana Mosley appeared soon after the latter's death in 2003.
† Hester Loyd of West Lockinge Farm, Wantage, Oxfordshire; m. 1944 Major Guy Knight, MC (b. 1919); equestrian personality.
‡ Christopher Loyd (b. 1923) of Lockinge Manor, Wantage; landowner and art collector.

When we all dispersed, Debo said, 'You will be distressed to hear that Gervase is dying.' 'Jackson-Stops?' I asked, incredulous. Yes, she said: Aids. Someone had just seen him looking ghastly ill. I am dreadfully sad. This dear little, extremely clever, gifted, jolly aesthete, with his incomparable knowledge; this tremendous asset to the N.T., stalwart defender of the right principles and critic of the wrong.

Tuesday, 7th February

Simon Blow, to whom I wrote asking for news of Gervase, telephoned this evening. Confirmed that G. had Aids, and had known since last summer. Simon guessed from the spots that appeared on his face. The friend living with him is HIV positive. Simon thinks the Aids virus may be human-invented, either manufactured by some nation for biological warfare, or deliberately disseminated among the blacks by white Americans to keep down their numbers, like myxomatosis to control the rabbit population. Unlikely in my view, though the wickedness of the world is without end.

Friday, 10th February

Dined at the House. Apart from the Beauforts, only Harry [Worcester], who has considerably improved. Talks sensibly, and is no fool. Caroline looking more beautiful than I have seen her for years. Her thinness so becoming, yet indicative of her deterioration. David's attention to her very marked. Is clearly very devoted, and concerned.

Monday, 13th February

Beanie Stewart-Jones* that was, whom I last saw in September 1939 going off to do war work in Egypt where she married a middle-class major, telephoned to say how much she had enjoyed 'my book'. And asking if I would write to a spinster friend of hers, who is a great fan and terribly lonely, about it. I spend hours each week answering fans, who often send me small presents such as hand-painted mugs which I don't want. Yet I am grateful, though bothered.

---

* Elizabeth Pulford (d. 2004); sister of J.L.-M's pre-war lover Richard Stewart-Jones (1914–57), architectural conservationist.

Thursday, 16th February

Decided to go to London just to see the recently discovered 'Irish' Caravaggio* during its short loan to the National Gallery. Indeed a most moving and spiritual painting. Face of Christ tragic, his hands tormented and so far away from his body that I at first thought they must belong to someone else. Indeed, much general confusion as to which limbs belong to whom. Reviewers remark on the 'homoerotic' look on the face of Judas, about to plant the kiss which Our Lord wishes to avoid, though I can't see it myself. The head of St John turned away from Christ, yelling and beckoning; and the artist surveying the scene.

Friday, 17th February

Peggy's birthday. Remembered just in time, and hastily packed the last of the pretty brooches I bought at the fleamarket into a gold Easter egg. Colonel and Mrs Crawford came at noon to discuss garden opening for American blue-rinses in June. Then dashed to Bath to lunch with the [Tom] Gibsons and meet the Floyds, he the grandson of the old Fullers of Great Chalfield.† Nice jolly hunting sort. He said his mother had told him I wore co-respondent shoes in the 1930s, which is absurd. Also present the Gibsons' handsome son Angus,‡ who talked of my novel about the German prisoner-of-war who seduces both a schoolboy and his mother.§ He said he thought it a fabulous tale. I agreed. He asked with apparent earnestness if I really believed a middle-aged woman, once aroused, would have an intense craving for sex. I said, 'You ought to know', for he was Don Juan incarnate. His mother then broke in, 'What are you two talking about?' 'Adultery, Mummy.' Then back to my library for Philippa Bishop¶ to choose two of my Beckford** books for an exhibition in the Tower.††

---

* *The Taking of Christ* (1602); purchased unrecognised by Irish Society of Jesus in the 1930s and recently identified as the work of Caravaggio (1573–1610).
† Major and Mrs R. Fuller; donors of Great Chalfield Manor, Wiltshire, to N.T., 1943.
‡ Angus Gibson (b. 1956); founder of Gibson Music Ltd.
§ *The Fool of Love* (Robinson, 1990).
¶ Philippa Downes (b. 1929); m. 1963 Michael Bishop; Bath historian.
** William Beckford (1759–1844); writer, traveller and collector, whose Bath library J.L.-M. had restored, collecting a number of the original books.
†† Lansdown Tower, built as a retreat by Beckford during 1820s, saved from ruin during 1970s by Dr and Mrs Hillyard who created a museum there.

Then rushed home to give tea to Imogen Taylor[*] and talk to her about John Fowler.[†] Too many things in one day. But Miss Taylor gave me amusing particulars of John, who in the office was a tyrant like so many men who are mild in society. I am including him in my book of sketches about friends.

Saturday, 18th February

Luncheon at the House to meet Tom Parr[‡] and Peggy De L'Isle.[§] Caroline much frailer, and extremely tired. She was so sweetly affectionate that my tears welled. Told me that, in a moment of gush, she had sent an affectionate postcard to Princess Diana. To her immense surprise she had a four-page letter from Prince Charles in reply, effusively thanking her and saying how devoted to her he was. How did this happen? Does he get to see her correspondence – or did she mischievously forward the postcard to the Prince? C. opened her arms wide when I left, and we hugged. Remember, she said, I don't want to be a bore to my friends.

Matthew Connolly and friend called to see the Somerset memorials in the church. Delightful they both were, so full of interest and curiosity, quick to observe and full of theories. We had an enormous tea of scones and cake, and they stayed until 6.30. Both OEs. Their chief interests genealogy, heraldry, sculpture, architecture, the world. *Simpatici.*

Sunday, 19th February

Peggy De L'Isle called. I asked if she would allow me to see the Bailey book, for I long to learn more about my great-grandfather Sir Joseph.[¶] She said she would bring it over and leave it with me next time she

---

[*] Interior Design Director, Colefax & Fowler (b. 1926); former personal assistant to John Fowler.
[†] Interior decorator (1906–77), partner of Colefax & Fowler, who did much work in N.T. houses.
[‡] Interior decorator (b. 1930); Chairman of Colefax & Fowler.
[§] Margaret Shoubridge; m. 1st 1942 (as his 2nd wife) J.L.-M's cousin Wilfred Bailey, 2nd Baron Glanusk (1891–1948) of Glanusk Park, Breconshire (eventually demolished), 3rd 1966 (as his 2nd wife) William Sidney, 1st Viscount De L'Isle VC (1909–91) of Penshurst Place, Kent; hunting personality, former friend of 'Master', 10th Duke of Beaufort.
[¶] Sir Joseph Bailey, 1st Bt (1783–1858); J.L.-M's great-grandfather on mother's side; Welsh iron and railways tycoon; MP for Breconshire; cr. baronet, 1852.

comes. She talked about how the 1st Lord Glanusk* and the then Duke of Beaufort were such friends in the last century, being the largest landowners of their time. I wonder. Oblique references to the Royals, for her daughter is Princess Anne's lady-in-waiting, and her granddaughter looks after the two young Princes. 'I must be careful what I say, being so involved with Them.' She is snobbish in the way that Jane Westmorland is, and very conventional, with her choker pearls. I asked her what Glanusk Park looked like. 'It was the size of that', she said, gesturing towards the House.

Tuesday, 21st February

Yesterday afternoon John K.-B. and I went to Gloucester to visit the Cathedral, neither of us having been there for twenty years. What a superb building. February is the best month to see a great cathedral. Hardly a soul besides ourselves, and those serious and elderly like us. We were deeply impressed by a monument in south transept arm to Alderman Abraham Blackleach, 1639. Mrs Esdaile† suggests Epiphanius Evesham or Edward Marshall as sculptor. Recumbent figures in alabaster of great refinement. Clothes beautifully carved, and their hands perfectly beautiful, long slender fingers, clearly by a great artist. Then Robert, Duke of Normandy, moved from centre of choir. (Why?) Red surtout repainted presumably, and well. Bold, brave face; crossed legs which irritates J. Then the chevet of the church, a miracle, with its curved end and huge Crécy window occupying entire wall. How is the vault supported?

Wednesday, 1st March

To Mary Keen's idyllic rectory at 10.30 to meet Charlotte Trumper and Peter Grover, chief executive and newsletter editor of Gloucestershire Gardens Trust, which wants to publish a memorial booklet about A's gardening. Mary offers to write it, if I can help her with data, which pleases me inordinately. When they left I had a snack

---

* Sir Joseph Bailey, 2nd Bt (1840–1906); grandson of 1st Bt; MP for Hereford; cr. Baron Glanusk, 1899.

† Mrs Arundell (Katherine) Esdaile (1881–1950); author of works on monuments in English churches, who had been of much help to J.L.-M. during his early years with the N.T.

luncheon with Mary, really the most delightful woman in the world, so natural, clever, amusing and devoid of affectation.

I was at home, typing my essay on Vita, when Jane Westmorland telephoned that she was expecting me for dinner, which I was unaware of. She said Caroline was coming, so I went. Jane the opposite side of the female coin to Mary, yet full of kindness and goodness, with her work for the Macmillan nurses. But the *grande dame* act doesn't ring true. Caroline sat facing me, and I noticed that her eyes had sunk since I saw her ten days ago. She talked of her cancer and approaching death; said she didn't want to die alone, and wished someone (David?) could accompany her.

Saturday, 4th March

No one can talk of anything but the Barings Bank disaster.* Sympathy was at first for the Baring family but is now veering towards Leeson, the rogue trader. Baring's must be greatly to blame for allowing this 27-year-old from nowhere to squander £700 million of their money. It is incredible. Nick [Robinson], who banks with them, tells me they telephoned him just before the news announced, assuring him that his deposit was safe. He was impressed by their decency in doing this on a Sunday morning.

Thursday, 9th March

The much-dreaded expedition to Mentone with Freda [Berkeley], Billa [Harrod] and Coote [Heber-Percy]. We fly through a dense blanket of cloud into the glorious blue. I am seated next to Coote who spills out into my seat, fairly squashing me. We are met at Nice airport by Nick Lambourne in his employer's large motor and kindly driven to Mentone along new *autoroute* high in the hills. Buildings all the way, a chain of concrete, virtually no country left. I recognise no landmarks; all swallowed up. Hôtel Méditerranée more a glorified *pension* than a hotel. No one to carry our multitudinous and heavy luggage from pavement to third floor. We stagger upstairs along corridors lit by automatic lights which switch themselves off, leaving one in

---

* Barings, Britain's oldest merchant bank, had collapsed after sustaining losses of one billion pounds, the result of unauthorised dealings in Singapore by the trader Nick Leeson (b. 1967).

Stygian darkness. We dine in, eating tasteless, NAAFI-style food. Billa says, 'We can't possibly stay here.' Coote is calm and says nothing. Modern, impersonal establishment, with disobliging teenage girl behind desk. We are miserable.

Friday, 10th March

We wake to glorious sunshine which never leaves us. My room faces enormous green tree with doves cooing therefrom. Coote has arranged for Paul Hanbury* to take us to La Mórtola at 10.30. The garden, which now belongs to Genoa University, splendidly restored from near-perdition. Within, one is unaware of surrounding horrors. We trek down to the villa, now used for conferences, where Paul gains us entry. Richly marbled in 1870s. A marble relief to Daniel Hanbury, younger brother of Sir Thomas and brilliant Fellow of Royal Academy; tablet commemorating visit of Queen Victoria; huge fresco recalling nearby stop of Charles V.†

We are then taken to see Waterfield gardens at Le Clos du Peyronnet. William Waterfield‡ now the resident, nephew of my Eton friend Humphrey. A dedicated horticulturist, with grey beard and whiskers, wire specs, and professorial, quizzical expression. I am rather captivated by this inscrutable man. He makes me sign copies of my works. An enchanted garden, specialising in rare South African plants and gladiolus species in pots of gravel. Fairy-tale overgrown terraces. An enormous wisteria, like Samson, has swallowed up the colonnaded front to the extent of smashing one of the columns in its arms.

Paul, who knew us at La Méridienne,§ is an affable bachelor, social, gossipy, kind, jolly. He is a contemporary and very old friend of Michael Luke,¶ who he says was a rogue even in his extreme youth. We give him lunch in excellent restaurant to which he introduces us. Afterwards I wander round town to get bearings. Much building

---

* Paul Hanbury (1921–96); grandson of Sir Thomas Hanbury (1832–1907), creator of gardens of La Mórtola near San Remo.

† Head of House of Habsburg; Holy Roman Emperor; ruler of Spain, Austria, the Low Countries and other territories (1500–58).

‡ Lexicographer and horticulturist (b. 1942); lived at Le Clos du Peyronnet, villa bought by his grandparents in 1913 (and the setting for the novel *The Long Afternoon* [2001] by his brother Giles).

§ House in Roquebrune where the L.-Ms lived during 1950s.

¶ Writer and film producer (1925–2005); estranged husband of Hon. Clarissa.

work, including building out to sea. Enormous lorry delivering stacks of concrete staircases to be hoisted into place nearby.

Sunday, 12th March

Freda and I walk to S. Michele Church in Old Town, scene of the Mentone Festival which was started by A. A woman in charge of sung Mass, waving arms as if conducting. Very low church ceremony, devoid of spirituality. No incense, no sanctus bell, paucity of holy water. Church packed by middle class in Sunday best. No sign of peasantry.

We now eat delicious restaurant food, fresh sardines, etc., instead of the ghastly hotel food, which is brought in from outside and micro-waved.

In afternoon I walk two miles along Promenade in direction of Roquebrune. What is so ugly is the horizontality of the modern blocks against the verticality of the hills, in themselves so beautiful.

Monday, 13th March

We walk to station to catch train for San Remo. All three women waddle slowly with extreme difficulty, which irks me. We change at Ventimiglia, but no longer any bother from frontier officials. After lunching at San Remo we catch filobus to Taggia. During journey, drunken man kisses Billa's hand and pats her head. B. behaves with aplomb like the lady she is. At Taggia, we take taxi to Convento di San Domenico, recommended by Derek [Hill], to see twelfth-century Spanish wooden crucifix. Stick-like arms and legs, tiny *cache-sexe*, agonised mouth, deep-set eyes. Moving.

Tuesday, 14th March

William Waterfield motors us to the Iliffes[*] at Villa Roquebrune. Edwardian house. Beautiful garden, once Norah Warre's.[†] Both Iliffes very friendly. Tea on terrace under cascade of white jasmine. Rich

---

[*] Edward Iliffe, 2nd Baron Iliffe (1908–96); newspaper owner; m. 1938 Renée Merandon du Plessis.
[†] Horticulturist (1880–1979), who created a famous garden at Villa Roquebrune from 1902.

chocolate cake. Butler in smart white jacket was air steward. We watch
hang-gliders over Monaco, like giant bats, and sun descending behind
Mont Agel, which I so often used to climb. Renée motors us home
via Cap Martin, passing the villas of Daisy Fellowes* and Empress
Eugénie.

Wednesday, 15th March

To Jean Cocteau[†] Museum in sea fortress on Promenade. Arranged by
him in his lifetime. Chalk drawings in simplistic style, influence of
Picasso.[‡] Mostly dated 1961, two years before C's death. Couples in
love, *Gli Inamorati*, and Harlequins. Large portrait of Cocteau in grey
by one McEvoy,[§] with firm, determined mouth and grizzled hair.
I saw him only once, in a restaurant. Eardley [Knollys] knew him at
Villefranche, and once slept with him. It was not much fun, he said,
too intricate.

In afternoon, we took taxi to Roquebrune. A pious pilgrimage,
and although rather sad with thoughts of A., I did not feel sentimental. The old *place* extended over cliff. A restaurant where we used to
garage the Topolino in the rock. Boutiques line the passage of entry,
where the old *épicerie* stood. But the little *place* in front of church and
post office, with war memorial where we got Winston Churchill[¶] to
unveil list of additional casualties of last war, and Simon Bussy's beautiful mosaic Madonna, unchanged. Church still delightful inside,
pretty and countrified. The nineteenth-century *crèche* with woman
knitting within pretty glass case; the twisting staircase to organ loft by
entrance door. We lit candles for A. and Lennox, with whom I used
to stand at Mass in the left aisle. Perhaps I am a little sentimental after
all, for I felt A's spirit everywhere. We descended under the vaulted

---

* Marguerite (1890–1962), dau. of 4th duc Decazes by his American wife Isabelle Singer
(sister of A.L.-M's friend Winaretta, Princesse Edmond de Polignac); Anglo-French
society figure, notorious for her malice; m. 1st Prince Jean de Broglie (d. 1918), 2nd Hon.
Reginald Fellowes.
† French poet, artist, librettist, dramatist, novelist and film director (1889–1963).
‡ Pablo Picasso (1881–1973); Spanish artist, founder of Cubism.
§ Eugénie McEvoy (1879–1975); French-born artist.
¶ During the 1950s, Sir Winston sometimes stayed in Roquebrune at La Pausa, a villa
owned by his literary agent Emery Reves and his wife Wendy. The L.-Ms occasionally
saw him there: J.L.-M. had been a friend of Churchill's son Randolph and nephew
Johnnie, while Churchill had been a friend of A.L.-M's father Tom Bridges.

arch (where I was once so impatient with Mama for making such a fuss over the climb), past the wagon-lit, to La Méridienne. Doorway unchanged. Peered over wall and noticed posh new descent. No change to *grenier* and weather-vane we put up. Did not, could not, would not enter. Continued along Mentone path as far as the ancient olive tree.

Thursday, 16th March

On arrival at station to take train to Nice, we are told of rail strike. So we lunch on Promenade. As I am talking to Billa of Molly Buccleuch,[*] a woman sits at adjacent table who is Molly in every feature and mannerism. On telephone, William Waterfield tells me I am his greatest literary hero, but he does not want to meet us again.

Friday, 17th March

Trains still on strike, so Freda lavishly hires a taxi for the day to take us to Nice, of which we all share cost. Sympathetic driver, to whom F. explains her purpose. I accompany F. to British Consulate while Billa and Coote dumped at café. Bright young woman receives us and assures us she will enquire about plot of land on Cap Ferrat once owned by Lennox's mother. We then drive to Cimiez cemetery in search of graves of Lennox's parents and grandparents.[†] We fail to find these, though we see graves of Raoul Dufy[‡] and Matisse.[§] Driving idly around Cap Ferrat, we come upon a pretty little chapel which I remember from visiting Rory [Cameron]'s[¶] villa in the old days, with

---

[*] Vreda Esther Mary Lascelles (1900–93); m. 1921 Walter Montagu-Douglas-Scott (1894–1973), who s. 1935 as 8th Duke of Buccleuch and 10th Duke of Queensberry.

[†] Lennox's father, Captain Hastings Berkeley, RN (1855–1934), and his mother, Aline *née* Harris (1863–1935), along with Aline's father Sir James Harris (1831–1904), HM Consul-General, Nice, were all in fact buried at the English Cemetery in Nice (now the Cimetière de Sainte-Marguerite) and not on Cap Ferrat – though the Hastings Berkeleys had lived on the Cap in their declining years.

[‡] French Fauvist painter (1877–1953).

[§] Henri Matisse (1869–1954); French artist.

[¶] Roderick Cameron (1914–85); garden designer and travel writer, who lived at La Fiorentina, Cap Ferrat; old friend of A.L.-M., of whom the L.-Ms saw much when they lived in South of France.

outsize Madonna-and-Child sculpture. Below, a small cemetery of Belgian soldiers killed in First World War. Mown terraces, cypresses, view of blue-blue sea. This solitary, tranquil spot just what Freda needs. She asks me to open bag of L's ashes, which I am carrying in my *sac-à-main*. In tears, F. takes handfuls and sprinkles them while I murmur, 'Dear darling Lennox whom we all loved, and who will be remembered by hundreds of thousands for ever and ever. Amen.' Scattered between hedges and over graves and grass. I watched the ashes float in a drizzle in the air before settling, some on my shoe. Cinders rather than ashes, whitish grey. A lovely occasion, F. very satisfied and happy.

Saturday, 18th March

Nick Lambourne calls and takes us to Villa Torre Clementina on Cap Martin, belonging to his American employer Koch (pronounced Coke). Poor man has had two shocks this morning – news that his mother has a shadow on a lung, and faxed letter from Koch giving him a fortnight's notice. Villa of unparalleled vulgarity. A Disney Castle outside. Floors and walls of shiny, slippery marble of every hue, including mauve and orange. Opaque stained glass in all windows. Metropolitan garden of no taste or interest. Swimming pool in Reckitt's Blue, below which a 'temple' for cocktails with glass wall through which to observe swimmers overhead. I telephone Lady Iliffe to ask if she might help Nick get another job on the Riviera.

In the evening, I remind the ladies that today is the anniversary of Alvilde's death. Am glad to be away from home.

Sunday, 19th March

Fly home. Peggy has put a bowl of camellias beside A's photograph in the drawing room.

Thursday, 23rd March

Peggy brings me a cutting from *Western Daily Press* – a very hostile article on centre page about me, calling me the National Trust's 'hijacker' who in 1936 formulated a policy of supporting the squirearchy at the expense of the people. Piffle, and I don't much care. Yet have sent a rebuttal to the editor, pointing out that in 1936 I was a mere twenty-seven, and no more than the humble servant of the distinguished committee that formulated the policies.

Saturday, 25th March

Eliza Wansbrough's* funeral at Carterton, Requiem Mass in barn-like church with open rafters, rather nice in Arts-and-Crafts way. Sat next to man stinking of drink at 2.30. So Catholic this – Catholic converts all drink in this country. The priest son Jo, small with distinguished profile, did the service well. Spoke of his deceased mother as 'our sister'. No tears – dear old Eliza was ninety-eight and had been without her mind for some years. I was fond of her. She travelled with us to the Near East. Would talk on any subject except her religion, about which she was as obdurate as a mule. I did not feel devout and indeed felt irritated by the congregation's mute superciliousness and cocoon of slushy devotion. I left the church with J.K-B. and stood talking with him beside the hearse. Felt rather beastly, as I had earlier refused his suggestion that he motor me to the funeral and take me home and stay the night. Miriam† came up to me and kissed me. We did not speak, yet understood one another. I did not go to the burial in Broughton Poggs churchyard and drove home, after exchanging some words with Zita and Teresa [the Jungman sisters]‡ who were already seated in their tiny white car, Zita at wheel. They are like two very old dolls, turning their heads this way and that in swift movements, and saying 'Yes' and 'No' in unison. Said they were sorry to be leaving Aynho§ for Ireland, where Desmond and Penny¶ have made a house for them. They laughed as they drove off perilously.

---

* Elizabeth Lewis (1897–1995); dau. of Sir George Lewis, 2nd Bt; m. 1928–38 George Wansbrough.
† Eliza's daughter (b. 1932).
‡ Teresa ('Baby') Cuthbertson and Zita James, daughters of the rich socialite Mrs Richard Guinness by her first husband, Dutch-born artist Nico Jungman; as girls in the 1920s, they had been prominent among the 'bright young things'.
§ Country house in Northamptonshire converted into flats.
¶ Penelope Cuthbertson, dau. of Teresa; m. 1985 (as his 2nd wife) Hon. Desmond Guinness (b. 1931), yr s. of 2nd Baron Moyne and Diana, Lady Mosley.

Sunday, 26th March

Drove fifty miles to lunch with the Charterises* at Wood Stanway. An easy household, without frills – and without servants that I could see. A sympathetic pair, whom I like much. He is a muddly bundle, untidy and red-visaged, his bald pate covered with red spots like mine. He drinks much, and seemed rather shocked by my abstemiousness. She is entrancing, and reminded me that we first met through Jamesey Pope-Hennessy during the war. Also Lord and Lady Plymouth,[†] he tall, gaunt and deaf, she pretty and sweet; and one Georgina,[‡] attractive, hard-drinking, opinionated woman who runs the Heritage Committee which dispenses public funds to worthy architecture. Martin is clearly fascinated by her, and is doing a bust of her. After luncheon, of which I could only eat an egg dish and apple pudding, both delicious, he took us to see his studio. He is a competent and dedicated amateur sculptor.

Tuesday, 28th March

Today I improved my new ghost story for Nick, and at first thought it quite good. Then re-read it and realised it was no good at all, and that I am now senile, and cannot write. Depressed by this and my tiredness. Struggled to walk in the park, made hideous by erection of shops for coming Horse Trials. A dull and very cold day, with driving sleet, the wind making a ghostly tremulous noise through the skeletal steel structures as yet unclad. Lit fire at four but unable to forget the day, for clocks have gone forward and it remains light at 7.20. I do not like the long evenings of daylight which accentuate my loneliness and restlessness. Am virtually waiting for death.

Wednesday, 29th March

A pretty young lady, Miranda Carter, came from London to see me in Bath to talk about Anthony Blunt.[§] Engaging. Curiously ignorant

---

* Lord Charteris of Amisfield (1913–99); Private Secretary to HM The Queen, 1972–7; Provost of Eton, 1978–91; m. 1944 Hon. Gay Margesson (b. 1919), dau. of 1st Viscount Margesson.
† Other Robert Ivor Windsor-Clive, 3rd Earl of Plymouth (b. 1923); m. 1950 Caroline Rice.
‡ Georgina Naylor (b. 1959); Director of National Heritage Memorial Fund from 1982.
§ Her book *Anthony Blunt: His Lives* was published by Macmillan in 2001.

for a biographer, but at least sympathetic to that arch-devil's sensitivity to and expertise in the arts. She said he destroyed all his papers before he died, save for an unfinished apologia regarding his treachery. It was left unfinished for the simple reason that he was unable to explain his motives, apart from boredom and lassitude. I can understand this. She has no doubt that his Bell's Palsy and internal cancer were both brought on by the strain of dissimulation. She has got more information from Dadie Rylands[*] than anyone else. I told her to get in touch with Bobby Gore.[†] As she said, he wasn't exactly a traitor in that Russia was our ally at the time, yet he may have caused the deaths of hundreds.

Friday, 31st March

Gerald appears at breakfast with the news that the village post office was broken into last night – on the very eve of the retirement of the postmistress, Betty Watkins, after forty-five years' service. This is pretty behaviour on someone's part.

I have read several reviews of the biography of Cyril Connolly which Deirdre set her face against, and wouldn't give papers to the writer thereof.[‡] Reviews favourable on the whole. One reviewer pointed out that, Cyril's besetting sin being sloth, his domesticity became the implacable enemy of his creativity. I think this is true. I am very domesticated and this has certainly had a deleterious effect on my writing.

Sunday, 2nd April

I gave a tea party, to which came Tony and Brigitte Mitchell, Rory Young and Judith Verity. They were all very kind and seemed to enjoy themselves. Judith belongs to the same type as Loula Gibson, Diana Menuhin,[§] Isabel Throckmorton, K. Kennet, the assertive female with a jolly air and no nonsense. And this is probably what Rory requires. He is vague, bubbling with enthusiasms, discursive; inclined

---

[*] George Rylands (1902–99); Shakespearean scholar and Fellow of King's College, Cambridge.

[†] Francis St John Gore (b. 1921); adviser on pictures to N.T., 1956–86; Historic Buildings Secretary, 1973–81.

[‡] Clive Fisher, *Cyril Connolly: A Nostalgic Life* (Picador, 1995).

[§] Diana Gould, ballerina (1912–2003); m. 1947 Yehudi Menuhin.

to be forgetful, and get carried away. He is thrilled to have been commissioned to sculpt saints and Old Testament figures for the Great West Door of York Minster. As models, he uses men and women of all ages encountered on the streets of Cirencester, who willingly give their services for free; and he hopes to produce a figure based on himself, if the Chapter will let him.

Monday, 3rd April

My painting of St Peter's returned this afternoon after an absence of a year and a half. It looks perfectly happy after visiting Venice and Washington DC. The carriers rehung it – I fear too high, but I did not have the heart to ask them to do it again. So the picture will remain wrongly hung, to irritate me each time I look at it, until it is taken down after my death.

Tonight I watched Dimbleby interviewing Mr Major on *Panorama*. D. behaved disgracefully, needling and insulting the PM and displaying all his socialist prejudices. The PM was calm, wary, collected and wise, displaying good manners and good judgement. I decided that I had lately been unfair in siding with the mass of the country in regarding him as a twerp. He is an honourable and decent man who would never do a rash thing, and if given the chance (which he won't be) might bring the country to its senses.

Thursday, 6th April

A Mrs Macdonald came to record my wartime memories of West Wycombe for the N.T. She was decent and polite, but without much humour or understanding. I failed to give her what I might have given in a lighter mood. This recording is to be kept in some archive for future generations to hear my voice and get some idea of what I am like – or rather, was like half a century ago.

At the request of his secretary, I rang up Gervase Jackson-Stops in hospital. A very painful business. He was clearly raving. Began by saying that everything was wonderful. He had seen the light. Roses from Heaven were falling all around him. Then he insisted on playing, over the telephone, extracts from the Beatles' songs. Was extravagant in praise of me and what I had done for the N.T. Raved about all the things still left for him to do. Insisted that I should stay with him at the Menagerie, and we would motor together to Flintham, Kedleston,

Chatsworth. Even mentioned a date. It was dreadful and embarrassing. The secretary, to whom I spoke afterwards, said he had his ups and downs, and was now 'up' to some tune, but was in a bad way, and would not recover.

Saturday, 8th April

Tom Gibson called, after going to the House to 'anoint' Caroline. He asked if she would like this and she said she would, very much. Anne [Somerset] was present. I am not sure whether anointing is the same as Extreme Unction. It is interesting how total agnostics will turn to spiritual comforts in crises. Tom also left a letter for David advising him what to do when the time comes. He fears it may come during the Horse Trials, and hopes there will not be too many people staying in the House, or luncheon parties.

Monday, 10th April

David Herbert died last week. A ghastly photograph of him in *The Times*, broadly grinning in his fancy hat, and an obituary making him out to have been a comic eccentric. Poor David. He sent me his love via the Revd John Foster who visited him in Morocco last month. I gather there was trouble with the Arab servant-companion, which I hope did not hasten his end. He was a great life-enhancer, and fun. But I could not keep up with his social life, and would not stay with him latterly in Tangier. We were contemporaries, he two months younger. He is the only person I can think of who never minded a jot what anyone thought of him, who wished to do nothing throughout life, and who was nevertheless blissfully happy from the beginning of it to near the end, when he became ill. A. adored him.

Tuesday, 11th April

I went round to see Caroline at midday. She showed me the illuminated scroll presented to her last week by some thirty charities she has been working for. When I admired it and congratulated her on it, she did not answer, and I saw she had fallen asleep. Rather miserably I waited, not wishing to disturb. When she woke, she said, 'It's dreadful. I can't keep awake. So embarrassing.' I said, 'If you can't sleep with an old friend like me, who can you sleep with?' which amused her a tiny bit, until she went off again. When next she came to, I left, saying merely, 'You know how devoted I am to you,' to which she replied, 'I too.' I felt utterly miserable as I walked home through the park, so bursting with life and promise, and thought, 'How can I continue to live here, where I have so much responsibility and no roots, with A. and C. gone?'

Thursday, 20th April

The Stuart-Menteths came to tea, having telephoned to say they had at last discovered the 'photograph' of Great-Aunt Jane which I had hoped to see when I had tea with them in Woodchester a couple of years ago. Jane Westmorland nobly agreed to come too, although she hates tea and regards it as an unnecessary meal. I hardly recognised the S.-Ms, who seemed much changed, though they were both charming. From the boot of his car he produced a huge framed picture of a dreadful mid-Victorian lady in ringlets, some kind of oleographic reproduction in monochrome. Jane later said that my face was a study when for a moment I feared they might be making me a present of this hideous likeness. I was expecting an 1890s photograph of a formidable lady in Court Dress and tiara. No doubt she was a generous old soul.

David drove up in his jeep and beckoned to me. I asked if I might see Caroline – for Rupert Loewenstein had told me that the House was now like some country house in a Russian play, with family and friends wandering in and out of the death chamber. But David said it was too late; she was now in a continuous coma. I was glad to be spared another harrowing visitation. 'I know how much you mind,' David said, adding that it was dreadful how difficult she was finding it to die.

Saturday, 22nd April

A terrible morning, pitch dark, blowing a gale and pouring. I huddle over the kitchen table, finishing the editing of my diary for 1974 before sending it to Misha to read. At midday, telephone rings. Tom Gibson in Bath to say that Caroline died an hour ago. David and all the family stricken. Tom to conduct the funeral here next week. Huge crowds expected, with loudspeakers in the orangery. I telephone Miranda to say I am at home all day if she feels like popping in. I hate the idea of her being alone and feeling rejected. And now (3.30) Freda [Berkeley] telephones that Jack Rathbone has just died. F. heard from his servant, who adored Jack and recently took him to America. Can't think why, because for years Jack has been quite senile.

Thursday, 27th April

Caroline's funeral. Was much moved when the coffin piled high with flowers was carried out of the church. That bright presiding spirit extinct. I did not go to the House for tea, but walked up the drive with the Morrisons. After embracing Rosalind in full view of the reporters at the gate, I was set upon by them asking banal questions. Was it a beautiful service? How would I remember the Duchess? When did I first meet her? I had controlled myself earlier, but now found myself on the verge of tears, and hoped to goodness I would not appear on the local news.

Paul Miles, who called to see me before the service, told me that as a young man he became fond of Charles de Noailles, and in writing to him asked if he might call him Charles. C. replied with a very courteous letter, saying that he had been brought up to address older men as 'Monsieur'; that after ten years' acquaintance one might address him as 'Noailles'; and that after another ten they might be on Christian name terms if he, the older man, felt so inclined, but not earlier unless they were close relations. Quite a lesson for the rather pushy young man.

Monday, 1st May

On Friday I took the train from Bristol Parkway to Port Talbot, where I was met at the station by Owen Lloyd George.* A very young septuagenarian, with wonderful manners. We drove some forty miles to Ffynone [Pembrokeshire], their house bought some eight years ago. I was not expecting a gem, but it has considerable beauty and interest. Built by Nash, who later added a colonnade to the façade. Several rooms, pretty cantilever staircase, and, above all, ceilings all as left by Nash. Built by Colby family. When Colonel Colby went bear-shooting in Russia in 1904, he felt guilty about leaving his pregnant

---

* Owen Lloyd George, 3rd Earl Lloyd-George of Dwyfor (b. 1924); m. (2nd) 1982 Cecily Gordon Cumming.

wife, and told her she might make any alterations she chose in his absence. He returned to find she had employed landscape architect Inigo Thomas to reface and extend the Nash fronts, turning a villa into a seat. Thomas laid a heavy hand on the house, inserting window surrounds, but his two additional wings of dining room and ballroom are interesting examples of Edwardian Baroque.

They were both extremely kind, and I took to them in a big way. She is pretty but not beautiful; he cherubic with turned-up nose, which gives him a quizzical look which misleads, because he is not quizzical. No one staying but me. Not a single servant to be seen in the enormous house. They disappear from Friday to Monday.

On Saturday, Owen took me to Picton Castle where we saw Hanning [Philipps],* now ninety-two and extremely frail. Snowy just alive and keeps to bedroom. Owen, a trustee of the estate, says the tragedy is the estrangement between them and their son Jeremy.† We went round the Graham Sutherland‡ Museum which is to close in the autumn owing to too few visitors. I am not surprised. Graham's landscapes now very dated, and disagreeable for the most part. Good if conventional portraits by Graham of Hanning and Snowy. Also loan exhibition of Picasso sketches of bestiaries and animals, simply lovely – I would adore to have just one of them.

On Sunday they gave a luncheon for the county. Included one Tom Lloyd,§ friendly man under forty who is Chairman of Welsh Historic Buildings Council and said he would send me his book on lost Welsh country houses. I sat next to one Mr Kemmis Buckley, old bachelor of Ted Lister type who is writing an article on St Rumbold. Who was he, I asked? He lived but three days, having delivered a sermon exhorting his listeners to follow Christ. There is a holy well in

---

* Major the Hon. Hanning Philipps (1904–98); yr s. of 1st Baron Milford (but inheritor of much of the family property, including Picton Castle, Dyfed, his elder brother being a Communist); m. 1930 Lady Marion ('Snowy') Dalrymple, dau. of 12th Earl of Stair.
† Jeremy Hew Philipps (b. 1931).
‡ Artist (1903–80), whom the L.-Ms knew in the South of France in the 1950s. He did much painting in Pembrokeshire, and in the 1970s was offered the service wing of Picton as a museum for his works. After the museum's closure in 1995, its collection was transferred to the National Gallery in Cardiff; in 2003, it was announced that a new home for it would be built at St David's.
§ Thomas Lloyd (b. 1955); solicitor; Chairman of Historic Buildings Council for Wales from 1992.

Northamptonshire sanctified by him, to which the owner, one Ewart of Astrop Park, denied Mr Buckley admission when he motored all the way from Pembroke to Northants to see it.

Thursday, 4th May

Suddenly we are plunged into summer, with high temperatures and burning sun. Grant McIntyre motored from London to lunch and we discussed the forthcoming double-volume reprints of my old diaries, one to come out this autumn, the other next spring. I fear the reading public will be sick and tired of J.L-M. I also gave him the eleven vignettes I have so far written for *Straight and Bent*.[*] Grant really is a man after my own heart, and I know that today I broke through the shyness barrier. He talked freely and is extremely sympathetic, well-informed and gentle, reserved yet expansive. Tells me his wife is also a publisher, and earns far more than he does.[†]

Sunday, 7th May

I went to Matins this morning, church full of gentry attending Horse Trials. Too many hymns, and sermon too long. On leaving the church I walked from the path into the enclosure to look at Caroline's grave. It seemed impossible that below the earth at my feet the adorable C. was lying, softly decomposing. And how awful the proximity for David, who now has the dreaded Event to cope with, a quarter of a million said to be attending today.

Sunday, 14th May

Freda [Berkeley] claims to be telepathic, whatever that means. At any rate, while she was here this evening with her two queer clergymen she talked about Bob Parsons and Nick Lambourne, from neither of whom I had heard for weeks. As she was leaving, first Bob rang out of the blue for a chat, and then Nick from Monaco to announce that he had taken a temporary job in Alexandria. 'What did I tell you?' said Freda.

---

[*] Working title of J.L.-M's 'book of sketches about friends' (17 February 1995).
[†] See entry for 17 May 1997.

Monday, 15th May

And today Barney Stewart-Jones,* who came from London for the day to talk about his father, mentioned that his grandfather, an insurance clerk, had married a Holland before the Great War, much to the disapproval of her relations. Suddenly the bell rang and Joanie Holland,† whom I have not seen or spoken to this year, telephoned, asking me to lunch in July to meet the Rowleys. Perhaps there is something in telepathy after all.

Barney is a delightful man, about the age of Rick his father at the time of his lamented death, but less nervy. He does not share Rick's architectural interests, or his looks, but is agreeable and lively. He is a director at the BBC, and spoke interestingly about his work and the people he meets. Strange talking with this middle-aged man whose father I knew and loved so well.

Tuesday, 16th May

Nigel Nicolson lunched in Bath. A dear friend and appreciative guest. Dusty and older, face expanded and mouth contracted, and rather deaf. He is lecturing in Bristol this evening. Said he immensely enjoyed lecturing because of the applause, 'which I know is very reprehensible,' he added laughingly. Told me that, during a visit to Sissinghurst, Stephen Spender discovered three letters he had written to Vita when he was young, and asked Nigel if he might have them back. Nigel refused, but Stephen took them anyway, because they contained indiscreet confidences of his youth. Being so much the gent, Nigel does not want to ask for them back. I would certainly do so.

Thursday, 18th May

To London for the night. Lunched with Derek [Hill] at Boodle's, Feeble [Cavendish] and Freda [Berkeley] also there. Derek boasted throughout about his painting and his friendship with Prince Charles. He has become a bore on these subjects. From there to Felix Kelly‡

---

* Barnaby Stewart-Jones; television producer.
† Joan Street; m. 1st 1945 Sir Guy Holland, 3rd Bt (1918–97), farmer and art dealer, 2nd 1999 (as his 2nd wife) 26th Baron Mowbray (b. 1923).
‡ New Zealand-born artist (d. 1996).

exhibition at Colnaghi's where I completely lost my head and bought one of the few unsold paintings, a landscape in Majorca, for £2,000. I don't think I have ever spent so much on a work of art in my life. In the evening saw *La Cenerentola** at Brooks's, taking Feeble as my guest. A dreadful scrum beforehand. Good performance but a silly libretto and I got bored. At supper in the Spencer Room, Feeble talked of John Betj[eman]. She has read through Volume 2 of Candida's *Letters*† and is pleased. Says that Candida's references to herself are tactful. 'After all, I could hardly be left out of the second half of his life.' That is what her friends have been trying to make her see for years.‡ She said that once, when Penelope§ had been to John's house, she, Feeble, from an upstairs window watched her walk away, looking so sad and weary that her heart bled. She admitted that John was often very difficult to live with because of his guilt over Penelope, about which he could never stop talking to her.

Friday, 19th May

Misha lunched at Brooks's, wearing a scruffy corduroy suit. I am all for individuality but I don't like scruff, as if to flaunt in a nest of orthodoxy. He was very charming, however, and I much enjoyed being with him. He returned my [1973–4] diaries with enthusiastic comments.

Saw Fabergé¶ exhibition at Queen's Gallery. Of course I coveted those eggs covered with diamonds and pearls and gold. Such poignancy in No. 252, the egg presented by the Tsar to the Tsarina in 1914, the 'surprise' within being profile heads of the five imperial children, the whole lot to be murdered within five years. Did George V feel guilty when he purchased it later?

---

* Opera by Rossini (1817), based on the story of Cinderella.
† The first volume of Candida Lycett-Green's edition of her father's letters, covering 1926–51, had appeared in April 1994; the second volume (1952–84) came out in October 1995.
‡ Lady Elizabeth had not approved of Bevis Hillier as Betjeman's official biographer, and had refused to help him.
§ Hon. Penelope Chetwode (1910–86); m. 1933 John Betjeman.
¶ Carl Fabergé (1846–1920); Russian jeweller.

Thursday, 25th May

I joined Debo in London and we drove to Chatsworth in her motor. Paddy Leigh Fermor there, all that a civilised man should be. Tells endless anecdotes, recites poetry, sings old music hall songs, looks up names in *DNB* and words in dictionaries. D's granddaughter Isobel Tennant* also staying, thirty and handsome indeed. Very intelligent girl, more Cavendish than Mitford. Was driven home in His Grace's magnificent glossy Bentley with ducal crest and coronet on door panels.

God deserts us in our old age when we most need him.

Thursday, 1st June

To Brompton Oratory for John Pope-Hennessy's memorial service. I arrived late, to find my old foe Father Michael Napier† holding the stage. He made a very good address, admitting, I hope ruefully, that John lamented the consequences of Vatican Council II, particularly the rejection of the Pauline liturgy. In fact, every sensitive, cultured, intellectual Catholic must deplore that Council's iconoclasm brought about by Pope John XXIII. I found the Oratory lugubrious despite its architectural merits. It has a dusky, dingy look.

Saturday, 3rd June

There is an evil in old men's faces. I catch a glimpse of my own in shop windows when not expecting to, and take a step backwards in horror and fear. The goodness, which must be there too, is not immediately visible. What an image to present to the world.

Sunday, 11th June

Nick lunches and we walk along the verge after. I wish I had the courage to rebuke him for his awful clothes, a bedraggled short tweed jacket, and he half-shaved. Yet absolutely sympathetic, and we talk of books.

---

* Er dau. (b. 1964) of Hon. Tobias Tennant and Lady Emma Cavendish; m. 1997 Piers Hill.

† Descendant of famous military family and convert to Roman Catholicism (1929–96), who as an Oratorian priest fiercely upheld the old Catholic rites. (He had required J.L.-M. to resign as an artistic adviser to the Oratory after the latter had signed an open letter against the encyclical *Humanae Vitae*.)

Tuesday, 13th June

Am re-reading letters from Jamesey Pope-Hennessy, whom Grant wants me to include in my book of sketches about friends. What a first-rate writer he was. His early letters are the best, before he became irredeemably dissolute and bellicose and unbearable. What humour, affection, sharpness. Never was a good man so lost to dissipation, and the lusts of the flesh. Towards the end I find myself becoming quite angry with him.

Wednesday, 14th June

Tony and Brigitte Mitchell picked me up at 9.30 and we motored to Croome [Court, Worcestershire]. There we met Jeffrey Haworth,* who has a laudable scheme to get the N.T. to acquire the surrounding land with church, Gothic castle, orangery, temples, Coade stone bridges and nymphs thereon. Went into the church which is simply wonderful and just as I remember: a pantheon of monumental sculpture, tombs to the Earls of Coventry, and Adam Gothic entirely – vaulted ceilings, soffits, stout oak door, clear glass windows, pews. Now redundant, but well cared-for and protected from vandals. One of the least spoilt and most nostalgic churches, vying with Hanbury [Hall, Worcestershire] and Badminton for family monuments. Then we walk along the ridge towards a domed temple, to obtain the Wilson view of the splendid, melancholy, now empty house. Views of the Malverns, and of Bredon Hill. This marvellous part of mid Worcestershire, as yet unspoiled, certainly ought to be acquired by the Trust; it is a second Stowe or Hawstone, and must be saved. The house, which we did not enter, is enormous. Ages since I saw inside. Much has apparently gone, one entire room including the famous Neilson-Boucher tapestries to the Metropolitan [Museum of New York].

Then on to Hanbury to see the new formal garden on the south front, a trumped-up restoration of the garden shown in the old engraving by London. Jeffrey warned me that I would not approve; and I don't. All the romance of Hanbury has gone with these finicky beds, gravel paths and galaxy of colour, also whimsy little latticed gazebos. I am a romantic and I prefer what the eighteenth century did, parkscape right up to the house. The Trust is becoming too antiquarian-

* N.T. Historic Buildings Representative for Severn Region, 1981–2002 (b. 1944).

horticultural, trying to recreate what they suppose the Caroline monarchs did at Hampton Court.

Then on to tea at the White House, Suckley, Jeffrey's doll's house circa 1700. A family home, with children and nice plump wife with shirt hanging out. And such a wonderful house, large contemporary staircase, uncarpeted, slippery treads, upstairs room of fielded panelling, and next door a closeted room with marquetried walls, all of the date. A joyful, tumbledown place, ungrand, enthusiastic, with some interesting furniture and Nash watercolours of the Olden Tyme. I have an 'up' on Jeffrey, with his firm chin, old-fashioned tweed suit, love of old things, and splash of a phrase or two on the harpsichord. Just the sort of man the N.T. ought to have on its staff.

Thursday, 15th June

This morning I was gratified to receive letters from four women asking to meet – Selina [Hastings], Jessica Douglas-Home,* Gay Charteris and Valerie Finnis.† I long to see them all, if I can face up to the meals. In old age I have become 100 per cent hetero-platonic. I prefer the company of women.

Friday, 16th June

To Deene [Park, Northamptonshire] for the weekend, motoring 135 miles. A beautiful day, stormy with sunlight. I love mid June, with the trees like tea cosies rimmed with a circle of shade, and powdery blue hills in the distance. I lunched off a banana and biscuit by the grand gate piers of Sarsden, the domain of Lord Clarendon of the Great Rebellion.‡ At Swerford I descended to the village and looked for Constantia Fenwick's§ grave. Did not find it, but in the church saw a nice little tablet to her adored husband Ralph Arnold which includes

---

* Jessica Gwynne (b. 1944); artist, stage designer, and biographer of her great-aunt Violet Woodhouse (see entry for 27 September 1995); m. 1st 1966 Charles Douglas-Home (1937–85), editor of *The Times*, 1983–5, 2nd 1993 Rodney Leach.

† Horticulturist; m. 1970 (as his 2nd wife) Sir David Montagu Douglas Scott, diplomatist (he d. 1986).

‡ Edward Hyde, 1st Earl of Clarendon (1609–74); Stuart grandee, who wrote a book on the Civil War period, *History of the Great Rebellion in England*.

§ Constantia Fenwick (1905–93); m. 1936 Ralph Arnold (1906–70) of Cobham, Kent; author and publisher.

her name. I also stopped at Haselbech [Hall] to see Aunt Con Ismay's*
grave next to her husband's – sausage-shaped, with a rather whimsy
inscription about birdsong etc., as I would expect. And beside it a little
round stone like a pepper-castor for the ashes of her daughter Del,
who died fairly soon after her mother in 1973. I wondered which of
the cottages Aunt Con moved to from the big and ugly house, where
I last stayed in the mid 1930s.

Finally reached Deene. Given Henry VII's bedroom at top of a
corner tower. Extremely cold, but with bathroom. When one sat on
the loo – the old-fashioned sort, the heavy top of which has to be
lifted and held by one hand all the time of micturation – the wind
whistled up one's behind, as on Mount Athos. Huge canopied bed.
The Brudenells welcoming but absurdly fogeyish. At dinner
Edmund fussing dreadfully because my neighbour, Swiss lady,
allowed herself to be engaged by him on her right instead of by me.
Too silly. Bobby Gore staying with his enchanting daughter Kathy
and husband. She as pretty as a picture, so clever and sensitive and
interested. Also Brinsley Ford,† very immobile and sparrow-witted;
Nancy Osborne Hill, rather sweet and extremely rich;‡ Edmund
Fairfax-Lucy, charming and stocky, with the smile of Brian through
the mouth of Alice.

This house is enormous and I have trouble finding my way about.
On Sunday, Communion was held in the chapel, the parish church
having been made redundant since my last visit. The household
jammed into one narrow pew, leaving the other side to two humble
ladies from the village, which I thought all wrong. Edmund handed
me an unwieldy prayer book with prayers for George II and Queen
Caroline. When I left my staff contribution in lacquer box in great
hall, as is the custom in this household, I noticed that the Swiss lady,
before departing in a hired London taxi, had left a £50 note. This
made me leave £20 instead of the £15 I had calculated enough.

---

* Matilda Constance Schieffelin of New York (1872–1963); m. 1900 Charles Bower
Ismay (1874–1924), partner of White Star shipping line; rich and sentimental widow
enamoured of J.L.-M. during 1930s.
† Sir Brinsley Ford (1908–99); sometime Trustee of National Gallery, Chairman of
National Art Collections Fund, and Hon. Adviser on Paintings to N.T.; Eton contemporary of J.L.-M.
‡ Seattle-based millionairess, who had surprised English friends seven years earlier with
the reflection: 'I honestly don't know how people can manage on less than £700,000 a
year' (*Beneath a Waning Moon*, 6 July 1987).

Tuesday, 20th June

Another extravagance. In Maggs's* catalogue received this morning, there is a letter in the handwriting of Bess of Hardwick.† It costs a fortune,‡ and doesn't interest me in the least, but the idea suddenly came to me that I should buy it for Andrew Devonshire. I shall be disappointed if they aren't interested – which they may not be, as Maggs have not had a bite from them.

Friday, 23rd June

I know that my interest in buildings is not scholarly, but that of the social historian. It is associative rather than architectural, and I am no longer interested in entablatures and quoins.

Tuesday, 27th June

To London for the day. Lunched at Sotheby's with George Plumptre,§ a nice, friendly young man. My neighbour a Mrs Fitzalan Howard, daughter of John Vernon of Sudbury.¶ She said how much her father resented the N.T's 'museumisation' of Sudbury. I opined that there had not been much else they could do, and that what they had done, they had done well. I told her that I had stayed at Sudbury during the war with her grandfather, a charming and sympathetic man who had fought in the navy during the First World War, who kept me up until 2 a.m. talking about pacifism and his hatred of Churchill. To Maggs in Berkeley Square where I saw the Bess of Hardwick letter which I asked them to post to Andrew Devonshire, to whom I have written separately about my great gift. Then to tea with Fanny Partridge. She was infinitely sympathetic, and when I left said that we seemed to agree about everything. I think this is true in a cerebral sense, though I don't

---

* Rare book and manuscript dealers in Berkeley Square.
† Elizabeth *née* Talbot (*c.*1527–1608); Elizabethan matron, ancestress of Cavendish family, who amassed a great fortune through four marriages, and founded both Chatsworth and Hardwick Hall, future seats of the Dukes of Devonshire.
‡ The price of the sixteenth-century autograph was £1,500.
§ Hon. George Plumptre (b. 1956), yr s. of 21st Baron FitzWalter; m. 1984 Princess Alexandra Cantacuzene; then on staff of Sotheby's; writer on gardening and social history.
¶ Hon. Joanna Venables-Vernon (b. 1965); o. dau. of John, 10th Lord Vernon (b. 1923) of Sudbury House, Derbyshire; m. 1992 Alexander Fitzalan Howard.

share her left-wing views. She is fussed about the film on Carrington*
and the exhibition of Carrington relics of which she has many. Said
that the film actor impersonating Lytton [Strachey] resembles him
almost perfectly except that he doesn't have the attenuated hands. I felt
a little sad on leaving Fanny, who says she is often lonely.

Thursday, 29th June

A fearsome heatwave, and the roses falling almost before they come
out, which is sad. Elspeth [Huxley] and the Levis come to tea in the
kitchen, which I have much ado in keeping cool. They are intoxicated
by the beauty of the garden, and A's sense of layout and colours.
Indeed how I hope the darling is proud of it.

Friday, 30th June

I visited the Acloques at Alderley† this evening and was bowled over
by the beauty of their garden. A depth, lushness and magic about it,
sheltered by its lovely walls, and denser than in our day. Now a
fulfilled garden, cut off from the world, Ariosto's secret garden of
Rinaldo and Armida. Overgrown, yet controlled. Another tribute to
A. – though she would doubtless have found much to criticise in it –
and tribute is equally due to Guy for maintaining it so faithfully in the
image A. imposed on it.

Thursday, 6th July

I have read three excellent obituaries of little Gervase, each praising
him for the inspiration he imparted to all who worked with him. He
was short and slight with the most animated little face imaginable. It
was never still. Flickering eyes, laughter, and the worst stammer ever
heard. He cracked his fingers as he struggled to get the words out.
Stammer improved after he underwent a cure in America following
the great success of his 'Treasures Houses of Britain' exhibition in

---

* Film about the artist Dora Carrington (1893–1932), and the complicated love relation-
ships connecting her to Lytton Strachey, Ralph Partridge, Frances Marshall and Gerald
Brenan.
† Alderley Grange; house in Ozleworth Valley where L.-Ms lived from 1961 to 1974, and
A.L.-M. created a noted garden.

Washington. No one knew more about every house of note than he. Prodigiously knowledgeable, yet absolutely unpedantic. The last time he rang up he implored me to stop the N.T. painting the sash bars of its Georgian houses brown. A pity he was so camp, and allowed his awful queer layabout friends to sponge off him. What will now happen to the Menagerie?

I went to London today to give lunch to Michael Mallon. He is very nice, and was clearly devoted to John [Pope-Hennessy], seeing him through his terminal illness. John has left everything to him, the apartment in Florence and pictures and furniture, much of which he is selling. He thinks he will live in Paris and write novels. We talked of the Pope-Hennessy trio – or quartet, as I insisted the General merited inclusion. He thinks a book could be written about them, or at least their correspondence should be published.

Monday, 10th July

After days of unbearable closeness, an apocalyptic thunderstorm. Catastrophic rain for an hour and a half, as if cascading from above. Vehement hailstones the size of gulls' eggs. I was at first pleased for the garden's sake. Then I saw the damage done to the roses.

Tuesday, 18th July

Stephen Spender's obituaries are well-deserved, for he became a great literary pundit and friend and encourager of young poets. He gloried in being a poet, said it was his earliest ambition as a child, and that it was a sacrificial act. Whether his poetry was any good or not I can't judge. I never knew him well, but shall always remember our last talk over that tiresome Marilyn Quennell's table, when he was so charming, sensible and funny. Of course, I hated him and his gang in the 1930s for joining the Communist Party, supporting the Republicans in Spain, and sympathising with the Soviets. They did incalculable harm which has not yet abated in left-wing literary and intellectual circles.

Friday, 21st July

Selina [Hastings] came for the night, blooming with success. Clear, soft complexion, liquid eyes. Her presence is very beguiling. Said she hates children and travels in smoking compartments of trains and planes just to avoid them. She is now engaged on Ros[amond Lehmann]'s life, and has a favourable opinion, I was pleased to learn. Admits Ros was good and generous, and a first-class novelist. Her friends enjoyed exchanging malicious stories about her, and Dadie [Rylands] and John [Lehmann]* would read extracts from her works roaring with mockery.

Saturday, 22nd July

Philip Ziegler† to tea. Wizened, quizzical face, smiling eyes though not smiling mouth. Does not wear heart on sleeve. Where is it, then? Says relations with his sons distant. No touching, not even an arm round the shoulder. The very idea turns him to stone. Admits this is sadly English. I recalled that Sachie [Sitwell] always called his sons 'darling', which led to odd looks in railway carriages. Philip is writing Osbert [Sitwell]'s life. I warned him that I hardly knew Osbert, or Edith.‡ We talked of the Sitwells' pretence of being Bohemian, whereas at heart they were true-blue landed gentry. They didn't really like Bloomsbury. Edith revered Osbert because he was head of the family, though she preferred Sachie. I piloted Philip round the garden, which he duly admired. I know very well now how A. felt when conducting ignorant people and having to listen to their inane remarks. 'How pretty those blue flowers are. Oh roses, really? I like a good show but am no expert' etc.

Sunday, 23rd July

The Henry [Robinson]s gave a lunch party at Moorwood for me to meet their friends the Shelburnes.§ I felt proud of Henry and Susy, such good hosts. No showing off, perfectly natural and delightful. A good luncheon of just two courses, Henry almost patriarchal with the carving knife. I was seated next to Shelburne. He is out to charm and

---

* Writer, poet, publisher and critic (1907–87); brother of Rosamond.
† Philip Ziegler (b. 1929); publisher, historian and critic.
‡ Dame Edith Sitwell (1887–1964); sister of Osbert and Sacheverell; poet and critic.
§ Charles Maurice Petty-Fitzmaurice (b. 1941); e. s. of 8th Marquess of Lansdowne (whom he succeeded as 9th Marquess, 1999); m. 1st 1965 Lady Frances Eliot, o. dau. of 9th Earl of St Germans, 2nd 1987 Fiona, dau. of Lady Davies and Donald Merritt.

succeeds. Very good-looking, almost film-starish, now inclining to broadness of the jowl. Dressed in well-cut light brown summer suit, with turned cuffs. Signet ring. Spoke of English Heritage, of which he is a retired Commissioner. Enjoyed it enormously. Said the Tories were indifferent to the cause, and Labour showed more interest. I said it was also thus in my day, that monster Dalton* being the benefactor of the N.T. She is enchanting, a sort of Penelope Betjeman type. Both are fans of my diaries and quote therefrom. I dropped two bricks. When I said that nothing good came from the United States, he remarked that his mother was American; and when I said I had heard that Ozleworth was overdone, he said his wife had decorated it. But we all seemed to like one another and they said I must come over to Bowood [House, Calne, Wiltshire].† He asked if I was an optimist or a pessimist. I said, 'How could I possibly be the first, having witnessed the ruination of the world?' 'I am an optimist,' he replied, 'although I agree with you.' Jane Westmorland who rang this morning said he suffered from terrible depressions.

Sunday, 30th July

Ian [Dixon] drove me to the wedding of Dale's son Tristan‡ at Silton church near Gillingham [Dorset]. An absolutely grilling day. Mercifully, as it turned out, we were late. Church was packed and we saw congregation fanning themselves furiously, so remained in the pretty porch with painted groining overhead, stencilling by Clayton & Bell, and a fairly cool breeze. Men in long tails and women in enormous hats. A thoroughly rural lot. When bridal pair about to march out and face cameras we, in order not to steal thunder, went and hid in the churchyard. Splendid view across old tombstones to a lake. Suddenly I remembered coming here thirty or more years ago with Mrs Esdaile, who showed me the marvellous Baroque monument to a Wyndham by John van Nost. There must have been a great house nearby. We knew no one but the Robinson brothers and their wives. I resolutely declined to go on to the reception; the sight of the

---

* Hugh Dalton (1887–1962); Labour politician, who as Chancellor of the Exchequer from 1945 to 1947 sought to bestow some fiscal advantages on the N.T.
† See entry for 15 June 1997.
‡ J.L.-M's great-nephew Tristan Sutton (b. 1966); landscape gardener; m. Catherine Louise Masters (b. 1972).

farmhouse festooned with balloons was enough to deter, heatwave or no heatwave. Instead I went back inside the church to look at the monument, followed by the family who seemed surprised that I knew about it and the sculptor. The heat so intense and the airlessness so oppressive that I was practically in a coma throughout and knowing not what I was doing or saying.

Wednesday, 2nd August

I am mad about Mr Peter Jones, the oculist. A very quiet and learned man, not liked by Peggy's sort who find him taciturn. I dare say he is with those to whom he has nothing worth his while to communicate. I like his authoritative manner. I happened to mention that I was rather colour-blind and had a devil of a job concealing it all the years I was responsible for the maintenance and decoration of N.T. houses. So he presented me with an album of many-tinted designs, as though of linoleum, in reds and greens, I having said that green was my chief uncertainty. He said, 'Tell me the numbers on each plate, one by one, as you flip through them.' I said, 'But there are no numbers.' 'Just as I supposed,' he said. Dead proof I am very colour-blind.

Thursday, 3rd August

I summon Chris Nash to examine my book room [at Essex House] because I contemplate another range of shelves if the wall will support them. I am amazed by his handsomeness and well-dressedness for a plumber who has been busily working all day. Yet there is something, not so much cocky, but smart-aleck about him which grates. He says the wall will support. Then tells that tomorrow, he, his wife and two kids are all off by road to Provence, where they have rented a house. They all do this. I suppose the Cotswolds will be brimming with Japanese and Chinese doing this here next year.

Friday, 4th August

Nick stays the night. I consult him about quitting Bath. He persuades me not to. Says I must not feel guilty about living here in three sitting rooms. He advises me to find out from Clarissa when I next see her whether she is truly in penury, and in need of my library floor. I have no mind of my own, that's the trouble.

Sunday, 6th August

My birthday. People telephone. In church I thought I might write my masterpiece about the Communion service, telling the history of each prayer, lesson and phrase, explaining how it took shape in apostolic times. Leaving the churchyard I was greeted by Miranda, who announced that '*We* are going to Scotland for a week.' I wonder what the vicar makes of her, the scarlet woman.

Seven [Robinson] great-great-nieces and nephews brought to tea by their parents, Susy providing food. Too many for me to take in. It was rather chaotic and I didn't enjoy it as much as I ought. I thought the little girls more attractive than the little boys, although Alexander* is rather engaging in a guttersnipe way. He is quite grown up and says, 'Uncle Jim, your garden is very tidy.' Then they sang 'Happy Birthday to You' out of tune, which I dislike whether in or out of.

Saturday, 12th August

This morning Nick motored me to inspect his new house which is finished, and empty awaiting their move thereto. I liked it. A bungalow in original style, yet traditional. Very spacious. One large room with high open-raftered ceiling. A sort of cottage *pas orné*, for no bargeboards where you expect them. Nice unvarnished floorboards. Clapboarding outside. Odd triangular dormer windows. I could be quite happy in it myself. Good situation with south view of Downs. It is certainly isolated, and may be windy and cold in winter. Perhaps a certain Japanese flimsiness about the structure, as though it might blow away in a high wind. But all in all I approve. Nick is the best man in the world, and the human being I am now most fond of.

J.L.-M. went with Debo Devonshire to spend a week with Diana Mosley at the Temple de la Gloire, Orsay, which he had last visited in 1986. They travelled through the Channel Tunnel, which had opened that summer.

Tuesday, 5th September

Leave for my visit to Orsay, staying night with Debo in Chesterfield Street. The Leigh Fermors and Nico Hendersons appear and Debo

---

* Alexander Robinson (b. 1985); e. s. of Henry Robinsons.

takes us all to Mark's Club. The purpose of this club is the entertain-
ment of multi-millionaires. The dining room arranged to look like a
stuffy old Victorian house, walls crammed with Landseers. Very good
food. Nico revealed that he was chairman of the Committee which
produced the Channel Tunnel. Said it was sobering to realise that, ten
years ago, not even the design was on paper. He was the only member
of the Committee who could speak a word of French, or had any idea
of human relations.

Wednesday, 6th September

Debo and I driven by Alan to Waterloo for 10.30 train to Paris.
Received by galaxy of young ladies and taken down long, tunnel-
shaped, glass-roofed way. We go first class. The Eurostar carriages a
smart blue and white outside. Inside, seats upholstered a dusky blue
velveteen, not chic. Numerous attendants in white shirts and braided
epaulettes. Almost immediately after leaving we are presented with
menus for luncheon. This soon comes and is pretty horrid, like aeroplane food. Motion wonderfully smooth and gliding. After the tunnel,
which takes twenty minutes and has no lights at all, like the tube only
darker, we shoot out into dull, flat landscape of northern France.
Open prairie; no pasture, scarcely a hedge. We are met at Gare du
Nord by Diana's [manservant] Gerry and motored to Orsay. A slow
drive in dense traffic, traffic lights every hundred metres. The Paris
streets with their nineteenth-century architecture are far wider,
grander and nobler than muddy old London.

Diana marvellously bright, her broken wrist mending. Upright,
slender, beautiful. When I present her with the prettiest imaginable
little plate, rather rare because of some Scottish factory, she says in
thanking, 'It will do very well for an ashtray.'

I said to D., 'Surely when Sir O. was active and after you had been
to prison you must often have been insulted by people?' She replied
in that Mitford voice, 'Insult was the most wonderful advertisement.
We never had the slightest difficulty getting servants. They flocked.'

Priscilla Hodgson,* recently widowed, lunched one day. Daughter

---

* Priscilla Bibesco; o. c. of Prince Antoine Bibesco and Lady Elizabeth Asquith, o. dau.
of H. H. Asquith by his 2nd wife 'Margot' Tennant (1864–1945); daringly escaped from
Romania, where her parents were trapped during Second World War, to join her grandmother in England.

of Antoine Bibesco and Elizabeth Asquith. Has affected Twentyish voice of her grandmother Margot. Clever, chain-smoking, drinking, dusty. When she is speaking, she carries her head slightly to one side, as I remember her aunt Violet Bonham Carter[*] doing.

The white swan seldom takes to the pond and sits at the kitchen door, for company and food. Treated like a pet dog or cat, and has been here twenty-five years.

Have immersed myself in Bertrand Russell's[†] autobiography and essays. Very witty man and devoid of prejudices. Although he wrote half a century ago, all his views are pertinent still. His message is that there is never any excuse for war. He wrote in the Sixties that the world was in the most parlous state in its history – though things may be worse now, with chaos in the East and the growth of unresolvable terrorism. Strange that he never makes any reference to the menace of over-population.

J.L.-M's diary was interrupted when he fell ill at Orsay. He did however write interesting descriptions of the main rooms at the Temple de la Gloire, which he considered redolent of Diana Mosley's wonderful taste.

The dining room is the original entrance hall, with clever fitted carpet of black and white squares feigning paving. Walls Etruscan red with a touch of orange. Fireplace of blood-red speckled marble (might be Brocatello) in Directoire Egyptian style, the supports being Pharaoh heads in white, feet protruding below. Marble hearthstone matching chimneypiece. Above hangs Tchelitchev[‡] oil of peasant with outsize folded hands – the only picture in this shaded room, which came from Geoffrey Gilmour[§] to whom D. was so devoted. The four corners of the room cleverly fashioned by D. as half-Ionic pilasters, in fact concealing unremovable downpipes within. Simple Louis XVI grey chairs with striped upholstery round a circular plain Directoire table, under a cylindrical hanging lantern of glass and brass. Pair of Directoire chests of drawers opposite a rustic Louis XVI table with marble top. Against east wall, where proper entrance is,

---

[*] Lady Violet Asquith (1887–1969); dau. of H. H. Asquith by his 1st marriage; political campaigner and broadcaster; m. 1915 Sir Maurice Bonham Carter; cr. life peer, 1964.
[†] Philosopher and social reformer (1872–1970); s. 1951 as 3rd Earl Russell.
[‡] Pavel Tchelitchev (1898–1957); Russian-born artist.
[§] Anglo-Argentine millionaire living in Paris (d. 1982).

stands a noble bust of Lord Chatham in bronze on marble plinth, occupying doorway. The west wall gives onto a substructure below the great Ionic tetrastyle portico with side perrons. The windows have white damask curtains tied by black loops. On either side of this garden entrance a pair of mirrors *appliqués*, with engraved figures of Orpheus and Eurydice.

Above this is the salon, a large high room facing east and west, approached from the garden front by a pair of side perrons in two short flights without handrails. It is approached from Diana's boudoir and the antechamber to the bedroom which Sir O. used by tall double-winged doorways on the south and north fronts. On the east wall a high central window with semi-circular fan. West side entirely glazed. (Formerly, judging by the Corot sketch, there were three attic windows, now indicated by plaster panels within.) The entrance door from the garden is between giant Ionic columns supporting a cornice of gentle brackets between little rosettes. Ceiling flat with quite simple central octagonal motif, from which a splendid glass and ormolu chandelier hangs. The high panelled walls have no paintings within their vertical gesso frames. A large worn Aubusson carpet covers wooden floor. In middle of room a circular Directoire table for folios, the cavetto sides enclosed within interlaced brass grilles, and buff silk hangings. Incised leather top; claw feet. Within east window a chaise longue of maplewood inlaid with rosewood Egyptian devices, upholstered in velvet. On either side a pair of delicious small inlaid marble tables. A wonderful pair of Directoire commodes, marble-topped, veneered, with central wreaths and ormolu embellishments on the front. They stand under a Louis XV clock and barometer, which came from D's grandfather Redesdale at Batsford [Gloucestershire].

He returned from France on 13 September.

Wednesday, 20th September

Am reading Henry James's *The Awkward Age* [1899], truly an awkward book and difficult to keep the attention fixed, especially when lying abed after luncheon. It is all dialogue and convoluted explanations as a small social clique talk around in riddles. Sentences are unfinished, or when finished end with interrogation marks, though no one bothers to answer. Yet I find it clever and rewarding, and am often amused. The prim, old-maidish James avoids the slightest reference to illicit love, yet the prurient can detect pointers.

Have done little since my return. Few letters to answer, mercifully. My reprinted diaries came out last Thursday.* Two young people from Bristol BBC came yesterday to interview me for a series on the aristocracy, speaking of aristocrats as if they were the atrophied and infertile grandchildren of dinosaurs. They asked if I thought they still played a small part in provincial life, having ceased to do so in national politics. They seemed quite sympathetic to the upper classes but did not have a vestige of understanding of the life they led before the war. How could they, a young man and young woman of middle-class background bringing up families in Bristol?

Monday, 25th September

Have read obituary of Princess Chichibu of Japan† who was a renowned philanthropist, rather an unusual thing to be in that country. I think she must be the widow of the Prince C. who was at Eton with me. He was a stocky, swarthy boy with an incipient moustache, large face, small eyes and a benign expression. I thought at the time that it was extraordinary to see at my school a boy from the Far East, even if he was a potentate's son. I remember staring at him as though he descended from the moon, something so alien that I wanted to pinch him to see if he were real. Japan so distant in those days, and I so provincial.

A bad dream last night. I was in some marvellous Italian *salone* with Gerry Wellington,‡ Sachie Sitwell, and Sachie's two sons. On two occasions, the Sitwell boys set fire to precious objects – first a canvas, then a tapestry panel. The fires were quickly extinguished. Gerry and I expressed horror at this vandalism, but Sachie took it calmly and did not rebuke the boys. This nightmare may have been provoked by the recent news of a fire at Tony Lambton's beautiful Cetinale, gutting the *salone* with its treasures.

---

* John Murray had reissued the four volumes of J.L.-M's 1940s diaries (originally published 1975–85) in a two-volume edition.
† Matsudaira Setsuko (1909–95); m. 1928 Prince Chichibu (1902–53), brother of Emperor Hirohito.
‡ Lord Gerald Wellesley (1885–1972); s. nephew 1943 as 7th Duke of Wellington; architect and architectural conservationist; m. 1914 Dorothy Ashton.

Wednesday, 27th September

To London. Most of my plans went awry. Grant who was to lunch telephoned that he had influenza; young man who was to come to tea to talk of Raymond Mortimer* also chucked; Derry [Drogheda] failed to turn up for breakfast. The car Radio 2 was due to send, for my appearance on the John Dunn show, never turned up, so I had to go to them by cab. Dunn† a nice man, looking forty though he turned out to be sixty-one. Asked me dull questions for ten minutes about my republished wartime diaries, to be broadcast in the intervals of dreadful music.

In the London Library, Adam Nicolson‡ came up for a chat. Sweet expression in the eyes of his oval, handsome face, which is Vita's, not Harold's. Laughingly said that everyone in his family had been divorced. The pictures of him in the newspapers convey an impression of him as complacent and uppity, but he is in fact amusing and sympathetic, liberal (like all his family) about both life and the things of the mind.

Freda dined at Brooks's. She talked about Father Michael Hollings, whom she has taken in following his disgrace.§ Showed me the wicked article in the *News of the World* with its allegations of homosexual gropings twenty-five years ago. A tall order for Freda, who nevertheless staunchly supports him as the holiest and best of men. He prays for two hours at 5 a.m. and then says Mass which Freda attends in her dining room. 'I have never prayed so much in my life.' The only time I met him, I was not attracted: drunken, dirty, and jealous of Freda's attention to others. Just like the late Father Illtyd Evans, and Father Napier-Hemy who received me,¶ batteners on the hospitality of old ladies and inclined to the bottle.

---

* Literary reviewer, sometime lover of Harold Nicolson, and co-tenant of Long Crichel (1895–1980).
† Broadcaster (1934–2005).
‡ Writer and journalist (b. 1957); o. s. of Nigel Nicolson; m. 1st 1982 (diss. 1992) Olivia Fane, 2nd 1993 Sarah Raven.
§ Having been accused by the *News of the World* of an alleged sexual indiscretion, Hollings was evicted from his parish by a nervous Westminster diocese, and offered refuge by Freda Berkeley, a devoted parishioner. After a police investigation, he was exonerated and restored to his parish; but the ordeal had affected his health, and he died in February 1997.
¶ At Westminster Cathedral in 1934.

Friday, 29th September

Lunched with the adorable Jessica Douglas-Home that was. Don't know her present name; no sign of current husband and no mention made. In spite of being middle-aged, Jessica has the same charm for me, with her strange elusive shyness and sweet affectionate manner. Walking around Henriette's* beautiful garden on the Coln River she tucked my arm in hers. She has a wistful, other-worldly way of speaking. Talked of her book about her Aunt Violet Woodhouse and her relations with her four husbands.† She believes Gordon Woodhouse was a homosexual, for whom Violet made a suitable wife as she was terrified of physical love. Is very excited by receipt of letter from archivist of Gordon's Cambridge college informing her that G. was sacked in mid-stream on account of some unmentionable conduct. Am haunted by Jessica's beauty. She is a faun-like creature of the woods, still the withdrawn little girl. She says I am now a cult figure among thirty-year-olds. Can it be?

Thursday, 19th October

Alec Douglas-Home‡ who has died at an advanced age is described by the press as the last upper-class prime minister. He was certainly a gentleman, which is more than can be said for any of the present cabinet, excepting Cranborne§ and Waldegrave. When I was a new boy at Eton he – Dunglass then – was in his last year. I remember him walking away from the 'fives' court putting on his long woollen scarf which reached below his bare knees, looking not handsome but distinguished. He was one of those rare Etonians admired by both masters and boys.

---

* Henriette, Lady Abel Smith (1914–2005; DCVO 1977), of Quenington, Gloucestershire.
† Violet Gwynne (1870–1948); m. 1895 Gordon Woodhouse; harpsichordist, who lived in a *ménage à cinq* with four men, as well as having lesbian associations. Jessica's biography, *Violet: The Life and Loves of Violet Gordon Woodhouse*, was published by Harvill Press in 1996.
‡ Conservative politician (1903–95); Prime Minister, 1963–4; s. 1951 as 14th Earl of Home but disclaimed peerages on attaining premiership, 1963; cr. life peer as Lord Home of the Hirsel, 1974.
§ Robert Cecil, Viscount Cranborne (b. 1946); e. s. of 6th Marquess of Salisbury (whom he s. as 7th Marquess, 2003, though sitting in House of Lords from 1992 under a writ of acceleration); Conservative politician, friend of John Major; Leader of House of Lords, 1992–7.

Today the dear Henrys called for me at nine and we drove to Uppark* in their smart and swift Mercedes. House even more marvellously reinstated than I imagined from the photographs. In fact it would be difficult to recognise that it had been burnt to a shell and rebuilt. Nearly all the contents back *in situ*. By some miracle the downstairs floors, one of Uppark's notable features, escaped burning. Gesso, carving, most beautifully reinstated. I was moved near to tears. I had a strangely warm welcome from the staff, not one of whom knew me personally, only by repute and from my damned diaries I suppose. A lovely day. View towards the Channel and Isle of Wight absolutely unchanged, not a building within sight.

Sunday, 22nd October

Have been alone this weekend and quite content, working at *Straight and Bent*. This evening, while shutting up, I distinctly heard A's voice calling to me, sounding urgent rather than frightened, as if she wanted me to come quickly. I answered, as I would have done, 'Yes, here I am. Coming.' I stopped and listened. There was no answer, and the house went cold and empty. Now, was she calling to me when she fell to her death? Did I hear some kind of ghostly echo? So dreadful to think of. Each time I pass the front door, I try not to look at the flagstones on which she fell, and concentrate my gaze instead on the incense rose.

Friday, 27th October

Tony Mitchell takes me in his motor to Flintham. Kind as kind. On the way we call at Farnborough Hall. The old Holbeches† show us round this enchanting house, in which they are allowed to live by the N.T. somewhat on sufferance. Very nice people, he looking older than his father looked when I was last here in 1955. It is a delightful place, though now disturbed by a motorway half a mile from the west front.

---

* William and Mary house in South Downs, donated to N.T. by Meade-Fetherstonhaugh family in 1954, J.L.-M. being involved in negotiations. The house had been devastated by fire six years earlier (as reported by J.L.-M. on 1 September 1989), though much of the contents was saved.
† Geoffrey Holbech (b. 1918), whose family had lived at Farnborough Hall, Warwickshire, for three hundred years; m. (2nd) 1950 Elizabeth Harrison.

A country gentleman's seat of Charles II's reign, of local orange Horton stone, decent and unpretentious. Entrance hall very splendid, niches filled with busts of emperors. Dining room *c.* 1740, Rococo plaster ceiling. John Cornforth here yesterday and they didn't much like him. I say to Tony, 'You can bet your bottom dollar that we shall read in *Country Life* that the ceiling relief work is not stucco but *papier mâché.*'

We reach Flintham for tea. Myles looking craggy and splendid. He amuses me by saying the only common drop of blood we have in our veins comes from the Crawshays. He says he is fed up caring for this huge house. All he wants are his pictures and his books. But he calculates he would need another house as large as Flintham to contain them, so is staying where he is. In fact he has made something stupendous of Flintham. It is stacked with family treasures. His parents thought it hideous and so hated it that they did not bother to mess it about. And the uncle from whom he inherited would alter nothing which his father had created. So it is still untouched, redecorated as it was when first built.

Simon Thurley,* an extremely handsome young man, stays the night. Runs those royal palaces which are not inhabited by the Court. Very bright.

Saturday, 28th October

To Gervase's Requiem Mass at All Saint's, Northampton. Two hours of superb music, Haydn. Seven hundred sign book. Gervase left a special request that all present should take the sacrament – and nearly all do. What an influence he had on his friends.

Then Tatton Sykes stays the night at Flintham. I fear a smartyboots. Not so. Great charm, and gentleness. I like him immensely.

We visit Bunney [Nottinghamshire]. Extremely eccentric house like a Vanburghian church with absurd belvedere rising from Baroque pediment. Effigy of boxing baronet in church, hands out, palms upwards.

Weather has been sublime during this visit. Mist and mellow fruitfulness, warm sunlight and long shadows. Sunday lunch in small drawing room, between open French windows and a roaring fire, delicious and memorable. Both Tony and I have thoroughly enjoyed ourselves.

---

* Dr Simon Thurley (b. 1962); Curator, Historic Royal Palaces, 1990–7; Director, Museum of London, 1997–2002; Chief Executive, English Heritage, from 2002.

Myles discloses that when in 1939 his regiment, the Sherwood Rangers, went to France to fight, they took not just their horses but their hounds with them. The French made them send the hounds back to England.

Saturday, 4th November

I am sad over Desmond [Shawe-Taylor]'s death. Though it is just as well, as Freda says, for he was going the same way as Lennox, and derived no pleasure from life. Des, so abounding in enthusiasms, so excitable, so fussy about a newspaper being crumpled instead of carefully folded, so very, very clever, so affectionate, sometimes in his enthusiasm laying his head on one's shoulder. I feel sure he knew more about music than any man has ever done, and his programme notes summed up every piece in exquisite prose and with perfect understanding. He is the last of the Long Crichel four* with whom I so often stayed, enjoying their hospitality, good food, talk and fun.

Thursday, 16th November

I lunch with Grant McIntyre in Italian restaurant in Albemarle Street. Good single dish and no drinks. I hand him the typescript of *Straight and Bent* which I regard as finished by me. I now await his comments. Grant tells me that his wife's car was attacked by a rutting stag in some park recently. The car a wreck, windows broken by antlers, though she and the two children within mercifully unharmed.

Diana Mosley and Nancy Osborne Hill, with whom she is staying at the Connaught, dined with me at Brooks's. Very enjoyable. Diana looking extremely distinguished and beautiful in Japanese velvet coatee. Talking of Dr Johnson's habit of debunking everyone and everything, we laughed till we cried. Nancy has a pretty face, but not a lively mind.

Ken Davison,† whom I ran into at Brooks's, tells me he is now Lord Broughshane – pronounced Bre*shane*.

---

* See entry for 24 December 1995.
† Hon. Kensington Davison DSO, DFC (b. 1914); yr s. of Sir William Davison (1872–1953), Mayor of Kensington, 1913–19, MP for South Kensington, 1918–45, cr. Baron Broughshane, 1945; s. brother as 3rd Baron, 1995.

Monday, 20th November

Jeffrey Haworth telephones that the N.T. Committee has agreed to purchase 700 acres of Croome Court park and gardens and temples, though not the house which will be saved by other means, as will the outlying Rotonda and Sham Castle. Says my letter was circulated to all and sundry and helped get this through. I am jubilant.

Tuesday, 21st November

Watched Princess of Wales on BBC last night. An astonishing performance. Never having heard her speak before, I imagined she would be like a silly little debutante. On the contrary, she was adult and articulate. A low, croaky voice slipping into Northolt 'eows'. Very beautiful, cocking her head to the left, lovely mouth, enormous clear eyes. Claimed that the cause of the marital breakdown was media intrusion, which became persecution. She did not criticise Prince or Family directly, yet left watchers with no doubt that she hated the lot. Venom visible in every gesture and look. Said they held her to be an embarrassment and a danger. I dare say. Won't consent to divorce on account of her sons. Respectful about the Queen, and in favour of the monarchy, which however must bring itself up to date. Admitted adultery with the disgraced major.* I don't know that I like her more than hitherto, and I am not particularly taken in by her professions of love for ordinary people, but I respect her for her candour and for so boldly confronting millions.

Thursday, 23rd November

I have received a letter from Alex Moulton telling me that he was most offended by what I had written about him in my diaries published last year.† I have read the entry and can't for the life of me find anything offensive. I have replied expressing bewilderment.

---

* James Hewitt of the Life Guards (b. 1958).
† On 8 August 1953, J.L.-M. describes their going on a jaunt on the river Avon, during which they admired 'idyllic youths bathing', and removed their clothes to lie in a field of cut hay.

Friday, 1st December

I am a little cross with Misha for passing on to Matthew Parris* some insalubrious material which the Bretts made me remove from the original manuscript of my Lord Esher biography. Parris has published it (fortunately without reference to me) in the chapter on Loulou Harcourt† in his book *Great Parliamentary Scandals*, and it has provoked a hurt letter from the grandson of Maurice Brett. Not surprising, for I do not forget the aggrieved letter I received from Maurice's daughters.‡ M. is an admirer of Parris, whereas I find his *Times* column facetious and irritating. Moreover, I don't like these flaunting homosexuals with their pleased-with-themselves attitude, as though they were deprived and stood for a noble cause. It isn't a noble cause. It is a mistake.

Saturday, 2nd December

This evening I dined at the House, the first time I had been there since Caroline's death. Dear Miranda present, and Eddie, and the silent Carol§ who rather oddly took Caroline's place at the foot of the table. David absolutely charming. Full of funny stories about local dinners he has to attend. He talked of Caroline's eccentricity, saying she was so unselfconscious as to be totally unaware of it. I said a person would not be eccentric if aware of it; it was the unawareness of their absurdities which made them eccentric. He said Tony Lambton was similarly unselfconscious, though it would probably be better if he were more 'aware' when he asked unknown young women whether they had yet been seduced, where and by whom. No awkwardness at all in this evening's meeting after so many months. They had all seen the Princess's broadcast and were very much against her, convinced she is

---

* Politician, writer and journalist (b. 1946); MP (C) West Derbyshire, 1979–86.

† Lewis, 1st Viscount Harcourt (1863–1922); Liberal statesman with paedophile interests; committed suicide at 69 Brook Street (now the Savile Club) after unsuccessfully attempting to seduce J.L.-M's Eton contemporary Edward James (1907–84).

‡ In his biography (*The Enigmatic Edwardian*, Sidgwick & Jackson, 1986) of Reginald, 2nd Viscount Esher (1852–1930), J.L.-M. made extraordinary revelations about his subject's intimacy with his yr son Hon. Maurice Brett (1882–1934). The family requested certain modifications; but enough remained to 'horrify' Maurice's daughters (see *Beneath a Waning Moon*, 19 October 1986).

§ Lord Edward Somerset and wife Caroline.

actuated by malice and mischief. David also spoke of how Mad Cow Disease* is ruining the beef farmers, merely because of a scare whipped up by the press.

David pointed out that he had had the fluted columns of the staircase hall painted white. It is certainly an improvement visually on the brown that was there before, probably introduced by Wyatville. D. said, 'I feel disloyal to Caroline who opposed the change, but was fortified in my decision by the approval you had given.' I don't remember venturing any opinion at all. Anyway it's done now, and the hall is brighter and the architecture more assertive.

Monday, 11th December

It occurs to me that I once knew an old lady – viz. Princess Winnie de Polignac – whose father-in-law had sat on the knee of Marie Antoinette before the fall of the Bastille.† He was seven at the time, and his mother was the Queen's favourite lady. He went on to become Prime Minister under Charles X. Clarissa, who also knew the Princess, will be able to tell her great-grandchildren of this link going back more than two centuries.

Wednesday, 13th December

Tony Scotland has confided to me his fears that Father Michael is taking Freda over. I verily believe there is something sinister about him. Tony once overheard Father M. being extraordinarily rude to F. He rounded on him and said, 'Never let me hear you speak to her like that again.' These Papist Fathers. Father Illtyd battening onto Eliza Wansbrough and Father Napier-Hemy onto old Mrs Astley Cooper,‡ eating and drinking these doting ladies out of house and

---

* The scare became a panic in March 1996 when the Government admitted that the disease might cause a similar fatal disorder in humans.

† In 1893, aged twenty-eight, Winaretta Singer had embarked on a short but happy marriage to the elderly, homosexual Prince Edmond de Polignac (1834–1901), whose father, Jules Armand de Polignac (1780–1847), chief minister under Charles X, was the son of the Duchesse de Polignac, Marie-Antoinette's lady-in-waiting.

‡ Evangeline Marshall (1854–1944); heiress to shipping fortune; m. 1877 Major Clement Paston Astley Cooper, yst s. of Sir Astley Paston Cooper, 1st Bt; châtelaine of Hambleton Hall, Rutlandshire, where she presided over a salon of young aesthetes including Noël Coward; see entry for 16 April 1997.

home. They get the old ladies in their clutches. And they drink like
soaks for all their vaunted piety.

Tuesday, 19th December

It is strange and gratifying to receive by post from Heywood Hill the
1813 edition of Byron's *Giaour*, with my book-plate therein and
Byron's inscription on the fly-leaf, which I lent Dame Una [Pope-
Hennessy] when she was writing about Byron in 1939. On her death
in 1949 I asked Jamesey if he had come across it among her books.
No, he said. And long after Jamesey's death, I asked John. Never seen
or heard of it, he said. Now Michael Mallon is selling all John's
possessions and it has turned up at Heywood Hill, and kind John
Saumarez rang me up to ask how it got among the Pope-Hennessy
books. For a moment I couldn't remember; then the loan to Dame
Una came back to my memory. The long and short is that Michael
Mallon, who has had the binding beautifully restored, has offered it
back to me. I am grateful, and have no compunction in accepting after
more than fifty years.

*J.L.-M. was invited to spend Christmas again at Chatsworth, but declined as
he felt he had been accepting the Devonshires' hospitality too often. He then
arranged to go to Venice with Derry Drogheda to stay with Anna-Maria
Cicogna, but cancelled in mid December owing to health problems. He finally
spent two nights at Long Crichel with Pat Trevor-Roper and Derek Hill.*

Friday, 22nd December

I take the little train from Bath to Salisbury, having to stand in a
crammed carriage. Very awkward and tiring. At Salisbury, no one to
meet me. Eventually Derek turns up, explaining that Pat's car has
broken down. Derek whisks me off in a taxi to Ted Heath's[*] house,
Arundell's, in the Close. In rather proprietary way, Derek rings bell at
much-barred iron gate. Nice detective and male servant come to gate.
D. explains that Sir Edward is coming to Long Crichel this evening,
and presumes he will gladly give both of us a lift. We are taken through
courtyard. Pretty Queen Anne front. A message is conveyed to Sir

---

[*] Sir Edward Heath (1916–2005); Conservative Prime Minister, 1970–4; possessed
musical interests.

Edward, who allows us to sit in a back room, like a dentist's waiting room, for two hours until he condescends to appear. Detective brings us each a cup of milky tea slopping into saucer and slice of inedible fruit cake. For two hours we lounge, chat to one another, and doze.

The inside of this house very disappointing, and has been much tampered with throughout the centuries. From a dreary flagged hall a long straight passage leads past a drawing room on left (unseen) to the sitting room in which we wait, which is totally without taste. Ceiling spotlights focus on nothing worth looking at. Several tiers of watercolours of yachts on green seas. On small tables stand photographs in silver frames of Queen, Duke of Edinburgh, Sir W. Churchill hideous in Garter robes. Shelves of neatly ranged books on music, mostly of coffee-table sort. Flesh-pink upholstered sofa. Chinese plate upright in fireplace. A nice lady housekeeper shows me with pride the dining room, a long narrow rectangle – nice John Piper* paintings, but room very ugly.

At 6.15 Heath appears at door wearing blue-and-white striped pullover. Enormous behind bulging over baggy trousers. Quite short he is, up to my shoulder. Appearance suggests a beer barrel aboard deck poised on two inadequate supports. Has his own snowy hair over that prominent proboscis. Is utterly without charm or grace. Shakes hands perfunctorily. No word of greeting. But drives us to Long Crichel. Chauffeur and nice detective in front; I wedged in excruciating discomfort between Heath and Derek on hard middle ridge of rear seat, almost crushed by their enormous, bulging bodies. Only twenty-five-minute drive, mercifully. Derek talks in very familiar terms across me. Has painted Heath and knows him fairly well. H. answers him in monosyllables until they get on to subject of some Japanese artist whose masterpiece H. has just bought for his collection.

On arrival at Long Crichel, Heath advances straight into drawing room, barely greeting Pat, who is after all his host. Within half an hour he has stuffed two sacks with music tapes from Desmond [Shawe-Taylor]'s collection, probably the most complete in the world, Derek having persuaded Desmond's nephew-heir to allow Heath to choose 'a few'. He leaves behind a very bad impression. The one thing in his favour is that he is scrupulously clean. On leaving he does shake my hand and says it has been nice to see me again. A man of no breeding,

---

* Artist and theatrical designer (1903–92).

spoilt by circumstances, and arrogant. Odd that such could rise to be Prime Minister. Desmond, whose judgement was unmatched, conceded that Heath was musically more than an amateur.

Sunday, 24th December

Two nights at Long Crichel. My name appears on the first page of the first visitors' book of this vastly visited house in 1945, the year that Eddy Sackville-West, Desmond and Eardley [Knollys] went to live there, soon to be joined by Raymond [Mortimer]. That was exactly half a century ago. Still the same beautiful deep-rose wallpaper of watered damask pattern in the drawing room. House inevitably a little gone to seed. They only have Mrs Best (whom Derek dislikes, the dislike no doubt returned). She is a wonderful cook, and meals are a joy. I have an 'up' on Pat, who is less debunking than formerly. Is tranquil, philosophical and calm, but maddened by Derek who has become extremely tiresome, bossy and self-centred. Pat told me that Derek never reads a book, listens to music, or goes to exhibitions except of his own paintings. On the whole I have enjoyed myself, but I just do not like staying in other people's houses any more. I read much of the time. On Saturday, a crowd of neighbours came for drinks, invited by Derek.

Tuesday, 26th December

Motored to lunch with Charles and Mary Keen. The nice clever actor son* there, and the rather severe-looking unmarried daughter. Mary mysterious about her career; she showed us photographs of her learning to be a pistol markswoman, but would not comment on the rumour that she had been a spy in Russia. The Henry [Robinson]s there too, with their children; so good of Mary to have us all. Lovely simple food, and the house so cosy. I drove home early, for I cannot see in the gloaming. I am content to be alone here in the warmth, at Badminton.

---

* William Keen (b. 1970); last mentioned 6 July 1992, when he was a leading light of OUDS.

1996

Between Christmas and the New Year the weather has been record-breaking for arctic conditions. The cold really agonising. How lucky, I keep repeating to myself, that I am at home and not stranded in someone else's house, nor someone else in mine.

Angelic Nick motored me to Bath and back in dense fog. I fetched the large folio books and the ottoman containing my diaries, and left a letter for Clarissa telling her that she really must make up her mind whether she wants to live in Bath, now that the Bath Preservation Trust are unable to take over my library.

Wednesday, 3rd January

I am reading the biography of Mrs Jordan* by Clare Tomalin.† Really, the Royal Dukes were ghastly, selfish, stupid, uncultivated and gross. Mrs J. an angel of sweetness. She must have had charm of a most elusive sort. All those children by Clarence – one a year for thirteen years. I have come to the conclusion that the aristocracy have always been shits, and that in my youth I was too beguiled by them. Nevertheless, I still maintain that the decent and educated ones attain a standard of well-being and good-doing which has never been transcended by any other class in the world.

Monday, 8th January

Desmond Briggs has lent me Mirabel Cecil's biographical anthology of her brother Sebastian Walker.‡ Rather good in a documentary way.

---

* Dorothea Jordan (*née* Bland; 1762–1816); Irish actress who was mistress of the future King William IV from 1790 to 1811, bearing him ten illegitimate children.
† Writer (b. 1933); literary editor, *Sunday Times*, 1979–86.
‡ Mirabel Walker; writer and journalist; m. 1972 Hugh Cecil (b. 1941), yr s. of J.L.-M's friend Lord David Cecil (1902–86). Her biography of her publisher brother, *Sebastian Walker, 1942–1991: A Kind of Prospero*, was published by Walker Books in January 1996.

He had reservoirs of charm and a great sense of fun, allied to a drive
to get on and make his fortune, not for love of money but for the sense
of power it gave him, and the opportunity to perform good works. I
didn't like him much, and his vulgarity and outrageous behaviour
made me squirm. He had no reserve, and wanted to experience every
sensation allowed by nature. Physically he was revolting, disguising
himself behind a hideous square beard so as to look like every other
middle-class aspiring philosopher. Terrible his death from Aids, when
he was doing so many worthy things.

Wednesday, 10th January

I said to Mr Davis, my dentist, that I will have incised on my tomb-
stone the words, 'Cut off ere his prime by his dentures'. He was not
amused. False teeth have caused me more discomfiture than any
other physical malevolence. Young people who think they are avoiding continuous trouble by having all their natural teeth pulled out,
and their mouths jammed with false, make a mighty mistake. There
is no end to the misery of gums and boils and inability to bite
properly.

Friday, 12th January

An unknown man rang this afternoon, writing an article for the
Daily Telegraph on visitors' books. Plunged into queries without a
by-your-leave while I had my eggs on the boil. Was it wrong to put
one's address? I don't know about wrong, I replied, but definitely
non-U.* How to avoid it happening? Only by standing over the
guest with a ruler in hand. I said it was strange how visitors' books,
even when consisting just of semi-legible signatures, were fascinating to read through − especially Edwardian ones, their Baroque
flourishes and underlinings evoking a whole age of elegance and
grandeur. I recalled the duc de Guermantes'† words, '*pas de pensées,
monsieur, s'il vous plaît*' − but in those days the visitor signed on arriving at a house.

---

* 'U and non-U' was a jocular 1950s coinage of Professor Alan Ross and Nancy Mitford,
referring to usages which were correct or incorrect from the upper-class point of view.
† Ultra-aristocratic character in the novel of Marcel Proust.

Tuesday, 23rd January

To London for the night. Hugh Massingberd fails to turn up to lunch with me. I am perfectly happy talking to a decent fellow called Tim Matthews, who lives in a whole house in Bath inherited from an old Mallet cousin. In afternoon I go to Sotheby's Country House Artists exhibition, organised by John Harris. Vast assembly of fascinating views from seventeenth century to present time. Hardly a work of art among them, but that's not the point, as the Knight of Glin and Olda* would say. What details of life they disclose. Several Julian Barrows towards the end, including me in my garden, which I believe to be one of his best.

Nick calls at Brooks's and takes me to dine at very expensive Italian restaurant. Says I should definitely call my book *Straight and Bent*. I have lately been having cold feet about this, and have asked Grant to help me find another title. Nick very sensible about my quandary over the Bath flat. Suggests I leave its future and Clarissa's to the discretion of my executors.

Wednesday, 24th January

Derry breakfasts. Always a joy to me. I go to exhibition of National Trust pictures at National Gallery. Excellently shown. Am most moved by *Christ and the Woman of Samaria* by Strozzi[†] from Dunham Massey [Cheshire], a house which came to the N.T. just after my time. Van Dyck's[‡] portrait of Sir Robert Shirley is marvellous, so impressionistic in the absurd dress. The Dutch landscapes rather bore me in their unsuitable Rococo frames.

Hugh Massingberd turns up today for lunch. Is on a very strict diet and only has a bowl of soup and a banana. Looks better already. Says he enjoys the self-martyrdom, being a masochist. He too begs me to keep *Straight and Bent*.

Saturday, 27th January

Ian [Dixon] lunches. I have never known a man so desirous of being loved by all and sundry. He tells me he sleeps with Aunt Dorothy's

---

* Desmond FitzGerald, 29th Knight of Glin (b. 1937); architectural and art historian; President, Irish Georgian Society; Christie's representative in Ireland; m. (2nd) 1970 Olda Willes.
† Bernardo Strozzi (1581–1644); Italian artist.
‡ Sir Anthony Van Dyck (1599–1641); Flemish-born portrait artist.

gold cigarette case, which I gave him for Christmas in gratitude for all his kindness, under his pillow.

Wednesday, 31st January

The Humphrey Stones come to lunch, bringing a huge dish of chicken pie, the remains of which they sweetly leave with me. Humphrey is designing Caroline's gravestone. He shows me the letter he is sending David, beginning 'My Lord Duke'. Dear people, they make me feel good and happy. Both have the appreciative eyes of artists, and regard every object with critical scrutiny. We walk to the church, all chattering with cold.

I have finished Mrs Langley Moore's excellent life of Byron's daughter Ada.* Doris Moore was a maddening lady, extremely pleased with herself and bossing us all over the Costume Museum,† but she can certainly write. Ada was interesting, vain, sensitive, dotty and unorthodox about love. Lady Byron of course a monstress, and Moore loathes her throughout. Ada came round to her father towards the end and stipulated that she should be buried [in the Byron family vault] at Hucknall [Nottinghamshire]. In fact Lord Lovelace arranged for her coffin to be put next to Byron's, almost touching.

I am appalled by the fire at the Fenice.‡ Of course, a fire in Venice can never be dealt with properly, even when the surrounding canals have not been emptied for cleaning. A. and I were present at the opening night of Stravinsky's *Rake's Progress* in 1951. A very hot evening. I did not enjoy it, finding it too astringent. It was a smart occasion, I in white dinner jacket, A. in jewels.

Friday, 2nd February

To London to see Grant at Murray's. We discussed photographs. It looks as if we are back to *Straight and Bent*. He made some sugges-

---

* Ada Byron (1815–52); m. 1835 William, 8th Baron King, cr. Earl of Lovelace, 1838 (1805–93); mathematician, said to have played a role in the development of the computer; her biography by Doris Langley Moore was published by John Murray in 1977.

† Doris Elizabeth Langley (1903–89); Byron scholar, scriptwriter of historical films and expert on the history of costume (who gave her own costume collection to the City of Bath to create a museum, opened in the Assembly Rooms in 1963); m. 1926 Robert Sugden Moore.

‡ The theatre had burnt to the ground on the night of 29 January in what was widely suspected to be an arson attack organised by Mafia elements.

tions for revision of preface. I hope he does not think my writing senile, as Harold [Nicolson]'s became towards the end. I met Stuart [Preston] at Brooks's, and for once lunched with him. He seemed very deaf, though this may be an affectation. Kept saying '*Comment?*' and '*Oui!*' Face like a wicked aunt's in a pantomime. We exhausted the common topics quickly. Still I am fond of him, and there was an occasional spark, though not enough to ignite the conversation. Dear old Sarge, I may never see him again.

Sunday, 4th February

I have consulted Debo, who is back from the United States, about *Straight and Bent*. She does not like the title, as 'bent' to her (and my) generation means dishonest or crooked. She suggests *Fourteen Friends*. (Her granddaughter proposes *Stale Mates*.)

Saturday, 10th February

It sickens me to read of the United Nations scooping up generals in the Balkans to arraign them as war criminals at The Hague. No doubt they are responsible for ghastly atrocities; but war is itself a crime, the ultimate evil, and all who engage in it must be regarded as accomplices to some degree. And how absurd to start trying war criminals even before the peace terms have been settled. No wonder the Serbs are furious, and may resume hostilities.

Wednesday, 14th February

Tonight I watched a programme about Pope Pius XII.* Fair, I think. Several aged cardinals and monsignores who worked for him during the war testified to his great inner conflict as to whether to be outspoken and thus risk the Germans invading and destroying the Vatican. The general opinion, however, was that he should have been much more outspoken in denouncing the appalling anti-Jewish atrocities, the most hellish things imaginable, all of which were reported to him. I thought of all the praise of him I used to hear from D'Arcy Osborne's lips.

---

* Eugenio Pacelli (1876–1958); Pope Pius XII, 1939–58; criticised for his conservatism and failure to speak out against Nazi atrocities.

Friday, 16th February

In the garden are scattered snowdrops and one bunch of aconites. An interesting contrast: snowdrops droop their heads; aconites thrust them upwards to greet the spring. Also a scattering of common daisies on the lawn. Daisies appear at all seasons and like sparrows are invincible, however much you cut off their jolly little heads.

Saturday, 17th February

On going out at 4.30 I found many police vans and much disturbance. The Woods told me that a gang of 'antis', wearing masks and armed with long sticks with knives on the ends, had arrived in old buses from Essex. These 'animal lovers' had slashed horses and hounds, wrecked horse boxes, attacked cars with people inside, and tried to drag David [Beaufort] out of his jeep with a view to kicking him to death. The leaders were apparently girls, and all wore masks. None of those who witnessed it had ever seen a more terrifying display of violence.

Sunday, 18th February

Alex Moulton came to lunch, I having written saying it was too long since we had met, two years in fact. He was very friendly and jovial as usual, but looked much older. Neither of us made any mention of the reference in my last diaries which offended him, for some mysterious reason. Alex less dogmatic than of old, and to my surprise inveighed against the fat cats of industry, saying that the disparity in pay between the bosses and the workers was unjustifiable. Very unlike Alex, this.

Monday, 4th March

To London for the day. Saw Lord Leighton[*] exhibition at Burlington House. Thought I should dislike it; but the portraits are good, some indeed beautiful. I can't abide the Quattrocento Renaissance stuff however.

---

[*] Frederic Leighton (1830–96); artist, President of Royal Academy, 1878–96; elevated to peerage the day before his death, the first artist to be so honoured.

Misha met me at Paddington and returned with me for two nights. He has become very eccentric. Seems to be in a continuous daze. Says he is studying the Alexander Technique* to rid himself of nervous habits. In London, he stays up all night, and the effect on his health is evident. I made no bones in telling him. But when he snaps out of his dreamy state and starts to talk, he is as clever and stimulating as ever.

He has just written another book about the Duchess of Windsor,† not that he wanted to, but her centenary is looming and he needs the money. The whole thing took him ten weeks. He is rather worried because the *Daily Mail* have paid him a large sum for the serial rights, and want to make great play with M's theory that the Duchess of Windsor may have been a man rather than a woman. In fact M. does not quite suggest this, but it is what the newspaper will try to say. At the same time, M. is looking forward to the reviews. He must walk on tightropes.

On Saturday, I asked Desmond Briggs to join us for lunch at The Salutation. Each liked the other very much. On Sunday, M. cooked himself an omelette for breakfast and finished off the previous night's pudding. Strange. I urged him to write a book about someone the reading public really wants to know about.

Friday, 8th March

I have been going through the typescript of *Fourteen Friends*, which has now been corrected by the lady Murray's refer to as 'Liz'.‡ She has made hundreds of suggestions, all of which I have so far accepted. I fear my syntax has become abominable; and I am grateful to this lady, though the idea of her terrifies me. I want to know who she is and whether she has written many learned tomes.

As the Bath Preservation Trust feel unable to take on Beckford's

---

* System of postural re-education founded by the Australian actor Frederick Matthias Alexander (1869–1955), whose biography by Michael Bloch was published by Little, Brown in 2004.
† Published by Weidenfeld & Nicolson in June 1996.
‡ (Jane) Elizabeth Tottenham (b. 1945); dau. of Lieutenant-Commander Lord George Tottenham, RCN (whose bro. s. 1969 as 8th Marquess of Ely) and Jane Martin; m. 1971 Captain Mark Robinson, RA; freelance editor (who adored J.L.-M. as much as she initially alarmed him).

library for the present, I have decided to vacate it this autumn in favour
of Clarissa, and to leave her my share of the property in my will, with
the proviso that, if she sells, the Trust should have first refusal. I wish
I could have found some way of preserving it for the future, and do
not feel tenderly towards C.

Saturday, 16th March

My diary has now become like Harold [Nicolson]'s in the last years of
his life, mere notes of little interest. Spotty; worthless. On Tuesday I
lunched with the Coopers,* on Wednesday with Jane [Westmorland].
Every day I go through a chapter of *Fourteen Friends*, revising and
retyping it, incorporating the recommendations of Liz. The prose is
now faultless, but reads like a professor of literature's.

  Derek Hill rang from Ireland to tell me about his holiday in
Morocco with Prince Charles. It rained every day, cats and dogs; they
sat under umbrellas, the Prince painting, D. not. At Marrakesh they
were guests of the Crown Prince, who is not allowed to marry (he is
already middle-aged) until the death of his father the King.† No press
allowed near them. Derek interested to hear that I am writing about
Robert [Byron], and mentioned a letter, unknown to me but published somewhere, which R. wrote for a future grandson. D. gave a
copy to the Prince, which he keeps in his pocket and reads repeatedly.

Wednesday, 20th March

To London today, where Susy [Robinson] sweetly invited me to see
the Cézannes,‡ having been given tickets by an obliging neighbour.
She met me at Paddington and drove us to the Tate. Our tickets
enabled us to avoid the enormous queue, doubling back and forth
like a serpent. It was nevertheless an exhausting visit owing to the
immense crowds, literally fighting for a stance in front of every paint-

---

* Sean Cooper, gardener and designer of garden furniture, and wife Evelyn.
† Eldest son (b. 1963) of King Hassan II; succeeded as Mohammed VI, 1999; married a
24-year-old computer engineer, 2002.
‡ Paul Cézanne (1839–1906); French artist. The Musée d'Orsay in Paris, the Tate Gallery
in London and the Philadelphia Museum of Art, which together owned many of his best
works, had jointly organised an exhibition which was shown successively at the three
museums and attracted vast crowds.

ing. I cannot learn what Cézanne was striving for without close scrutiny of individual paintings, which was impossible. Still, it was an experience I would not have missed for the world. The landscapes are wonderfully evocative of Aix as I remember it; and I think *The Card Players* one of the greatest genre paintings I have ever seen.

Monday, 25th March

To bed in utmost depression, unable even to read. But unable to sleep either, so I took up *As You Like It* and turned to Act 2. I was bowled over by Amiens' lamentation over the death of a stag and the right of animals to be left to themselves in their environment. Even Shakespeare in 1600 was an environmentalist. Then I listened to two piano sonatas, one of Mozart's, and Beethoven's last. I thought, what matters the life or death of one miserable individual, if such works of genius are permitted to us?

Tuesday, 26th March

To London for Desmond [Shawe-Taylor]'s memorial service at St Martin's-in-the-Fields. Entirely non-religious, presumably allowed by tolerant vicar. Pat Trevor-Roper had organised excellent service sheets showing photographs of Desmond at various ages and giving extracts from his brilliant reviews. Principal address given by Lord Harewood,[*] with snow-white, spade-shaped beard. Then Fanny [Partridge], who was too small to reach microphone and remained inaudible. Whereas Dadie [Rylands], aged 93, positively boomed. I left before the end for Brooks's, in time to change into black tie and get to Marcus Worsley's[†] N.T. retirement dinner at Ham House [Richmond]. Stood in freezing hall for half an hour talking to the others, not knowing who most of them were. Finally dinner in Orangery, where acoustics so dreadful that I could neither hear nor make myself heard. Good speech by Marcus. I was somewhat lionised, introduced to lady custodian, and to new

[*] George Lascelles, 7th Earl of Harewood (b. 1923); e. s. of 6th Earl and HRH Mary, Princess Royal; musical personality, successively Director and Chairman of English National Opera, 1972–95.
[†] Sir Marcus Worsley, 5th Bt (b. 1925), of Hovingham Hall, Yorkshire; sometime MP for Chelsea; Chairman of N.T. Properties Committee, 1980–90; Deputy Chairman of N.T., 1990–2.

Chairman and wife. Others came up to shake my hand and mouth compliments. These things embarrass me and make me feel a fraud. The Nuttings kindly drove me back to Brooks's, where I was soon asleep.

Wednesday, 27th March

Woke feeling unusually well. Derry breakfasted. He is looking forward to making his maiden speech in the Lords tomorrow; has already visited the chamber, and says there are few hereditary peers to be seen. I visited the Doria Pamphili* exhibition, all in one large room. Wonderful, all great works of art. Bernini's splendid bust of Innocent X, and the great Velázquez of that Pope which inspired Francis Bacon.† Wonderful Claude. Raphael, Guercino, Titian, all great artists to be sure.

Sunday, 31st March

I have spent all weekend writing a short article for George Plumptre's *Sotheby's Magazine*. This sounds ridiculously slow, but to condense the history of Ickworth and the Herveys‡ into five hundred words is no easy task. Meanwhile am cheered by today's appearance in *Sunday Times* of my little article in the 'Bookshelf' column on Logan Pearsall Smith's *On Reading Shakespeare*. It reads well, I think.

Wednesday, 3rd April

The Henry [Robinson]s dined, bringing with them a delicious casserole. Both very affectionate. They fly to Namibia tomorrow with the three children. Henry told me that living at Moorwood costs him £250,000 a year. He has to make this from the farm, which is why he worries so much over the harvest. After dinner we drove to the Slates to look at the stars, though the glow from Bristol interfered with our

---

* Italian noble family which had married into English families for several generations, still inhabiting much of their thousand-room palace in Rome with its famous art collection.
† Francis Bacon (1909–92) based his 1953 paintings on Velázquez' portrait of Innocent III (1650).
‡ Following a rake's progress, John Hervey, 7th Marquess of Bristol (1954–99), life tenant of the east wing of Ickworth House, Suffolk (the whole of which had been donated by his grandfather to the N.T. in 1956), was about to sell many of his remaining family possessions at Sotheby's.

gazing. We thought we saw the comet, but it might have been Venus. Total eclipse of the moon due to begin at 12.30, but we all agreed we could not sit up until then.

Wednesday, 10th April

Shall I, shan't I go to London today? I went. A satisfactory and enjoyable day. Saw three exhibitions and ran into several old friends – Burnet [Pavitt] descending from a taxi at Coutts, Simon Houfe* emerging from London Library, Nico Henderson lunching upstairs at Brooks's. To National Gallery to have another look at the Doria pictures. The Caravaggio Angel which David Beaufort so much admires is without sex, and quite celestial. To British Museum to exhibition of Sir William Hamilton's Volcanoes. The rooms in darkness, lights trained on exhibits only, which was irritating for me with my poor eyesight, unable to read the notices. Then to see the Caillebottes† at Burlington House. Very interesting, a mixture of Expressionism and traditional Salon artistry. I particularly liked the Haussmann street scenes and iron bridges. Returned home in the evening on a high.

Wednesday, 17th April

My luncheon party caused me much angst; but Lavinia Unwin supplied good food, and Michael and Isobel Briggs came early to help. The others Elspeth [Huxley], Mary and Charles Keen, Jane Westmorland. All dear friends. As the Keens were leaving, Charles said shyly to Mary, 'Should I really give it to Jim?' She replied, 'Yes, go on, don't be absurd,' and he handed me a slim volume of poems entitled *Quick Fox-Trot*. It is marvellous, witty and satirical, a mixture of Pope and Byron – surprising from this most unassuming man.

Sunday, 21st April

Our dear and good Queen's seventieth birthday. So I go to Matins at Didmarton. Vicar announces death of Nancy Dill.‡ She attended the

---

* Grandson of J.L.-M's friend Sir Albert Richardson (1880–1964; Professor of Architecture, London University, and adviser to N.T.).
† Gustave Caillebotte (1848–94); French artist.
‡ Nancy Charrington; m. 1st Brigadier Dennis Furlong, 2nd Field Marshal Sir John Dill (1881–1944).

Easter Sunday service, and soon afterwards held a party for her nine-tieth birthday, during which she had a sudden premonition, said goodbye to her friends, and five minutes later died. She was a staunch old girl of the old-fashioned sort, who rarely called people by their Christian names, and always referred to her late husband as 'the Field Marshal'.

Tuesday, 23rd April

Reading the letters of my Bailey grandparents* to each other at the time of their engagement, I am amazed to learn that my grandmother asked my grandfather to see to the redecoration of the drawing room, dining room and hall at Coates before their marriage. 'I know your cousins have excellent taste and if you will allow them to offer their advice I know I should be pleased and they will go about it much more economically than I could.' So strange that this lady should not have supervised the redecorations herself. No one in her circum-stances today would ever do such a thing. I imagine she was much in dread of the awful old man, who was old enough to be her father, and whose main interests were huntin' and shootin'. I don't suppose she loved him one bit. On 22 August 1884 she writes to him from staying with the Anstruthers in Perthshire that it will be some time before she sees him again as she is going on to the So-and-Sos. My mother was born on the 29th of that month, in his absence.

Music seems to have been their only shared interest; she writes to him to 'bring some songs for the evenings'. She always refers to herself as 'Scotch' rather than 'Scottish', which confirms my natural tendency to use the former adjective.

Friday, 26th April

My reading of my grandparents' letters inspired me to visit Coates to look at their graves, this year being the centenary of her death. I found it. It is well-kept, the headstone a typical Victorian cross, the letter-ing of incised zinc or lead, still readable. He died on 10 August 1889 aged sixty-six, having caught a chill after bathing at Weymouth; she followed him on 24 August 1896 aged forty-seven, of Bright's Disease,

---

* Henry Bailey (1822–89), of Coates near Cirencester; 5th and youngest son of Sir Joseph Bailey, 1st Bt; m. (2nd) 1881 Christina Thomson (1849–96).

when my poor mother was not yet thirteen. I suddenly had the idea that we – that is to say, the Robinson brothers and myself – might partake of a picnic above the grave this coming 24 August, as pagans used to do, pouring wine through a funnel onto the grave for the benefit of the defunct. The church was open, and I entered. Fine Norman columns on arches; nineteenth-century pews; no memorials. An indifferent window in memory of Thomas Gibbs, *ob.* December 1914, 'for 64 years Rector of Coates'. He is often mentioned in their letters, and surely buried them both.

Saturday, 27th April

I was invited to dine at the House, on the anniversary of Caroline's funeral. The Loewensteins staying, and all the children present. I sat next to Anne [Carr], who said her mother's diaries had been left to her – luckily not to Bunter,* so Tracy could not get her hands on them. These family antipathies. David surprised me by saying that Andrew Devonshire had been given the Garter. I would not have thought he was considered respectable enough. Debo would have been a worthier recipient. I shall have a difficult letter to write.

Friday, 3rd May

J.K.-B. for the night. Was delightful throughout. He seems to have acquired a new interest in life through becoming a Fellow of the [Society of] Antiquaries. We motored to Owlpen [Manor, Gloucestershire], which alas is no longer the remote, cosy, unspoiled, lived-in manor house which inspired Vita. The Manders lack taste. Environs undisturbed, thank goodness, but it is sad that the removal of the great yew hedge has opened the gabled house to distant views.

Sunday, 5th May

Lunched with the Keens at Duntisbourne Rous. Magnus and Veronica Linklater† there. They live in Edinburgh's New Town, support the Kirk, and devote themselves to conservation. She is a

---

* Her brother Harry, Marquess of Worcester.
† Journalist (b. 1942); Chairman of Scottish Arts Council, 1996–2001; m. 1967 Veronica Lyle (b. 1943), cr. Baroness Linklater of Butterstone, 1997.

beautiful woman, a chairman of educational trusts. He writes the 'Times Diary', and we spoke of diaries. He said to me, 'Doubtless when you get home you will write, "Met boring couple; unprofitable occasion; didn't know who or what they were."' We also talked of Monty Mackenzie,* whom she knew well. How is this possible, she being so young?

Debo telephoned. She has been staying at Highgrove, but could not come to me because of the Event. Said the cold at Highgrove was dreadful, and there was little to eat. The young princes and their friends were present, all starving. No meat course for dinner.

Monday, 6th May

Simon Blow came to interview me for the *Spectator*. There is a tiresome side to him, but I like him, and he understands the clan spirit. Having stayed all afternoon, he suddenly announced that he had forgotten to put a tape in his machine, and would have to come again. Says he lives on journalism and nothing else.

Sunday, 12th May

Yesterday Liz Robinson, the mystery editrix of *Stale Mates*, was brought to tea by Gail Pirkis. She is tall, large, rather butch in tight trousers, with fair hair scooped in a tail, and rather pretty face which becomes pleasant when relaxed. We had tea in the kitchen and then went into the garden. She is very knowledgeable on plants. I was pleased to see them. They had visited Westonbirt before coming to me.

Monday, 13th May

To my surprise, Pompey† telephoned this evening from Euston [Hall, Norfolk]. Fortune had just gone off to Buckingham Palace for Chirac's visit tomorrow. Pompey irritated that she aged seventy-five

---

* Sir Compton Mackenzie (1883–1972); novelist, who had once declared his passion for J.L.-M.; a biography of him (omitting all mention of his homosexuality) by Magnus Linklater's brother Andro had been published by Chatto & Windus in 1987.
† Hugh Fitzroy, 11th Duke of Grafton (b. 1919); m. 1946 Fortune Smith, Mistress of the Robes to HM The Queen from 1967.

should have to drive herself and not have a car sent. 'After all, she is the Mistress of the Robes.' He then added, 'I gather from Billa [Harrod] that you're on the way out.' He was very solicitous, and we had a good nostalgic talk about old times.

Sunday, 26th May

Simon's cousin Detmar Blow[*] invited me to lunch at Hilles. I thought we might be alone, but not so. A number of young people, including a clever niece of Rosemary Chaplin.[†] Sat next to young Detmar who treated me as though I was an ex-prime minister, and at the end of luncheon, to my embarrassment, asked the company to drink my health. He is half-Sri Lankan and very like Simon in his class-consciousness and love of gossip. When we had eaten, his wife who had been cooking came and took his place. She was wearing a long black gown with train that skimmed across the boards, and a hat of orange ostrich feathers with pigeons' feathers stuck askew among them. She talked inconsequentially in an upper-class manner which embarrassed me somewhat. The strangeness of the young. Yet again very welcoming and kind. This house, by the elder Detmar Blow,[‡] has enormous charm, and is absolutely in accord with the Cotswold landscape, while showing much originality. Huge rooms, clad with cosy lugubrious tapestries and full-length portraits of Kings and Queens. A living house.

Saturday, 1st June

Julian Barrow called, having come from Lyegrove where he is painting the latest owners. The two bachelor owners since Diana[§] have both died of Aids. New owners are immensely rich Jews from Hampstead. Their visits are occasional, and this Saturday they are having seventy to luncheon. It is only non-country people who buy

---

[*] Of Hilles House, Gloucestershire (b. 1963); art dealer and boulevardier; m. Isabella Delves Broughton, dau. of Sir Evelyn Delves Broughton, 12th Bt.

[†] Hon. Rosemary Lyttelton (1922–2003), dau. of 1st Viscount Chandos; m. 1951 3rd Viscount Chaplin (formerly husband of A.L.-M.).

[‡] Country house architect (1867–1939); sometime friend and adviser to 2nd Duke of Westminster.

[§] Diana, Countess of Westmorland, until whose death in 1983 J.L.-M. had been a frequent visitor to the house.

large houses now. Julian plans to paint in India again. He is pleased that his little painting of our garden will appear on the jacket of *Ancient as the Hills*.*

Thursday, 6th June

Arctic weather has turned to Saharan. Debo, who has a meeting at Highgrove, asked if she might stay the night. Overjoyed, I welcomed her at 5.30 with a cup of tea. It was lovely having her. She looking very beautiful in thick pearls, bearing presents of cake, jam, etc., as well as the main course for our dinner, and her breakfast, in a huge case, as she rises at 5 a.m. I poured out my health woes, very tiresome for her. She listened and advised wisely. This morning she walked to post a letter, chatting to all and sundry. She fears that Diana may never come over to England again. She turned down an offer from the benefactress[†] to have her motored to Gare du Nord, collected by private car at Waterloo and driven to the front door of Chatsworth. The fall at Waterloo Station has deprived her of all confidence.

Friday, 7th June

In reading Gombrich's fascinating *Story of Art*,[‡] I realise the mistake I made in my sightseeing days in burying my head in guide books instead of soaking myself in the surroundings, like A. Nowadays there are books of excellent illustrations of every work of art in the world, so that I no longer need to revisit the haunts of my past.

Monday, 10th June

Richard Robinson comes to lunch, bearing gifts of chocolate orange slices and books which I don't want to read. Unliterary people in their kindness are apt to do this. They think that any old book will do.

---

* Title chosen for forthcoming volume of J.L.-M's diaries, covering 1973–4.
† Nancy Osborne Hill.
‡ The popular history of art by Sir Ernst Gombrich (1909–2001), one of the most successful books to appear during the twentieth century, was first published in 1950.

Saturday, 15th June

James Knox,* staying with his sister Lucy Abel Smith† at Quenington, called this afternoon to talk about Robert [Byron]. He read me extracts of letters from Desmond‡ to Robert which were interesting, full of pertinent comments on friends and work. James has absolutely understood Robert, by whom he is still fascinated, although some early illusions have been dispelled. He is aware of Robert's brutish sexual behaviour, and persecution of friends. I came quite clean about all that. James looks eighteen whereas he is over forty. Very charming, and devouring every titbit which he jots down in a note-book. He is going to Birr [Castle, Co. Offaly] where he has discovered there are hundreds of Robert's letters to Michael [Rosse] and Desmond.

Monday, 17th June

Stephanie Allen§ telephones that Cheltenham Literary Festival want me to lecture in the autumn about Vita and Sissinghurst. I have no hesitation in turning down this idea. I sense in her voice not so much disappointment as polite disbelief. Stephanie, the publicity girl at John Murray's, is immensely tall, stately and beautiful. John Betjeman would have flung himself at her feet.

Saturday, 22nd June

I discussed my wishes with Nick, and told him that he would have to mingle A's and my ashes and scatter them. 'Where?' he asked. I suggested the garden, for it was here that we both finished our lives together very happily. But he must tell no one, not even David Beaufort, because people don't like the idea of others being interred on their property. I told Nick that he would be in sole charge here until the lease was surrendered. He accepted all this in his usual sweet, unperturbed, optimistic way.

---

* Writer and artistic consultant (b. 1952); his biography of Robert Byron was published by John Murray in 2003.
† Lucy Knox; m. 1982 David Abel Smith (b. 1940) of Quenington Old Rectory nr Circencester.
‡ Hon. Desmond Parsons (1910–37).
§ On staff of John Murray, 1990–2002 (b. 1967).

Wednesday, 26th June

Yesterday Clarissa and Billy came for tea. C. very sweet, he very accommodating as usual. We exchanged little gifts and we parted friends. She was greatly taken by the garden. Indeed it is at its annual zenith, and will never be more luxuriant than this day. Roses proliferating like a tapestry of Burne-Jones.

Liz Robinson came again this afternoon. Handsome, massive, a little forbidding. Masks her omniscience behind a slightly kittenish manner. We went through the diaries she has been editing. She misses little, having read the erasures.

Saturday, 29th June

I drove to Alderley to be shown round the garden, just as I was last year. It is marvellous. Particularly striking the *Buddleia alternifolia*, but unlike ours the drooping stems spout little poufs of racemes. These, Guy said, were planted by A. All her layout just the same. A joy to see it so mature and flourishing. The Acloques showed me two portraits just bought at the Ickworth sale,[*] including one of John Hervey[†] the diarist from whom Milly is descended.

Sunday, 30th June

No church for me today. Worked hard at my diaries for Liz. Then to lunch with Veronica,[‡] Bamber and Christina at Veronica's farmhouse, Ashcroft, prepared by her son Ben and girlfriend. V. still a beauty, her auburn hair streaked with grey. Bamber as full of enthusiasms as ever. His eagerness very appealing. He is currently writing, all by himself and with no contributors, a *History of the World* in 850,000 words, to be available on computer and finished by 1998. An extraordinary mind he has, and compulsions. Works like a tiger. On their way back to London, he and Christina stopped to visit the garden here, and showed keen interest and botanical knowledge. There is nothing low-brow about these Gascoignes. All politically to the left, the girl working for an institution advocating Britain's reception of all appli-

---

[*] See note to 31 March 1996.
[†] J.L.-M. presumably refers to the flamboyant Lord Hervey (1696–1743; 2nd son of 1st Earl of Bristol), courtier to King George II, known as a writer of memoirs rather than a diarist.
[‡] Veronica Gascoigne (b. 1938); sister of Bamber; m. 1960 Hon. William Plowden.

cants from foreign countries irrespective of their reasons for wishing to come here.

Saturday, 6th July

When I spoke to Debo to accept her invitation to go to Chatsworth later this month, she informed me that Decca* was riddled with cancer on liver, chest and brain, and being treated with chemotherapy. Dreadful news which evokes my latent affection and sympathy for Decca. I wonder if the fall of Communism had the same effect on her as Vatican Council II had on Evelyn Waugh, driving her to despair and illness.

Wednesday, 10th July

The great Liz returns to finish off my diary manuscripts. We get on well and I like her much. She seems fascinated rather than revolted by the society of my olden days.

Friday, 12th July

The kind Hollands motor me to Deene. With ineffable politeness, Guy insists I sit in front with Joanie who is driving, whereas I would much rather sit in the back to relax.

We arrive for tea in the great hall. The following guests are staying: Lord Stockton,† who is touring the country for the Conservative Party, but not a good advertisement for it, having the largest belly on a man I've ever seen; Laurence Kelly,‡ writer, and brother Bernard,§ former incapacitated by a stroke; the wives of these two, Linda and Lady Mirabel, both delightful; dear Nathalie Brooke;¶ pretty Russian

---

* Hon. Jessica Mitford (1917–96); m. 1st Esmond Romilly (1918–41), 2nd 1943 Robert Treuhaft (1912–2001); satirical writer living in USA, the 'Communist Mitford sister'.
† Alexander Macmillan, 2nd Earl of Stockton (b. 1943); grandson of Harold Macmillan (1894–1986), Prime Minister 1956–63, cr. Earl of Stockton, 1984; President, Macmillan Ltd, from 1990; a member of the European Parliament from 1999.
‡ Businessman and writer of works on Russian subjects (b. 1933); m. 1963 Linda McNair Scott.
§ Banker (b. 1930); m. 1952 Lady Mirabel Fitzalan Howard, sister of 17th Duke of Norfolk.
¶ Countess Nathalie Benckendorff; granddaughter of last Imperial Russian Ambassador to London; m. 1946 Humphrey Brooke, Secretary to Royal Academy, 1951–68.

Ambassadress (her husband unable to come at last moment), knowing little English but speaking Russian with Nathalie and the Kellys; Kenneth Rose, much older and hunched like a dormouse, his head resembling a bust by Nollekens;* Drue Heinz,† the Harrises, the Hollands and myself. I enjoyed myself on the whole, and was overwhelmed by the kindness of Edmund and Marian. Given Henry VII's room as before. Lovely to be woken by morning sun on my pillow.

I walked in the garden with Kenneth who is writing the life of Victor Rothschild,‡ whose son has just killed himself in a Paris hotel.§ He explained to me that Victor's greatest achievement was a scientific discovery concerning the behaviour of the male sperm. Kenneth's conversation is peppered with references to 'my great friend the King of Greece' and 'the Duke of Kent, as you know my great friend', yet I am not sure he is entirely snobbish. His ingratiation has a fiendish charm. Very nice to me.

On Saturday after tea, Marian took the Ambassadress, John Harris and me to look at Southwick church, its forest of tombstones lit by the dying sun. Box pews with polished brass handles and hinges; in the chancel, six huge black memorial stones with beautifully incised writing, eighteenth-century, covering graves of Lynn family. Then Fotheringay church with its beautiful perpendicular architecture, to which I remember being taken by dear old Lady Ethelreda Wickham in 1944. Ambassadress kept talking on mobile telephone. Outside the porch in the graveyard she had a long conversation. When asked with whom, she said, 'The dearest old lady who is like a mother to me, outside of Moscow.' She telephones and is telephoned all the time. But reception at Deene is indifferent owing to low-lying land, and she has to climb to the attics or the roof. I met her outside my bedroom door endeavouring to get through to Kiev.

I was very pleased to be with the Harrises. John now distinguished

---

* Joseph Nollekens (1737–1823); English sculptor.
† Drue Maher; m. 1953 as his 2nd wife Jack Heinz II (1908–87), Chairman of international food company H. J. Heinz; benefactress of literature and the arts.
‡ 3rd Baron Rothschild (1910–90); zoologist, industrialist, intelligence officer, and government adviser; his biography by Kenneth Rose, *Elusive Rothschild*, was published by Weidenfeld & Nicolson in 2003.
§ Amschel Mayer James Rothschild (1955–96); he was found hanging by the cord of his bathrobe, the conclusion of the Paris police that he had killed himself being questioned in some quarters.

with wavy hair, she much improved in looks. He made a discovery in Deene church: found name of William Kent's* plasterer and identified his work with that of ceiling in billiards room. An affectionate pair, I have an 'up' on them.

On Sunday morning, the Eucharist in the chapel. House party sit on right against wall, villagers on left. We take Communion first. All this rather shocks me. Ambassadress attends and says it is just like the Russian Orthodox Church. I wonder if she can be religious.

Wednesday, 17th July

Alan [the Devonshires' chauffeur] motors me to Chatsworth. Am welcomed by Debo and present my plants to her, which are immediately sent off to head gardener. After tea I wander to kitchen garden and admire D's layout of vegetable and herb beds in concentric rings, herbs raised to within sight level and labelled. Andrew appears for dinner, wide-armed and welcoming. I take care to respect his taciturnity. He has little appetite on account of his having watched golf on television all day. He says that Derek [Hill] has invited himself to Chatsworth during Prince of Wales's next visit, saying, 'I am sure H.R.H. would like me to be present when I have my eightieth birthday.'

Thursday, 18th July

D. takes me to the blessing of the well at Pilsley. Whole village assembled in Sunday best. Revd Mr Beddoes in long white chasuble officiating. Lady with portable harmonium accompanies immensely long Alleluia hymn. Children in evidence. Copy of a Pre-Raphaelite window made of tightly-packed flower heads in clay. Took four days in the making.

We enter cottage of pretty old lady Mrs Dean, retired housekeeper of State Rooms, and before the war housemaid to the Duchess of Windsor, whom she much liked and respected for her 'fairness'. Says Duke very democratic, calling staff by first names, but also moody. Mrs Dean a great reader; has several of my books, one of which I sign. Nice old lady, chair-bound by multiple sclerosis.

---

* Artist, architect and landscape gardener (1685–1748).

Sunday, 21st July

Sir Edward Ford* has been staying two nights, taking himself to Buxton Opera for *Beggars' Opera* and Handel. Is eighty-five and very musical. Most delightful man, widower. At luncheon yesterday I hear with left ear Debo being told by Feeble of an entry in her father's diary of 1919 that he expects announcement within a few days of his sister Dorothy Cavendish's engagement to Prince of Wales, and with right ear Andrew discussing with Sir Edward particulars of King George VI's final illness. Like all courtiers, Sir Edward is discreet, though amused by foibles.

Debo tells me that Decca is dying in New York. We return from a short stroll in great heat at 5.45 and hear telephone ring. D. says, 'Stay with me'. Decca recites lines from *Maud* about how the black bat has flown, which Debo continues.

After church we look at Sir William Cavendish's† tomb re-erected in the 1860 Edensor fabric. An old lady guardian points out what I would never have noticed, namely the marble toes of angel holding open two-winged lapidary encomium of deceased, projecting below. A true Baroque touch yet executed presumably in Jacobean times.

Tuesday, 23rd July

I surrender totally to Henry [the butler]'s ministrations. Evidently I did not bring enough shirts and underclothes, for he allows me to wear a shirt for no more than a day before taking it away to be washed. Although he is Irish, Henry is one of the most decent friends I have ever had. His patience, readiness to oblige, kindness and loyalty are unsurpassed. But having to tip him causes me embarrassment and unease, of which he is well aware. For a week's sojourn I have given £35 to him, £20 to Stella the housekeeper, and £20 to Jo for motoring me home. Nothing to Alan who motored me from home because he has gone off on his holiday, and this worries me.

Andrew stalks around the house in dressing gown at 11 a.m. A sort

---

* Courtier (b. 1910); Assistant Private Secretary to the Sovereign (1946–67).
† Treasurer of the Chamber to Henry VIII, Edward VI and Mary I (d. 1557); husband of Bess of Hardwick and father of 1st Earl of Devonshire.

of dread comes over me here from time to time. I feel that Chatsworth is just too grand for me. I can't live up to it. I am inadequate, notwithstanding the ineffable kindness I receive.

This afternoon the Ds and I are motored at 2.30 to the Tram Museum, oddly situated at Crick in remote heart of Pennines. We leave Chatsworth in unbroken, sweltering sunshine. We buy tickets for tram ride and are in mid journey when thunder and lightning begin and hail descends in noisy torrents. Instantly tram lights go out and vehicle halts, the electricity having been struck by lightning. We are stuck for almost an hour, unable to move. Finally a diesel truck comes and pushes tram home. Chatsworth has entirely escaped the storm, receiving not one drop. Debo in halted tram makes friends with fellow travellers with utmost ease and interest.

On my last evening, telephone rings at dinner. Debo jumps up saying, 'I know that will be Decca.' Returns, sits down, and says, 'She has just died.' Talk of other things. Then she says she must do some telephoning, and leaves the dining room. I walk with Andrew towards her sitting room, but say good night to him at my bedroom door and go to bed.

Friday, 2nd August

Received sweetest letter from Nigel [Nicolson] to whom I wrote, hoping he would not disapprove of the chapter on Vita in *Fourteen Friends*. He says he has already read proofs and is reviewing for the *Sunday Times*. Is also writing in his autobiography that I ought to have been his mother's son, as there was so much affinity. Nigel is a generous man.

I went to London yesterday, calling at Murray's and going to Jean Hugo exhibition in Bond Street. Also saw the Queen's Leonardos which are rather disappointing, his scientific drawings not meticulous, his human sketches exceeded by Michelangelo and others. At Brooks's I lunched with John Jolliffe, whom I introduced to Toby Hildyard as an Old Catholic. Not so, said John; it was through his grandmother K. Asquith, who converted, and his Hylton grandparents disapproved to the extent of not going to their son's wedding to John's papist mother Perdita. John told me that his brother Raymond Hylton*

---

* Raymond Jolliffe, 5th Baron Hylton (b. 1932).

received £250,000 for one of the six Seymour horse paintings[*] recently displayed at 1 Royal Crescent [Bath].

Saturday, 3rd August

How regularly the seasons thread their relentless way. There is a faint whiff of autumn already. At 7 p.m., in a slanting sun from a clear and windless sky, I watch a multitude of bumble bees, brown and black, buzzing in the lavender, and cabbage whites in abundance.

I relish the continuity of old family feuds and jealousies. Have received a very formal letter from Squire Davie-Thornhill of Stanton, demanding to know why, in my life of the Bachelor Duke, I have referred to his great-great-aunt Mary Thornhill as 'egregious'. The fact is that the lady, though a local friend of the Duke, was rather a pest to him, always demanding favours.

Tuesday, 6th August

My unblessed [eighty-eighth] birthday. People telephone with congratulations, including Anne Hill who says she had no idea it was my birthday, but had an urge to call me. Then Nick motors me to Wickhamford. On the way we stop at Upper Slaughter to look at new memorial window in the Witts chapel. As I expected, it is a hideous gash of uncompromising colours. Typical of the Wittses and Wrigleys,[†] old-fashioned country folk with aspirations to avant-garde-ness.

We get to Wickhamford at four. Welcomed most kindly and warmly by Jeremy and June Ryan-Bell. Too blustery to sit on the terrace, so we go into hideous plastic tent erected on the lawn for recent performance of *Much Ado about Nothing*. They propose to make this structure, with imitation Georgian windows of waving perspex, a permanent feature in the once pretty sunken garden, now deprived of pool and fountain. Nevertheless they both love Wickhamford and are eager for any information on its days of yore. An enormous tea provided – birthday cake and three others sorts of cake, three jams and scones galore. The darkness of the house, smallness of the rooms.

---

[*] James Seymour (*c.* 1702–52); English artist.
[†] Alice Wrigley (1902–90); second cousin of J.L.-M.; m. 1929 Major-General Frederick Witts (1889–1969), whose forebears had been Rectors and Lords of the Manor of Upper Slaughter for three generations.

Pond much improved since last visit, weeds and lilies removed. They have cleared a welcome view beyond the pond of a park-like field with sheep. Nick for the first time seems interested in the childhood home of his grandmother Audrey, and impressed with the church. The kindness we receive from these nice people is really overwhelming. Nick says when we get home, 'I have never seen a man more nervous of you than him.' Nonsense, surely, for I was all sugar.

Thursday, 15th August

Did possibly a wicked thing. Was so irritated by ants climbing up my trouser leg while I was reading under the parasol that I poured boiling water over their entry between the flags of the terrace, exterminating them. Acting like the Allies in oblitering Hiroshima, and relatively as culpable.

Saturday, 17th August

David Beaufort telephones at 8 asking me to meet him at Swangrove at 11. Of course I agree, though busy with other matters. He has put this *maison de plaisance* back to what it should be, with his infallible eye. Calls it his gloating house. I don't blame him. He says he can hardly bear friends walking round it lest they spoil it. He has fitted it out with three bedrooms, complete with beds and furniture from the House attics. A very complete and ravishing little house. All it wants is a library.

Tuesday, 20th August

At breakfast, Patricia rings in tears to say that Elaine* died early this morning. I write to Simon telling him he need have no remorse as so many people do on the death of a parent.

Thursday, 22nd August

J.K.-B. stayed last night. Very kind, good, and tolerant of my quick temper. He is a mini-sage, with his knowledge of the classics, literature and theology. I fear he is taken advantage of by many researchers

---

* Elaine Brigstocke (1911–96); m. (2nd) 1938 J.L.-M's brother Richard Lees-Milne (1910–84); mother of Simon L.-M. (b. 1939; m. [2nd] 1976 Patricia Derrick).

and art historians, who drain him of his knowledge and do little for him in return. He finds writing difficult to embark on, and so others reap his harvests.

Friday, 23rd August

Dined at Swangrove. An experience. Some twelve guests in the ground floor dining room. This house is larger than mine. Sat between Miranda and Josephine [Loewenstein]. Andrew Parker Bowles making teasing jokes at one's expense, yet very friendly. David explained that his collection of framed Claude* sketches comes from the famous *Liber Veritatis* which Andrew Devonshire was obliged to sell to meet death duties on succession. Master wanted to scrap them, and David persuaded him to sell to him. A large fire burning in upstairs saloon. Much draught from the high front door. It could never have been a cosy pleasure retreat, though ravishing.

Sunday, 1st September

Freda [Berkeley] came to stay last Tuesday, motored by Coote, for what turned out to be five days of unremitting society. We went out to meals with Gerda Barlow,† Jane Westmorland, the Hollands, and the Revd John Foster, and I gave a luncheon party here to which came Jane, Desmond Briggs and the Duff Hart-Davises. I am ashamed to say that I used the long-planned luncheon with Gerda on Wednesday as an excuse not to attend Elaine's cremation at Worcester. Freda never stopped telephoning or being telephoned. Her Catholic priest Father Michael [Hollings] rang twice a day. She could not have been kinder or sweeter, but is not very well, and fatter in spite of a much-vaunted diet. Two horse-loving lesbians called this afternoon to motor her back to London.

Monday, 2nd September

Though not due out for weeks, *Fourteen Friends* is already receiving reviews. A good one yesterday by Ziegler in the *Telegraph*; and today

---

* Claude Lorrain (1600–82); French landscape artist.
† Widow of Basil Barlow (1918–91) of Stancombe Park, Gloucestershire.

that gorgeous lamp-post Stephanie rang to announce a favourable and prominent one by Anne Scott-James in today's *Standard* – generous of her in view of some of the things I wrote about Osbert [Lancaster]. Also an indulgent note from Louisa Young assuring me that she 'does not entirely disapprove' of my disparagement of her grandfather and father.

Thursday, 5th September

Nick lunches and is as comforting as ever, as good as gold. I have been reading my diary for 1978, when I felt I had broken through to him and that he would be a companion for the rest of my life. And so it has proved. But little did I realise that in my last years he would become my dearest friend and counsellor in whose company I am happiest. Little too did I realise that a book of mine would receive exaggerated praise in the literary pages of *Country Life*. I would now be very content, were it not for my health. I am reconciled to the loss of A., though I feel remorse when reading my old diaries for having treated her so ill.

Sunday, 15th September

Diana [Mosley] writes that she is drained of all vitality by the unsolicited and fatuous communication of acquaintances. I know just how she feels.

Tuesday, 17th September

Derek [Hill] telephones. 'Are you doing anything on November 15th? Then Prince Charles wants you to lunch. I am going to stay there the night before. I hear you have written a book.' All rather peremptory.

Thursday, 19th September

Grant [McIntyre] motored down from London this afternoon to talk to me. We had tea in the kitchen, and he went straight back again. I knew something unexpected was coming. First, he congratulated me on successful reception of *Fourteen Friends*. Secondly, he asked me to sign twenty more copies for Stephanie. Thirdly, would I consider a reprint of *Another Self*? Then, shyly, 'Would you consider being subjected to a biography?"* I said no, no, no. The whole idea was preposterous. He suggested James Knox, whom I like. But the idea of unbosoming myself to this nice young man is repugnant. All those skeletons in my cupboard which I now recoil from with a shudder, but know are still unburied. But as Grant pointed out, if I decline to cooperate while I am alive, it will very likely still happen after my death. I shall wait until James has finished his life of Robert [Byron]. Meanwhile, with whom can I consult? Grant suggested Debo. The very idea.

Friday, 20th September

A fascinating experience today, reminding me of my wartime visits to remote country houses and harassed owners. Susy [Robinson], who is on the local CPRE committee, has been much concerned with the condition of Barrington Park, the Wingfields'† house near Burford, but in Gloucestershire. Architectural historians have been denied admission to this house for years while hearing rumours of its slow deterioration. Now the son, Richard, twenty-five or so I should guess, bright-eyed, good-looking, beautifully mannered, fairly ignorant, eager for information and guidance and a prey to antiquarian rogues, has taken possession of the house, and is prepared to restore it. This means demolishing wings added in the 1870s and 80s by the mediocre architect McVicar Anderson, leaving the 1735 core,‡ a typical George II villa attributed to William Kent and one of the Smiths of Warwick.

We were greeted in the courtyard by young Richard, his parents Charles and Mary Wingfield, and their architect. Politenesses and recollections of former meetings. She a dear bewildered lady who is sister of Lord Sandys of Ombersley and daughter of the benevolent Colonel Arthur Sandys who once gave me a box of cigars. The whole house draped with plastic sheets under scaffolding, so exterior cannot be seen. The parents live in darkness relieved by an occasional one-horse-power electric bulb. Beautiful central hall, deep square panelled ceiling

---

* The idea had already been put to J.L.-M. five years earlier, the proposed biographer then being his former editor Ariane Bankes (see *Ceaseless Turmoil*, 24 February 1991).
† Charles Talbot Rhys Wingfield (b. 1924); m. 1954 Hon. Cynthia Hill, dau. of 6th Baron Sandys.
‡ Built by the Wingfields' forebear William, 1st and last Earl Talbot (1710–82).

of stucco, two chimneypieces with pictures in overdoors (temporarily removed). Impossible in the dimness to see colour of walls. The hall looks more or less intact, but the rest of the 1735 core as well as the Victorian wings in appalling condition. Riddled with dry rot. The Wingfields' vast bedroom ceiling collapsed in one corner. The same in practically all rooms. Went upstairs to see once delightful children's nurseries, in same state. Stone roofs decayed into rubble. In the drawing room, the Flemish tapestries seem miraculously to have survived, having been protected from the light. Unfortunately Anderson obliterated the original staircase, substituting his own. His dining room and billiards room admittedly decent Victorian, but two-a-penny.

The public enquiry to be held in ten days' time is anticipated to go against the Wingfields, who are facing opposition from English Heritage and the Victorian Society. Yet I see absolutely no alternative to demolition of the Anderson additions in order to preserve and reinstate the Kentian villa. The family are asking for no financial assistance from the state, and would be unable to live in the present house, were it to be reinstated. Susy and I given tea in large drawing room. We had a long talk with Mrs, a charming, gentle, slightly giggly woman who is clearly at sea and has long since thrown up the sponge. Says they suffer from ramblers claiming the right to long-forgotten footpaths. In all my days of country house visiting I don't remember a more tragic case than Barrington. The scenario of a Russian novel. I kept wondering how they managed to keep so clean and tidy, living as they do.

Tuesday, 24th September

Myles motors me to Flintham. We doodle up the Fosse Way and arrive at tea-time. Nothing has changed. Myles says he could never have improved Flintham without David. All the ideas, the craft, the artistry came from him. He is the perfect housekeeper; has all the feminine inclinations.

Wednesday, 25th September

In the morning, Myles takes me to Doddington, now inhabited by Ralph Jarvis's* delightful son and daughter-in-law. The beauty of this

---

* Colonel Ralph Jarvis (1907–73) of Doddington Hall, Lincolnshire; Eton contemporary of J.L.-M.; merchant banker and wartime secret service agent; m. Antonia Meade.

glowing red-brick Elizabethan house, with its pleasant Georgian interior. After tea to Winkburn Hall, a pleasing old mill house with Queen Anne front, Georgian front, Regency front, bought back by present owner, by name Richard Assheton-Pegge-Burnell-Craven-Smith-Milnes, whose father sold estate which had been in the family since 1500s.

Thursday, 26th September

We meet Hugh Matheson who has inherited the Thoresby estate. House now rotting, but Matheson, a lithe and enthusiastic fifty, is in the process of building a replica of Palladio's Villa Caldogno, an enormous affair, roofed but not yet finished. No staircase yet. Of decent modern bricks, it is to be rendered in the Palladian way.

Friday, 27th September

Henry Thorold* came to luncheon, bringing dreary friend from Victorian Society who is an expert on railway stations. He was looking much better than formerly, plump and spruce. M. took him around Flintham and he displayed much ignorance.

After tea, Myles took me to Holme Pierrepont, having bought tickets for a lecture and supper. We were welcomed like VIPs and I was conducted around this fragment of a medieval palace. Owner Robin Brackenbury† and wife, sister of Hugh Matheson. They inhabit what was the 'lodgings', a fair-sized fragment in red brick. Effusive, and slightly boring about their ancestors.

These days of country house visiting are like old times. I imagine the Nottinghamshire and Lincolnshire landed gentry, now thinly spread, are lonely folk.

Myles has become a marked character. Very squirearchical, and philistine in that he ignores arts such as music that do not interest him. If you ask him what a room he has just seen looks like, he will not know. Yet he has sure natural taste, and can discern the good from the

---

* The Revd Henry Thorold (1921–2000); squire of Marston Hall, Lincolnshire; bachelor antiquarian and writer of guide books; sometime housemaster and chaplain of Lancing College.
† Robert Brackenbury (b. 1929); m. Elizabeth Matheson (b. 1936), half-sister of Hugh Matheson (b. 1949).

bad. Sculpture is the art which most appeals to him, because it is tactile. He is the kindest old bear alive, proud of his ancient status in the County of Nottingham, and I love his society.

Tuesday, 1st October–Friday, 4th October

With Debo to stay three nights [with Diana Mosley] at Orsay. We travel from City Airport on eastern edge of London, rather romantic – wide expanses, take-off over river and sea, ultramarine under deep blue sky.

On the Thursday, the Feray* brothers lunch. They are incorrigible socialites who behave as Hamish Erskine behaved, amusing, sharp, *à la page*. I don't feel absolutely happy because I can't respond, and feel I am a drag on their jollity.

Have long talks with both Debo and Diana. One evening, Debo and I go for a walk and peer over walls of hideous and vulgar middle-class villas, with concreted lawns and pretentious ironwork. We talk about her problems over the future of her beloved cottage in Swinbrook, and mine over the future of my library. Debo with all her responsibilities makes time for lame ducks, and even feels occasional loneliness.

Sunday, 6th October

One hundred years ago today, a haycart drew William Morris's[†] body from Lechlade station to Kelmscott church. I joined a party of the Antiquaries to commemorate this event. His tomb in the churchyard is still isolated and sheltered under drooping trees. Made by Philip Webb[‡] in Viking style. Striking, and very *de l'époque*. Beside it in the grass, a round slab with 'M.M.' carved – this to May Morris,[§] daughter, whom I remember sitting on the platform at N.T. and SPAB annual meetings in London, a little dark old lady with a frown. None

---

* Jean and Thierry Feray; unmarried French brothers, officials of the *Monuments Historiques*, who lived together in the rue Cambon, Paris, and died together in a car crash in 1999.
† British craftsman, designer, writer, typographer and socialist (1834–96).
‡ Architect and designer (1831–1915); co-founder with William Morris of Society for Protection of Ancient Buildings (1877).
§ Designer and craftswoman, and editor of her father's works (1862–1938).

of the other Fellows present known to me. We lunched in the barn close to the manor house. I walked through the village to the church service at 2 p.m. and was given a seat in front row at the crossing. Very old church, Norman, with a transept. Several readings, one with Morris's beautiful description of the church. Several substantial houses in the village, one with stone slab fencing on the road, like tombstones. Never seen this before. The manor makes an enticing group of rooftops, tall diamond-wise chimneys, pointed gables with ball finials, and wooden guttering projecting several feet from the eaves. Little windows in attic have tiny pediments which give the Elizabethan structure a faintly Renaissance air. The outside is as lovely as any Cotswold house known to me. Inside no longer a lived-in manor house, but a well-ordered museum. Blue-and-white William de Morgan tiles inserted by Morris in the grates. Several flashy late seventeenth-century fireplaces of carved garlands. Tapestry room upstairs remembered by me from 1942, the panels ruthlessly cut to shape the walls. When last seen, this room was musty and romantic. Now tidied up somewhat.

J.L.-M. moved out of his Bath library in the course of October.

Tuesday, 8th October

John Saumarez Smith came down for the day to Bath. A great help to me, because he makes up his mind at once. He has separated those books I want to get rid of into two piles, the majority, which he will sell in his shop, and the rest, to be disposed of to some trash bookseller. He is a breathless talker, which tires me somewhat. The same is true of Tony Mitchell, who kindly came to the library to advise Pickford's men on how to remove large items of furniture. It was amusing to watch these giants talking and waving their arms like characters in a comic opera.

Thursday, 10th October

Simon [Lees-Milne] came to Bath for the day, and gratefully took away all I had got out to give him, unreadable books relevant to the family and odd assortments of china. Mercifully he is passionate about the dreary Lees family. He has conventional views on every subject, and is jocular, middle-class and happy with his lot. He told me that, as Elaine lay dying, his American half-sister asked her if she would like to see her eldest son David Guthrie, now living in Cheltenham, aged sixty-two, with whom she had never so much as communicated since she deserted his father for Dick when he was three. 'Oh well, I suppose I might,' she said. He saw her at the hospital, but Simon has no idea what they talked about, as she said nothing about it before falling unconscious soon after. He turned up at the funeral but left as soon as it was over.

Saturday, 12th October

Nick Robinson and Jamie Fergusson lunched. I gave the latter the little bust of a bald man by W. Jones dated 1838, which I used to think was of Lord Melbourne until I discovered that M. maintained a shock of hair into old age. Jamie seemed to be touched. He is so devitalised that he sits silent, unable to make up his mind to move away. Yet when interested rouses himself and is clever and wise. Nick and I went to Bath, where he chose many family books and the table from which I have eaten my meals there these past twenty-two years.

Thursday, 17th October

Telephoned Debo this evening and breezily asked her how things were. 'Haven't you heard of our dreadful tragedy?' she retorted. Their beloved [chef] Jean-Pierre drove himself into a tree and killed himself outright, in full view of visitors to Chatsworth. He was indispensable, and they are dreadfully upset. Debo nearly in tears in the telling. They have fourteen of his French family staying in the hotel for the funeral.

Saturday, 19th October

Hugh Massingberd came to luncheon alone, dropped by Andrew Barrow, his friend from Harrow. Has abandoned his diet, and polished off the whole of a sweet, sticky pudding left by Nick. There is no one I am happier talking to. He wants to write a book about the heroes he worships and longs to emulate.*

---

* It was published by Macmillan in 2001 as *Daydream Believer: Confessions of a Hero Worshipper*, and includes a chapter on J.L.-M. ('Saint Jim').

Wednesday, 23rd October

Grant writes accepting my next batch of diaries – 1975–8 – which Murray's will publish in 1998.* Shall I be alive? Nice however to have some work ahead of me. I need not be at a loose end for the remainder of my days. Oddly, if he had rejected them, I do not think I would have minded much.

I am almost ashamed of the pleasure I am taking in rearranging my furniture, pictures and objects from Bath at Essex House, where they replace A's things taken away by Clarissa. The Isfahan carpet looks well in my book room. Spent hours positioning Marie Antoinette on her pedestal in my downstairs room, eventually deciding she would have to look out of the window. This is a thoroughly bourgeois pastime which most British people lapse into on their retirement.

Wednesday, 30th October

The *Independent* and *Telegraph* both ring to announce death of Sylvia Chancellor,† and ask if I will obituarise. I decline, but write to Susanna [Johnston] about her wonderful, eccentric, clever, funny mother.

Friday, 1st November

J.K–B. stays the night, and tells me that tomorrow he becomes an old age pensioner. The pace of time.

Wednesday, 6th November

Lunched with Hart-Davises at Owlpen. All the other guests were friends whom I much like – Charlie Morrisons, Keens, Gerda [Barlow]; yet I was in a daze after reading proofs of my 1973–4 diaries, which froze me with horror over my criticisms of friends who are either still living or have children. It is too late now to make more than minimal changes. John Saumarez Smith assures me that they are 'compulsive reading'.

---

* They appeared posthumously that year as *Through Wood and Dale*.
† Sylvia Paget, dau. of Sir Richard Paget, 2nd Bt, and Lady Muriel Finch-Hatton, dau. of 12th Earl of Winchilsea and Nottingham; m. 1926 Sir Christopher Chancellor (1904–89).

John says that Heywood Hill will pay me £15,000 for the books they have taken. I am amazed by this huge sum. I said I would accept £3,000, the rest to be donated to the National Trust for their scheme to re-establish libraries in country houses.[*]

Thursday, 7th November

Peggy prepared a good luncheon for Clarissa and Billy, to whom I was to hand over the keys to No. 19 [Lansdown Crescent]. I said, don't be late. They were. He telephoned from Acton Turville to announce that their car had broken down near Tormarton. I fetched them. Luncheon ruined while Billy feverishly telephoned a rescue service. A van eventually arrived with their car hoisted on it, and they went off together, having forgotten to take the keys.

Tuesday, 12th November

Mark Bence-Jones's[†] book *Life in an Irish Country House* deals with some dozen houses, several of which I have known, such as Curragh[‡] and Mount Stewart.[§] All Irish houses are deeply romantic, and on the verge of disintegration even when splendid. The book culminates in the period of the Great War, in which all elder sons were killed, the widows lingering on. All tragic, mournful, nostalgic. The atmosphere dead, breathless, green and dank. Queen Alexandra, in signing the visitors' book at Mount Stewart, added the comment, 'A beautiful place, but damp.'

Wednesday, 13th November

To London for the night. In the library at Brooks's I meet Stuart [Preston], who has just come from Heywood Hill where he bought two of my discarded books, one of them given to me by Stephen Spender with a flowery *dédicace*. I am upset by this, John Saumarez

---

[*] It was eventually used to restore a dismantled library at Gunby Hall, Lincolnshire.
[†] Writer (b. 1930), of Glenville Park, Co. Cork.
[‡] Curragh Chase, Co. Limerick, seat of the de Vere family until gutted by fire in 1941.
[§] Seat of Marquesses of Londonderry, on shores of Strangford Lough, Co. Down; donated to Northern Ireland National Trust 1977 by Lady Mairi Bury, yst dau. of 7th Marquess.

having assured me he would advise me if he came across anything which looked personal and I might wish to keep.

Then to Grosvenor House for Foyle's luncheon to celebrate Mrs Major's* book. A grand triumph for Christina† after sixty-six years of these luncheons to have as guests of honour the Prime Minister and wife, a former Prime Minister (Heath), a former Deputy Prime Minister (Whitelaw),‡ two Prime Ministers' widows (Clarissa Avon and Mary Wilson),§ and the former Foreign Secretary (Hurd).¶ As we enter Stratton Room, Clarissa says to me, 'I don't know a soul, but am sitting next to Heath and someone else thrilling.' I find I am sitting on the right of Christina, already seated. Much older and rather deaf, though still pretty. Slumped with head just above table-top, wearing black velvet dress and jewels, very smart. Tells me she is eighty-five. Mrs Major comes up to chat. I rise on being introduced. She has a sweet face. Is followed by husband. With difficulty, I rise again, though he beseeches me not to. He has a nice firm handshake, and beams. As he bends over Christina, his greying hair brushes my chin. Lucky man to have hair. On my right sits Lord Armstrong of Ilminster,** the civil servant who was 'economical with the truth'. Jeffrey Archer†† makes bland introductory speech. Followed not by Mrs Major but Mr, who delivers charming impromptu speech paying wife unqualified praise for her research and writing. I understand how Mr Major is two persons in one. Today he displays his off-duty private persona – natural, funny, nice and engaging.

Dinner at Brooks's for Diana [Mosley], Selina [Hastings] and

---

* Norma Wagstaff (b. 1942; DBE 1999); m. 1970 John Major (Prime Minister, 1990–7); her book *Chequers: The Prime Minister's Country House and its History*, was published by Collins and illustrated with photographs by Mark Fiennes.

† Bookseller (1911–99), Managing Director of W. & G. Foyle Ltd (founded by her father); started Foyle's Literary Luncheons, 1930; m. 1938 Ronald Batty.

‡ William Whitelaw (1918–99); Conservative politician, Deputy Prime Minister to Mrs Thatcher, 1983–8; cr. Viscount, 1983.

§ Mary Baldwin (b. 1918); poet; m. 1940 Harold Wilson (1916–93; Prime Minister, 1964–70 and 1974–6; cr. life peer as Baron Wilson of Rievaulx, 1983).

¶ Douglas Hurd (b. 1930); Conservative politician, Foreign Secretary, 1989–95; cr. life peer as Baron Hurd of Westwell, 1997.

** Robert Armstrong (b. 1927); Cabinet Secretary, 1979–87 (who used the notorious phrase during the 'Spycatcher' case in Australia in 1986); cr. life peer as Baron Armstrong of Ilminster, 1988.

†† Conservative politician and novelist (b. 1940); Deputy Party Chairman, 1985–6; cr. life peer as Baron Archer of Weston-super-Mare, 1992; imprisoned for perjury, 2001.

Richard Shone. Diana as beautiful as ever, with new tooth which cost a thousand pounds. I give her the book which my grandfather* received from her Mosley grandfather-in-law† as a leaving present at Eton. She and I find it very difficult to hear each other, but Selina bawls and is heard. Nevertheless all enjoy it I think.

Thursday, 14th November

To exhibition at National Portrait Gallery of English picture frames throughout the ages. Interesting. Then to lunch at Partridge's‡ in private dining room. Hosted by Mrs Partridge, second wife, and her stepson John, whose mother must have been a Cust,§ for he spoke of Belton as his grandfather's house. Mrs a typical smarty-bootess, much name-dropping and talk of grand houses. 'We often stay at Blenheim. As Bertie¶ said to me . . .' These women all the same, shallow. Said that today's young were all savages; standards were slipping, whereas her generation . . .

Friday, 15th November

Not having heard further from Derek, I turned up at Highgrove at 12.55, asking the policeman on duty whether I was expected. 'Your name, Sir? . . . Yes, you are. Please go ahead.' On arrival, I asked the nice footman where the gents was, for being very old I might suddenly have need. He was about to show me when Prince Charles crossed the hall to welcome me. On the left the drawing room, with a huge fire and Derek sitting hugely in front of it. For once well-groomed, and decently dressed. He is very good with the Prince, on the easiest terms verging on familiarity. Almost cheeky, which is doubtless enjoyed. 'Now, Sir, what will happen to Royal Lodge and the Castle of Mey – not that I care for the last much – when the sad day comes and we lose Queen Elizabeth?' 'Oh, don't!' Derek complimented the Prince's equal facility with brush and pen, saying that he

---

* James Henry Lees-Milne (1847–1908).
† Sir Oswald Mosley, 4th Bt (1848–1915).
‡ Art gallery in Bond Street, founded in Edwardian times.
§ Hon. Caroline Elizabeth Maude Cust (b. 1928), dau. of 6th Baron Brownlow; m. 1954 (as his 1st wife) John Arthur Partridge.
¶ Bert, 10th Duke of Marlborough (1897–1972).

(D.) can't write and his autobiography, though penned by a competent ghost, has been refused by every publisher.

The Prince has exquisite manners as host, yet is very shy and uncertain. Speaks hesitantly without finishing sentences. Is wary, wondering whether he can trust anyone in the world. No longer youthful in appearance, though his countenance is clear. He said he was going to be fifty next birthday. I told him I cried when I turned fifty. 'Did you really?' Calls me by my first name, but I suppose he does this with everyone he meets socially. Has a strange scar on his left cheek of the sort which German students used to acquire from duelling. He is lonely, afraid of experts yet seeking to keep up with them. Told me he was reading *Fourteen Friends*, and asked if Diana [Mosley] was one of them; so he has not got as far as the Table of Contents. 'I wouldn't have dared even if she were dead, which thank God she isn't.' He asked if any loved ones' widows or children, had complained. I said that Anne Lancaster may have been slightly aggrieved. I am not sure if he knew who Osbert Lancaster was. Said he liked looking for and eating wild mushrooms from the woods.

We lunched at the small round table in the window of the small breakfast room overlooking the garden and the hornbeam avenue. Luncheon consisted of a rather dry quiche of the bought kind and his own vegetables, ice cream and stewed peaches for pudding. I felt very at ease, and was enjoying myself. He talked of his recent visit to Russia. Remarked on the pinched faces of the inhabitants. Said all old buildings swept away by the Soviets, to be replaced by the usual modern muck. Even now they sweep away what's left with positive pride in their vandalism. I asked if he saw anything created since Tsarist times which was covetable. Nothing, he replied. We talked of George IV and Wyatville* destroying the Verrio† rooms at Windsor, which he thought deplorable. He asked if I liked Pugin.‡ Moderately, I said – though I liked the wallpapers much.

He showed me all round the downstairs rooms and is very proud of them. Took me to see his framed watercolours in the loo. (Here was my opportunity, but I had no need.) Some I thought very pretty.

---

* Sir Jeffry Wyatville (1766–1840; *né* Wyatt); architect who remodelled Windsor Castle for George IV.
† Antonio Verrio (1639–1707); Italian decorative artist working in England.
‡ A. W. N. Pugin (1812–52); architect and designer in the Gothic style.

Memories of his incognito travels in Greece and Italy with Derek and others. This is what he enjoys and wishes he had more time for. He explained that most of the house's contents come from the lumber rooms at Windsor. Walls are crammed, which I like to see. Frederick, Prince of Wales* in superb Rococo frame with bold feathers atop. Tables also crammed with gifts, huge seventeenth-century bible with silver facings and clasps given by wife of Laurens van der Post.† Spoke highly of him, and 'that dear man Gervase'. Treasures everywhere. His own office filled with piles of unread art books and paintings by young artists.

The Prince clearly very fond of Derek. Gave him a copy of his recent diary. While I was saying goodbye soon after three, Derek asked for Camilla's telephone number, which the Prince rolled off his tongue. A car at the door to take Derek back to London. Derek said he must take a photograph of us both, and that the Prince must put on his fox-fur, red-velvet-lined mantle with matching hood. Prince Charles expostulated, but was bulldozed by Derek. He shyly donned these wonderful garments which I had seen him wearing in newspaper photographs. We walked onto the drive in the sun. I discreetly distanced myself from the Prince as Derek snapped away.

What a sweet man. Heart bang in the right place. Earnest about his charities, and writhes in misery at the destruction of the world. Not very clever in spite of praiseworthy intentions. Lays himself open to criticism because he contends with intellectuals and specialists in fields of which he can inevitably have only superficial knowledge. He deserves all our encouragement and support. A figure of tragedy with abundant charm.

Saturday, 16th November

Derek on the telephone, asking how I liked Him. Oh very much indeed, I replied. And he liked you too, said D. I said, you are a bully. You simply drove him to put on that garment and be photographed. 'Did I really?' he said, and laughed. 'So like me.'

---

* Son of George II and father of George III (1707–51); the first Hanoverian to show a serious interest in the arts.
† South African-born writer (1906–96; ktd 1981) interested in mysticism and the Jungian concept of the collective unconscious; m. 1928 Marjorie Edith Wendt (d. 1995).

Tuesday, 19th November

Filthy day of continuous rain and wind. Misha came for the night. He has his fads, and like all Londoners hates the cold. We lunched indoors, and in spite of rain, wind and dark I took him to dine at the King's Arms at Didmarton. Rather frightening, as I could hardly distinguish the road from the verge because of the fallen leaves. I told him how much distaste I have for homosexuality now. He seemed rather shocked, and reluctant to believe me.*

Sunday, 24th November

I drove in pouring rain to lunch with the Norwiches, down their inundated lane. Very kind they are to ask me, but I don't think I'm fit company any more. They had Elizabeth Jane Howard,† Moira and Ludovic Kennedy, and Fram Dinshaw,‡ deserted husband of the beautiful bolter Candia.§ E. J. Howard, at whose wedding to Peter Scott I was an usher, is now a stout matron and a great-grandmother, with flowing aluminium hair. Very friendly, and invited me to stay with her in Suffolk next summer. Ludovic K. now bent over a stick, his handsome head turned downwards; but Moira still very pretty and tiny, with the supple figure of the dancer she was. Faultless profile which I do not remember from the days when she visited us at Roquebrune. Perched on a high stool in front of the fire, hugging her delicate feet. Full of self-confidence, her voice somewhat affected. Talked of Freddy Ashton,¶ whose biography she has just slated in the *Spectator*. Said he was no genius, and lazy; never had an idea of his own. Everyone present united in complaint of the *Spectator*'s new editor, Frank Johnson.** Conversation turned to us all

---

* During this visit, J.L.-M. mentioned to Michael Bloch, his designated literary executor, Murray's proposal to commission his biography (see 19 September above), saying that he dreaded it being undertaken in his lifetime, as it would inevitably involve discussion of his homosexual past, of which he now felt bitterly ashamed. (Details from M.B's own diary.)

† Novelist (b. 1923); m. 1st Peter Scott, 2nd James Douglas-Henry, 3rd Kingsley Amis.

‡ Fellow of St Catherine's College, Oxford (b. 1954).

§ Candia McWilliam (b. 1955); writer; m. 1st 1981 (diss. 1984) Hon. Quentin Wallop (who s. 1984 as 10th Earl of Portsmouth), 2nd Fram Dinshaw; admirer of J.L.-M., who had known her father, Colin McWilliam, architectural historian.

¶ Sir Frederick Ashton (1904–88); choreographer.

** Journalist (b. 1943); editor, *Spectator*, 1995–9.

reciting limericks. I found this luncheon rather a strain, yet was pleased to be there.

Monday, 25th November

Derek has sent me the photograph of Prince Charles accoutred in his fur-lined gabardine, smiling and looking self-conscious. Very charming picture.

I am beside myself with shame correcting the proofs of my diaries for 1973. A catalogue of complaints and nonsensical verbiage. 1974 is better.

Wednesday, 27th November

Lunched with Bruce Hunter at Athenaeum. Very civilised. Club has recently had marble floor of hall relaid at great cost, old floor having been ruined by kitchen trolleys trundling to dining room. Bruce persuaded me to allow Murray's to republish *Another Self*.* I hope it will not come out before my death. I don't want to face the inevitable question, 'Is it true?'

Wednesday, 4th December

I sit in my three rooms admiring the improvements I have made, and wondering what A. would think of them.

This journal has become extremely boring. I think I may stop it at the end of this year, before my operation.

Saturday, 7th December

Debo telephones that she is awaiting arrival of Prince Charles and Derek for the famous weekend. She has prepared dinner in the library and erected some sort of flowered aedicule in which to ensconce Derek, with little bells attached. Hold on, she interrupts. Oh, that was Henry to say that the Prince has rung from his car that his arrival is imminent.

---

* J.L.-M's much-praised autobiographical novel, originally published by Hamish Hamilton in 1970, was reissued by Faber & Faber in 1984, John Murray in 1998 (two months after J.L.-M's death), and Michael Russell in 2003.

Tuesday, 10th December

Debo telephones to tell me about weekend. She evidently has some reservations about Derek's proprietary attitude towards the Prince. Indeed is mystified as to why the Prince puts up with his cheekiness. For instance, D. keeps telephoning the P. when the latter withdraws to his bedroom between tea and dinner. Camilla is also at Chatsworth, and the Prince blossoms in her company. It was there that they first met, twenty-four years ago.

Saturday, 14th December

A sparkling sunny day after a night of severe frost. To Langford to lunch with Hardy [Amies]. I must say his house is *bien*. Charming the way he has looped a tapestry panel over entrance door to the big room, as at Cotehele [Cornwall]. The Faringdons present. She is one of the greatest beauties, but cold and stiff. He jolly and roaring at every word one utters. Both very friendly to me. They spoke of the problems they have had choosing a new vicar. Out of fifteen candidates, ten had been through the divorce courts. They have moved out of beautiful Barnsley to make way for their second son,* and are having a sort of prefabricated chalet erected at Buscot where they will live in summer to avoid the visitors to the house. They evidently don't care much for the N.T. regional committee. She complained that, when thirty of them lunched at Buscot, ten demanded vegetarian food and some insisted that the peacocks be shut up.

Sunday, 29th December

Christmas at Chatsworth. The moment Coote and I arrived we sensed there was something wrong with Debo. She looked flushed and unusually wan. Next morning, Christmas Eve, she was in bed with virulent 'flu, and stayed there, save for coming down to dinner on Christmas Day. I sat next to her and was in terror of catching the bug because of my impending operation. (Debo calls my condition 'Before the Bombardment'.†) In her absence, Andrew was a

---

* Hon. Thomas Henderson (b. 1966).
† Title of novel by Osbert Sitwell (1926), set in Scarborough during the First World War.

perfect host. Staying were Alastair and Sophie Morrison, with two children, Pat Trevor-Roper, Margaret Budd, Paddy [Leigh Fermor] (having left Joan at Dumbleton, she also down with 'flu), Coote and self. Debo gave me the Canning bedroom because it has a bathtub and loo in it. Yet it was miles from drawing room and dining room.

Walked with Paddy. He told me that his father was a geologist in India. P. seldom saw him, but adored his mother who loved reading and poetry and communicated this love to him. I marvel at his knowledge. One has only to recite a line of poetry and he will continue the quotation for half an hour. How handsome he is, at eighty-one. Still has firm profile, and all his hair.

On Friday Coote and Paddy and I were driven home by chauffeur in Andrew's luxurious Bentley, which he is about to discard for a new one. We lunched at Mill House, Dumbleton. Most lugubrious, Joan's brother Graham* (whose arrangements she won't alter) obviously having had little taste.

Watched Jan Morris† on television visiting three cities she has written about. Her female role is unconvincing. Looks like a camp old man in drag. Deep masculine voice, large head. The citizens of Cairo seemed bewildered by her as she stalked around the souks.

Tuesday, 31st December

Since return, I have spent most of my time answering unsolicited letters and thanking people who have sent me their books. Charles Keen sent me his *Daphnis and Chloe*, Edward Fawcett‡ a volume of poems, Julian Fane his *Obiter Dicta*, and Nicholas Shakespeare his life of Bruce Chatwin. I have also been writing an introduction for Heywood Hill's sale catalogue of my books.

Today the customary New Year's Eve luncheon at Old Werretts. I have accepted much hospitality this year from Desmond and Ian, who are unfailingly kind to me. When I got home, Bath Clinic telephoned asking if I might come in tomorrow instead of Thursday, to undergo the op. on Thursday at one o'clock. Saw no reason why not, so agreed.

---

* Graham Eyres Monsell, 2nd and last Viscount Monsell (1905–93).
† Writer (b. 1926), known as Morris prior to a much-publicised sex change in 1973.
‡ Director of Public Relations at N.T., 1969–88.

This evening Peggy Willis* rang to ask if the Derek Hill who has been awarded the CBE in New Year's Honours is our Derek. I said to Peggy, 'Derek won't be pleased. CBE isn't much.' 'What do you mean?' she replied. 'I was awarded it.' I had no idea. 'But in Derek's eyes it won't mean much,' I said. 'He would expect the KG at least.' She referred to my mention of her missing right hand. Said no one she knew ever referred to it, and her mother taught her never to do so herself. She was happy that I had at last recorded the fact of her disability. Is pleased that her younger son has been appointed Lord-Lieutenant of Warwickshire, the elder one already being Lord-Lieut of Herefordshire.† This is unusual, possibly unique.

---

* Margaret Anne, dau. of T. Walker; m. (1st) 1930 Philip Dunne MC of Gatley Park, Herefordshire. The mention of her referred to is in *A Mingled Measure*, 3 December 1972, when J.L.-M. found her 'very civilised and sympathetic . . . so beautiful a woman she must have been, with two if not more husbands and beaux galore'.
† The brothers Sir Thomas Dunne (b. 1933; KCVO 1995; Lord-Lieutenant, Hereford and Worcester, 1977–2001) and Martin Dunne (b. 1938; Lord-Lieutenant, Warwickshire from 1997).

1997

On New Year's Day I went into the Bath Clinic. The anaesthetist, Mr Suter – who is incidentally the most Apollonian man I have ever encountered – decided not to give me a full anaesthetic, but to numb me from the waist down with a spinal injection. Great relief, as I had been dreading the coming-round and consequent effects. So I was wheeled in my bed down to the theatre and given a prick in the base of the spine. I kept wondering when it was going to begin, when a voice said it was all over. Incredible. I slept, had tea, and remained jolly for the rest of the day. Next day I felt awful, and thought I would never be able to pee again. But when I did so, the gush and flow were as strong as they used to be when I was eighteen.

On Sunday, Mr Smith came to tell me I could go home the next day at 7 p.m. He is a very intelligent man. Says there will always be unemployment because there will always be a class of drones, and we live in an age when only skilled workers can expect employment. The problem is how to keep the drones partially content.

Home since yesterday. I don't feel ill, just exhausted and unable to concentrate, or do anything except moon around in my dressing gown and lie on the bed.

In my current state I have refused two commissions – to write the *DNB* entry for Brian Fothergill,* and do a review for the *Oldie*. Nor do I feel much like tackling *Bruce Chatwin* for the *TLS* – but I must accept, or it is a total giving up.

Finished *Oliver Twist*. Academically speaking, a bad novel. Improbable sequences, exaggerated horrors, political bias, too much moralising, often deplorable syntax. Of course the picture of London in William IV's reign is deeply depressing and indeed terrifying, if

---

* Historical writer (1921–90) who had treated several of J.L.-M's favourite subjects – including William Beckford and the Jacobites – and like him twice won the Heinemann Prize.

true. Yet the characters – Fagin, Sykes – stand out like Shakespeare's. Oliver Twist himself is cardboard. I didn't enjoy.

Sunday, 12th January

Suddenly I feel well again. Walked to Little Badminton across the park and back by the road. Not the least tired. The Arctic cold has gone, and it is mild and damp. A streak of sun, enough to bring a sniff of the damned spring.

In my new Smythson's diary, I have only one engagement down for this year – Coote's birthday party in March, to which I may not go. I haven't yet answered Maureen Dufferin's* card for her ninetieth, tiaras and white ties. The very idea. Yet I wish I felt like going.

Tuesday, 14th January

Greatly distressed on opening *The Times* to be confronted by Elspeth Huxley's obituary. A month ago she seemed frailer than usual, although full of spirit, muttering provocative political opinions. How I shall miss her. One of the very few neighbours whose society I truly enjoyed. She was eighty-nine. It seems just yesterday that her mother Nellie died at ninety-two.

Watched documentary on Tracy Worcester. Not bad at all. To my surprise, she did and said nothing idiotic. Can look very beautiful, and smiles becomingly. Shots of her with the Newbury by-pass protesters. She does not seem to have any constructive suggestions as to how to prevent the world sliding into environmental ruin. Deploring and protesting is not enough. Then saw a very upsetting film on the last years of Nureyev.† He never ceased to be adored and venerated, for all his faults. No wonder – for the flashbacks to his heyday take the breath away. A Byron of our time.

---

* Maureen Guinness (1907–98); m. 1st 1930 Basil, 4th Marquess of Dufferin & Ava (schoolfriend of J.L.-M.; d. 1945), 2nd 1948–54 Major Desmond Buchanan, 3rd 1955 Judge John Cyril Maude; continued to call herself Maureen, Marchioness of Dufferin during her later marriages.
† Russian dancer (1938–93); died of Aids.

Monday, 20th January

Henry [Robinson] came to dine on his own. Extremely sweet he was. He talks all the time, not about books like Nick, for he does not read, but he has interesting views on life. Is disappointed that his boy Alexander, aged ten, has failed to get into Eton. He is just the decent sort of country boy who would benefit from Eton, but because he puts country life before learning, he failed. Henry feels very lucky, with Moorwood which he adores, wife and three sprogs. He thinks it important that the children should get away from home, at least for an interval. Henry himself was unable to do so; his mother died of cancer when he was twenty-one, and he had to look after his alcoholic father while attending agricultural college.

Wednesday, 22nd January

The Victoria Gallery in Bath has excellent exhibitions to which few Bathites go. Today I looked at *The Room in View*, containing pictures of writers and artists in their everyday surroundings. Photograph of Mr Gladstone reclining on chaise longue, concentrating deeply on an open book. An oil of Raymond Mortimer at Long Crichel by Edward le Bas,* quite unrecognisable.

Lunched today with the dear Levis at Prospect Cottage. Excellent meal – caviare in cream, calves' liver and delicious pudding. Anthony Hobson† was the other guest, and brought a pile of books of mine for signature. Flattering, from one of the great bibliophiles. Deirdre is adorable, always smiling, like a radiant golden moon. How I love her. The mysterious little Matthew present, silent yet missing nothing. I rushed away to get home before dark.

Sunday, 26th January

A beautiful day. In early afternoon I drove along the lane from Badminton to Sopworth, left car on verge and walked through the village. Church locked, but Pevsner‡ says nothing within. Nevertheless very pretty on summit overlooking a vast field. Graveyard full

---

* English artist (1904–66).
† Bibliographical historian (b. 1921); m. 1959 Tanya Vinogradoff.
‡ Sir Nikolaus Pevsner (1902–83); Professor of Fine Arts, Cambridge (1949–55) and Oxford (1968–9); originator of *The Buildings of England* series of county guides.

of wool merchants' tombs. Sopworth, two miles from Badminton as the crow flies, is in Wiltshire. I talked to an old lady with a spotted dog, who asked if I was 'a local man'. When I replied that I lived in Badminton, she expressed astonishment that I had walked all the way. I had to disabuse her. Ten years ago I would have done so, and back.

Although I don't want to go to parties or even to see anyone, nevertheless I am often assailed with a sense of imprisonment in my ivory tower. So I venture out, as I did today, for a drive or a short walk. But after a while, discomfort assails me. No one who has not been through their late eighties can conceive of the hell of them. It is as though one is being subjected to a different torture every day.

Wednesday, 29th January

Watched 'Born to Rule', first part of BBC2's *Aristocracy* series. Fine views of Chatsworth, Christmas feeding of tenants' children in Painted Hall. Debo excellent, looking so pretty. Programme dwells too much on eccentricities of peers like the pansy Lord Anglesey,* and frivolities such as the Devonshire House Ball.† Not so much hostile as ignorant. No mention of contribution made by aristos to architecture, fine arts, the landscape, nor of their performance of public duties, rural and national. They are treated as though remote from ordinary people, and solely devoted to pleasure.

Thursday, 6th February

Received outraged letter from Rick Stewart-Jones's surviving sister Beanie taking exception to my quoting Robert Byron's description of the S.-J. establishment in Cheyne Walk, where I lodged in the late Thirties, as 'that refined brothel'.‡ I did in fact deprecate the bad taste of this remark in my book, but thought it worth quoting as it is so

---

* Henry Paget, 5th Marquess of Anglesey (1875–1905); 'the Dancing Marquess'; m. 1898 (diss. 1900) Lilian Chetwynd.
† Legendary costume extravaganza of 1897.
‡ An ardent architectural conservationist, Stewart-Jones had used a legacy to purchase a row of fine but dilapidated houses in Cheyne Walk which had once formed part of a great seventeenth-century residence, with a view (never realised) to restoring and reuniting them. Lacking money for their upkeep, he had turned them into boarding houses, the lodgers including several bohemian couples.

typical of Robert. In apologising to Beanie, I said I felt like a war criminal being accused of something done fifty years ago.

Sunday, 9th February

Re-read J. T. Smith's life of Nollekens, bought by me in 1941 from the second-hand bookshop in Evesham kept by the delightful lady with fuzzy lip and dyed red hair. Smith exceedingly caustic about Nollekens and Mrs, both misers and living in appalling squalor.

The Chandors to tea, bringing me a delicious chocolate cake, and showing me a book they had bought which belonged to Beckford. She told me that, during her debutante days, she worked for MI5. Would go every morning to HQ in Curzon Street from where she and other junior staff would be driven to a 'secret' address in Burlington Gardens, above a tailor's shop. Her duty was to listen in to telephone conversations of people known to be living beyond their earnings. She said it was fascinating work for a time, but eventually got on her nerves. Anything suspicious overheard was taken down in pencil, there being no instant recording equipment in those days. I did not like to ask which days those were as it would have revealed her age.

During their visit Debo rang in a great state about the forthcoming show at the Lyric Theatre in commemoration of Decca, details of which have been revealed in the 'Times Diary'. She agreed to back this show, but was not told about the content, put together by Decca's old Communist friends and involving hearses and coffins on stage. I strongly advised her and Andrew not to attend.

Monday, 10th February

I am always amused by the rules which old people set themselves. Gerry Wellington would never allow himself a drink before the clock struck six. Taking out his watch, he would say, 'Only another five minutes before we can have a cocktail.' Whereas I say to myself, 'It's nearly four o'clock, when the radiators come on.' My besetting vice is not drink but meanness.

Wednesday, 12th February

I have made a Lent resolution – to be nice to someone every day. Went to Communion at Little Badminton in the evening, and was irritated by the four hymns and the churchiness of the usual congregation.

Another of the *Aristocracy* programmes this evening, entitled 'Letting in the Hoi Polloi'. Better than the previous ones, and Lord Lichfield really good, pointing out how much tougher the upper classes were, taking the lead in a crisis and putting their lives at risk. I came on. What I said was not too bad, but I was horrified by my appearance, with drooling lower lip and dead sheep's eyes. Made to read extracts from my diaries. Mere snippets of the interview shown – the usual treatment. Someone in the village said to Peggy afterwards, 'Poor old soul.'

Saturday, 15th February

I telephoned Miranda yesterday asking if she would dine with me at the Didmarton pub. Result was that I was invited to dine at the House today. We were about sixteen. David very charming and sat with me afterwards. I remarked that every other person seemed to be a millionaire these days. You only have to own a house and some nice possessions. 'Yes,' said D., 'every vicar is now a millionaire because of his furniture. But he can't eat it. It's very unfair.' I sat next to Lord Mancroft* at dinner, whom I much liked. He talked of his great friend Roger Scruton,† whom he described as tactless and opinionated, but the cleverest man he knew.

Tuesday, 18th February

To London, staying night at Brooks's, for dinner given by Henry Hoare‡ at Hoare's Bank, Fleet Street for Tony Mitchell's retirement from N.T. About twenty present. I was placed between Mrs Hoare and Alastair Laing.§ What with the dim light, the old, unfamiliar or unrecognisable faces, blindness, deafness, muddle, fuddle, I didn't enjoy it as much as I ought to have done, and could not take in the treasures displayed, such as Jane Austen's correspondence with her

---

* Benjamin Mancroft, 3rd Baron Mancroft (b. 1957); campaigner for the homeless, the rehabilitation of drug addicts, and field sports.
† Writer and philosopher of libertarian views (b. 1944).
‡ Henry Cadogan Hoare (b. 1931); Chairman, C. Hoare & Co.; owner of that part of Stourhead estate in Wiltshire not bequeathed to the N.T. by his distant cousin Sir Henry Hoare in 1947; m. (2nd) 1977 Caromy Maxwell Macdonald.
§ Adviser on pictures to N.T.

banker. I left at 10.30, escorted to the door most politely by my host. It is a fact that I can no longer attend such festivities.

Friday, 21st February

Have been reading Emily Lutyens[*] on her infatuation with Krishnamurti.[†] Strange how educated people could have believed that this Indian youth was a Messiah, and sad the disillusion that ensued. Wish I had an opportunity of discussing with Mary Lutyens,[‡] who knew him as a child and loved him too, and even contemplated marrying him. K. must have had great charisma and a gift of tongues. Yet on reaching manhood he dissolved the Theosophical movement and disclaimed his own divinity. Longed in fact to divest himself of the aura, his followers, the foolery.

Sunday, 23rd February

I heard from Joanie Holland that Joshua Rowley[§] died on Friday. Of all those I knew who are dead and gone, he was one of the best. Always that large, round, beaming face, sweet smile, twinkling eyes, gurgling laugh. Not intellectual, just a simple country gentleman; an absolute gentleman. Dutiful, Lord-Lieutenant, on every right committee, especially those associated with Suffolk. I remember him coming to the N.T. for a job soon after the war. He took the lowly one of curator of Packwood [House, Warwickshire], then a little-visited property. He was still suffering from having been a prisoner-of-war, almost a psychological case. We all loved him in the office. And what fun he was.

Wednesday, 26th February

The Levis came to tea, Deirdre bringing biscuits and a pot of marmalade. She said she kept a diary of her early life when living in these

---

[*] Lady Emily Lytton (1874–1964), dau. of 1st Earl of Lytton; m. 1897 Sir Edwin Lutyens (1869–1944), architect.
[†] Indian sage (1895–1986); adopted in childhood and educated in England by the Theosophist Annie Besant; recognised as the movement's 'world teacher' until his dissolution of it in 1929.
[‡] Writer (1908–99); dau. of Sir Edwin and Lady Emily Lutyens; biographer of Krishnamurti; m. (2nd) 1945 J. G. Links (d. 1997), royal furrier and expert on Canaletto.
[§] Sir Joshua Rowley, 5th Bt (1920–97), of Tendring Hall, Suffolk; Deputy Secretary of N.T., 1952–5.

parts, which I begged her to let me read. I showed her and the silent Matthew the book room. Matthew has a furtive manner, all eyes, although tongue so seldom loosened. In book room he was immediately drawn to the volumes on genealogy.

Am reading Phyllis Grosskurth's large biography of Byron, which claims to be the first for forty years. Just as Richard Holmes in his enormous book makes Shelley out to be a fiend, so this lady does the same for B. I dare say they are both right, having rootled out a lot of compromising papers unavailable to their predecessors.

Sunday, 2nd March

Back from cruise down the Nile, which she adored, Debo telephones. She has at last received directions from Diana about what to do on her death. Diana wishes to be cremated in France, no one to attend, her ashes to be brought to England for burial at Swinbrook after a full, proper Christian service. It's true, I said, that everyone wishes to return home in the end. 'Yes, but she hated life at home,' says Debo. I said that was nonsense really; she had a lovely time, with the sisters and Tom and indulgent parents, until she left to be married at eighteen.

Tuesday, 4th March

Graham Kinnaird,* whose obituary is in *The Times*, was a good old soul. I met him in ARP work at the beginning of the war, and often subsequently at Brooks's. He was the King of Mollycoddles, always avoiding draughts and wrapping himself in scarves and topcoats. Did not belong to his generation; spoke in a slow, old-fashioned way, deplored the degradation of manners. Large shapeless mouth, teeth like broken eggs. The last of his line, which is sad. Surprising that no heir produced by his late brother George,† who resembled their great-great-uncle, Byron's friend Douglas Kinnaird,‡ a jolly drunken rake.

---

* 13th and last Lord Kinnaird (1912–97).
† Hon. George Kinnaird (1914–73); literary adviser to John Murray; m. 1950 (diss. 1963) Lady Elizabeth Olive James, dau. of 8th Earl of St Germans.
‡ Hon. Douglas Kinnaird (1788–1830); yr s. of 7th Lord Kinnaird; Byron's London banker who also acted as his literary agent.

Friday, 7th March

When Duff Hart-Davis rings, I fear the worst and imagine that Rupert has died. Not that, thank God, but he is very downcast by having his last volume of memoirs turned down by Murray's. It strikes me as rather shocking that Rupert, the highly venerated biographer, publisher, man of letters, literary executor of Walpole,[*] Sassoon[†] and other great writers, should be rejected,[‡] whereas I, whom Rupert once refused to publish and who have always felt exceedingly humble in comparison, am one of Murray's favoured authors. Of course, I must remember that I am no more than the Godfrey Winn[§] *de nos jours*.

Monday, 10th March

This is the most wonderful moment of thrusting spring. The rusty lichen on the stone at a peak of beauty. How does it get there? The tiny leaves of the incense rose budding by the front door. Amelanchier trees likewise. A brimstone butterfly, more ginger than rust. Small bees in the acid green centres of upturned white crocuses.

Wednesday, 12th March

To London for the day. To exhibition at Wartski's of tiaras. Two tiny rooms crammed with old women in pearls, drooling over glass cases. Several items of great beauty, I admit, but I decided that one hundred tiaras were too many. At Brooks's fell in with Francis Sitwell, who is excitedly awaiting publication of Aunt Edith's letters. I said rather apologetically that I was coming round to her poetry. Lunched upstairs with Angus Stirling, now retired from both N.T. and Covent Garden and devoting himself to giving funerary addresses. Then to National Gallery to see Denis Mahon's[¶] exhibition of Baroque paintings. I can't enjoy Carlo Dolci's simpering sibyls with eyes upcast to Heaven, though the startling colours, so bold and uncompromising, delight those whose palates relish gusto and flavour.

---

[*] Sir Hugh Walpole (1884–1941); novelist.
[†] Poet and writer (1886–1967).
[‡] His memoir was finally published in 1998 by Sutton as *Halfway to Heaven*.
[§] British journalist (1908–71); star writer in women's magazines from the 1930s to the 1960s, notorious for his tone of sentimental whimsy.
[¶] Sir Denis Mahon (b. 1910); art historian.

Sunday, 16th March

Lunching with Jane Westmorland I met a Mr Drinkwater, nice florid businessman who is chairman of his Tory constituency party. He is a fan of mine. 'You've no idea what this occasion means to me.' We spoke of Jessica Douglas-Home's book on Violet Woodhouse. Drinkwater's father John was Gordon Woodhouse's first cousin, but they quarrelled over an inheritance. John was brought up by Gordon's two old sisters and given to understand that he was the heir to their house, Burghill Court in Herefordshire. Both sisters made wills under which the survivor would leave everything to John. One day they were murdered by their butler, who laid out their corpses on the billiard table before fleeing. It transpired that the elder sister had died first and the younger had forgotten to sign her will. The property therefore passed on intestacy to their next of kin – i.e., Gordon. Gordon wanted to do the decent thing and waive the inheritance in favour of John; but Violet would not let him, as they were quite hard up at the time. The shock of the whole affair drove John Drinkwater to drink, misery and untimely death.

Friday, 21st March

The Poës came to lunch. I told him that he had a distinct look of his mother Frida.[*] He said a man does not relish being told that he resembles his mother. I said that such a thing had never worried me. Emma spoke to me of her walk to Rome, door to door from Westminster Cathedral to St Peter's, crossing the Alps by the Brenner Pass, never once cheating by taking public transport or accepting a lift. Her parents-in-law much disapproved of her for being a Catholic, and divorced. Now, how did she get away with being divorced in the eyes of the Church?

Monday, 24th March

To London for the night. Went to three exhibitions, Braque[†] the best. He was a friend and contemporary of Picasso, but they ultimately fell out, presumably because B. was serious and scholarly whereas P. was

---

[*] Frida Lees, first cousin of J.L.-M's father.
[†] Georges Braque (1882–1963); French artist.

a showman. During the war B. remained in Paris under German occupation, his muddy, colourless canvases reflecting the misery and deprivations of that time. One feels that B's extravagances were never to *épater le bourgeois*, as were P's.

I lunched at Brooks's with Martin Drury to meet new Chairman of the N.T., Charles Nunneley,* who presented me with the Trust's medal, a hefty gold object designed by female Chinese art student, in form of jagged oak leaves and acorns. Nunneley very sympathetic, but appears to know little of the properties and purposes of the N.T. I liked his modesty and gentleness.

Andrew Devonshire called at Brooks's and took me in his grand new motor to Festival Hall to hear Debo lecture to N.T. on Hardwick [Hall, Derbyshire]. Packed. She spoke for over an hour to splendid slides. Extremely interesting talk, as good as could be. She complained afterwards that the audience did not laugh at her jokes. These however were so esoteric, and thrown in so casually, that I doubt whether anyone noticed them. I was made dizzy before and after the lecture by half-familiar faces coming up to me.

Richard Shone dined with me at Brooks's, by which time I felt exhausted. But he was so charming, funny and delightful. Wants to write a book about twentieth-century portrait painting.

Monday, 31st March

Although early, this Easter as beautiful as any remembered. Glorious sun and coldish wind. Garden bursting forth. Having lunched out four days running, I am wondering whether to retire totally from social life.

Received enchanting letter from Mary Lutyens. For an eighty-eight-year-old with whom I have never been intimate, she is delightfully frank. Wrote that Peter Rodd† was a marvellous lover. And that her mother got tired of Lutyens' sexual demands, worshipping Krishnamurti because their relationship was absolutely pure.

---

* (Sir) Charles Nunneley (b. 1936); Chairman, Nationwide Building Society; Chairman, N.T., 1997–2002.
† Hon. Peter Rodd (1904–68); yr s. of 1st Baron Rennell; m. 1933 (diss. 1958) Hon. Nancy Mitford; the model for Evelyn Waugh's egocentric character Basil Seal.

Friday, 4th April

To London to attend Ambrose Congreve's ninetieth birthday luncheon at Warwick House. Party of twelve. Ambrose larger than life, with
healthy complexion. The first fellow guest I met was Lady Heald,*
who I could have sworn died years ago. She too is unchanged at
ninety-six, and making eminent sense. She still lives in a large house
and runs a large garden. Talked of A. and her understanding of plants.
Sir Lionel, who went mad and bad, long since dead. He led her a
dance. Other nonagenarian Monsignor Gilbey, more bent than ever
and inaudible to me. Sat next to Ambrose's charming lady friend, full
of fun and frolic, and Lady Waterford.† Table groaning with silver and
opulence. Four long, drawn-out courses, followed by enormous
birthday cake with single candle which emitted melody of *Happy
Birthday to You*. Everyone amused except Ambrose. At 3.45 the
women withdrew, oddly for luncheon. I found myself talking to nice
brother of duc Decazes, nephew of Princess Winnie. He told me that,
as she had no children, most of her estate had to be divided among
some seventy descendants of her siblings. When time came to leave,
Monsignor and I were borne away in very smart Rolls – Monsignor
to Travellers', I to Paddington. On halting at Travellers' I made a show
of getting out so as to escort the ancient man up the club steps, but
he forbade me, and was escorted by chauffeur. Whereupon he stood
watching the car as we drove away, Don Basilio hat in hand, bowing
slightly. Such exquisite manners. The only remark of his I could hear
was in praise of David Watkin's‡ new book. Wonderful sparkling blue
sash round his waist.

Tuesday, 15th April

Drove in the evening to Charlfield churchyard to see memorial to
those killed in a railway accident of 13 October 1928. A list of ten
persons, ending with 'two unknown' – presumably the two well-

---

* Daphne Price; m. 1929 (as his 2nd wife) Sir Lionel Heald QC, sometime Attorney-
General (d. 1981).
† Lady Caroline Wyndham-Quin (b. 1936), yr d. of 6th Earl of Dunraven and Mount
Earl; m. 1957 John Hubert de la Poer Beresford, 8th Marquess of Waterford (b. 1933).
‡ Historian of architecture (b. 1941); Fellow of Peterhouse, Cambridge; his recent book
on the architect Sir John Soane (1753–1837) had been awarded the Sir Banister Fletcher
Prize.

dressed children whom ticket collector remembered seeing in a compartment on their own. A pretty little church, locked and key unobtainable. Pevsner calls it nineteenth-century, but it looks mediaeval to me, with white harled tower, Perpendicular slit windows, ancient oak door to porch. On return stopped at Wickwar church on its prominent site overlooking town, likewise locked and bolted, as it ought to be. I fear my idea of visiting all churches within a twenty-mile radius of Badminton will come to nothing owing to difficulties of access.

Wednesday, 16th April

Man telephoned from BBC, making a programme about Noël Coward.* I assured him I didn't know N.C. Oh, but you must have met him. Yes, but I didn't know him. But you knew Mrs Astley Cooper. So for twenty minutes we talked of her and Fred her butler, and her habit of picking up young people in need of help and promotion, such as Malcolm Sargent, Scott Moncrieff[†] (she hadn't read his sonnet to her) and Isabel Surtees.[‡] I put him on to the last. He asked whether I would appear on the programme to talk about Mrs C. I enjoy these talks with strangers out of the blue.

Thursday, 17th April

Debo made me go to London to see Padshahnama[§] exhibition at Queen's Gallery. The attendants most polite and correct, old gentlemen in top hats and gold braid, ladies in gowns. Good decoration in show room, dark, matt red walls painted with Muslim arches supported by slender columns in dull gold. Forty miniature panels displayed under dimmed lights, chronicles of Shah Jahan, contemporary of our Charles I whose life like his ended in tragedy. Minutely delineated scenes of tournaments and battles. Human figures shown in profile like Egyptian art, with no perspective or shading. One had to

---

* Actor, playwright, singer, songwriter, poet, novelist and possessor of other talents to amuse (1899–1973).
† C. K. M. Scott Moncrieff (1889–1930); poet, writer and aesthete, best known for his translation into English of the novel of Marcel Proust.
‡ Isabel Surtees (b. 1906); m. 1931 Sir Joseph Napier, 4th Bt; second cousin of J.L.-M.
§ Illustrated manuscript in Royal Library, describing first ten years of reign of Mughal emperor Shah Jahan (1628–58).

shuffle right up to the barrier to see anything. Since the panels were
all pretty alike I soon gave up and left.

On return home, watched Mr Major on television. Very amiable,
charming, smiling, polite, assured he was. He's my man. One old
woman in the audience said to him, 'You are a good, honest man.
Can't you get rid of all the bastards which surround you, and rule us
on your own?' My sentiments entirely.

Sunday, 20th April

I have finished Edith Sitwell's letters. They cast light on Sachie's fits of
profound melancholy, which I fear I ignored in my sketch. He could
not see that other writers were as underrated as he was himself, and
was deeply wounded when Osbert and Edith went off to lecture in
America without him, not realising it was Georgia they wished to
avoid. Edith was far too pleased with herself in her writing, like
Nancy Mitford – a very female trait. Her longing for the love of
Tchelitchev, who rejected her, presents her in a pitiable light. She
chopped and changed in her feelings for friends, sometimes gushing
over them, sometimes reviling them. She was disloyal and vain, but
suffered dreadfully from her lack of physical appeal. Indeed her
appearance was grotesque.

I am mentioned, with high praise, in reviews of Peter Mandler's
Rise and Fall of the Stately Home by Paul Johnson in the *Spectator* and
Brian Masters in the *Daily Mail*. Brian draws attention to a mischievous footnote, which I missed, referring to my 'genius for retro-
spective self-fashioning'. I can't think that, in any of my writings, I
have ever claimed to have done anything remarkable. But it is perhaps
true that my having written so much about the National Trust and its
efforts to save historic buildings may have drawn undue attention to
the small part I played in the process.

Thursday, 24th April

Tea with the Levis at Frampton. Matthew has gone from home; flown.
Undoubtedly good for him, but Deirdre observed that everyone
congratulated him on the break whereas I am the only one to have
commiserated with her on losing him. Well, I know how sad it must
make her, though like the others I see it is best for him. Didn't ask
how the poor boy was supporting himself. Peter murmured some-

thing about genealogical research. A wonderful tea looking out on the dear little garden at the back.

Returned to receive Derry [Drogheda] for the night, just returned from Hong Kong, where he went with Clive Aslet to take photographs. With Derry, conversation flows deliciously, and there are no barriers or awkward silences. I really love him. He said that the breakdown of decency and honesty in this country took place simultaneously with the vandalism of city centres and historic buildings in the 1960s. Life by 1970 was quite different from life in 1960.

Sunday, 27th April

On the way to lunch with the Littles, I stopped at North Wraxall church which I had never seen before. A gem, worthy of Simon Jenkins,* and open this Sunday morning. Splendid Norman arch to entrance door within porch, with zig-zags. Pretty graveyard, old stones and toppling tombs. Memorial tablets to thirteen killed in First World War and two in Second. Victorian stained glass windows, of anthemium-like pattern as of a carpet, very attractive. Old hanging oil lamps, so homely. Grand Jacobean pulpit. Floor of stone flags throughout. The Methuen chapel on north side extremely grand. Ceiling decorated with armorial painted panels as in the dining room at Corsham, obviously by same artist. Alone in the middle an ultra-grand table tomb by Westmacott, to an early eighteenth-century Paul Methuen. Really fine, like a good Chantrey. Nave ceiling barred. A lovely church.

Monday, 28th April

Obituary in *The Times* of dear Joan Camrose, born the same year as me. Senile in recent years but always sweet to me. I wonder what has happened to Hackwood [Hampshire], which she made a splendid house. She was a great gardener too, cramming the rooms with enormous plants in flower.

Tuesday, 29th April

The telephone rang while I was reading this afternoon. Are you J.L.-M.? Yes; and who are you? Man named Gorman, speaking from

---

* Writer and journalist (b. 1943; ktd 2004); an enthusiast for architectural conservation, particularly of English churches (his work on which appeared in 1999).

Ireland, wartime officer in Irish Guards, though years younger than me. Charming old county voice. Asked whether the story about marching the men over the cliffs at Dover* was true. More or less, I answered. We then had a long conversation about friends we both remembered in the Brigade – Patrick O'Donovan, and Hugh Dormer† who took over G's company when G. was sent off on secret missions behind enemy lines. Gorman a Catholic. Said that Cardinal Hume was his contemporary at Ampleforth, and a very unsatisfactory boy who was constantly swished for misdemeanours. Gorman most friendly and talked to me as if I were a chip off the old regimental block, whereas of course I am nothing of the sort, and look back on my brief army career with shame and embarrassment.‡ He said that Dormer's diaries had inspired his grandson to join the Irish Guards. How splendid, I said, I wish him well. Rather touched by this unexpected encounter.

Thursday, 1st May

I cast my vote in the village hall this morning.

Jeremy Lewis§ writes that he is doing an introduction to Murray's forthcoming reprint of *Another Self*. He is having wonderful notices with his 700-page biography of Cyril [Connolly], to which I look forward immensely.

With one foot in the grave, I listen with revulsion and dread to the moans and groans of my contemporaries: to Daffers Moore¶ who is disintegrating in beastly homes; to John Mordaunt who has had a knock-out stroke and is wheelchair-bound, all feeling gone but mind unimpaired, which makes it worse; to my ancient neighbour Mr Greenway, whose dotty wife has just died. I sympathise yet I run away, cowardly and revolted, fearful of disaster overtaking me too at a moment's notice. I hope that I do not then solicit sympathy, and can disappear from view.

---

* Recounted in the final chapter of *Another Self*.
† Soldier killed in action (1919–44), whose diaries were published posthumously in 1947.
‡ Having been commissioned in the Irish Guards in the summer of 1940, J.L.-M. was invalided out after an illness brought on by being caught in a London bomb blast in October that year.
§ Writer, publisher, journalist and literary editor (b. 1942).
¶ Daphne Moore (1910–2004); Gloucestershire hunting personality; former resident of Badminton and friend of Mary, Duchess of Beaufort (d. 1987).

Saturday, 3rd May

The magnitude of the Tories' defeat is only beginning to dawn.* It means they will be out of power for possibly two decades. I had little regard for the last government, while developing a progressive respect and liking for Mr Major. There were too many spivs in his government, non-gents in every sense. I am not surprised by the defeat, for latterly I have noticed an absolute hatred of Toryism among the masses, evident in TV programmes such as *Question Time*. I shall not live to see another change. What appals me is the jubilation, the ringing of church bells as though Great Britain had been delivered from Hitler, Stalin or President Mobutu† rather than good, honest and wise Mr Major who has improved the lot of the working classes. My fear now is not so much of extremist socialism as of the insidious liberalism which will overlook the appalling scandals of bogus social security claimants, kowtowing to the IRA and all criminals, encouraging rather than limiting more coloured immigrants, and the general descent into American-style vulgarity and yob culture.

Julian Berkeley and Tony Scotland lunched. They were enchanting. I gave them a pile of A's old gramophone records which she wanted them to have. Tony gave an amusing account of Father Michael Hollings,‡ the beloved of Freda. He was a monster of arrogance and dogmatism, and treated her like dirt. Ordered her about, accepted her hospitality as his due, subjected the boys to headmasterly dressing-downs for presumed misdemeanours. The impertinence of it. He shouted at Freda for his drink, complained when he disliked a dish she had cooked, and when given a Christmas present by Tony and Julian, a carefully chosen clerical pullover, said he would give it away to the first comer. I met him once and cordially took against him. He was proprietary, gluttonous, boozy and dirty, like other intellectual RC priests I have known.

---

* The general election on 1 May ended eighteen years of Conservative rule; as a result of tactical voting, the Conservatives, with 31 per cent of the popular vote, won only a quarter of the seats, while Tony Blair's 'New Labour Party', with 43 per cent of the vote, was swept to power with a massive parliamentary majority of 179.

† Mobutu Sese Seko (1930–97); the notorious dictator of Zaire (later Democratic Republic of Congo) since 1965, then facing a rebellion: he fled the country on 16 May and died four months later.

‡ He had died on 21 February, aged seventy-five.

I like the way Julian pauses, stands still, and observes, scrutinises. A dark horse.

Sunday, 4th May

Lunched at Little Sodbury Manor with the Killearns.* Fourteen of us, mostly county and unknown to me. Jane [Westmorland] and Gerda [Barlow] present. I sat on left of Melita. I like her very much, and am intrigued. She is immensely shy and diffident, with strength in her chin. I must get her to come and advise on the garden. Victor can be rough. When I said goodbye, I added, 'You won't be pleased with this, but you look very much like your mother, Jacqueline.' 'Oh, that woman!' 'Yes,' I said, 'but she was very attractive when I first met her.' 'She gave you the brush-off when you met her here last year, and wasn't in the least interested,' riposted he. 'You are quite right,' I admitted. 'She wasn't, was she?'

Wednesday, 7th May

I am reading Goethe's† journal of his Italian tour [in 1786]. How qualified is he to pontificate on the merits and authenticity of works of art? Angelica Kauffmann‡ has bought an old master, attributed to Correggio.§ There can be no doubt, states Goethe, that it is by Correggio. Plants, meteorology, politics, human behaviour, everything fascinates him. He cannot bear wasting a moment from improving his mind. Rather touchingly, he admits that he has not the talent to be a painter. Modestly, he has endeavoured to learn from the young artist colony in Rome. It is no use, a waste of time, yet his studies have taught him how to look at works of art. Sculpture particularly intrigues him, so long as it is antique. A great admirer of Michelangelo as a painter, he makes no reference to M's sculpture. Only Medusas, Belvedere Apollos, Venuses will do. I see I gave quite a good review to this volume of the *Italienreise* in 1962,

---

* Hon. Victor Lampson (b. 1941); s. of 1st Baron Killearn by his 2nd wife Countess Jacqueline Castellani; banker; s. half-bro. as 3rd Baron Killearn, 1996; m. 1971 Melita Morgan-Giles.
† Johann Wolfgang von Goethe (1749–1832); German poet, writer and philosopher.
‡ Swiss artist (1741–1807).
§ Italian artist (1489–1534).

which I stuck into the back cover at the time. The great universal man lacked humour.

Surely most old people become indifferent to what others, notably the young, think of them and their utterances. On the contrary, I mind more than ever to the extent of avoiding the clever young. Polite though they are, and indulgent, I cringe before the sensed curl of their lips. Moreover, I feel more and more ashamed of my past shortcomings, particularly in my writings.

Having read through the small copy of *De Profundis** which I bought while at Eton in 1926, I thought I would compare it with the original of Oscar Wilde's long letter to Bosie Douglas from Reading Gaol in Rupert [Hart-Davis]'s *Collected Letters* published in 1962. The real letter is twice the length of *De Profundis*. Robbie Ross left out all mention of Bosie and cheated like mad, so as to create the most poignant apologia ever published. And it did arouse sympathy even in that hard-boiled Edwardian generation. In fact the real letter does not strike me as at all sincere. O.W. makes out that he never admired Bosie, on the contrary despised him from the word go, and consorted with him only out of sympathy for his dreadful lot in being the son of Lord Queensberry.† Whereas the embarrassingly erotic letters he wrote Bosie in the early 1890s make it clear he was besottedly in love with him.

Received this morning a very sweet packed postcard from Peter Levi about *The Moat*,‡ which I had the audacity to send him. Beautifully he gets round his opinion of it by declaring it 'exactly of its date' (1950) between Walter de la Mare§ and John Fuller.¶ I value this card and shall cherish it. Could it be privately published as a

---

* Self-justification by Oscar Wilde (1854–1900), written in Reading Gaol, 1896–7, in the form of a long denunciatory letter to his former friend Lord Alfred ('Bosie') Douglas (1870–1945), contrasting the latter's selfishness with the loyalty of Wilde's other friend Robbie Ross (1869–1918); published by Ross (then Wilde's literary executor) in drastically edited form, 1905.

† John Sholto Douglas, 8th Marquess of Queensberry (1844–1900); formulator of the 'Queensberry Rules' of boxing; father of Lord Alfred Douglas and persecutor of Oscar Wilde, whom he goaded into bringing the libel action which resulted in the latter's downfall.

‡ Unpublished narrative poem by J.L.-M.

§ Poet and novelist (1873–1956).

¶ English poet (b. 1937); son of Roy Fuller (1912–91), sometime Professor of Poetry at Oxford (who may be the person meant).

pamphlet, he asks? 'In a sense it is a barrier because its psychological depths cannot be further exploited or explored.' What exactly does this mean? So good of him.

Richard Ingrams has asked me to review Roy Strong's diaries for the *Oldie*.

Friday, 9th May

Billa [Harrod] comes for the weekend. Adorable she is, and the very same to me as when I first met her in the early Thirties, though very bent. But bright, and faculties unimpaired. Her grandson Huckleberry rings up and asks to speak to her in a very common voice. B. deplores this, and cannot understand where he picked it up. His elder brother, who is the same, runs a band in America called 'Fucking is Fun'. He could never bring it to England, opines Billa. She looks very distinguished. I tell her that her saintly image ought to be recorded on a panel of the rood screen of her favourite Norfolk church.

Monday, 12th May

Mr Blair's new government already irks me with its bogus bonhomie ('Call me Tony'), refusal to wear white tie at Lord Mayor's Banquet, and abandonment of traditional way of referring to MPs in the Commons (My Honourable Friend the Member for Wherever) in favour of Reggie and Mo. I loathe such rejection of traditional courtesies and downgrading of long-accepted modes and manners in the supposed interest of democracy. Yet I am in favour of their policy to ban export of armaments to third-world tyrannies, and curb big business exploitation of the environment.

Thursday, 15th May

Bishop Bill Llewellyn called on me at 11.45, ushered through door by lady minder. A sad old spectacle in thick tweed jacket with pectoral cross on long chain. For an hour he sat, glass of sherry in hand, murmuring inaudibly at snail's pace. He is very far gone. Desperately I tried to jog his memory about McNeile's house [at Eton] where we were together until he left in 1925. As I watched his expressionless face, I tried to retrace the handsome, cherubic lineaments of more than seventy years ago.

By dint of immense patience and straining of the ear, I managed to catch the gist of a story he told about Master, when Bill was Vicar of Badminton. One day when they were out hunting, Master left the field and beckoned Bill aside, saying he had something extremely serious to impart to him. Quaking in his stirrups, Bill wondered what enormity he had committed. Master said to him, 'It has been brought to my attention that you no longer patronise Drewett's Stores (the village shop). Is this so?' Bill admitted it was, because he found them too expensive. Immediately the stores were told to reduce their prices.

This afternoon, Ambrose Congreve's secretary telephoned, asking if I would dine with him next Thursday in London. I hate being asked point-blank on the telephone, and said no. Then thought I might have been stupid, for I would have enjoyed it, and could have stayed at Brooks's next door. But I need time to reflect. As it is, this fine weather and these long days make me melancholy and lonely. Walked in park for first time since horse trials. The mess unbelievable. Appalling litter, drive churned by lorries, grass verges looking as if they would never grow again. Wandered towards the coppices, vainly listening for the cuckoo. Not a sound. They have all gone, I suppose. Within the past ten years, 60 to 70 per cent of our song birds have been eliminated.

Saturday, 17th May

Grant [McIntyre] came to tea, bringing first copy of *Ancient as the Hills*, and his family. Luckily I provided a rich spread of cake and scones. Party included wife Helen Fraser* and three daughters. Nice, well-behaved girls, of whom one was just grown-up and so communicated. I liked Helen immensely. Very sympathetic and, considering her high status in the publishing world, modest. Has a clever, perpendicular face, beautiful in its way. She said that, before her recent promotion, she had been Anne de Courcy's publisher, and so read her biography of Diana Mosley in manuscript. Said it was brilliant, affectionate and fair, dextrously interweaving Diana's political views with episodes showing her gentleness and hatred of violence and cruelty. When I asked the McIntyres where they were on their way to, supposing Wales or Cornwall, they disclosed that they had come all the way from West London just to see me, and were returning home.

---

* Publisher (b. 1949); then Publishing Director of Heinemann, subsequently Managing Director of Penguin UK; m. 1982 (as his 2nd wife) Grant McIntyre.

Which they did soon after six. Grant said that Hilary Spurling* had already been engaged by Tony Powell for his biography. He wanted it in three volumes, but she stuck out for two. I should think so too. Spurling would not begin the book so long as Tony was still living, which I gather he is barely doing, poor old boy. Grant says he is rather beastly to Violet, his sainted wife, and beastly about everyone now it seems. Quite evident in his latest diaries, I find.[†]

Tuesday, 20th May

Am deep in Tony Powell's third volume of diaries. His cleverness and learnedness fill me with veneration and awe. His personality freezes me up. I have always liked him and loved Violet, but A. never felt at ease with him. From his few references to me, he was clearly bored with me. Writes that Jim is never interested in his own work. Truth is that I never wanted to discuss my writings with him. The difference between our diaries is that between a highbrow and a middle-brow. I suppose I'm a poor man's Anthony Powell.

Wednesday, 21st May

I now have proof that cockroaches are cannibals. I killed one stone dead the night before last. Next morning, the corpse had been moved a foot from the scene of slaughter. Following morning, all but the legs had disappeared.

Saturday, 24th May

Selina [Hastings] lunched on her way to London. Affectionate and sweet, as always. Said her last visit to Diana [Mosley] exhausted her dreadfully, the deafness being far worse. We think we may visit her together in the autumn.

Sunday, 25th May

I lunched with Tony Scotland and Julian Berkeley, a surprise for Freda who is staying with them for her birthday today. I motored sixty miles

---

* Writer of biographies (b. 1940).
† *Journals, 1990–1992* (Heinemann 1997); he describes J.L.-M. (26 July 1991) as 'oddly uninterested in his own life'.

there and back, too long. No lorries on this Bank Holiday Sunday, but Newbury a nightmare of jams. Pottery Cottage [near Aldermaston] much improved, a large, open-roofed room having been added since my last visit. It contains a tall late Georgian Gothick organ from Markenfield, given Julian by late Lord Grantley,* large Bechstein grand given him by Joan Leigh Fermor, and a harpsichord. He is very musical, and played the organ after luncheon, beautifully I thought. I presented Freda with an advance copy of *Ancient as the Hills*.† Large party, more than a sprinkling of queens. Their mannerisms, their social contacts, their sharp little jokes are the same the world over. How is it they do not recognise that they are artificial, shallow, slick, sophisticated, absurd? Julian never says a stupid thing. Is withdrawn, a thinker, has depth, is hard to connect with. Whereas Tony is extrovert, open, bubbling. They have made this cottage into a 'place', with lovely orchard garden and pretty things inside and out.

Wednesday, 28th May

Bevis Hillier writes to ask if I will support his campaign to establish a national memorial to the Millennium. But I don't care a fig about the Millennium, which is a totally unreal landmark of time undeserving of any notice.

Thursday, 29th May

John K.-B. sends me a half-page of information relating to the AD dating system. In 550, Dionysius Exiguus, Greek-speaking monk, suggested the counting of years should date from the conception of Christ; but not until many centuries later did this become common practice. Until mediaeval times, years were counted from the succession of the monarch. So typical of John to have this information. He is a standby where anything to do with the Christian religion and classical mythology is concerned, having been brought up in his parents' RC prep school, then Ampleforth. Still, I don't understand how, say, an educated Englishman might settle by missive on what date he intended visiting his cousin in Languedoc.

---

* John Richard Brinsley Norton, 7th Baron Grantley (1923–95), of Markenfield Hall near Ripon, Yorkshire.
† Published by John Murray on 10 July.

Friday, 30th May

American garden society party of twenty visited at 9.30 a.m. Were nice and polite. The moment they left I went to London for the night. On the train, I tried but failed to summon ideas for the book Grant wants me to write about my youth. In walking to Coutts in the Strand, I wondered if I would ever get there, so weary was I, dragging one foot after the other. Then walked back to National Gallery and bought for £40 their complete catalogue, each single painting illustrated in colour, postage-stamp size. Weighs a ton. Derek [Hill] dined at Brooks's. Very good and affectionate he was, and amusing. He hopes to go to Mount Athos in September with Prince Charles.

Sunday, 1st June

Asked to lunch by Elsie Gibbs* at Sheldon to meet Jamie Fergusson and his new wife Maggie Parham,† who is her cousin. They seem a very happy pair, and I liked her immensely. I expected her to be middle-aged, angular and somewhat dour. On the contrary, she was short, very pretty, and shy. He's a lucky fellow, and looks it. We ate in the barn off delicious food cooked by Elsie, who was so busy in the restaurant that we hardly saw her. Maggie runs the Royal Society of Literature, and is also writing the biography of her friend, the recently deceased Scotch poet.‡

Thursday, 5th June

Yesterday I entertained to luncheon Heck Knight, Gerda Barlow and Hardy Amies. Great success. Heavenly day, sitting out on the terrace. Heck a very sympathetic lady, grand in a county sense. Driven here by attractive daughter Henrietta and husband, latter an unexpected rough diamond.§ Hardy came all the way from London. Very old now, but

---

* Elsie Hamilton-Dalrymple (b. 1922); m. 1947 Major Martin Gibbs (1916–95) of Sheldon Manor near Chippenham, Wiltshire.
† Secretary of Royal Society of Literature from 1991 (b. 1964); m. Oct. 1996 James Fergusson.
‡ George Mackay Brown (1921–96); the biography is due to be published by John Murray in 2006.
§ Terry Biddlecombe; former champion National Hunt jockey; m. 1995 Henrietta Knight (b. 1946), they being known in the racing world as 'the Odd Couple'.

not gaga. Like me he forgets much. He has become an institution, a 'character' who speaks his mind. 'Please don't interrupt me.' Darlings trill from his lips. He thrice expressed his gratitude to Essex House for introducing him to Selina [Hastings], now his most beloved friend.

The garden at its peak. Roses beginning en masse; deutzia, honey-suckle, aquilegia, peonies full out. It no longer has the groomed, trimmed look that A. liked, but is *belle au bois dormante*, luscious, almost blowsy-looking.

Friday, 6th June

In the morning young lady from BBC arrived, a sweet and pretty girl, tossing her hair from eyes. As usually happens, the machine she had brought failed to work, and she had to telephone an engineer. For half an hour she questioned me about K. Clark. Nice though she was, she knew little about K's career and only seemed interested in his relations with his wife Jane and his lady friends. This suggests the programme will be valueless. The BBC ought to send someone who recognises that K. was an important figure, who qualifies in reputation with Ruskin.

I slept in the afternoon. Then at five Rory Young appeared, having advised Simon Dring,* how to re-harl the walls of the House. He brought photographs of the biblical figures he has devised for west doorway of York Minster. And beautiful they are, in full relief, now being carved by the Minster stonecarvers. Although not derivative from the Gothic, they are finely explicit of Adam and Eve (slightly Sloane Square), Noah and the Flood, Abraham, etc. Most carefully considered and thought out, fine figures and faces based on residents of Cirencester. After finishing them, he said to himself, 'At the age of forty-three I have produced my *magnum opus*, with which I am well pleased.' Then instantly wished to embark on new themes. He is now recognised as a considerable sculptor. I relish his enthusiasm.

Sunday, 8th June

Yesterday evening John Julius [Norwich] and Mollie came for a drink and to see the garden. Both very appreciative of it and seeming to like

---

* Of the Badminton estate office.

its slightly rugged look. J.J. said he was determined to win the [National] Lottery and had worked out to the last detail how to spend the winnings, for he says one simply must have more money for one's old age. As if he did not earn a lot from his many activities, and she had not inherited a fortune from her exceedingly rich father. He thinks Jeremy Lewis's biography of Cyril [Connolly] one of the best of the century. Picked up my copy from the footstool and read aloud the first paragraph, saying 'It is genius.'

In Acton Turville church today I was one of a congregation of two. Meanwhile in this parish, which is larger than Badminton and full of rich Bristol commuters, no one has volunteered to be church warden. And if no one does, the church will be declared redundant. I suggested to the Vicar that a letter should be delivered to every resident explaining that they face having no church for their baptisms, weddings and funerals. Vicar responded with vacuous smile of indulgence, assuring me that 'it will turn out all right in the end'.

In the afternoon, Jerry Hall telephoned to say they had been staying at the House for the weekend and would drop in on me at once. After I had waited an hour, she turned up in large, chauffeur-driven motor with two small children. The youngest, aged five, the most advanced infant I have ever encountered. Hearing the kitchen clock striking, she demanded to examine the mechanism, and then sang a song about a clock, while her doting mother led her into the garden. Then Mick [Jagger] appeared with son James in second limousine. He looks handsomer now he is past fifty, somewhat rugged but very lithe and healthy. Wearing that absurd American cap and chewing gum. Whisked around the garden politely and asked me to stay at La Fourchette in August, saying that David [Beaufort] would fly me out. Somehow I don't think so.

Monday, 9th June

Very enjoyable day. Alex [Moulton] calls for me at 10.30 and drives me to Worcester in his brand-new Bentley, enormous and prominent, bringing villagers to their doors. I don't know whether to wave or look straight ahead, and just smile. Interesting walk round Porcelain Museum, the modern gallery containing hideous wares. Then to the dark, forbidding Cathedral, grim inside and totally Victorian. Talked to delightful lady guide, probably a canon's widow. Scott's rood screen a delightful object. Unfortunately Bishop Hough's Rococo monument by Roubiliac* invisible, as is Mrs Sherwood's memorial, owing to repairs to north transept.

Alex, who has a highly-placed German friend, says that Chancellor Kohl† is obsessive about the European currency, and indeed European federation, out of terror lest Germany be driven by irresistible subterranean forces to go to war again. Others of his generation feel the same way, though this feeling is not shared or even understood by the younger generation who did not know the horrors of the last war.

Wednesday, 11th June

Charles and Mary Keen motored me to see *Mrs Warren's Profession*‡ at Bath Theatre. Title role taken by Penelope Keith,§ who was marvellous, as were the rest of the cast. I enjoyed it hugely. Mary had taken a box from which we only saw a quarter of the stage, but during first interval she saw some empty seats in the front row of the stalls to which we moved for the remaining acts. Heard every word; so did Charles, who is deafer than me.

Thursday, 12th June

The Royal Librarian telephoned from Windsor, inviting me to lunch with him and look at the Library and help him identify the rooms Lord Esher occupied. I said I could no longer motor so far in the day. We left it that I might accompany John Saumarez Smith from London, where I could stay the night. I would much like to meet this nice man and be shown around by him. He told me that he had bought my signed copy of Bamber Gascoigne's book on the Mughals from Heywood Hill, and presented it to Princess Margaret. I said I was glad it had found a good home.

---

* Louis-François Roubiliac (1702–62); French tomb sculptor.
† Dr Helmut Kohl (b. 1930); Chancellor of German Federal Republic from 1982 to 1998, who presided over German reunification and was an enthusiast for ever-closer European union.
‡ Written by George Bernard Shaw in 1894, but censored in the UK until 1925 owing to its theme of prostitution.
§ British actress (b. 1940), known for her appearance in television sitcoms.

Saturday, 14th June

Lunched at Prospect Cottage with the dear Levis. The fourth was John Byrne,* slim, gaunt-faced young man with scarred left cheek. He is a cataloguer of books and first editions, who did Cyril's books for Deirdre. An intellectual and a scholar. Disclosed that he is on medication which gives him a matutinal hangover. I explained that I too had taken a drug for over fifty years and suffered similarly until midday. Having at last reached the end of Jeremy [Lewis]'s biography of Cyril, I wanted to discuss it, but had to tread carefully, for C. treated D. abominably, yet she adores his memory. Peter said that Matthew had not disclosed what his feelings about the book were. He also told me that Cyril devoted much of his life to correcting the manuscripts of his friends. Had I noticed how well-written Barbara Skelton's† novels were? (I had not.) Whereas her recent memoirs, written since Cyril's death, were stylistically disappointing. I gave them a copy of *Ancient as the Hills*, and he returned *The Moat*, repeating that I ought to have it privately published. I suspect he is being polite and kind.

Sunday, 15th June

The Henry [Robinson]s motored me to Bowood for luncheon. Greeted warmly by Charlie Shelburne, who was extremely affable and kind. Took me to the gallery to see family portraits – Reynoldses galore, Gainsborough, Romney, the lot. Returning to the drawing room we were confronted by an enormous party of guests of whom I knew none. Astors of Hever, relations without end, coming up with 'Are you still writing?' And a man with long white hair and beaming countenance, who introduced himself as Adrian Linlithgow.‡ Sat next to Laura someone, handsome lady under a shadow, and Elizabeth Lambton,§ who is Kitty Nairne's¶ younger sister. Delightful. I asked, 'When you

---

* Bookseller and archivist (b. 1945).
† Novelist and writer of memoirs (1916–96), whose work was largely based on her own tempestuous love life; m. 1st 1950–6 Cyril Connolly, 2nd 1956–61 George (later Baron) Weidenfeld, 3rd 1966 Professor Derek Jackson (formerly husband of Pamela Mitford).
‡ Adrian Hope, 4th Marquess of Linlithgow (b. 1946).
§ Lady Elizabeth Petty-Fitzmaurice (b. 1927); yr dau. of 6th Marquess of Lansdowne; m. 1950 Major Charles Lambton.
¶ Lady Katherine Petty-Fitzmaurice (1912–95); m. 1933 Hon. Edward Bigham, later 3rd Viscount Mersey; succeeded brother to Lordship of Nairne, 1944.

were a child here, did you live in the whole house?' 'No, we lived in this part, except over Christmas when we moved to the Adam block', now gone. There were forty servants in the house. We hung around afterwards. I found it terribly tiring. All the guests finally left, except for the Robinsons who had to wait until children rounded up. A lesson, never be taken by the young with children. Always be independent, child-free.

Charlie, looking complacently out of window, cigar in mouth, said, 'I positively like seeing the visitors enjoying themselves. They do not interfere with me.' Then, 'You remember how you at one time thought it was all up for the aristocracy? And now it isn't. We are still here.' 'Some of you, I'm glad to say,' I said. He continued, 'We were the bogey. Then it was the trade union bosses. Now it is the fat cats. We shall be all right.' I thought, but did not say, 'Don't be too sure. The public are notoriously fickle and stupid. You could easily be thought to be doing what they disliked, and the arsonists would turn their attention to your marble halls.'

Sunday, 22nd June

Midsummer Day and cold as Christmas. Lit drawing room fire. To Alderley to see garden which was open for nurses. A wonderful display of Paul's Himalayan musk rose over dead tree at the front and a mountain of mock orange. Everywhere profusion and lusciousness. Guy [Acloque] exudes county names until I almost become left-wing. But I forgive him all for keeping the garden in perfection.

Got home in time to receive the Levis and Andrew Barrow and friend, beautiful lady who is granddaughter of famous war hero General Freyberg.* She works with Jamie Fergusson on *Independent* obituaries and is very bright and *au fait*. Noticed everything, the Venetian glass obelisks, even Eardley's little still life, which she recognised as by him. We had a good talk.

Wednesday, 25th June

Bevis Hillier came from London for the day, I'm not sure why, though I enjoyed seeing him. Has become rather beefy in appearance.

---

* Hon. Annabel Freyberg (b. 1961); m. 2000 (as his 2nd wife) Andrew Barrow; her grandfather, the New Zealander Bernard Freyberg, VC (1889–1963; cr. baron 1951), distinguished himself as a commander in both world wars.

A sensitive man, devoted to the memory of his parents. Is in favour of the proprieties and established traditions, yet contemptuous of toffs. I could not think how to respond when he said he regarded me as the best living writer of English prose.

Thursday, 26th June

Ghastly day of storms, non-stop rain and bitter cold. I received a letter from John Byrne announcing that it was he, then with Rota,* who catalogued my letters sold to Yale, and asking if I would like to sell more papers. Have replied that I may well do so. It may be a good idea to part with the packed drawerful in my lifetime, so as to spare executors, and build up some funds to meet future health bills. I told John that I always hoped never to meet the young man who catalogued my letters of the past.

Saturday, 28th June

Tom and Gloria Gibson to tea, talking of Badminton in ye olden dayes. How Mary Beaufort's guests invited to tea in Raglan Room were surprised to see table laid with unmatching cups and saucers, and Mary going on hands and knees to pull the lead out of the socket when the water boiled. How, when Master died, Leslie the old butler laid out his personal effects – rings, cuff links, wallet – on the kitchen table, and asked David what to do with them. D. replied, 'Just get rid of them as you think fit.' When Tom heard this he was appalled, and told L. that he would be well-advised to make an inventory of them and lock them in the safe.

Sunday, 29th June

I drove to Chastleton† today, arriving before one o'clock. A favourable day for my eyes, neither dark nor dazzling. A good thing that the

---

* Bertram Rota Ltd of Long Acre, dealers in rare books and manuscripts.
† Chastleton House near Moreton-in-Marsh, Oxfordshire; Jacobean manor built by the wool merchant Walter Jones; a rare late twentieth-century acquisition of a country house by N.T., thanks to its wonderful state of preservation; the money to endow and restore it provided by the National Heritage Memorial Fund; following six years' conservation work, it was now ready for limited opening to the public.

N.T. have made a car park 250 yards from the house on top of a wooded hill and totally screened from view. A long yellow path descends towards the four-gabled dovecote, the tiny church and the great bulk of purple-grey stone flying the Union Jack. The epitome of an old manorial setting, remote, isolated in quiet Oxfordshire country. I entered the pretty church, walking over shiny black memorial gravestones enscrolled with flourishes to Jones family. Several wall tablets which I couldn't read for darkness. Nice fusty smell.

Ushered into a dark downstairs room, where found Martin Drury and some thirty friends of the N.T. Couldn't distinguish a soul. Buttonholed by friendly Hugh Roberts;[*] then embraced by Fortune [Grafton] whom I had to ask who she was. And Hugh G. – rather diminished and bent over a stick, but full of funny stories – with whom my group went round house after luncheon. Samantha Wyndham[†] acted as hostess and was very attentive and helpful.

The rooms at Chastleton still left bleak, dusty and rather empty despite the N.T. having spent £2 million on structure. Bedroom of former châtelaine, Mrs Whitmore Jones, still smells of cats. Remarkable how much of what we take for Jacobean was supplied in the nineteenth century by the antiquarian Squire Jones. Hall screen bogus Victorian. Best room the High Chamber with genuine ceiling. In next room I asked Alec Cobbe whether he thought the ceiling Jacobean. Not so, also early Victorian. Martin Drury displayed the Jacobite wine glasses which he cleverly managed to buy back from a dealer. The late Clutton-Brock[‡] sold many items to pay his taxes and wine merchants. I pick my way gingerly in these old rickety houses with slippery floors and uneven stair treads, feeling with my stick what I fail to see.

Martin D. and the officials who have reinstated Chastleton were amused to hear that I went to a children's party here in the 1920s. All I remember is that the house, which the Richardsons rented for thirty years, did not strike me as any less well-maintained or cosy than any other manor house we frequented in the Cotswolds; that we danced

---

[*] Art expert (b. 1948); Director of the Royal Collection and Surveyor of the Queen's Works of Art from 1996 (Deputy Director, 1988–96).
[†] On staff of N.T. and Georgian Group (b. 1962); Secretary of Chelsea Society.
[‡] Alan Clutton-Brock (1904–76); Slade Professor of Fine Art, Cambridge, 1955–8; author of *A History of French Painting* (1932); inherited Chastleton House from a cousin, 1955.

and played hunt-the-slipper in the long gallery; and that there was a hole in the plaster ceiling. Apparently John Arkell, not there today, remembers similar parties, his father having been a neighbouring vicar.

Friday, 4th July

Desmond Briggs motored me to St David's for three nights, a jaunt planned months ago. He drives his Volvo at immense speed, seeming to be more interested in his driving than the places we passed through. Wales gives impression of prosperity. Many houses with slate roofs and dingy grey façades have recently been painted white on the cob, which is jollier. We stayed at Warpool Court Hotel, ten minutes' walk from St David's. Bill including dinners, rather pretentious food, £345. Hideous building, redeemed by interesting heraldic tiles showing arms of local Welsh families, found in bedrooms as well as downstairs fire-places. Rained nearly all the time. The Cathedral splendid. Uniform dark granite, speckled with purple and grey. All the interior wood-work of oak left unvarnished, blending well with walls. I remembered the steep climb from west door to east end. Stands in a bowl. Desmond a very kind and attentive friend, and an excellent compan-ion with all his erudition.

On Thursday I listened to Radio 4 documentary on K. Clark. Not at all bad. Some good speakers, including Derek [Hill] whose voice I could hardly distinguish from my own. The closing words came from me – 'He may not have had a great soul, but he had a great mind.'

On return found a note from David [Beaufort], who had read my latest diaries and thanked me for what I wrote about Caroline, and asked me to dine this evening. But I felt so worn out that I declined.

Monday, 7th July

Listened to broadcast on Violet Woodhouse. Very interesting and well-produced, by experts on harpsichord and clavichord. Jessica spoke well. Several ancient recordings of V. playing in 1920s, sound-ing a harsh jangle. When she spoke her voice was not feminine, but authoritative. Rosemary Chaplin spoke as a survivor who attended her concerts in Mount Street. I suspect Sachie and Osbert slightly exaggerated the poetry in her playing.

Felt so worn out, unable to walk further than end of garden, that I thought I must chuck Jane's dinner party. Pulled myself together. John Julius there, full of brio. Sat next to Micky Nevill* whom I could not hear and Mollie [Norwich] whom I could. Micky's half-American walk-out sat with me later. Visits Russia as representative of some American body. Says chaos reigns in every institution except the mafia. Poverty among civil servants awful.

Sunday, 13th July

Weekend at Deene, driven there by Liz [Longman]. It must have been the largest house party I've attended since the war. Women Katie Macmillan,† Clementine Beit, Mary Roxburghe, Anne Wyndham,‡ Fortune Stanley,§ Liz; men Edward Ford, Derek Hill, John Cornforth, Steven Runciman, Miles Gladwyn,¶ self. (Dear Anthony Hobson chucked for influenza.) I may have left a few out, and there were neighbours in addition at luncheon and dinner.

Whole visit beautifully staged. Delicious food and good chat, but little conversation. One could not get to know all. Mary R. very affable but stiff. Her grandfather Monckton Milnes was born in 1809. Asked me to visit her at West Horsley [near Leatherhead, Surrey], which I would like to do. K. Macmillan formidable and ugly but undoubtedly clever. Told me how miserable she was having to sell Highgrove [to the Prince of Wales] in order to live with her father-in-law the ex-Prime Minister in hideous Birch Grove [Sussex]. Clementine simply enormous and totally changed in face, but sweet as of old.

---

* Lady Camilla Wallop (b. 1925), er dau. of 9th Earl of Portsmouth; m. 1944 Lord Rupert Nevill (1923–82), yr s. of 4th Marquess of Abergavenny, friend and aide of HRH The Duke of Edinburgh.

† Hon. Katharine Ormsby-Gore (b. 1921; DBE 1974); dau. of 4th Baron Harlech; m. 1942 Maurice Macmillan, Conservative politician, who d. 1984, having assumed courtesy title Viscount Macmillan of Ovenden earlier that year on his father, Harold Macmillan, former Prime Minister, being cr. Earl of Stockton; Vice-Chairman of Conservative Party, 1968–71.

‡ Anne Winn (b. 1926), dau. of Hon. Reginald Winn, yr s. of 2nd Baron St Oswald; m. 1947 (as his 1st wife) Hon. Mark Wyndham, yr s. of 5th Baron Leconfield.

§ Fortune Smith; m. 1951 Michael Stanley (b. 1921), Cumbrian landowner, s. of Hon. Oliver Stanley, yr s. of 17th Earl of Derby.

¶ Miles Jebb, 2nd Baron Gladwyn (b. 1930); o. s. of Sir Gladwyn Jebb, 1st Baron, diplomatist, whom he s. 1996; writer and former British Airways executive.

Steven Runciman like a feather. Or rather like a crisp old leaf, that's what he is, bent and hollow in the middle as he scuttles like a crab upstairs. Yet in talking to one alone he is very spry. We agreed that hunting can't be justified, any more than hereditary peers, or for that matter religion – yet they are all good things. The arts may also be included in this category. He can no more read Scott than I, and can't stomach Dickens; re-reads Thackeray, but finds George Eliot impossible.

The one I find most sympathetic here is Edward Ford. After dinner he said to me, 'You didn't like Winston, did you?' I began to explain why when Miles joined in, claiming that unconditional surrender was the only course to be adopted in 1945. I think Edward did not agree with him, but rather with me.

Wednesday, 16th July

William Burlington* came to photograph me for the National Trust, bringing beautiful Chilean assistant with raven hair and perfect teeth. He took infinite pains, unlike so many young photographers these days who just flourish the camera at one without preparation and fire off fifty snaps. He spent almost two hours choosing the site, finally taking me sitting on a garden chair by the buddleia, wearing straw hat. He has wonderful manners, an enquiring mind, and is absolutely natural. Handsome, busy, eager, shirt-tails flying; more Mitford than Cavendish in appearance.

David telephoned asking me to dine tonight with him and Miranda, who received me at the door. Ushered me into the old Raglan Room which D. is transforming. He has got rid of the black Jacobean panelling of which Master and Mary were so proud, revealing beneath early Georgian panelling which he has painted pale buff. He is very pleased with this, his new toy. He has hung huge landscape paintings across the fielded panels, one a vast Landseer of a Somerset dog. I could not criticise because he is so pleased, and doubtless when the room has shaken down a bit it will look charming as all his rooms do. But when he asked me what he should do with the clumsy Victorian window projection, now bare, I did suggest either vertical paintings or a pair of marble obelisks or similar high-standing ornaments, to relieve the horizontal emphasis of the room.

---

* William Cavendish, Earl of Burlington (b. 1969); s. and heir of 12th Duke of Devonshire.

Sunday, 20th July

Lunched with Anne Wyndham at Chilson. Edward Ford, the Martin Charterises, the Faringdons, and Liza (of Lambeth) Glendevon.* I sat next to the last and told her how fond A. and I were of her father Willie Maugham, who was so kind and hospitable to us on the Riviera. To which she replied, 'Humph!' Then I added tactlessly, 'I believe there is a new book about him.' Yes, she said, I don't think I shall read it. We talked about the Villa Mauresque which she sold, and then, getting tactless again, I said, 'I suppose Alan Searle is dead.'† She replied, 'Yes, I don't grieve over that.' I asked if her mother was American. 'Certainly not, she was the daughter of John Barnardo.'

Thursday, 24th July

After lunching with Desmond at The Salutation, I joined Georgian Group party at [Badminton] House. Found them in the dining room being lectured by Lucy Abel Smith and other learned authorities. David had escaped. Warmly greeted by John Martin Robinson‡ and Samantha Wyndham, who introduced me to new chairman, Lord Crathorne.§ I accompanied party round the rest of the rooms, and learnt much I did not know before. Standing before the Tudor portraits, I wished I had written a history of the Somersets. They even had Jacobite connections – the 4th Duke was apparently prepared to meet Prince Charlie at Derby, but died two days before.¶

---

* Elizabeth Mary Maugham (1915–98); ostensibly dau. of William Somerset Maugham (1874–1965; novelist, playwright and short story writer), and Syrie Wellcome (1879–1955; dau. of Dr John Barnardo [1845–1905], founder of children's homes; interior decorator; married to W.S.M., 1917–28), known as 'Liza' after W.S.M's early novel *Liza of Lambeth*; m. 1st 1937–48 Vincent Paravicini, 2nd 1948 Lord John Hope (1912–96), yr s. of 2nd Marquess of Linlithgow, cr. Baron Glendevon 1964.

† Alan Searle (1904–85); secretary and companion to W. Somerset Maugham, 1945–65 (known to the L.-Ms who were friends and neighbours of W.S.M. in South of France); inherited much of Maugham's property following an acrimonious dispute with Lady Glendevon.

‡ Librarian to Duke of Norfolk, and writer and consultant on architectural and genealogical subjects (b. 1948); Maltravers Herald of Arms Extraordinary, and Vice-Chairman of Georgian Group.

§ James Dugdale, 2nd Viscount Crathorne (b. 1939); art dealer and architectural conservationist; President of Georgian Group, 1990–9.

¶ J.L.-M. presumably means to refer to the 3rd Duke, who died in February 1746 (Bonnie Prince Charlie's brief occupation of Derby having taken place in December 1745).

Tuesday, 29th July

Have been reading Ruskin's[*] lectures on architecture. His loathing of Greek and Renaissance architecture intense. Did not loathe the Romans so much because they introduced the round-headed arch, which led to the Anglo-Saxon and Gothic. He argues that mediaeval craftsmen had opportunities to express their individuality in sculpting trees, etc., whereas Renaissance and Georgian craftsmen had to follow repetitive, conventional patterns in friezes and all carved surfaces. He deduces that mediaeval workmen, poor and subjected though they were, yet loved their labour and took pride in it. Not entirely convincing, this.

Debo telephoned to propose herself for luncheon. It happened that I had Susy [Robinson] lunching, who had always longed to meet Debo. The meeting a great success, Debo delighted with S's keenness and interest in all things. Both brought mercy bags of food. Debo as usual enhancing my cling to life.

Wednesday, 30th July

Lunched with the Keens at Duntisbourne Rous to meet the couple who have bought Daneway [House, Sapperton, Gloucestershire]. Very rich Hong Kong tycoon called Spencer, and Thai wife. Then Mary, who is a sport, motored me at terrific speed to meet Debo and Andrew at Asthall,[†] which is now on the market. Debo, who was six when her father sold it in 1926, wanted to look around for old times' sake. I stayed there twice with Tom, and cherish rose-tinted memories of the interior. Now empty, drear and desolate. Dark, shapeless rooms, no Jacobean furniture left. Mr Hardcastle, whose parents bought the place from Lord Redesdale, died last year. A bachelor whose prime interest was in luxurious Rolls-Royces. His bedroom littered with shoe boxes. His housekeeper, who showed us round, told us that, after his death, seventy-five pairs of unworn shoes came to light. He had an order with Lobb's to provide two pairs a year, which he didn't like to cancel. A rich Englishman's eccentricity.

---

[*] John Ruskin (1819–1900); poet, artist, critic, social revolutionary and conservationist.
[†] Jacobean manor on river Windrush, owned by Lord Redesdale from 1919 to 1926, where J.L.-M. stayed as a schoolboy with his friend Tom Mitford.

Monday, 4th August

I listened on Radio 3 to a performance of Schumann's *Papillons* on a pianola roll. I remember playing the pianola at Ribbesford* as a child under thirteen, pressing madly at the pedals which motivated the machine, and running my fingers like a zany along the keys as if I was actually performing, while watching fascinated as the perforated roll unfolded before my eyes. I don't know why the pianola was despised. True, there was something a bit mechanical and impersonal about the playing, the sensibilities apparently not transmitted as they are in the recordings of today. Anyway, the Schumann sounded pretty good I thought.

Wednesday, 6th August

I enter my ninetieth year. Motored to Moorwood to lunch with the Henrys, dispensing money to the children and chocolate to the adults. Henry present because bad weather prevents him harvesting. Susy then motored me to Rousham† [near Oxford] where we joined a Georgian Group party. Pouring rain. No sign of Cottrell-Dormer owners. Samantha Wyndham greeted and took charge of me. J.K.-B. present among group. Several come up to me to congratulate on *Ancient as the Hills*, and my enormous age. A charming old house, still a home, though not wholly so, the large rooms evidently not much used. Bad-taste carpet of Reckitt's Blue on staircase and in drawing room. Long hall sympathetic, walls lined with good family portraits in Sunderland frames. The two Kent rooms splendid, the low ceiling derived from Villa Madama colonnade in Rome. The larger room with high ceiling very strange for England, in recessed caissons that call to my mind the architecture of Guarini and Juvarra‡ in, say, the Turin Chapel of the Shroud.

I stopped at Bagendon churchyard to pay respects to little Audrey's

---

* Ribbesford Hall near Droitwich, Worcestershire, J.L.-M's grandmother's house during his childhood (recreated as 'Wribbenhall' in his novel *Heretics in Love* [1973]).

† Manor near Oxford, built 1635 by Sir Robert Dormer, redecorated *c.* 1740 by William Kent who also designed gardens. In *Another Self*, J.L.-M. writes that he resolved to devote his life to architectural conservation after witnessing an orgy of vandalism there; but this has been questioned by some contemporaries, and he never mentions the alleged incident in writing about Rousham in his diaries.

‡ Guarino Guarini (1624–83) and Filippo Juvarra (1678–1736); Italian Baroque architects.

grave, reading the sentimental inscription which describes her so exactly, kissing my fingers which touched the stone that I cannot easily reach with my lips, and moved to love and prayer for her precious soul.

Saturday, 9th August

At six o'clock I sit on the white bench facing the pool, the sun in my eyes. A background of darkest green, lush from recent rains. The fountain burbling gently, the refractions on the water like broken glass at the instant of splitting. A long, slim dragon-fly darting across the pool. The tranquillity and the relentless heat almost too pressing. No breath of air. No birds singing. A red admiral has just alighted for a moment on my open left hand.

Sunday, 17th August

Nick lunched to discuss my wishes. He was still here when the Levis came for tea, bringing Matthew, who seemed more adult, yet with the same taciturnity; less handsome, hair shorn and ears protruding. He and Nick talked together and I hope N. may help him find a job.

Monday, 18th August

I went to George Bayntun's bookshop* [in Bath] which I have meant to visit for ages. The basement where the second-hand books are kept was so dark that I couldn't scour as I wished. Bought William de Morgan's *Joseph Vance* and Meredith's poems for little, but forgot to pay, and they forgot to ask for the money. This caused by my being introduced to James Williams the Bath Wonder,† described by local press as cleverest man in Britain. Aged eighteen he has gained four first-class degrees. I shook hands and congratulated this wire-spectacled youth, with hollow chest and limp air, while Bayntun said to him, 'You can say in 2070 that you met James Lees-Milne.'

---

* Founded by George Bayntun in 1894, and owned at this time by his great-grandson Hylton Bayntun-Coward (1932–2000).
† He was doing a part-time job in the shop, having failed to gain admission to Jesus College, Cambridge despite his remarkable attainments.

Tuesday, 19th August

Day of horrid torpidity, answering letters before tomorrow's operation at [Bath] Clinic. One from owner of Rainscombe Park, Oare, Wilts, who has just bought a pair of Holland & Holland guns inscribed J.H.L.-M. and wants to know if a relation. My grandfather, who died March 1908. Another from Sutton Park, Tenbury Wells, Worcs about recent diaries. I reply to all and take my time.

Dined alone with Jane Westmorland. She was very sweet and we had the perfect dinner, sorrel soup, scrambled eggs with smoked salmon. All so beautifully presented in her exquisite house. She spoke of Kitty Kelley's book on Prince Philip, which she is dreading, knowing him so well. Admitted that she is less than frank at times. We agreed that to be a good liar one has to have a long and accurate memory.

Monday, 25th August

Had to have a proper anaesthetic this time, and stay in the Clinic for two nights. Felt and still feel awful. I was diagnosed as anaemic, and given a blood transfusion lasting six hours. Am rather worried about such future as remains, and feel several new symptoms of decline. O the tiresomeness!

Am grieved by death, *aet.* 70, of Christopher Harley* of Brampton Bryan, a true legacy of English squiredom. Public duties galore and life dedicated to salvation of B.B., which has come by descent (not always male) since the Conquest. A dear, welcoming, happy, courteous, wonderful man. Has three sons.

Tuesday, 26th August

Francis Russell† came to tea on his way to Ross-on-Wye, to look at my pair of Naples paintings. He confirmed they were Fabris, but evidently thought them not of the highest class. Thought they might fetch £50,000 on the market. I made it clear I had no intention of selling. He is very charming, well-groomed, slight in build and good

---

* Landowner in Shropshire and Herefordshire and member of N.T. Severn Regional Committee (1926–97); High Sheriff of Hereford and Worcester, 1987–8.
† Director of Christie's (b. 1949).

looking; has good manners with the aged, and loves old ladies. Said that John Pope-Hennessy a great scholar and far exceeded K. Clark in that respect – though K. a mind of magnitude and a great showman who succeeded to a phenomenal degree in reaching the ears and eyes of the man in the street. When Francis was at Oxford, his bedmaker watched the *Civilisation* TV series, and said to him, 'I now understand why you're so keen on that there art.' Says Michael Mallon totally honourable; admired J.P.-H. above all other men, and ministered to him without thought of benefiting. Then J.P.-H. had a blood-row with the Ashmolean, which was to have been his heir, and so he left his treasures to Mallon.

Monday, 1st September

The grieving over Princess Diana is beyond all belief.* Radio and telly totally given over, and today's *Times* contains not one paragraph which is not devoted to her. Now undoubtedly she was a great beauty, and had star quality of the film actress sort; also seems to have had a genuine caring side. Q. rang yesterday to ask what I felt. I said the tragedy seemed pre-ordained; and dreadful though it was to say, it would be recognised as a mercy in the long run. Q. admitted that to see her with old or mortally ill people was a revelation; yet it was terrifying that the world regarded her as a saint. People did not realise that few of her staff could abide her, and that she was odious to the Prince ever since they became engaged. She was shallow and devious, as cunning as a vixen, determined to do him down, motivated by malice and spite. She took no part in his interests and his intellectual friends, never read a book and was totally uneducated and stupid.

Wednesday, 3rd September

Misha telephones to say that, in the London streets, one must not be overheard saying anything critical of the Princess, or one risks being lynched.

---

* She had died in Paris in the early hours of 31 August, when the car in which she was travelling with her new friend Dodi Fayed, driven by a drug-fuelled alcoholic and speeding to avoid press photographers, crashed in an underpass.

Friday, 5th September

Susy [Robinson] is all for Diana and critical of the Royal Family for being stuffy, out of date and out of touch. But I say that the Queen, who has been endlessly meeting her subjects for forty-five years and has weekly contacts with the Prime Minister etc., knows more about the people than anyone else in the country. S. accuses her of lack of 'care' and of not welcoming Princess D. from the start. How does she know? In my opinion the thing most wrong with the Queen is her hats. They are awful, and always have been. They suggest the stuffiness which is not really there.

Saturday, 6th September

Owing to Diana funeral the roads empty this morning, when I motored to lunch with Anne Cowdray at Broadleas. I was early and halted in Devizes, it being the best day of the year to appreciate the architectural beauties. The war memorial in the centre strewn with flowers in plastic bags, with messages such as 'Diana, we will always love you, Bert and Rosie' and 'You will live for ever. We shall join you.'

Wednesday, 10th September

One of the most beautiful days ever. Lunched with Gerda [Barlow] in her conservatory at Stancombe. Delicious food. She is the sweetest and most gallant of women. Afterwards we walked down the path to the pond garden. I got down all right but could not climb back, so she got a builder at work to motor us up again. With help of English Heritage, the 1820s temple has finally been restored, every mould reproduced where missing. The transverse roof lantern rebuilt and glazed with coloured glass which dapples walls and floors when sun is shining. Gerda told me she would retire the moment Nicky married, which he shows no sign of doing as yet.

Thursday, 11th September

Debo called on me at 3 on her way to Highgrove. Much talk about Princess Diana, whose behaviour was utterly unpredictable. She dropped her friends like plummets and then behaved vengefully to their hurt. Quarrelled with both sisters, and with her brother Spencer who offered her a house at Althorp which she declined to take up. Till the last day of her life she kept in close touch with the press, asking them to send photographers and advising them how to get the best pictures of her in action.

Saturday, 13th September

Lunched with Desmond and Ian off the grouse Debo brought me, beautifully cooked by Desmond with all the trimmings – bread-crumbs, jellies, sauces.

I thought I would ring Duff Hart-Davis to ask how Rupert was. A gentle female voice answered, not like Phyllida's clarion tone. I asked to speak to Duff. 'He's not here,' answered the voice. 'I want to know how Rupert is feeling at ninety,' I said. The voice, puzzled, said, 'You can speak to him. He's beside me.' 'Oh,' I said, surprised. 'Is he staying with you, then?' 'I don't understand,' said the voice. 'He lives here.' I then cottoned on to fact that, in my dottiness, I had rung Rupert rather than Duff. Rupert's voice little changed, with that slightly stifled last syllable. He asked to know my ailments, and then told me of his – arthritis, inability to walk, and heart troubles. Said he was kept alive by his angel, his wonderful June.

Monday, 15th September

Interviewed today for Welsh radio by fuzzy-wuzzy Father Christmas, Ian Skidmore, who brought wife and producer. They were so kind and easy that I acquitted myself fairly well I think. I am rather tired of being asked to re-tell the same boring incidents such as my visit to Longleat by bicycle.* Gave them tea and we parted friends.

Tuesday, 16th September

Lunched today with Bill Llewellyn, ninety last month. His sad wife Inez scowling and silent; but Bill rather better, sprightly movements and looking handsome. Two very attentive girl minders, saying Bill this and Bill that. I kept wondering how in Bill's circumstances I could bear it. Bill has family portraits in every room. There is no doubt that

---

* Recounted in *People & Places*.

eighteenth-century portraits, especially when true ancestors, are the fittest adornment of walls in small country houses. The fuzzy, bewhiskered Victorians have to be good art to be acceptable; the Edwardian ancestors jollier.

Wednesday, 17th September

Misha [Bloch] came to lunch, motored by Philip Mansel.* A great success. Good luncheon of Covent Garden soup, Ian's kedgeree and a blackberry and apple pie of Peggy's. M. very good and rather less eccentric than on last visit. Philip a charming man, nice looking, gentle, not forthcoming. Speaks only when obliged to, and always pertinently. He is not happy, according to M., despite his renown as a historian, and ownership of ancestral Dorset seat; has never got over death of his devoted companion five years ago. They stayed until four; got stuck in the mud motoring through the park afterwards, and had to be helped out.

At this point, J.L.-M. ceased to type his diary, though he continued to keep it for the next six weeks in his neat, artistic hand.

Saturday, 20th September

Leafing through current *Country Life* I come upon a coloured photograph in 'For Sale' pages of South Luffenham Hall, Rutland, which I once visited in 1950s and was quite smitten by. Very little known, and merely mentioned in passing by Pevsner. Yet the photograph evoked in me a tug at the heart. It belongs to that scarce breed of small country house of Restoration or even Commonwealth date, of the school of Roger Pratt† and Inigo Jones,‡ free from Jacobean extravagances, proto- rather than neo-classical. Thrilling on account of its rarity (perhaps Thorpe Hall, Cambs, the prototype, though a few to be found in the Northants area), a sort of epitome of solid British culture and squiredom. I was irrationally moved. This particular house

---

* Historian (b. 1951), then writing a book about Constantinople; owner of Smedmore estate, Dorset, which had descended by inheritance since the 14th century.
† English architect (1620–84).
‡ Architect (1573–1652), Surveyor of the King's Works from 1613; introduced the Italian style to England; J.L.-M. had written a book about his work, published in 1953.

had, I remember, nearly all its rooms with the original wainscot, stairs, etc. intact. Far more moving than any Georgian house of the size.

Sunday, 21st September

Lunched alone with Briggses at Midford. What a dear couple. The composure, wisdom, erudition of Isobel, and total lack of society affectation, stimulates me. Always worthwhile conversation, not untinged with malice of unharmful sort. Michael delighted with recent expansion of his estate, and has bought and brought back into use the straight drive from castle to road.

Monday, 22nd September

Dr White said today, 'You have been through a rough time lately.' Touched me by adding that he was always glad to see me, and that I must never hesitate to make an appointment whenever inclined.

Tuesday, 30th September

Gordon Brown* yesterday reiterated the old Labour assurance that by the Millennium there would be no more unemployment. No government except a Communist one can promise such a thing, for it depends on the labour required by business. As the need for labour grows less because of technology, and the pool of labour grows with the rising tide of immigrants without qualifications, so unemployment will persist until Mother Earth's yields are exhausted. Whereupon uprisings, anarchy, and starvation will occur, if the physical world has not yet imploded.

Thursday, 2nd October

Tony Mitchell called at 9 and off we drove to Lyme [Park near Stockport], leaving Badminton in balmy Indian summer weather as we headed for the grey, cold north. Lyme improved since my old days, but house still rather stark and institutional. Very nice young N.T. rep., James Rothwell, his smile and slight laugh at end of state-

---

* Chancellor of Exchequer in Labour Government (b. 1951).

ments reminding me of Francis Dashwood in his young days. A perky and efficient lady custodian, arch and rather forward (kissed Debo), provided lunch. Inner courtyard by Leoni* just like a Roman palazzo, pavement of mauve and pink polished stone, central well-head, grand flight of steps leading to hall which John Fowler decorated in white and gold, doing away with mustard graining which was probably more suitable. Yet I cautioned against scrapping any of John's decoration. My Khorassan carpet from Bath looking splendid on floor of ante-library, a good place for it. Some bad treatment lately received from Stockport Corporation (from whom lady curator inherited) in stripping of Stuart staircase and Grinling Gibbons† carvings.

Motored with Debo to Chatsworth, Tony following and staying night. He was very appreciative, saying it was an experience ever to be remembered.

Dreadful how tottery I have become. Sightseeing wears me out. After tea lay on my bed in the Centre Dressing Room, not even reading, but listening to Pizetti's‡ seductive incidental music to d'Annunzio,§ and admiring the curtains of rich, pea-green moiré silk, fringed with appliqué galloon three inches broad, upheld by stout clasps of gold foliage and draped and tasselled festoons. The opulence of the Bachelor's taste.

Friday, 3rd October

Andrew relates how in extreme youth he attended a ball at Lyme with his cousin, the present Lord Salisbury.¶ The cousin, drunk, sawed off the legs of a buffet for fun, an act of sheer barbarism in the tradition of the Mohawks. Debo admitted that, when first married, she would wear Bess of Hardwick's wedding dress in which she frisked and frolicked about the house. Today the dress is kept under lock and key, considered as holy as the Turin Shroud.

---

* Giacomo Leoni (1686–1746); Venetian architect who came to England with George I in 1714.
† Wood carver (1648–1721).
‡ Ildebrando Pizetti (1880–1968); Italian composer.
§ Gabriele d'Annunzio (1863–1938); Italian poet, dramatist and adventurer; Pizetti composed the incidental music to his play *La Nave* (1908).
¶ Robert Cecil, Viscount Cranborne (1916–2003); s. 1972 as 6th Marquess of Salisbury.

Saturday, 4th October

Andrew to Newmarket for the day, racing. There came to luncheon from the hotel, where staying, Sir Robert and Lady Jane Fellowes.* Also a couple called Greville Howard,† Mrs having been brought up at Luckington, one mile from Badminton. I sat in Andrew's place, between the two wives. Fellowes praised *Fourteen Friends*, and on leaving said, 'It has been an honour to meet you.' I assured him the honour was all mine. Nice friendly man who is Queen's private secretary and soon to retire. Having been enjoined to make no reference to Princess Diana I trod warily, whereas Fellowes and Debo launched into chat about Morton's latest scurrilous publication.‡ I talked to Lady Jane about her grandfather Jack Spencer,§ of whom as a child she went in deadly awe. He never addressed a word to his grandchildren when they stayed at Althorp, and ate voraciously while scowling at them. Lady J. quite unlike her sister, not pretty but jolly and decent. Easy to chat with. We got onto subject of decapitation by the sword in Saudi Arabia. Then I thought that, bearing in mind the Princess's death, we were treading on sensitive ground, and changed subject. She then told me that pheasants killed while under stress were less tasty and made tougher eating than those shot while unawares. Does this mean that, in shooting for the pot, one should kill them sitting?

Monday, 6th October

The Mlinarics arrived dinner time, and William Burlington. David and William are photographing garden chairs and benches for a catalogue of their commodities. The shop in orangery full of tapestried cushions, taken from Bayeux Tapestry and *Dame à la Licorne* scenes, very reasonable at about £20 each. I bought two and a supply of Debo's honey.

Have read Turgenev's *House of Gentlefolk*, deeply moving. Lavretsky the typical Russian country gentleman, all at sea, beneficent, spiritual

---

* Sir Robert Fellowes (b. 1941); Private Secretary to HM The Queen 1990–9; m. 1978 Lady Jane Spencer, elder sister of Diana, Princess of Wales; cr. life peer, 1999.

† Owner (b. 1941) of Castle Rising, Norfolk; m. (3rd) 1981 Mary Culverwell; cr. life peer, 2004, as Baron Howard of Rising.

‡ Andrew Morton's *Diana: Her True Story*, written in collaboration with the Princess, originally published in 1992, was about to appear in a more 'unrestrained' new edition.

§ 7th Earl Spencer (1892–1975).

yet unbelieving. Now halfway through Paddy L. F's *Between the Woods and the Water*.* Like a rich birthday cake, too much descriptive writing for easy reading, yet the descriptions inimitable – how he arrives on foot with knapsack at grand Hungarian castle to join a game of bicycle polo with Hapsburg archdukes and footmen; how Count Jeno, unable to resolve some point by consulting theological books in his library, utters a phrase learnt from his Glasgow nanny, 'I ken it noo.'

Tuesday, 7th October

Breakfast at 9 suits me, giving me an hour of extra sleep. Can I introduce it at home with Peggy? Eat two helpings of porridge and cream, two slices of toast with butter and honey. Barely one cup of coffee now, too rich for me. Pore over newspaper with magnifier. Knock half-full glass of orange juice over Andrew's place. Mop up with napkin and bolt to drawing room. Read at window. Andrew passes through at 10 and out again at 10.45 without recognising me. Henry comes, and I own up to him. 'It doesn't matter in the least,' he assures me. Andrew weighed down by newspapers of which he reads every line through his sawn-off telescope. I give him as wide a berth as possible, knowing his disinclination for early morning chat.

Wednesday, 8th October

I am whizzed home by the taciturn Jo in brand-new Bentley in greatest comfort. On unpacking 'sandwiches' I discover whole dishes of minced lamb, vegetables, pâtés and white grapes. I thoroughly enjoyed visit in spite of abysmal tiredness throughout. I hope Andrew and Debo didn't find me too languid and dotty.

Deaths while away of Joe Links and Leslie Rowse, both very remarkable men. Joe Links of ineffable sweetness and worshipped by poor Mary Lutyens to whom I have sent a line.

Friday, 10th October

Feeling absolutely awful I nevertheless go to London for day. Not a success. Went First Class for once. Full of businessmen glued to

---

* Second volume of P.L.F's epic account of his walk in 1933, aged eighteen, from the Hook of Holland to Constantinople, published by John Murray in 1986.

telephones, very irritating. Failed to find a cardigan, chief object of expedition. Nearest approach to what I wanted was priced at £430 in Burlington Arcade. Lunched Brooks's opposite Merlin Sudeley,* who on recognising me at once launched into boring talk about Toddington [Manor, Gloucestershire] which he has done these thirty years at least. Was almost made gaga by dodging the blazing sun and blinding shadows of the streets. Tired to death. I fear I can never go to London again. Just not up to it. Found the weight of my rolled umbrella and overcoat almost too much for my feeble shoulders and stick-like arms.

Saturday, 11th October

Beloved Nick comes to lunch. After which I retire to bed. Then over mug of tea we resume our heavenly talk. He grows portly.

Marvellous obit. of Joe Links in today's *Times*. How a furrier (to HM The Queen) becomes the writer of the best guide to Venice† and greatest authority on Canaletto. And remains withal the sweetest, modestest character.

Am reading letters of Joyce Grenfell‡ and Virginia Graham. I love their humour and wish I had seen J.G. perform. Her sheer goodness shines through the jokes and gossip. Beloved by all she was, and I could have met her had I tried. Not that she would have cared much for me. Virginia, her greatest friend since they met aged seven and sharing same fun and sympathies, does not emerge as quite so good.

Sunday, 12th October

To morning service at Boxwell. Packed, with gentry rather than peasantry. I love the remoteness and secrecy of this church.

The Levis came to tea, bringing Matthew, who is evidently home again and has abandoned London. Desmond joined us and was talkative, but Matthew never uttered. What can the matter be?

---

* Merlin Hanbury-Tracy, 7th Baron Sudeley (b. 1939); author of *The Sudeleys – Lords of Toddington* (1987); in *Who's Who*, gives recreation as 'ancestor worship', and mentions that he is 'Patron of Association of Bankrupts'.
† *Venice for Pleasure*.
‡ Joyce Phipps (1910–79); actress and entertainer; m. 1929 Reginald Grenfell; her correspondence with her lifelong friend Virginia Graham had just been published by Hodder.

Tuesday, 14th October

Carmen Silva's* book of short stories *Pilgrim Sorrow*, taken out of London Library, is the greatest rubbish. Translated from German, she born Princess Wied. How even sentimental Victorians could digest such tosh, in which all the characters are Sorrow, Art, Jealousy, Fortitude, Revenge, not a human being among them, beats me. The good Queen of Romania doubtless suffered childhood and domestic miseries galore.

Sidney Blackmore† to tea. I enjoyed his company and chat about Beckfordiana, in which he is deeply versed. I said I would let him know within a fortnight whether I could write preface to the Christie's exhibition catalogue. He was very informative about Sir William Hamilton's‡ Neapolitan abodes, and my Fabri paintings.

Wednesday, 15th October

I am immersing myself in Julien Green's§ diaries, which Diana [Mosley] urged me to read. They are marvellous like Roger Hinks's¶ in that they are introspective, self-analytical, not gossipy at all, even when he dissects his intimate friend Gide. He says his greatest desire is for Truth. I'm not so sure about this. What is truth? Something which, once found, remains unmalleable, immovable, dried up, a tablet of stone, a Nazi *Diktat*. Green the most self-centred of men. His pessimism and melancholia accord with mine. He is a mystery man, part French, part American. Says French his natural language; that to write in English, he feels confused by the diversity of words and meaning, while the French language is so concise, rational, intellectual, unwoolly. He hardly mentions the war, despite fleeing France for USA in 1940, except to express his homesickness for Paris.

I asked Simon [Lees-Milne] if his future daughter-in-law is what

---

* Pen name of Queen Elizabeth of Romania (1843–1916), consort of King Carol I (1839–1914).
† Civil servant and art history lecturer; Secretary of Beckford Society.
‡ Sir William Hamilton (1730–1803); diplomatist and archaeologist, British Ambassador to Naples, 1764–1800; his wife Emma was the mistress of Horatio, Lord Nelson.
§ French novelist, playwright and academician of American parentage (1900–98).
¶ Roger Packman Hinks (1903–63); British Council official; his *Journals, 1933–1963* were published by Michael Russell in 1984.

my grandmother would have called a lady. He replied, 'Not exactly – but then they aren't these days.'

Saturday, 18th October

Most beautiful day. At Acton Turville tried to enter church. Locked, and no notice how to obtain key. Thence I motored by lanes to Tetbury. Passed another car too closely, and it knocked against my side mirror, shattering the glass. For some reason I didn't mind a bit, and continued singing.

J.K.-B., who stayed Friday night with an appalling cold, told me that he once lunched alone with Julien Green in Paris. It was not a success. Green was kind – for J. was young – but taciturn. J. wanted to watch Part II of Tony Powell's *Dance* on telly.* I had missed Part I, about Eton days. What I saw of Part II revolted me. The snobbery, arrogance, hauteur, stupidity, insolence of the young people were ghastly – except for Widmerpool, who was meant to be ghastly, but seemed good. I feel ashamed to have grown up in the 1920s and to have been a young adult in the 1930s. Thank God that generation is now extinct.

Monday, 20th October

Green asks, 'What do I mean by prayer?' He says that, until middle age, he prayed glibly. Now decides that silence on his knees the best method – the way I have usually followed. The trouble is that silence leads to invasion of one's devotion by secular thoughts. In other words, religious faith and communication with God need either a priest standing over one or attendance at church services.

Green recounts that, after twenty years' ownership of his waste-paper basket, he actually looked at it for the first time, to find it was made of honey-coloured wicker sticks. As for me, after sixty years in some cases, I have never really looked at my treasures. Have become so over-familiar with them that I pass them by unnoticing. For the rest of my life, and so long as they are not stolen, they can satisfy my curiosity for craftsmanship and art. I need not go in search of other and far greater treasures in the world's galleries.

---

* The four-part adaptation of Powell's 12-volume novel *A Dance to the Music of Time* was produced by Alvin Rakoff and starred James Purefoy as the narrator Nicholas Jenkins and Simon Russell Beale as Widmerpool.

Wednesday, 22nd October

And today came Fiona MacCarthy* to lunch with me. Had imagined an elderly, frumpy, academic Miss. On the contrary, attractive late forties with dulcet manner. Object of her pilgrimage to talk to me about Byron, about whom I know no more than the average educated man. Well, when it came to talking I seemed to know rather more, because he has always been an icon. She is visiting every surviving house and building lived in or visited by Byron in Switzerland, Italy, Greece, having already seen every English or Scotch house. Recently saw Melbourne House, Whitehall, which retains all its eighteenth-century decoration. Apparently old Lady M., to whom B. wrote many indiscreet letters, lived on one floor, and William Lamb and Lady Caroline on another.† Thus B. flitted from one floor to the other. Fiona has identified all their rooms. I advised her to write a specialised book, and not to repeat the well-worn tales about treatment of Lady B. and so forth. We parted firm friends.

Friday, 24th October

I now know the operating theatre at the Bath Clinic like the back of my hand. The porter wheels me in and wishes me good luck, which confirms my alarm over what may be in store. I see a platoon of doctors, assistants, nurses in tight blue overalls and pale blue caps. From these emerges Britton, brightly ejaculating, 'I much enjoyed your book' (*Ancient*, which I had given him). 'And now,' wielding a syringe concealed in his palm, 'here is just a little prick.' I did not become unconscious, yet was blissfully unconcerned with what they were doing. In bed upstairs I was in euphoria, drank tea, ate delicious fish and chips and told the nurses I had seldom enjoyed a day more. Euphoria continued when at home drinking more tea and eating chocolate biscuits with Gerald and Peggy.

---

* Her book *Byron: Life and Legend*, arguing that the poet's nature was predominantly homosexual, was published by John Murray in 2002.
† During 1812, Byron conducted simultaneous relationships with Elizabeth, Viscountess Melbourne (*née* Milbanke [1751–1818]) and her daughter-in-law Lady Caroline Lamb (*née* Ponsonby [1785–1828], wife of Hon. William Lamb [1779–1848], later 2nd Viscount Melbourne and Prime Minister).

Saturday, 25th October

Very low and depressed all day. I decline in rapid successive spurts. Three whole days with no engagements. Work on editing next volume of diaries.

Tuesday, 28th October

Rushed down to Post Office to have expired passport (luckily noticed yesterday by me) renewed. Presented with piles of bumph. Practically in tears I turn to lady behind desk. She takes pity, fills in forms, takes me to automatic photo kiosk, tells me to smile. Then this saint leads me to guichet behind which saintly young man stamps form, assuring me I shall receive passport by registered post on Friday.

To London. Raeburn exhibition at National Portrait Gallery shows him to be a sensitive portrait artist, as good as Lawrence, without the magic. All his exhibited subjects wearing colourful garments – men in tartan trews, women in dresses – unlike my humble, unadorned great-great-grandfather.

Staying night at Brooks's, I find I am unable to read in any of the downstairs rooms. So dark; no single strong lamp. Dine alone, as I wish. Very tiring day on feet, dodging traffic like a strayed sheep.

Wednesday, 29th October

Pick up John Saumarez Smith. Taxi to Paddington. We take train to Slough. At Slough, dreadful mishap. Crossing bridge over the lines J., in volubly talking to me as we start descending steep stairway, face turned to me, misses step, tries desperately to recover rhythm of the treads, fails, falls headlong from top to bottom. Lies spreadeagled on stone platform of station. I follow as fast as I can. People gather round him. I fear he may be dead, surely limbs broken. But no, greatly shaken, ashen white he is raised. No benches on modern platforms. I guide him to a seat where he recovers. He still dazed, cheek bruised, we board taxi for Windsor Castle. At entry to Royal Library greeted by Oliver Everett* who summons Castle nurse. She and doctor, ever

---

* Royal Librarian and Keeper of the Queen's Archives, 1985–2002 (b. 1943), with whom J.L.-M. had had dealings over his biographies of Reginald, Viscount Esher and the Bachelor Duke of Devonshire.

on the ready day and night (Prince Philip said to keep finger smartly on the button at all times), pronounce John not to be injured, bar teeth. His courage exemplary. It gave me the shock of a lifetime to witness.

I liked Oliver Everett immensely. Calm, modest, no scholar, but has courtly manners. Alas our time limited because joined by Michael Meredith,* Eton librarian and archivist, who takes us on to Eton. Could only get a glimpse of treasures without end – Charles I shirt worn on scaffold, lace trimmings and unfaded blue ribbons; music score by Mozart *aet.* 11, work of an adult. Shelves of books given to royalty with subservient dedications by Tennyson, Disraeli, Hardy, every known author. Princess Margaret the royal most interested in library. Queen only comes when visitors conducted. Library mostly made by Prince Albert out of Elizabethan Gallery on North Front. Whole room contains Leonardo drawings in neat boxes, white gloves worn for handling. So many treasures that the mind boggles.

Michael Meredith quite a card, eccentric enthusiast, gets carried away, dances with excitement. Funny twisted corner of lower lip. Extraordinary that after thirty years as Eton Librarian he has never been inside Royal Library until today. Also extraordinary that he has got Eton Library to acquire largest collections of Hardy correspondence, Browning papers and Gordon Craig† papers – all his favourite writers and artists, but having no association with Eton. Necessitates large extensions to College Library over Lupton's Tower, spreading into South Wing. I wonder why the Trustees allow this. Where will it end? In twenty years another wing will be needed at this rate.

Under Lupton's Tower we were talking about the power of public opinion in the present world, and this led to discussion of national hysteria following Diana's death, not a subject I would normally have raised with a servant of the sovereign. Oliver E. expressed strong feelings about encouragement of hysteria by the press. I said it was the most astonishing phenomenon of my lifetime, and frightening. 'Yes,' he said, 'if only they knew. I worked for her, you know. She was not genuinely dedicated to charitable works like Princess Anne, who gets

---

* Head of English, housemaster, and School (later College) Librarian at Eton (b. 1936), whom J.L.-M. had befriended when he had visited Eton on 8 July 1992 (see *Ceaseless Turmoil*) to present the library with lockets of Dickens's and Byron's hair.
† Theatrical producer, critic and stage designer (1872–1966); son of the actress Ellen Terry and of the architect E.W. Godwin.

little public recognition. It was simply a case of a pretty face.' 'Hollywood values,' I said. I don't think he grieved over her death, though he attended funeral in the Abbey because he received an invitation, and admitted he found it moving. Said public had no idea how well the Queen behaved when she learnt of the death at Balmoral. Non-mention of it at Crathie Church that morning was deliberate to spare the boys' feelings. He evidently feels extremely sore over treatment of the Queen and Prince Philip.

Had no time to see my gold locket containing Byron's hair, though glad to see it acknowledged and described in new catalogue.

Thursday, 30th October

Motored to Burford for Guy Holland's memorial service. In great angst lest I be late, and on arrival over whether I should find parking place. Desperately I left motor where I should not have done, and bolted. Crowds of county gathering at porch, several recognised by me, all in black or mauve. A good service in beautiful building. But as I watched the afternoon waning through the patchy unstained windows, was again in angst as to how I should get out. Beautiful singing, Handel and Haydn for this good, absolutely honourable deceased English baronet with a taste for classical music, literature and the arts. Dreadful difficulty escaping throng and when porch reached heard my name called by Joanie, wearing enveloping cloak in white. Poor face wracked by anguish. We embraced and she promised to telephone me soon.

Friday, 31st October

Felt really ill with fatigue all day. Could barely walk in the house. Ate little and slept. Then in the bath before bed felt a new lump in pit of stomach. True to custom, discovery made on eve of weekend.

Saturday, 1st November

Made appointment to see doctor Monday morning before departure. Am philosophical and resigned. How long has this growth been festering? I know that I am riddled. Growths on bladder, prostate and bowel cannot be eliminated, only kept at bay. No wonder am so often extremely tired. My ailments are so many that I can no longer enumerate them. Trouble is that I have no one in neighbourhood whom I can bore with problems. Nick and Susy are my nearest confidants, poor things, apart from Peggy who listens, is as wise as a peasant, but cannot *advise*.

Spent morning writing on favourite books read this year for *Spectator*. And *Oldie* have asked me also.

On Tuesday 4 November, with some foreboding, J.L.-M. set out with Debo Devonshire to stay with Diana Mosley at Orsay. The next day, he was taken ill there; and on 6 November he returned to England with Debo, going straight into the Royal United Hospital in Bath. It was there that he wrote his last diary entry in a marbled notebook, headed simply 'Nov 1997'.

New arrival in hospital ward with wife. They sit in silence for hours before he is allotted a bed. Speechless. She goes. He sits beside bed alone. Tall poker-faced attendant, evidently doctor [under] Mr Britton, comes to bedside. Says without expression of sympathy: 'Tomorrow morning you are to undergo a serious operation. They will cut your stomach (indicating with hand a vertical foot's length) and remove part of bowel. To rejoin the two intestines will be a del icate job. You may wake up in the intensive care unit to find you have a bag beside you. All right?' And he moves away. The patient looks out of the window and likewise walks away, probably to tell the wife.

The food in the Royal United is utterly disgusting. And yet in a way less ghastly than at the [Bath] Clinic which is sheer middle-class pretentious Trust House style. This is sheer plebeian – a sort of dog's dinner tonight, such as what we gave to Fop and Chuff. While [I was] stuffing it down a nurse injected something into my left arm.

Debo telephoned at 6.35. Walked away elated by talk with her & went into the wrong ward. Approached what corresponded with my bed by the window & was about to get into it when a terrified lady gave a yelp of horror.

My handwriting is very shakey [*sic*]. Damn it.

The doctors were unable to do much more for J.L.-M. At the end of November he was moved to Tetbury Cottage Hospital, where he died in the early hours of Sunday 28 December.

Index

Works by James Lees-Milne (JL-M) appear under title; works by others under author's name